WALTER PATER: THE CRITICAL HERITAGE

THE CRITICAL HERITAGE SERIES

GENERAL EDITOR: B.C. SOUTHAM, M.A., B.LITT. (OXON.)
Formerly Department of English, Westfield College, University of London

For a list of books in the series see the back end paper

WALTER PATER

THE CRITICAL HERITAGE

Edited by
R. M. SEILER
The University of Calgary

ROUTLEDGE & KEGAN PAUL
LONDON, BOSTON AND HENLEY

First published in 1980
by Routledge & Kegan Paul Ltd
39 Store Street,
London WC1E 7DD,
9 Park Street,
Boston, Mass. 02108, USA, and
Broadway House,
Newtown Road,
Henley-on-Thames,
Oxon RG9 1EN
Printed in Great Britain by
Redwood Burn Limited
Trowbridge and Esher

British Library Cataloguing in Publication Data

Walter Pater, The critical heritage—(Critical heritage series).

1. Pater, Walter—Criticism and interpretation
I. Seiler, R. M. II. Series
828', 8'08   PR5136   79–42837

ISBN 0   7100   0380   3

General Editor's Preface

The reception given to a writer by his contemporaries and near-contemporaries is evidence of considerable value to the student of literature. On one side we learn a great deal about the state of criticism at large and in particular about the development of critical attitudes towards a single writer; at the same time, through private comments in letters, journals or marginalia, we gain an insight upon the tastes and literary thought of individual readers of the period. Evidence of this kind helps us to understand the writer's historical situation, the nature of his immediate reading-public, and his response to these pressures.

The separate volumes in the *Critical Heritage Series* present a record of this early criticism. Clearly, for many of the highly productive and lengthily reviewed nineteenth- and twentieth-century writers, there exists an enormous body of material; and in these cases the volume editors have made a selection of the most important views, significant for their intrinsic critical worth or for their representative quality—perhaps even registering incomprehension!

For earlier writers, notably pre-eighteenth century, the materials are much scarcer and the historical period has been extended, sometimes far beyond the writer's lifetime, in order to show the inception and growth of critical views which were initially slow to appear.

In each volume the documents are headed by an Introduction, discussing the material assembled and relating the early stages of the author's reception to what we have come to identify as the critical tradition. The volumes will make available much material which would otherwise be difficult of access and it is hoped that the modern reader will be thereby helped towards an informed understanding of the ways in which literature has been read and judged.

B.C.S.

For my parents

Contents

CONTENTS

CONTENTS

Obituary Notices and Tributes

Posthumous Publications

'Greek Studies' (1895)

'Miscellaneous Studies' (1895)

'Gaston de Latour' (1896)

Preface

Shortly after Pater's death the 'Athenaeum' (11 August
1894) announced the proposal 'that several friends of Mr.
Pater should prepare reminiscences, to be gathered into a
single volume' (p. 196). One month later Arthur Waugh
(1866-1943), critic, editor and publishing executive,
printed a similar notice in the 'Critic' (1 September
1894): 'It is ... proposed to evolve a memoir of Pater
from a series of appreciations from the hands of the various friends who were best acquainted with him in private
life' (xxv, 145). The principal initiators of this scheme
obviously included Lionel Johnson, Edmund Gosse and Arthur
Symons, who published individual reminiscences in the following years. For some reason the book never materialised.
The present collection of reviews, notices, obituary notices, tributes and extracts from letters, journals and
books is offered in lieu of that volume; its aim, however,
is to provide a critical profile of Pater's reputation in
the period which spans the publication of his first book
in 1873 and the publication of the Library Edition of his
works in 1910. As Waugh predicted in his London Letter,
the problem of selection is a difficult one, for there are
many critiques from which to choose and many are by his
friends, from whom he solicited notices and reviews. Ultimately, I have attempted to strike a balance between those
by his admirers and those by his detractors. Items which
repeat established opinion are omitted and the most significant of these are discussed in the Introduction. The
order is chronological and anonymous reviewers are identified wherever possible.

Acknowledgments

For their suggestions and help in preparing this volume,
I should like to thank Dr Ian Fletcher, Dr Lawrence Evans,
Mr Samuel Wright, Professor J.D. Jump, Professor U.C.
Knoepflmacher, Professor R. Breugelmans, Professor A.A.
Long, Dr Ian Small and Dr Stuart Sykes. I should also
like to acknowledge the assistance of Professor Walter
Houghton of the Wellesley Index; Dr P.J. Blake-Hill of
the Department of Manuscripts, the British Museum; Mr
Richard Garnett of Macmillan & Company; Miss Marion
Fleisher, Librarian for the 'New Statesman'; Mr C.A.
Seaton, Librarian for the 'Spectator'; Dr Albert Mit-
ringer, Der Direktor der Wiener Stadtbibliothek; Mr R.B.
Miller, Librarian for the Catholic University of America;
and the staffs of the British Library, Colindale, the
Bodleian Library, the New York Public Library, the Boston
Public Library and the Harold Cohen Library at the Uni-
versity of Liverpool. Thanks are also due to Mrs Joan
Welford and Mrs Christine Moneypenny for typing the manuscript. Finally, I am most indebted to the University of
Liverpool for awarding me the William Noble Fellowship,
which made this book possible, and to the late Professor
Kenneth Allott and to Professor Miriam Allott for their
encouragement and constructive criticism of my work.
Every effort has been made to obtain permission from
copyright holders, but the editor and publisher regret
that it has proved impossible to trace some of them. We
wish to thank the following for permission to reprint
copyright material: W.H. Allen & Co. Ltd for an extract
from 'Feasting with Panthers' by Rupert Croft-Cooke; The
Bodley Head for No. 66, from 'Renaissance Fancies and
Studies' by Vernon Lee, published by The Bodley Head;
The Principal and Fellows of Brasenose College, Oxford,
for No. 63; Cambridge University Press for No. 38, reprinted from 'The Journals of George Sturt: 1890-1927',

ed. E.D. Mackerness; Cassell and Company Ltd for No. 29,
reprinted from 'The Letters of Ernest Dowson', ed. Desmond
Flower and Henry Maas, pp. 21-2, 144-5, 146, 257;   The
Clarendon Press, Oxford, for material from 'Letters of
Dante Gabriel Rossetti', ed. H. Oswald Doughty and John
Robert Wahl, © 1965 Oxford University Press, and from
'Letters of Walter Pater', ed. Lawrence Evans, © 1970
Oxford University Press; Mrs Pamela Diamand, Chatto &
Windus, and Random House, Inc., for No. 70, from 'Letters
of Roger Fry', ed. Denys Sutton, copyright © 1972 by Mrs
Pamela Diamand;   The Garnstone Press Ltd for No. 72;   Mrs
Nicolete Gray and The Society of Authors on behalf of the
Laurence Binyon Estate for No. 99; Macmillan & Company for
material from the Macmillan Letter Books;   J.C. Medley and
R.G. Medley, the owners of the copyright in George Moore,
for No. 28;   The Nation Associates for No. 100, a signed
review by P.E. More, 'Nation', 13 April 1911, copyright
1911 The Nation Associates; the 'New Statesman' for Nos
42, 75 and 94, reprinted from 'The Athenaeum' of 14 December 1889, 23 February 1895, and 12 June 1897, respectively;
H.F. Read for Nos 35 and 58; The Estate of George Saintsbury for No. 68; The Society of Authors as the literary
representative of the Estate of Havelock Ellis for No. 16;
The Society of Authors as the literary representative of
the Estate of Richard Le Gallienne for Nos 30, 53 and 62;
The Society of Authors on behalf of the Bernard Shaw
Estate for No. 73;   the 'Spectator' for Nos 44 and 97; 'The
Times' for No. 98;   Wayne State University Press for Nos
2, 21 and 48, reprinted from 'The Letters of John Adding-
ton Symonds', ed. Herbert M. Schueller and Robert L. Peters,
vols ii and iii, copyright 1968, 1969 by Herbert M.
Schueller, Wayne State University, Detroit, Michigan, and
Robert L. Peters, University of California at Riverside,
California; Yale University Press for No. 11, from 'The
George Eliot Letters', ed. Gordon Haight, and for an
extract from 'Letters of Swinburne', ed. Cecil Lang.

List of Abbreviations

All references in the reviews and notices to the text of Pater's published works are to the first edition, unless otherwise indicated. Other references are to the ten-volume Library Edition of the 'Works of Walter Pater', originally published by Macmillan & Company Ltd in 1910 and reprinted in 1967 by Basil Blackwell with the permission of the original publisher. The titles are abbreviated as follows:

R	'The Renaissance: Studies in Art and Poetry'
ME	'Marius the Epicurean: his Sensations and Ideas'
IP	'Imaginary Portraits'
Appr	'Appreciations, with an Essay on Style'
PP	'Plato and Platonism: A Series of Lectures'
GS	'Greek Studies: A Series of Essays'
MS	'Miscellaneous Studies: A Series of Essays'
GdL	'Gaston de Latour: an Unfinished Romance'
EG	'Essays from "The Guardian"'

References to other works are abbreviated as follows:

Benson	A.C. Benson, 'Walter Pater' (1906)
LWP	'Letters of Walter Pater' (Oxford, 1970), ed. Lawrence Evans
VLL	'Vernon Lee's Letters: With a Preface by her executor' (privately printed, 1937), ed. Irene Cooper Willis
Wright	Thomas Wright, 'The Life of Walter Pater' (1907)

Chronological Table

1839   4 August: Pater born in Shadwell, East London
1844   Death of Pater's father
1848   Death of Pater's grandmother, Hester
1853   3 February: enrols at King's School, Canterbury
1854   25 February: death of Pater's mother
1858   11 June: matriculates at Queen's College, Oxford
1861   Lent term: 'coached' by Benjamin Jowett
1862   11 December: BA, with second class honours in
Literae Humaniores. Moves to 9 Grove Street (Magpie
Lane) and works for two years as a private coach;
elected a member of the Old Mortality Society
1864   5 February: elected probationary Fellow of Brasenose
College, Oxford
20 February: reads an essay advocating 'self-
culture' before the Old Mortality Society
July: reads Diaphanéité before the society
1865   Awarded the MA degree
Summer: journeys with C.L. Shadwell to Italy
(Ravenna, Pisa, Florence)
1866   January: first publication, Coleridge's Writings,
in 'Westminster Review'
1867   Spring: becomes Lecturer of Brasenose College
1869   Autumn: moves to 2 Bradmore Road, Oxford
1873   1 March: 'Studies in the History of the Renaissance'
published
1874   Unsuccessful in his try for the Junior Proctorship
1875   29 November: lecture on Demeter and Persephone delivered at the Birmingham and Midland Institute
1876   June to December: satirised as 'Mr Rose' in W.H.
Mallock's 'The New Republic'
1877   March: withdraws his candidature for the Oxford
Professorship of Poetry
24 May: second edition of 'The Renaissance' published, with Conclusion omitted

1878 Autumn: delivers first lectures on classical archaeo-
      logy at Oxford
1882 Winter: visits Rome and works on 'Marius the Epi-
      curean'
1883 Summer: resigns his tutorship at Brasenose College
1885 4 March: 'Marius the Epicurean' published
      July: candidate for the Oxford Slade Professorship
      August: moves to 12 Earl's Terrace, Kensington
1887 24 May: 'Imaginary Portraits' published
1888 June to October: 'Gaston de Latour' published
      serially
1889 15 November: 'Appreciations' published
1890 May: second edition of 'Appreciations' published,
      with Aesthetic Poetry omitted
      15 November: delivers Prosper Mérimée as the
      Taylorian Lecture at Oxford
      24 November: repeats the lecture at the London
      Institute
1892 2 August: delivers lecture on Leonardo at the Fifth
      Summer Session of the University Extension, Oxford
1893 10 February: 'Plato and Platonism' published
      13 July: moves to 64 St Giles's, Oxford
1894 13 April: receives the honorary degree of LLD of
      the University of Glasgow
      28 July: delivers a lecture on Rubens before the
      Sixth Summer Session of the University Extension
      30 July: dies at Oxford and is buried in Hollywell
      Cemetery

Introduction

Walter Pater's literary output during his lifetime amounted
to only five books; his first was sufficient to guarantee
him a distinct place in the history of English letters.
Initially, he made his mark at Brasenose College, Oxford,
where he had been elected to a classical fellowship in 1864.
Yet for the thirty years he spent at Brasenose College as a
writer and teacher he met with suspicion and hostility from
those in authority — from Benjamin Jowett (see p.255
n.1) downwards — who 'felt instinctively that he was
inaugurating a mode of thought and feeling which would
prove irresistible to a troublesome type of young man'.(1)
   For a short time after his election Pater was relatively
unknown to the undergraduates and seniors of his college,
but when the essays on Coleridge and Winckelmann appeared
in 1866 and 1867 respectively, 'there at once began, in a
very small group in Oxford and in London, that curiosity of
admiration which became general when the Lionardo article
appeared in the "Fortnightly Review" (1869)'.(2) Among
the first to notice the latter article were D.G. Rossetti
and A.C. Swinburne, whom Pater held in high regard. In a
letter dated 26 November 1869 to Swinburne, Rossetti wrote:
'What a remarkable article that is of Pater's on Leonardo!
Something of *you* perhaps, but a good deal of himself too to
good purpose.'(3) Two days later Swinburne replied: 'I
liked Pater's article on Leonardo very much. I did confess
there was a little spice of my own style as you say, but
much good stuff of his own, and much of interest.'(4) This
group of admirers expanded with the publication of his
first book, 'Studies in the History of the Renaissance'
(1873), and with his next, 'Marius the Epicurean' (1885);
it included many young men who were to become prominent
literary figures in the 1890s, most notably, perhaps, Oscar
Wilde, William Sharp, George Moore, 'Vernon Lee', Lionel
Johnson, Arthur Symons, Richard Le Gallienne and W.B. Yeats.

1

His remarkable personality and almost military appearance,
the novelty of his lectures,(5) his philosophy of approaching life in the spirit of art and his unique prose style
made an indelible impression on the undergraduates. One
acquaintance later recalled: 'No man ever came into the
presence of Mr Pater without feeling a certain spell come
over him.'(6)

After the publication of his second book Pater abandoned
'the jealous professionalism of Oxford' and attempted to
launch himself as a man of letters in the 'wider and world-
lier audience' of London.(7) In August of 1885 he moved
from his Oxford residence to 12 Earl's Terrace, Kensington.
It is revealing that he lived four doors from the home of
the poetess Mary Robinson, later known as Madame Duclaux
and then as Madame Darmesteter (1857-1944), whose father
entertained the literary and artistic personalities of the
day.(8) He made many new friends, gave dinner parties,
contributed to the leading magazines and newspapers and
published three more books, 'Imaginary Portraits' (1887),
'Appreciations' (1889) and 'Plato and Platonism' (1893),
which added to his reputation. According to reports,
however, Pater became 'averse to being lionised'.(9) At
first he found London stimulating, but his anxieties and
despondency, which were reflected, for example, in the
melancholy of 'Imaginary Portraits', returned.(10) He admitted the failure of the experiment by returning to the
academic seclusion of Oxford in the summer of 1893.

With the publication of his last book, 'Plato and
Platonism', he secured the academic recognition for which
he had struggled all his career. Jowett, who had predicted
in 1861 that Pater had a mind which would come to 'great
eminence' and who had later identified him 'with the advanced aesthetic school', healed the breach in their friendship by warmly congratulating him on the book (Benson, 54-5).
Pater was finally accepted as a son of Oxford and proclaimed
by some to be 'the first of our living critics' (No. 55).

Pater's reputation reached its height in the twenty
years following his death. In the Introduction to his
'Oxford Book of Modern Verse' (1936) Yeats observed that
Pater had become the 'only contemporary classic', the one
writer who had his generation's 'uncritical admiration'.
Yeats and his literary friends regarded 'The Renaissance'
as the most influential of Pater's books; 'Marius' as his
masterpiece. Symons spoke of the former as 'the most
beautiful book of prose in our literature' (No. 35); Wilde
called it his 'golden book' and always travelled with a
copy.(11) Moore referred to the latter as 'the book to
which I owe the last temple in my soul' (No. 28). They
believed that Pater's influence did much to rescue them

'from the dangerous moralities, the uncritical enthusiasms
and prejudices, of Mr Ruskin'.(12)

As literary taste shifted Pater fell out of intellectual
fashion. When in 1930 T.S. Eliot described him as 'the cultivated Oxford don and disciple of Arnold, for whom religion was a matter of feeling and metaphysics not much
more',(13) he 'fixed' the image by which Pater has been
known for four decades. Today he is a shadowy figure, and
in many people's minds his reputation is entangled with
the notoriety of Oscar Wilde and the Aesthetic Movement.
The following judgment is typical:

> For years Pater's books were considered a part of a young
> man's academic education, for years they stood unread on
> the shelves of aesthetic undergraduates who would argue
> about them, profess to be guided by them, anything but
> read them. The words in them are manipulated with a
> cunning almost unprecedented in English prose, but they
> have no guts. If Pater had anything to say he never
> dared say it.(14)

Pater has been much misunderstood by his critics. He stood
aloof from the critical debates which his early works provoked, left few letters and no diaries explaining his intentions and became more and more elusive.

PATER AND THE REVIEWERS

Pater was keenly interested in the reception of his books,
and, like many Victorians, he was sensitive to adverse criticism in the press. It had long been his ambition to have
them included in Macmillan & Company's list of 'high' literature (LWP, 56) and to have them favourably reviewed in the
leading journals.

Periodicals and newspapers flourished during his career;
'The Times', the 'Spectator', the 'Saturday Review' and
the 'Athenaeum' in particular rose to a position of considerable power. Almost every new book attracted critical
attention in the press and 'a favourable notice in "The
Times" could make all the difference to a book's sales'.(15)
As the press proliferated, reviewing became a professional
occupation, and eminent reviewers like Richard Le Gallienne,
Edmund Gosse, R.H. Hutton, Andrew Lang and George Saintsbury exerted an immense influence upon the educated reader.
By the 1880s the dogmatic 'sermon' of the first part of the
century was giving way to the informal article, which
stressed 'appreciation'. Consequently, a variety of literary standards prevailed. Some writers, like Havelock Ellis,

eschewed critical systems or theories altogether, but many
adopted the common practice of judging a writer by his sincerity.

The nature of Pater's work, which 'seems to lie in a
twilight of categories between criticism and creation',(16)
perplexed many reviewers. The traditional, neo-classical
school of criticism viewed his 'aesthetic' or 'synthetic'
technique with distrust. John Morley identified it as a
sign of a new school and Arthur Symons praised it as a
fine art, but Mrs Pattison, Mrs Oliphant, W.J. Courthope
and Andrew Lang regretted that it lacked objectivity.
Pater's fiction puzzled many critics because it did not
conform to the realistic tradition established by such famous novelists as Dickens, George Eliot, Thackeray and
Trollope. To Philistine readers his esoteric themes and
serious treatment of them were indigestible. They found
Pater insincere because he seemed to stress form above
matter. The more probing critics, however, commended the
originality of his 'imaginary portraits'.

Pater was often thought to be a member of the Aesthetic
Movement because his writings seemed to suggest the separation of art and morals. By 1882 this movement had
gained considerable notoriety as a result of the satire
on the Aesthetes, the Fleshly Poets and the Pre-Raphaelites
in George Du Maurier's cartoons in 'Punch', Gilbert and
Sullivan's comic opera 'Patience' (which was first produced
on 23 April 1881) and F.C. Burnand's 'The Colonel' (which
was first produced on 4 October 1881). Earlier, Pater had
been satirised as 'Mr Rose' the arch-aesthete in the 'New
Republic' (see p. 227, n.1), which first appeared in
'Belgravia' from June to December of 1876. 'Patience' and
'The Colonel' were written, Walter Hamilton tells us in
'The Aesthetic Movement in England' (1882), 'with the
avowed purpose of ridiculing a certain school, known as the
AESTHETIC'. Hamilton writes:

> No doubt some of the popular ridicule of the Aesthetic
> School has been brought about by the zeal of Mr. Oscar
> Wilde, whose somewhat unguarded utterances, and pecu-
> liarities of garb have been seized upon by sapient
> critics, who find it easier to laugh at his knee
> breeches than his poetry, which for the greater part
> they appear not to have read. (P. 99)

In order to avoid further misunderstanding Hamilton identifies Rossetti, Morris, Swinburne, O'Shaughnessey and Wilde
as members of this school, 'who pride themselves upon
having found what is the really beautiful in nature and
art, their faculties and tastes being educated up to the

point necessary for the full appreciation of such qualities' (p. vii). Those who did not see the true and the
beautiful were called 'Philistines'. Significantly, Pater
is omitted from this study.

Pater's works were widely reviewed in the American
press, but as late as 1896 critics were still saying that
he was not as well-known as he should be (No. 90). 'Harper's Magazine' (No. 24), the influential journal devoted
to the printing of literature which would not offend women
or religious sensibilities, explained that his seriousness
would irritate as many readers as it would please. It
appears that, in the period between the Civil War and the
Chicago Fair (1892), the new culture-conscious middle-class
reader preferred the architectural writings of the prophets
John Ruskin and Charles Eastlake, together with the art of
the Pre-Raphaelites and William Morris, in his attempt to
design and furnish 'The House Beautiful'.(17) This is not
surprising, as Ruskin's disciples included W.J. Stillman
and C.E. Norton, two of the most powerful figures in nineteenth-century America. During this period George Woodberry,
along with his small group of critics known as the last of
the 'defenders of Ideality' (see headnote to No. 26), promoted Pater's reputation and in fact appropriated many of
his aesthetic views in their crusade against the materialism of the age, but Pater's alleged connexion with the
Aesthetic Movement aroused deep hostility in Philistine
minds. The Catholic Church repeatedly denounced Pater as
a dilettante and 'the literary hierophant of that aesthetic school in England' (No. 90), a view which was shared
by Stillman, Sarah Wister and Agnes Repplier. It was widely
believed that his influence was morally subversive, and
this trend culminated in P.E. More's attack on 'Paterism'
in 1911 (No. 100).(18)

After the turn of the century Logan Pearsall Smith (1865-
1946), man of letters, and his friend Bernard Berenson
(1865-1959), art historian, critic, connoisseur and author
of 'The Italian Painters of the Renaissance' (1930), became
Pater's most devoted American disciples. Both left Harvard
in 1888 to become students at Oxford; Berenson asked to
attend Pater's lectures, but was told that they were 'drawing to an end' (LWP, 172). The influence of 'The Renaissance' on Berenson's career has been discussed by Sylvia
Sprigge in her book, 'Berenson: A Biography' (1960).
Pearsall Smith's adulation of Pater is rather fulsome and
in the 'Paterian' style, which was denigrated by More. In
On Re-Reading Walter Pater, which first appeared in the
TLS for 3 February 1927, he attempted to recapture the
enthusiasm that his undergraduate colleagues felt for the
'expressiveness and beauty' of Pater's writings and his
gospel for 'a new way of living'.

On the Continent, however, Pater's books generated
little serious attention until the 1890s, when artists and
writers on both sides of the Channel began to exchange
ideas (the French, for example, borrowed the word 'aesthete'
from England). Pre-Raphaelitism and the Aesthetic Movement
were topics which aroused much interest, and of course many
of Wilde's aesthetic views were traced back to Pater. The
publication of the memorial articles by Edmund Gosse and
others (see p.38) introduced the author of 'The Renaissance' to many European readers.

In France, Hippolyte Taine (1828-93), the critic, historian and author of 'The History of English Literature'
(1863), inspired a number of writers to study the English
literary scene. His Notes on England, a series of articles
on such topics as Oxford, painters and criticism and the
Pre-Raphaelites which appeared in the Paris 'Temps' between 1860 and 1870, were very popular and were reprinted
in extract form in the world press. Taine's notes prompted
the aesthete Paul Bourget (1852-1935) to investigate the
English version of Gautier's *l'art pour l'art* at first
hand. Bourget visited England in 1884 and printed his impressions in 'Études Anglaises' (Paris, 1887). In the
chapter entitled English Aestheticism, really a review of
'Vernon Lee's' 'Miss Brown' (see headnote to No. 25), he
speaks of Pater as 'a writer of delicate prose', whose
'book on the Renaissance contains twenty of the most beautiful pages which have ever been consecrated to Leonardo
da Vinci' (p. 293). In 1889 Theodore de Wyzewa (see headnote to No. 67), Bourget's colleague on the 'Revue des
Deux Mondes', began to call attention to Pater as a much
undervalued writer. De Wyzewa printed three articles in
his Foreign Literature section and these are the first
serious appraisals of Pater's work. He warms to Pater as
the typical Oxford recluse and the pre-eminent disciple of
Flaubert (No. 67). The first translation to appear was
G. Knopff's 'Portraits Imaginaires' (Paris, 1899), which
included an introduction by Arthur Symons. Others followed
between 1917 and 1930. Brief mention must be made of
another volume of 'Études Anglaises' (Paris, 1910).   This
book was written by Raymond Laurent, a poet who died at
the age of twenty-one. Laurent regretted that de Wyzewa's
articles and Knopff's translation were the only demonstra-
tions in France of interest in this 'indefatigable craftsman' and Oxford recluse. In this book he traces the Romantic tradition which runs through Coleridge, Morris, Pater
and Wilde and shows the parallels between English and
French aestheticism.

In the period between the wars critical attention concentrated on the investigation of 'aestheticism' and

'decadence' in general. This vogue produced a variety of
studies which dealt indirectly with Pater; they included
Albert Farmer's 'Le mouvement esthétique et décadent en
Angleterre' (Paris, 1931) and Louise Rosenblatt's 'L'idée
de l'art pour l'art dans la littérature anglaise dans la
période victorienne' (Paris, 1931). One influential critic,
however, noted in his journal entry for 2 February 1923
that there was almost a 'total lack of response' to, and a
'total lack of understanding' of, Pater in France.(19)
This was the view of Charles du Bos (1882-1939), who had
become a disciple while studying at Oxford as a young man.
Du Bos shared his enthusiasm for Pater with his close
friend André Gide (1869-1951), who had met Oscar Wilde in
1891. Du Bos went so far as to model his own criticism on
Pater's technique of finding the 'formula' or 'active
principle' that penetrates a work of art. He proposed to
remedy the situation by writing a book entitled 'Walter
Pater: ou l'ascète de la beauté', which would deal with
'Marius', 'Plato and Platonism' and the essay on Pascal,
as well as explore the Pater-Wilde problem. This ambition
did not materialise until he included a chapter on 'Marius'
in the Fourth Series of 'Approximations' (Paris, 1930).

In Germany, Pater's aesthetic and philosophic theories
first attracted the attention of a small group of intellectuals which included Hugo von Hofmannsthal and his
friend and mentor, Hermann Bahr (1863-1934), the Austrian
critic, novelist and dramatist. Hofmannsthal announced his
'find' to Bahr, the spokesman for the group, in a letter
dated 6 August 1894. He looked to Swinburne, Wilde and
Pater as sources of inspiration for his own brand of 'romantic' aestheticism; what interested him was 'The psychology and purpose of the artist and the mystery of the creative process'.(20) He found Pater a congenial spirit - a
lover of Goethe and German culture, a writer whose imagination was visual and a critic who was, especially in 'The
Renaissance', 'the very rare man who is born to understand
the artist' and to present him 'as a whole' to the reader
(No. 64). In this respect Hofmannsthal, elevated 'the
great English critic' above Goethe. While he adopted
Pater's critical method to make his own more objective,
Hofmannsthal rejected the philosophy of approaching life
in the spirit of art.

In the following decades Hofmannsthal's newspaper articles on aestheticism undoubtedly aroused some interest in
Pater's work among other German aesthetes, but until the
1920s this literary activity consisted primarily of seven
translations of his books. Critical studies date from
Eduard Boch's 'Paters Einfluss auf Oscar Wilde' (Bonn,
1913) and culminate in Wolfgang Iser's philosophical study,

'Walter Pater: die Autonomie des Ästhetischen' (Tübingen
1960).

What emerges from the critical response is the image of
Pater as a 'writer's writer'. Critics often regretted that
he was more concerned with his own consciousness and sensibility than his subject-matter (No. 69). These reviewers
failed to detect in his writings 'a prolonged quarrel with
himself'; they interpreted his philosophy of self-unifi-
cation through aesthetic contemplation as an advocacy of
selfishness and sensuality. In the essay on Style (1888)
Pater repudiated his former 'art for art's sake' position
and declared that great art depends not on form but matter.
Nothing irritated Pater more than to be known simply as
the 'high priest' of style. As William Sharp pointed out
in 1894, Pater wanted to be known as a 'thinker'(21) with
a message for an age dominated by materialism.

At the outset of his literary career Pater addressed
himself to 'a comparatively small section of readers', but
the largely unsympathetic response to 'The Renaissance',
together with the malicious caricature of him in the 'New
Republic', put him on his guard. What really 'ruffled'
Pater was 'the persistence with which the newspapers at the
time [1876] began to attribute to him all sorts of "aesthetic" follies and extravagances'.(22) As he informed
George Saintsbury, 'very few of his critics had seen what
he was aiming at'.(23) When many of them labelled him a
'hedonist',(24) he protested to Edmund Gosse that the word
produced 'such a bad effect on the minds of those who did
not know Greek'.(25) Consequently, in 'Appreciations' and
in 'Plato and Platonism' he attempted to reach beyond
literary and artistic circles to what he called 'average
readers'.

In order to clarify his meaning, and thus remove grounds
for misunderstanding and offence, Pater incessantly revised
his works. For the second edition of 'The Renaissance' he
altered the book's full title from 'Studies in the History
of the Renaissance' to 'The Renaissance: Studies in Art
and Poetry', modernised the spelling of Mirandula, Michael
Angelo and Lionardo, toned down his expression of aestheticism, excised passages plainly provocative or critical of
religion, and, most significantly, suppressed the Conclusion, because, as he said later, 'it might possibly mis-
lead some of those young men into whose hands it might
fall'. Many of these alterations and suppressions were
made in response to specific criticisms, as in the case of
Mrs Pattison's attack on the 'misleading' title (No. 6).

Many of the changes made to the four versions of 'The
Renaissance' were too subtle to be noticed by the critics.
One important instance was the alterations Pater made to

the Conclusion, which recommended 'the supreme, artistic
view of life', before he reprinted it in the third edition (1888); he restored the Conclusion because he had
'dealt more fully in "Marius the Epicurean" with the
thoughts suggested by it'. Pater calls these changes
'slight' and says they were made 'to bring it closer to
my original meaning'. There are at least thirty-eight
points of difference in the first and third edition printings of the essay; five are significant, while the rest are
basically stylistic variations. For example, in the first
edition Pater wrote: 'we have an interval, and then our
place knows us no more. Some spend this interval in listlessness, some in high passions, the wisest in art and song'.
This is one of the passages which annoyed Mrs Oliphant (No.
10). In the third edition Pater altered the last phrase to
read: 'the wisest, at least "among the children of this
world", in art and song'. A collation of the third and
fourth edition (1893) printings of the Conclusion reveals
seventeen variations, the majority of which involve refinement of expression. One of the most significant is the
following. In the third edition the last sentence reads:
'For art comes to you frankly to give nothing but the highest quality to your moments as they pass, and simply for
the love of art for art's sake.' The last phrase was
altered to read: 'and simply for the love of art for its
own sake'. Interestingly enough, the Library Edition
(1910) gives a different version again: 'and simply for
those moments' sake'.

   Almost immediately after the publication of 'Marius'
Pater began to revise the book for a second edition. He
made more than one hundred alterations, primarily in word
order and punctuation, but they are insignificant in comparison with the changes he made for the third edition
(1892). Pater considered this revision so important that
he abandoned 'Gaston de Latour' and spent four more years
on the book. Edmund Chandler claims that there are six
thousand textual variations from the previous editions and
that 'the great majority of the alterations are made within
the context of the original sentence in meaning and shape'.
(26) Richard Le Gallienne examined some of the alterations
to the third edition and concluded that Pater had been
'overcome by a grammatical affection of nerves' (No. 30).

   In response to criticism of 'Appreciations' Pater suppressed the essay on Aesthetic Poetry from the second
edition of 1890 and from all subsequent editions. In a
letter of May 1890 to Herbert Horne (see headnote to No.
36), Lionel Johnson remarked that 'there were things in it;
which some people, pious souls! thought profane, yes!
profane' (see LWP, xxiii). 'Michael Field' offers a

slightly different account in the journal entry for 25
August 1890: 'Pater has ... struck out the Essay on
Aesthetic Poetry in "Appreciations" because it gave offence
to some pious person — he is getting hopelessly prudish
in literature and defers to the moral weakness of everybody. Deplorable!'(27) Pater may have been thinking of
the criticism of William Watson or C.L. Graves (see Nos 43
and 44), who thought that, in emphasising the atmosphere
of William Morris's poetry as reverie, illusion and delirium, Pater was encouraging the 'pagan spirit'.

Pater also tried to forestall disapproval by arranging
to have notices written by his influential friends. In
each case he wrote a letter of gratitude, but curiously
refrained from taking up the 'literary points' which individual critics identified (see headnote to No. 23).

Some weeks before publication he 'leaked' a bound copy
of the proofs of 'Marius' to William Sharp, so that his
favourable notice would set the tone for subsequent
critiques.(28) Sharp printed two premature enthusiastic
reviews. The first appeared four days before the book
was released and on the day of publication Alexander Macmillan wrote to Pater regretting these early reviews. 'We
take pains that all papers have their copies for review
as nearly as possible at the same time. We certainly sent
early copies to neither "The Athenaeum" nor "Time". How
did they get them?'(29) Pater's reply is missing.

Pater intensified his log-rolling campaign after the
publication of 'Appreciations', partly because the reviewers
had criticised him for directing 'Imaginary Portraits' to a
small audience. Because he had heard that Lionel Johnson
was likely to write an article on the book for the 'Century
Guild Hobby Horse', on 24 December 1889 he wrote to its
editor, Herbert Horne, a mutual friend, expressing interest
in the next number of the journal (LWP, 105-6). In his
letter he enclosed a clipping of Watson's favourable review.
Immediately after hearing some of the details of Johnson's
article from A.H. Galton (1852-1921), the scholar, critic,
priest and assistant editor of the 'Hobby Horse', Pater
called on Johnson at nine on the morning of 18 February
1890. He was agitated and insisted on knowing what was
said in the article (see LWP, 108n). Johnson quickly
wrote to Galton, who sent Pater a copy of the journal containing the article. On 4 January 1890 Pater wrote to
Oscar Wilde (see headnote to No. 50), expressing a keen
interest in the 'Speaker'. This review of politics, letters, science and the arts had appeared for the first time
that day (Saturday), and in advance notices in the 'Athenaeum' Wilde was listed as a contributor. This hint did
not go unheeded, for Wilde printed an enthusiastic notice
of 'Appreciations' in the March issue (No. 50).

Pater was sensitive to adverse criticism throughout his career. This fact is illustrated by the following story, which was recorded by an Oxford acquaintance, D.S. MacColl (1859-1948), who was art critic for the 'Spectator' from 1890 until 1895:

'Plato' appeared, and one morning I was called from a scandalously late bath by a visitor. It was Pater with a copy in his hand. He gave me this, and explained that he was concerned about its reception by the reviewers. Could I arrange to deal with it in the 'Spectator'? I stammered my astonishment that he should care what any reviewer said, and urged the difficulty of invading Mr Hutton's domain. It would fall, I was certain, into more competent hands, but I would find some less preoccupied corner to say my modest word. Evidently he was conscious, even in '93, of disapproval and suspicion.(30)

It seems likely that he also persuaded J.M. Gray (No. 20), Clement Shorter (No. 39), William Sharp (No. 40), Arthur Symons (No. 42), L.C. Moulton (No. 47), J.R. Thursfield (No. 52), Richard Le Gallienne (No. 53) and Edmund Gosse (No. 55) to write their favourable reviews.

PUBLICATION AND SALES

Pater's contemporaries attributed the fact that he published comparatively little to his conscientiousness and 'passion for perfection'. Many acquaintances concurred with Edmund Gosse in his belief that there never was a writer 'to whom the act of composition was such a travail and an agony'.(31) Actually, he made many false starts in different directions in the period 1873 to 1885 and promised or undertook too much in the period 1885 to 1893.

When Pater introduced himself to Alexander Macmillan (1818-96) in June of 1872 he had published seven articles, three of which had attracted much attention. On 29 June 1872 he sent Macmillan ten essays (one in manuscript form) and suggested that they might make a book of 300 pages. (32) A few days later Macmillan proposed an octavo volume and terms of 'half profits' (the publisher would carry the risk and the author would share the profits). He accepted this handsome proposal, but when he received the proofs of the essays in September he had doubts about their suitability. He thought the essays 'short', 'slight' and 'only suitable' for a volume costing about five shillings (LWP, 8).

He was also concerned about the book's physical appearance. In his letter of 2 November 1872 to Macmillan he said he liked 'the look of the page, but not altogether the paper'. He suggested that the book be bound in the old-fashioned pasteboard covers of greyish-blue and that the title be printed on a paper back of olive green. Macmillan disagreed, arguing that booksellers would be reluctant to stock such a book, and pressed for cloth binding and gilt lettering.(33) Pater was determined to give his book the 'artistic appearance' which a volume on art required and attempted to overcome Macmillan's objections in his letter of 11 November 1872:

> Something not quite in the ordinary way is, I must repeat, very necessary in a volume the contents of which are so unpretending as in mine, and which is intended in the first instance for a comparatively small section of readers. For a book on art to be bound quite in the ordinary way is, it seems to me, behind the times; and the difficulty of getting a book bound in cloth so as to be at all artistic, and indeed not quite the other way, is very great. (LWP, 10)

Macmillan continued to argue for cloth binding and on the following day he sent Pater a sample volume with imitation 'wirewove paper' in 'mock rib' to persuade him (LWP, 10n). These materials convinced him and 'Studies in the History of the Renaissance' was bound in dark blue-green cloth lettered in gold and issued on 1 March 1873 in an edition of 1,250 copies (a size commensurate with its limited appeal).

During Pater's lifetime the book went through four editions. On 13 November 1876 Macmillan suggested that he pursue his plan to issue a new and revised edition of the book. Pater made a number of revisions (see pp.8-9) and included an engraved vignette of 'Head of a Youth', once ascribed to Leonardo (LWP, 20n). He also felt that it 'should be thoroughly advertised when it does appear' (LWP, 21).(34) 'The Renaissance: Studies in Art and Poetry' was issued on 24 May 1877 in an edition of 1,250 copies. Pater thought that only 1,000 copies should be printed, but was informed by Macmillan in a letter dated 26 February 1877 that 'the last 250 makes a considerable difference in the money matter and they are sure to sell'.(35) The third edition, with the Conclusion restored, was issued in 1888 in an edition of 1,500 copies; the fourth was issued in 1893 in an edition of 2,000 copies. American editions, each of 1,000 copies, were issued in 1887 and 1890.

He next contemplated writing a book on Shakespeare, an orthodox subject by which he might restore his somewhat tarnished reputation. Pater 'leaked' word of this plan to the 'Academy' (7 November 1874), which announced his intention 'to continue his short aesthetic studies of Shakspere's Plays in the "Fortnightly", the present month's one on "Measure for Measure" being the first of a series that will some day make a book' (vi, 506). A short while later the 'Academy' (12 December 1874) stated that his next 'study' for the 'Fortnightly Review' would be on 'Love's Labour's Lost' (vi, 630). Evidently he found Shakespeare an uncongenial subject and soon abandoned this path. Early in 1875, F.W. Furnivall (1825-1910), founder of the New Shakspere Society (1873), asked him to edit one of Shakespeare's plays. In his letter of 18 May 1875 to Furnivall, Pater said that, although he wanted to edit a play for schoolboys, possibly 'Romeo and Juliet', he could see no prospect of doing so for some time (LWP, 15). The essay on 'Love's Labour's Lost' remained unfinished for a number of years. It was read before the New Shakspere Society on 13 April 1878 (LWP, 15n), but was not published until 1885, when it appeared in 'Macmillan's Magazine' (December 1885).

Pater then proposed writing a book on Greek mythology, a subject to which his mind had turned by November of 1875. Within three years he had written the lectures entitled The Myth of Demeter and Persephone and A Study of Dionysus. In his letter of 1 October 1878 to Alexander Macmillan he proposed to print early in 1879 a volume of miscellaneous essays collected from various periodicals. This book, which he planned to call 'The School of Giorgione, and other Studies', was to include essays on Giorgione, Wordsworth, the myths of Demeter, Persephone and Dionysus, Romanticism, 'Love's Labour's Lost', 'Measure for Measure' and Charles Lamb. On the following day Macmillan wrote to say that he would be very glad to publish this new volume of essays uniform with the second edition of 'The Renaissance'. Pater was more confident about this book than the last one and he approached the 'Academy' and the 'Athenaeum', both of which announced on 5 October 1878 that it could be expected early in the following year. On 18 November 1878 he said that the book was ready to be printed, but five days later he asked Macmillan to call it 'Dionysus and Other Studies' (LWP, 34). The paper was specially made and proof copies were printed later that month, but when he revised the proofs he changed his mind again and decided to stop the publication of this volume altogether. Macmillan was concerned about this decision because the book had been

advertised in the press. He wrote to Pater, arguing that
there was no reason for his apprehension since the volume
would make a worthy successor to 'The Renaissance'. (36)
Nevertheless, the type was broken up at his own expense.
Curiously, he advised Macmillan not to 'announce, in any
way, that the book is not to be published' (LWP, 34).

In the midst of his Greek studies Pater discovered his
métier, the 'imaginary portrait', a fictional device which
derived from the critical technique he had employed in the
Renaissance studies, namely realising the personality behind the philosophical idea or work of art. The 'imaginary' portrait provided greater artistic detachment. He
published his first piece of fiction, Imaginary Portraits.
I. The Child in the House, in 'Macmillan's Magazine' in
August 1878. In a letter dated 17 April 1878 he wrote:
'I call the M.S. a portrait, and mean readers, as they
might do on seeing a portrait, to begin speculating — what
came of him?' (LWP, 30). At the same time he began, but
never completed, the second portrait of this series, An
English Poet, which was published by Mrs Ottley in the
'Fortnightly Review' (April 1931). On a slip of paper that
survives among the Harvard manuscripts he wrote: 'Child in
the House: voilà, the germinating, original, source, specimen of all my *imaginative* work' (LWP, xxix).

By the end of 1881 Pater was working on a new portrait,
'Marius the Epicurean', which is dated '1881-1884' in the
second and subsequent editions. The book was 'designed to
be the first of a kind of trilogy, or triplet, of works of
a similar character; dealing with the same problems, under
altered historical conditions' (LWP, 65). 'Gaston de
Latour' was meant to be the second work of this series.
Perhaps an expanded version of An English Poet was meant
to be the third.

He began research for 'Marius' in the spring of 1881.
(37) In his memorial article William Sharp pointed out
that this book 'had been begun, and in part written, long
before Walter Pater went to Rome'.(38) In 1882 he spent
seven weeks in Rome, collecting material, and in 1883 he
put off his continental holiday, remaining in Oxford to
work on the book. He first disclosed his plans to his
blue-stocking friend, 'Vernon Lee', who informed her
mother on 24 July 1882 that Pater 'seems to be writing ...
a novel about the time of Marcus Aurelius' (VLL, 105).
In his letter dated 22 July 1883 he observed that he regarded the completion of the work 'as a sort of duty' and
that he wanted to show 'that there is a fourth sort of
religious phase possible for the modern mind' (LWP, 52),
over and above the three presented in her article on The
Responsibilities of Unbelief in the 'Contemporary Review'

(May 1883). While she stayed with the Paters in Oxford
from 18 to 21 June 1884 he read her some of the novel,
presumably the first two chapters, but she thought that
they lacked 'vitality' (VLL, 147).

Characteristically, Pater tried to publish the work
serially. He submitted the first two chapters to his
friend John Morley, who had become the editor of 'Macmillan's Magazine', but they were found unfit for serial publication. Pater acknowledged their unsuitability and early
in July sent them to Alexander Macmillan,(39) with the view
to having the work published in the spring of the following year. He also hoped that the book might be taken 'on
slightly more favourable terms' than in the case of his
former volume. He was informed on 11 September 1884 that
Macmillan & Company 'would greatly like to publish' the
new book, but could not offer better terms than 'equal
division of profits' because of the uncertainty of the
book's sales'.(40) As an expression of his confidence in
this book, Macmillan offered to pay him, on publication,
£50 on account, whether his share reached this amount or
not. Pater accepted this offer, but asked that the book
be precisely similar to the second edition of 'The Renaissance' with regard to 'size, quality of paper, and binding'.
'Marius' was printed in two volumes, bound in dark blue
cloth lettered in gold (as were his subsequent books) and
issued on 4 March 1885 in an edition of 1,000 sets.

A second edition was soon required. He was notified on
11 June 1885 that the first edition was almost sold out.
Macmillan & Company made two proposals for a less expen-
sive edition, either in one volume on thinner paper or in
two volumes uniform with the Eversley Edition of the works
of Charles Lamb. Pater chose the latter and the second
edition of 2,000 sets was released on 13 November 1885.

'Marius' went through three editions during his lifetime.
A third (in the original form) of 2,000 sets was issued in
June of 1892. Three American editions of 1,000 sets each
were released in November of 1885, December of 1890 and
January of 1893. Frederick Macmillan (1851-1936) informed
him on 8 December 1890 that 'Our people in New York want
the book badly'.(41)

From March of 1885 to spring of 1887 Pater was at work
on a collection of 'imaginary portraits', publishing one
portrait a year in 'Macmillan's Magazine'. At first he
planned to include The Child in the House in 'Imaginary
Portraits', but at the last moment decided that it required
too many alterations and settled for the portraits of Jean
Baptiste Watteau, Denys l'Auxerrois, Sebastian van Storck
and Duke Carl of Rosenmold. On 24 May 1887 the book was
issued in an edition of 1,000 copies. Three years later,

on 30 May 1890, Frederick informed him that there were
fewer than forty copies left.(42) A second edition of
1,250 copies was released in November of 1890.

In June of 1888 he began work on 'Gaston de Latour',
the second book of his proposed trilogy. He published the
first five chapters in 'Macmillan's Magazine' from June to
October, and the greater part of chapter vii (The Lower
Pantheism) as Giordano Bruno in the 'Fortnightly Review'
in August of 1889. He temporarily abandoned this work to
complete one of the most difficult compositions he had
undertaken, namely the essay of Style, which he printed in
the 'Fortnightly Review' (December 1888). Pater never gave
up hope of publishing 'Gaston', for he struggled with
this work until late 1891.

He made a third attempt to publish a collection of miscellaneous essays in June of the same year. He proposed
that this book, provisionally entitled 'On Style, with other
studies in literature', should be printed for publication
before the first of November and that it should appear in
all respects similar to the third edition of 'The Renaissance'. Under the title of 'Appreciations, with an Essay
on Style', the book was released on 15 November 1889 in an
edition of 1,000 copies. The book sold very rapidly. On
23 December 1889 George Macmillan (1855-1936) informed him
that there were only 120 copies left. He felt that, although sales would slacken a little after Christmas, a reprint should be issued without delay.(43) For some reason
Pater lingered over the correction of the proofs and the
second edition of 1,500 copies was not released until May
of 1890. In July of that year 1,000 copies were printed
for release in America.

Pater was heavily 'over-burdened with work' by July
of 1890. In August he planned to visit Italy, but the trip
was postponed due to his work on Art Notes in Italy, which
appeared later in the 'New Review' (November 1890), and
on 'an Imaginary Portrait with Brescia for a background'.
Lawrence Evans notes that the latter is the manuscript
fragment entitled Gaudioso, the Second, now at Harvard.

He preferred writing 'imaginary portraits', for in 1890
he contemplated publishing a second series with the same
title. Apparently he meant to include Hippolytus Veiled,
a study based on Giovanni Moroni's 'Portrait of a Tailor',
a portrait set in the time of the Albigensian persecution
and a modern study.(44) On 22 January 1892 he announced
that a revised version of this series was near completion
and by December the volume was tentatively called 'Three
Short Stories', which would have included Hippolytus
Veiled, Emerald Uthwart and Apollo in Picardy (Benson, 123).
This book did not materialise. Pater died with four pub-

lished portraits still uncollected: The Child in the
House, Hippolytus Veiled, Emerald Uthwart and Apollo in
Picardy, and unpublished fragments of at least four more:
An English Poet, Gaudioso, the Second, Il Sartore and
Tibalt the Albigense (see LWP, xxx).

In December of 1890 Pater began writing the lectures
on Plato and Platonism, which were published under that
title three years later. These undergraduate lectures
began on 21 January 1891 and were delivered at noon on
Wednesdays of the Hilary term. Typically, he attempted to
secure a wider audience by publishing the chapters separately as articles. On 21 December 1891 he sent 'The
Genius of Plato (ch. vi) to Percy William Bunting (1836-
1911), editor from 1882 to 1911 of the 'Contemporary Review'. In his letter he remarked: 'I have treated the
subject in as popular a manner as I could' (LWP, 124).
Bunting liked the article and it appeared in the February
1892 issue. During 1892 Pater sent four more: Plato and
the Doctrine of Motion (ch. i), Plato and the Doctrine of
Rest (ch. ii), Plato and the Doctrine of Music (ch. iii)
and Lacedaemon (ch. viii). The first appeared in 'Macmillan's Magazine' (May 1892) and the last in the 'Contemporary Review' (June 1892). Bunting and his colleague,
William Canton (1845-1926), pointed out that these lectures required alterations and subdivision of the text
into paragraphs. Although Bunting found The Doctrine of
Plato (ch.vii) particularly interesting, Pater decided on 1
November 1892 that it was too long and unsuitable for publication. He believed that if the lecture appeared as an
article it might prejudice his proposed volume with 'average readers'. Macmillan & Company accepted the book and
on 13 December 1892 they drew up a contract, awarding him
an additional bonus of 10 per cent of the American sales.
'Plato and Platonism' was issued on 10 February 1893 in
an edition of 2,000 copies.

Soon after Pater's death George Macmillan informed
Pater's sisters Hester (1837-1922) and Clara (1841-1910)
that 'if there is an idea of collecting unpublished papers
whether in MS or otherwise it would be a great pleasure to
us to publish them'.(45) Hester pursued this offer and
three posthumous works were published in the following
three years. These were edited by C.L. Shadwell (1840-
1919), Pater's close friend and literary executor and
later Fellow and Provost of Oriel College, Oxford. Shadwell prepared, with Lionel Johnson's assistance (see No.
95), 'Greek Studies' for release on 11 January 1895 in an
edition of 2,000 copies; 'Miscellaneous Studies' for release on 18 October 1895 in an edition of 1,500 copies;
and 'Gaston de Latour' for release on 6 October 1896 in an

edition of 1,500 copies. Shadwell wrote a short Preface
for each book and inserted in the second a chronology
(somewhat inaccurate) of Pater's writings. With these
volumes he hoped to bolster Pater's reputation by dis-
pelling the popular belief that he was merely 'a consummate master of style'. Edmund Gosse prepared and wrote a
short Preface for 'Essays from "The Guardian"', which was
printed in an edition of 100 copies on 6 October 1896 for
'the inner circle of [Pater's] friends'.

On 24 January 1900 Frederick Macmillan proposed that
an edition of Pater's works might be published in the handsome and profitable *Édition de Luxe*. Macmillan maintained
that such a limited edition would be 'at once bought up by
collectors'.(46)   Hester welcomed this proposal, but was
undoubtedly disappointed to learn that terms could not be
altered. On 4 September 1901, 775 sets of the *Édition de
Luxe* were issued;   1,000 copies of 'Essays from "The Guardian"', printed from the private edition of 1896, were included.

Save for the posthumous works, Pater's books were reprinted frequently in the period 1901 to 1910. Three were
very popular;   'Marius' sold well in England (5,100 copies
were released, as compared to 2,500 in America), while 'The
Renaissance' and 'Appreciations' sold well in America
(4,600 and 4,000 copies were issued, as compared to 3,750
and 2,750 in England).

In addition to the many reprints released by the New
York office of Macmillan & Company, a large number of
pirated editions of Pater's works were included among the
'little-known masterpieces of literature' which T.B. Mosher
(1852-1923) introduced to the American reading public.
Mosher, the book-collector and founder of Mosher books,
specialised in the printing of beautiful books at low
cost. Aside from reprinting a great many essays and imaginary portraits separately, or in his monthly magazine
the 'Bibelot' (1894-1914), he printed 425 copies of 'The
Child in the House' in 1895;   400 copies of 'Essays from
"The Guardian"' in 1897; 450 copies of 'Marius' in 1900;
450 and 700 copies of 'The Renaissance' in 1902 and 1912
respectively;   and 925 copies of 'Gaston' in 1906. He
also printed 450 copies of 'Uncollected Essays' (1903):
this book included the eleven uncollected reviews identified by Arthur Symons (see p. 390), together with Pater's
Introduction to 'The Purgatory of Dante Alighieri', which
Shadwell published in 1892.

On 2 February 1910 Frederick Macmillan informed Hester
that a new and uniform edition of Pater's works had been
suggested by several large booksellers. He explained in
his letter that this possibility arose because the stock

of 'The Renaissance' was low and it would have to be reprinted in a few weeks. Moreover, he pointed out, another
edition would have to be printed in a year or two because
the copyright expired in 1915.(47) Hester agreed to this
suggestion and 1,250 sets of the Library Edition were
issued late in 1910.

THE CRITICAL RECEPTION: 1873 TO 1894

'The Renaissance'

For a first book by a relatively unknown writer, 'The
Renaissance' created a considerable stir in the world of
art and letters. Not unnaturally its unconventional attitude provoked a storm of criticism in Oxford. Mrs Ward,
who was twenty-three years old at the time, wrote in 1918:

> I recall very clearly the effect of that book, and of
> the strange and poignant sense of beauty expressed in
> it; of its entire aloofness also from the Christian
> tradition of Oxford, its glorification of the higher
> and intenser forms of aesthetic pleasure, of 'passion'
> in the intellectual sense — as against the Christian
> doctrine of self-denial and renunciation. It was a
> gospel that both stirred and scandalised Oxford. The
> bishop of the diocese thought it worth while to protest.
> There was a cry of 'Neo-paganism', and various attempts
> at persecution.(48)

Generally speaking, the book excited as much censure as
praise. On the one hand, there were those who, like John
Morley, found the essays pleasant and instructive reading
and saw in them a significant contribution to literature;
on the other, there were those who, like Mrs Oliphant,
attacked Pater for his dilettantism and regarded the book
as 'pretentious' and 'artificial', a 'mixture of sense and
nonsense, of real discrimination and a downright want of
understanding' (No. 10). Sarah Wister went so far as to
claim that it lacked originality and that its popularity
derived from its subjects, names and themes, which were in
themselves magical or 'incantations' (No. 14).
     When viewed as an historical work, the book met with
much opposition from the specialists. While some critics
commended Pater's unorthodox interpretation of the Renaissance as 'an uninterrupted effort of the middle age', many
believed that students of the period would learn little
from the book. The 'Spectator' (14 June 1873) observed

that 'after most carefully perusing Mr Pater's book, we
find ourselves gravely doubting whether he has rightly
apprehended the Renaissance at all' (p. 765). W.J. Stillman and Sarah Wister quarrelled with his definition of the
term as a 'revival'; they felt that the term had lost the
significance of its traditional meaning, namely 'new
birth'. Probably through the influence of her husband,
Mrs Pattison protested that the book was 'in no wise a
contribution to the history of the Renaissance' (No. 6).
She attacked its title and lack of 'scientific' method:

> The title is misleading. The historical element is
> precisely that which is wanting, and its absence makes
> the weak place of the whole book.... For instead of
> approaching his subject, whether in Art or Literature,
> by the true scientific method, through the life of the
> time of which it was an outcome, Mr Pater prefers in
> each instance to detach it wholly from its surroundings,
> to suspend it isolated before him, as if it were indeed
> a kind of air-plant independent of the ordinary sources
> of nourishment.

Sidney Colvin pointed out that the choice of subjects was
in fact too fragmentary for the purpose of a complete history (No. 1). J.A. Symonds was sufficiently perceptive to
remark that 'each article treats of some phase of the Renaissance through a representative character or work of
art' (No. 3).

The connoisseurs of art likewise failed to agree on the
merits of the book as art criticism. Reviewers were enthusiastic about the essays on Leonardo, Michelangelo,
Botticelli and Winckelmann. Most readers regarded Leonardo
da Vinci as the best essay in the book and they called the
description of the formula of his painting ('Curiosity and
the desire of beauty — these are the two elementary forces
in Leonardo's genius') 'a first rate analysis'. Colvin and
Morley expressed the consensus of opinion when they declared that the Mona Lisa passage reflected delicate poetry
and imaginative charm. Even Mrs Oliphant, one of his
strictest critics, applauded this passage as 'a really fine
description' (No. 10). Sarah Wister concurred with these
remarks, but attributed its popularity to the fact that
the subject-matter afforded Pater great 'scope for speculation and paradox' (No. 14).

Despite the laudatory comments on these essays, many
specialists viewed Pater's 'aesthetic criticism' with suspicion. For Symonds, his 'aesthetic temperament' caused
him to make mistakes, particularly in the interpretation
of Botticelli's Madonnas as 'peevish-looking', apparently

overcome by a burden too heavy to bear (No. 3). Sarah
Wister questioned the theory that 'incompleteness' served
as an equivalent for colour in Michelangelo's sculpture
(No. 14). While Stillman dismissed his 'aesthetic criti-
cism' as nothing but the expression of his personal taste,
Mrs Oliphant and Sarah Wister more astringently noted that
Pater read too much into a picture (No. 10). The 'Atlantic
Monthly' (October 1873) stated the problem in the following
words:

> modern art-criticism is attributive when it supposes
> itself interpretive. The sight of an old painting in-
> spires the critic with certain emotions, and these he
> straightway seizes upon as the motive of the painter.
> It *may* happen that both are identical; or it may hap-
> pen that the effect produced was never in the painter's
> mind at all. Very likely it was not; but this vice,
> which Mr Ruskin invented, goes on perpetuating itself;
> and Mr Pater, who is as far from thinking with Mr Rus-
> kin as from writing like him, falls a helpless prey to
> it. (xxxii, 497-8)

More than one reviewer traced his critical method to the
influence of Ruskin.

Pater's 'poetical prose' stimulated considerable controversy. Many reviewers like W.J. Courthope referred to the
Mona Lisa passage as 'plain, downright, unmistakable
poetry' (No. 12). As the 'Saturday Review' (26 July 1873)
noted, however, 'The reader runs no doubt some danger of
being carried far away by an alluring imagination and by
a singularly seductive diction' (xxxvi, 123). Readers frequently compared this effect with Ruskin's word-pictures.
Mrs Pattison, for example, praised Pater's gift for match-
ing his language with the quality of the paintings he chose
to describe:

> He can detect with singular subtlety the shades of
> tremulous variation which have been embodied in the
> throbbing pulsations of colour, in doubtful turns of
> line, in veiled words; he can not only do this, but he
> can match them for us in words, in the choice of which
> he is often so brilliantly accurate that they gleam
> upon the paper with the radiance of jewels. (No. 6)

For Sarah Wister, however, Pater 'has the peculiar eloquence which goes with insobriety of style, and all the
charm and force which can be snatched by breaking rules'
(No. 14). She called this fault his 'trick of iteration',
which consisted primarily of variations *ad nauseam* on the

words 'comely' and 'sweetness'. But, rightly, she also
pointed out that one of his chief characteristics was the
'power of giving to his theories — and some few of those
about art are perfectly sound — the clearness of chiselled
marble'.

The *carpe diem* theme of the Conclusion produced a tor-
rent of rebuke from religious and conservative circles in
Oxford. Morley tried to ward off the attack by explaining
that the 'pagan' element of the book was 'one more wave of
the great current of reactionary force which the Oxford
movement first released' and that Pater's theory of art for
art's sake was 'a protest against the mechanical and graceless formalism of the modern era' (No. 5). Indicative is
the fact that Jowett regarded him as a 'demoralising
moraliser' and resolved 'to subvert his influence' (Benson,
55). Writers as different from each other as John Wordsworth, Mrs Oliphant and George Eliot declared that his
philosophy of self-culture was logically incompatible with
Christianity. In his letter of 17 March 1873 to Pater,
Wordsworth voiced the widespread disapproval of the theory
'that no fixed principles either of religion or morality
can be regarded as certain, that the only thing worth
living for is momentary enjoyment' (No. 4). In his sermon
preached before the University of Cambridge on 11 May 1873,
F.W. Farrar (1831-1903), the distinguished Anglican clergyman, Fellow of Trinity College, Cambridge, and Dean of
Canterbury (from 1895), attacked as 'wretched' and 'base'
this ideal of crowning life 'with the greatest number of
pleasurable sensations'.(49) Two years later the Bishop
of Oxford attacked the Conclusion as an advocacy of selfishness and scepticism (No. 13). These protests echo
Colvin's warning: 'By all means, let the people whose bent
is art follow art, by all means refine the pleasures of as
many people as possible; but do not tell everybody that refined pleasure is the one end of life' (No. 1).

'Marius the Epicurean'

Pater's next book, which had been expected with eagerness
and suspense, fascinated most readers. Reviewers on both
sides of the Atlantic greeted this unique work with considerable respect. 'Harper's New Monthly Magazine' (No.
24) called it 'one of the most interesting books of the
decade'. Many commentators concurred with J.M. Gray in
his belief that 'Marius' was 'the most important and sustained work' that he had so far offered to the public
(No. 20). Highest praise came from Mrs Ward, who declared
that there is 'added to the charm of style, and deftly

handled learning, a tenderness of feeling, a tone of
reverence for human affections, and pity for the tragedy of human weakness worthy of George Eliot' (No. 23).
The critic for 'The Times' (No. 22) voiced the general
impression when he described the book as 'fine writing
and hard reading'. Many reviewers concluded that its
esoteric theme and grave tone would appeal only to a
limited audience.

'Marius' fell uneasily into the category of a novel
and was called variously an 'historical' or a 'philosophical' romance. Many critics regretted that it was a
record not of actions but of thoughts and sensations.
Julia Wedgwood argued that its subject-matter was too intellectual for the novel form (No. 25). Gray explained
that, despite its lack of reference to ordinary human
emotions, it scarcely fails to interest because it throws
'the processes of thought into a concrete and pictured
form' (No. 20). Many reviewers, however, agreed with the
view expressed by Ernest Dowson in 1889: 'It is a pity ...
that Pater can not write a *real* novel. If he had the force
of concentration necessary it would be a book unsurpassed
& not surpassable' (No. 29a).

Two of Pater's friends called attention to the autobiographical aspect of the book. While Gray spoke of
Marius as an altered and expanded version of Florian
Deleal, Mrs Ward observed that 'Marius' was a more successful attempt than The Child in the House to secure a
disguise for the autobiographical matter and an impersonal
form for the free expression of his ideas (No. 23). Particularly revealing, in her view, is the fact that Marius,
'as a young man, starts in life on the principles expressed in the concluding pages of the "Studies"'.

Most reviewers approached 'Marius' as an historical
novel and they generally praised the richness of his
scholarship and the power of his interpretive imagination.
'Harper's New Monthly Magazine' (No. 24) remarked: 'As a
student of the age of Marcus Aurelius ... Mr Pater shows
wide and deeply attentive reading.' H.N. Powers in the
'Dial' (August 1885) spoke of the book as the work of 'a
scholar breathing our modern air while charged with the
free spirit of antiquity' (vi, 90). The majority of commentators isolated for special praise the Latin translations, especially the story of Cupid and Psyche and the
passages from Lucian and Marcus Aurelius. Mrs Ward regarded the former as a 'masterpiece' and 'evidence of brilliant
literary capacity'. J.M. Mackail predicted in the 'Oxford
Magazine' (6 May 1885) that the dating and attribution of
the 'Pervigilium Veneris' to Flavian (in ch. vi) would
fascinate many readers (iii, 207).

What pleased most readers, however, were the graphic
descriptions of Rome, the classic banquet in honour of
Apuleius at Lucian's house, the view from the house of
Cecilia, the rituals of the early Christians and Marius'
visit to the Christian tombs. The 'Westminster Review'
(January 1886) expressed what may be called the Philistine response in these words:

> we should find the ceaseless introspection and self-
> communing of Marius simply unendurable were they not
> relieved by the occasional introduction of very vivid
> and realistic pictures of Roman life, manners, and
> scenery, during the latter part of the second century
> of our era: these to our thinking, constitute the real
> charm of the book, shining out like gems from their
> somewhat dreary setting of fruitless dissertation.
> (N.s. lxix, 594-5)

Obviously many readers equated Pater's historical scholarship with these 'impressionistic' pictures of Roman life
and manners.
    A number of critics noticed a striking resemblance
between Pater's Antonine Rome and Victorian England. G.E.
Woodberry, for example, remarked: 'Mr Pater, while he
imagines in Italy, always thinks in London; he has modernized his hero, has Anglicized him, indeed, and nevertheless has not really taken him out of the second century'
(No. 26). Only Mrs Ward formulated the true significance
of this resemblance, namely that 'Marius' represented a
trenchant and indirect analysis of the problem of belief
in Victorian England.(50) In her view, Marius expressed
the reflections of 'a real mind' not of the second but of
the nineteenth century.

> It is in books like 'Sartor Resartus', or 'The Nemesis
> of Faith', 'Alton Locke', or 'Marius', rather than in
> the avowed specimens of self-revelation which the time
> has produced, that the future student of the nineteenth
> century will have to look for what is deepest, most
> intimate, and most real in its personal experience.
> (No. 23)

Mrs Ward added that the book voiced the subtleties and
elusiveness of 'English feeling' at a particularly troubled
time — a time when intellectuals who had repudiated orthodox Christianity constructed world views or beliefs for
themselves which would satisfy their emotional cravings
for the certitude of the old dispensation.

Some reviewers interpreted the book as a philosophical novel. Mackail for one thought that it would be regarded as 'a serious contribution to the highest philosophy'. Curiously, Alfred Goodwin in 'Mind' (July 1885) found it a renunciation of philosophy altogether (x, 444). Most commentators, however, concurred with William Sharp in his belief that Pater was now the chief exponent of Epicureanism (No. 18). Like Gray, readers frequently regarded Epicureanism as Pater's 'guide to a right practice of life', his antidote against modern scepticism (No. 20). In 'Time' (March 1885) Sharp identified the chapter on The New Cyrenaicism as 'an essay of the utmost value to all striving to work out for themselves the difficult problem of how to make the most of life' (n.s. i, 350). Many readers were misled by the ethical drift of the book, as Pater pointed out in his letter to Sharp (see headnote to No. 18).

Mrs Ward was not misled, however, for she contested the view that 'Marius' represented a reassessment of the sceptical philosophy of life expressed in the Conclusion to 'The Renaissance'. She claimed that Pater still spoke of religion in terms of aesthetics and that he still sought 'exquisite moments'. After pointing out that in the Conclusion he protested against submitting to 'some abstract morality we have not identified with ourselves', she observed that he 'now presents obedience to this same morality as desirable, not because of any absolute virtue or authority inherent in it, but because practically obedience is a source of pleasure and quickened faculty to the individual' (No. 23). Mrs Ward cites as the 'principal intellectual weakness' of 'Marius' 'the further application of this Epicurean principle of an aesthetic loss and gain not only to morals, but to religion'. She goes on to argue that it advocates 'acquiescence in the religious order' without assenting to the claims of religious belief' (LWP, 61n).

The ending puzzled most readers. As Woodberry put it, 'A sense of failure, or rather of incompleteness, oppresses one when he lays down the volumes' (No. 26). Clearly, Marius' 'aesthetic' conversion to Christianity lacks cogency. Marius is brought to the threshold of faith by the aesthetic charm of the liturgical solemnities of Christianity, that element which is essentially human in character and which Christianity has in common with all other religions (Benson, 111). A few critics thought that he died a Christian, but William Sharp, Mrs Ward and Julia Wedgwood believed that he died an optimistic agnostic. Sharp argued that, had Marius lived, he would have been

unable to reconcile two teachings as antagonistic as
paganism and Christianity (No. 18).

Nearly every reviewer commended the 'grace and chastened
beauty' of Pater's prose. Only J.A. Symonds, his arch-
rival, could not easily bear 'the sustained monotonous refinement in his style' (No. 21a). Sharp spoke for many
when he ranked Pater as one of the chief masters of English prose (No. 18). Mackail noted: 'The style here is
different from that of the "Renaissance"; it has in some
degree matured, acquired more amplitude, and at the same
time a more delicate reserve.' 'Marius' was judged to
be a great success, for in place of the sceptical paganism
and aggressive rhetoric of 'The Renaissance' it offered
readers a quantum of religious optimism and a more measured prose style.

'Imaginary Portraits'

Pater's third book was his favourite (Wright, ii, 95). It
was warmly received by the English and American press, but
stimulated less discussion than either of his previous
books, presumably because it failed to equal their power
and charm. Some critics felt that Pater's name alone
guaranteed its favourable reception. Gamaliel Bradford
Jr declared in the 'Andover Review' (August 1888) that
this book was the most delicate work that he had so far
produced (x, 152). Others felt that he never intended it
to be a 'popular success'. The writer for the 'Oxford
Magazine' (No. 37) observed: 'In a newspaper age this
book, with its handsome margin, rich paper, and writing
beautiful for writing's sake, will be prized by too few.'
These readers believed that the book would attract only
the confirmed admirers of his writings.

Reviewers recognised that the book was no ordinary
collection of short stories. As the critic for the
'Saturday Review' (25 June 1887) stated: 'The distinctive
merit and characteristic of the whole book will be missed
if the reader does not appreciate what the author has evidently tried to do' (lxiii, 921). Lady Dilke, formerly
Mrs Pattison, and George Sturt adopted the most obvious
approach and stressed its autobiographical aspect. Lady
Dilke claimed that Pater had once again turned his 'eclectic philosophy of sensation ... to account in a fashion
intensely personal and attractive' by presenting in the
individual portraits 'images' of himself seizing 'exquisite moments' (No. 32). Writing in 1892, Sturt observed
that these 'character pictures represent ... only one
order of character, which one might suppose to be Pater's

own seen in various lights' (No. 38g). While Oscar Wilde
also interpreted the portraits as attempts to seize
'exquisite moments', Lady Dilke emphasised their broader
significance. Echoing Mrs Ward's comment on 'Marius',
she claimed that they contained the record of 'one of the
most intellectual phases of the modern mind', one which
'should be read by all lovers of psychological problems'.
Obviously she had in mind the concluding statement of the
first portrait: 'He has been a sick man all his life. He
was always a seeker after something in the world that is
there in no satisfying measure, or not at all' (IP, 44).

To the majority of readers the book represented the
fusion of Pater's 'critical insight' and 'imaginative
sensibility'. As the critic for the 'Westminster Review'
(July 1887) pointed out, the portraits deal almost exclusively with 'sensations and ideas' (n.s. lxxii, 515). Some
reviewers stressed their scholarship. Arthur Symons and
Oscar Wilde treated them as 'a series of philosophical
studies' (No. 31). In the 'Academy' (18 June 1887) T.W.
Lyster claimed that each of the personalities represented
an attempt to grasp and typify one historical period,
Denys l'Auxerrois, for example, representing the Renaissance theme of the 'outbreak of the human spirit' (xxxi,
423). G.E. Woodberry found the impressionistic sketches
of the social backgrounds which surround the protagonists
most striking (No. 34). E. Price pointed out that the portraits expressed Pater's 'impressions' and not his 'convictions' (No. 33). The 'Saturday Review' (25 June 1887)
summed up this view when its critic warned readers not to
expect to listen to a story-teller but to watch 'an artist
gradually adding stroke to stroke, and producing, not so
much a successive effect, as in narration, but a combined
and total impression, as in drawing' (lxiii, 921).

The reviewers ranked the portraits (according to their
interest and charm) as they appeared in the book. Despite
Wilde's claim that the portrait of Jean Baptiste Watteau
was too 'fanciful', most critics found it the most skilful
in characterisation and the most highly finished. What
appealed to Woodberry was the originality of the imaginative reconstruction of the personality and work of an
unpopular painter, who was generally associated with fri-
volous delicacy of grace (No. 34). E. Price, however,
detected a flaw in characterisation when the girl in the
portrait is made to define the 'formula' of his artistic
success. She explained that the girl's observations were
too subtle for a woman of the period and that she in fact
represented Pater's 'aesthetic critic' (No. 33). Readers
generally agreed that the girl emerged as the most developed and interesting character in the portrait.

While Woodberry found the portrait of Denys l'Auxerrois
'too obviously managed' and over-crowded with details, most
commentators were delighted by Pater's treatment of the
myth of Dionysus. Arthur Symons called it a 'poem' because of its suggestiveness (No. 35) and drew attention
to the fact that here he was on his favourite 'Renaissance
ground', which he first explored in Aucassin and Nicolette. E. Price praised this portrait as the 'most striking' of the four. The 'Saturday Review' (25 June 1887) expressed their reaction in these words:

> Few may recognise the skill with which he has adapted
> and combined the various traditional elements of the
> Dionysiac character; fewer, perhaps, the exactness of
> his adjustment of these to mediaeval conditions. But
> the most competent judges of both are likely to give
> him the highest praise. (lxiii, 920)

Wilde, who juxtaposed Denys, the symbol of the passion of
the senses, against Sebastian, the symbol of the passion
of the intellect, remarked that 'In its rich affluence of
imagery this story is like a picture by Mantegna' (No. 31).
Most readers found the portrait of Sebastian van Storck
'too cold'. Only Wilde praised it as the most striking
and fascinating, undoubtedly because he sympathised with
Sebastian's ideal of 'intellectual disinterestedness' and
attempt to separate himself from the transient world of
sensation (No. 31). Wilde claimed that Pater had never
written 'a more subtle psychological study'. Many reviewers contended that its circumstances were gross and that
its 'intellectual parts' lacked cogency. According to
Woodberry, in trying to re-create the 'thought history'
of the period, he was out of his depth (No. 34).
Reviewers generally regarded Duke Carl of Rosenmold as
the least successful of the four. Woodberry regretted the
'lack of that substance in the midst of picturesqueness
to which Pater has accustomed us'. He lamented that, in
defending 'those poor people who go into raptures and
enthusiasms over third-rate things', Pater was too much
like his disciple 'Vernon Lee'. While he called the portrait a third-rate study, the writer for the 'Critic' (24
September 1887) maintained that it was distinguished by
its 'power of word painting' (n.s. viii, 149).
Much of the adverse criticism sprang from a misunderstanding of Pater's intentions. E. Price regretted the
lack of background to the figures portrayed in the book.
Woodberry, however, praised the 'landscapes' as the aspect
of the book most successfully treated. Lady Dilke identified as the book's fundamental weakness its lack of dramatic

tension. Symons agreed with this observation, but pointed
out that Pater never had attempted to demonstrate, either
in 'Maurius' or 'Imaginary Portraits', that he possessed
'the genuine dramatic power of creating characters which
shall live and move and have a being independent of their
creator' (No. 35). In his view, the book should be appreciated in the light of its primary aim, which he defined as
an attempt 'to give concrete form to abstract ideas'. Many
readers were struck by its melancholy tone. According to
E. Price,

> The book leaves upon our mind a vague sensation of
> pleasure, and a stronger sensation of a very great
> want.... From its very quietness, which makes it so
> great an advance on 'The Renaissance', it is the sad-
> dest book that Mr Pater has yet written. (No. 33)

To her mind the book lacked the optimism of 'Marius'. Lady
Dilke complained that it was incomplete. She argued that,
although Pater gave expression to 'the most interesting
currents of thought of the day', he evaded (due to his
characteristic 'hesitancy' or 'suspense of judgment') the
important question of how to live in the modern world
(No. 32).
    Many reviewers found the book 'more carefully chastened
and subdued in style than "Marius"'. Symons explained that
Pater spent as much time over his prose as Tennyson gave
his poetry. E. Price remarked that 'we can now read his
books without longing to dash cold water over them and
ourselves, and to call Dr Johnson to the rescue'. Although
Arthur Symons and Selwyn Image extolled him as the foremost
prose-writer in the English language, Oscar Wilde regretted that 'at times it is almost too severe in its self-
control' (No. 31).

'Appreciations'

'Appreciations' met with a mixed response; in England the
press responded immediately and enthusiastically, but in
America the press viewed his 'preciosity' and 'aestheticism' with some suspicion and disappointment. The 'Pall
Mall Gazette' (No. 41) expressed the consensus of opinion
on this side of the Atlantic when the reviewer claimed
that the book contained some of Pater's finest work. William Watson called Pater 'one of the most catholic of
living critics' (No. 43). The 'Atlantic Monthly' (March
1890), however, judged 'Appreciations' to be of less consequence and originality than any of his previous books

(lxv, 424). Agnes Repplier found it difficult to read
because Pater's sentences lacked direction and point (No.
49). The reviewer for the 'Critic' (8 February 1890) spoke
of the book as an 'excellent and delicate critical work',
but wondered why so much of it had been devoted to 'talents
manqués', namely the Lake School of Poets, Sir Thomas
Browne and the Aesthetic Poets of the age (n.s. xiii, 61).

Like the writer for the 'Saturday Review' (28 December
1889), many readers hailed the title as eminently appropriate and indicative of the author's special sensibility
(lxviii, 745). Oscar Wilde interpreted 'appreciations' in
its Latin sense, by which he meant 'an exquisite collection of exquisite essays' (No. 50). For some critics the
term meant simply admiration and sympathy, but for Lionel
Johnson and Arthur Symons it defined a critical technique.
To Johnson, it promised 'a quality of reserve, a judgment
very personal, a fine tolerance towards the reader' (No.
46). Symons defined the term in 'the sense of the French
appréciation, a weighing, a valuing, more even than in the
general English sense of valuing highly' (No. 42). In
his view, Pater carried Goethe's theory that the critic
should be concerned with the merits and not the faults of
a work of art to its furthest possible limits and he made
his subject come to life again by expanding his work to
the full measure of its intentions. The 'Pall Mall
Gazette' pointed out that these essays were 'appreciations'
and not 'depreciations'. W.J. Courthope attacked this
romantic tendency to 'expound to the world the nature of
the artist's motives' (No. 51). He preferred Pater's 'sympathetic criticism' to the criticism of antipathy, which
had been directed by 'Blackwood's Magazine' and the 'Quarterly Review' against the Lake Poets and against Shelley
and Keats at the beginning of the century, but he regretted
its lack of judgment.

Most commentators thought Wordsworth the best essay in
the book and perhaps the finest of all Pater's critical
studies.(51) Symons praised the essay because it rectified
the injustices that Wordsworth had suffered at the hands of
his previous interpreters (No. 42). Critics agreed with
Courthope's admission that Pater had approached the poet
with 'real inspiration' and that the definition of his
'formula' as the expression of an intimate consciousness
in natural things had captured the 'essential character of
Wordsworth's genius' (No. 51).

Mention of Wordsworth inevitably invited discussion of
Coleridge. The 'Oxford Magazine' (26 February 1890)
claimed that Coleridge would 'probably be regarded as the
most important in the book' (viii, 233). Courthope praised
it because the appreciation of the poet-philosopher was

more severe and therefore more just. Most reviewers believed that it showed a 'masterly grasp' of Coleridge's
theories and temperament and they concurred with the view
that the pursuit of the Absolute impaired Coleridge's
poetry. Watson, however, differed strongly with the description of Coleridge as the typical 'flower of the *ennuyé*',
the mouthpiece for the modern *Weltschmerz* (No. 43).

The essay on Style, with its defence of poetic prose,
caused the most controversy. Many critics regarded it as
Pater's 'most ambitious essay' and his most interesting
attempt to say something new on a hackneyed subject. William Sharp considered it the most important essay of the
collection and worth the price of the book (No. 40). Oscar
Wilde and Lionel Johnson praised Pater's canon of style
(the precise identification of word with object) as a
reminder of 'the real scholarship that is essential to the
perfect writer' (No. 50). Some reviewers, however, attacked the essay as the least successful in the book. The
'Oxford Magazine' warned readers that Pater tended to be
'too regardful of exactness in representing his impressions' and too inconsiderate of his public. Mrs Oliphant
found his 'literary creed' very thorny reading and his
'scholarship' of words an affectation (No. 45). Courthope
believed that a search for the exact word would only result in Flaubert's 'artistic impotence' (No. 51). American readers generally agreed with the writer for 'Scribner's Magazine' (May 1890), who claimed that, in pursuing
'poetic prose', Pater 'frittered' away his talents, becoming 'one of the most irritating of obviously artificial writers' (vii, 525). Many reviewers concluded that
he was better reading when he was not dealing with abstract subjects.

The other essays aroused scant attention. Most critics
believed that the Postscript contributed nothing new to
the old feud between classicism and romanticism and that
the 'aesthetic studies' of Shakespeare were too subtle.
Some readers commented on the 'imaginative sympathy'
reflected in the essays on Rossetti, Morris, Lamb and
Browne, but they were primarily interested in their autobiographical impress. Watson objected to Aesthetic Poetry
because Pater spoke unpleasantly 'with the falsetto of a
school and the accent of an epoch' (No. 43). C.L. Graves
said that there were certain passages in the essay in
which he persuaded 'the plain person to be a Philistine'
(No. 44). Graves may have been thinking of the disturbing
sentence in the opening paragraph in which Pater says that
the secret of the enjoyment of 'aesthetic' poetry 'is that
inversion of homesickness known to some, that incurable
thirst for the sense of escape, which no actual form of

life satisfied, no poetry even, if it be merely simple and
spontaneous'.

Despite Watson's belief that the faults of 'Appreciations' were 'few and slight', some critics raised a number of points for comment. The 'Nation' (26 December 1889),
for example, deplored the lack of originality in such essays
as Style and Postscript (xlix, 542). Graves took exception
to the musical imagery, especially the inappropriate comparison of Richard II, who attained 'contentment finally
in the merely passive recognition of superior strength',
with Handel's indulgence in grief (see p. 210). Graves
also dismissed as simplistic the theory that all the arts
strive towards the condition of music. Mrs Oliphant attacked as pretentious Pater's 'theory of language' and his
advocacy of following French models of prose style (No.
45). She claimed that he used more words than his subjects demanded and was at a loss to know what he meant by
the 'finer edge' of such words as 'ascertain', 'communicate' and 'discover'. Watson likewise found the 'religiously accurate and anti-popular use' of such words as
'complexion' and 'mortified' academic to the verge of
pedantry. Courthope contended that his criticism suffered 'from the same defect as Lamb's — excess of sympathy'. Many readers concurred with Courthope in his view
that

> In his fine perception of the motives of his authors,
> and in his delicate description of their styles, his
> 'Appreciations' are all that can be desired; but he
> seems to me to flinch from the severe application of
> critical law. He exhibits invariably the taste of a
> refined literary epicure. But the taste of an epicure
> is not always that of a judge.

Finally, Graves detected a lack of sincerity. He argued
that Pater frequently thought 'less of what he wanted to
say than the effect that his periods would produce on his
audience' (No. 44).

The book's 'chastened' prose style was highly commended
by most reviewers. Symons praised its tendency towards
'emancipation, breadth, naturalness' (No. 42). Watson
said that Pater had the 'gift of saying what is emphatically the right thing with unerring precision of phrase'
(No. 43). Wilde noted that over the years his style had
become 'richer and more complex, the epithet more precise
and intellectual' (No. 50). He called attention to the
pleasure to be derived from tracing the 'constructive intelligence' through the intricacies of long sentences,
which seemed 'to have the charm of an elaborate piece of

music'. C.A.L. Richards caught the American response
in the 'Dial' (June 1890) when he described Pater's
prose, in the essay on Style especially, as over-refined
and meaningless to an intelligent reader (xi, 38).

'Plato and Platonism'

The unanimous acclaim which greeted Pater's last book confirmed his established literary reputation. He thought
that of all his books it alone would stand the test of
time (Benson, 162). Classical scholars on both sides of
the Atlantic (see Nos 56 and 59) hailed 'Plato and Platonism' as delightful and stimulating reading. Edmund Gosse
described Pater as the very 'oracle' of Oxford (No. 55).
The critic for 'Mind' (April 1893) observed: 'If the young
student is capable of becoming interested in Plato, he is
certain to be powerfully attracted by this book' (n.s.
ii, 251). Paul Shorey recommended it as 'the first true
and correctly proportioned presentation of Platonism that
has been given to the general reader' (No. 56). E.J.
Ellis claimed that neither the student nor the general
reader would put the book down (No. 54). Like the writer
for the 'Westminster Review' (April 1893), most commentators believed that it would attract a much wider reading
public than any of Pater's previous works (n.s. lxxxiii,
447).
     Critics welcomed the 'popular' treatment of Plato and
they read the book as a literary rather than a philosophical work. Lewis Campbell spoke of it as Pater's last
and longest Appreciation (No. 59). R.H. Hutton noted that
he had written 'a very fine and delicate study ... of a
scholar and an artist even more than the study of a metaphysician' (No. 57). The 'Saturday Review' (25 February
1893) agreed: 'To most of those who read Plato at all,
he is probably welcome as an artist rather than as a philosopher' (lxxv, 212).
     Like Ellis, readers thought Pater's mixture of scholar-
ship and imagination refreshing (No. 54). The 'Nation'
(30 November 1893) expressed the consensus of opinion when
its reviewer said that no previous treatise as compact as
this had produced such a life-like portrait of the philosopher (lvii, 414). What particularly interested Hutton
and Gosse was how 'eminently apposite' it was to the 'intellectual and political life' of the time. To Hutton,
one of the most stimulating aspects of the book was the
translation of Plato's theory into 'its true modern equivalents', especially the explanation of 'how the scientific knowledge of species and genus adds even to the ima-

ginative, as well as to the intellectual, apprehension of every individual specimen of a class' (No. 57).

Reviewers attributed the book's appeal to two aspects of Pater's approach to his subject: the lecture method and the critical essay. Ellis claimed that the reader would miss 'half the effect and most of the true value' of the work if he failed to look on its author as a lecturer. Richard Le Gallienne explained that the lecture method, with its frequent interjections and asides, established an intimate rapport with readers (No. 53). Gosse and Ellis emphasised the great attraction of Pater's 'personal presence'. The latter remarked: 'We seem to hear the voice of a personal acquaintance giving impressions that he has an authoritative right to convey' (No. 54). To a few critics, it was Pater's literary *métier* which contributed to the book's success. Campbell called it 'a brilliant critical essay', because the essay was (as Pater said) the best vehicle for modern philosophic thought (No. 59). The 'Nation' claimed that the book evinced 'the same literary gifts and graces, the same penetrating and vital sympathy with the Hellenic spirit' which were revealed in the essay on Winckelmann.

Readers were especially enthusiastic about the chapters on Plato and the Doctrine of Motion (ch. i), The Genius of Plato (ch. vi) and Lacedaemon (ch. viii). Le Gallienne found the first chapter the most charming of the book and thought Pater's style was at its best when he dealt with the theme of the Heraclitean flux (No. 53). Many critics regarded the sixth chapter as particularly 'sympathetic' in its representation of 'a living Plato' and in its unravelling of 'a complicated and fascinating personality'. Most reviewers, however, hailed the chapter on Lacedaemon as the most original part of the book. Le Gallienne called it an 'imaginary portrait' and Campbell described it as a 'prose poem'. To Shorey, the sympathetic picture of the imaginary Athenian's visit to Sparta owed a great deal to Oxford's ascetic atmosphere (No. 56). This last point is significant, because it foreshadows the subsequent American view of Pater as a typical Oxford man (see No. 100).

Most commentators felt obliged to qualify their praise by isolating a few minor points for censure. In the 'Athenaeum' (18 March 1893) A.D. Innes detected a 'touch of Philistinism' in the inordinate emphasis on Plato's 'richly sensuous nature' (p. 339). The 'Saturday Review' regretted that Pater took for granted 'a very considerable knowledge of philosophy and history' and avoided such academic problems as determining the chronology of the 'Dialogues'. The 'Mind' reviewer claimed that the account of the pre-Socratic philosophers was not up to date because

Pater failed 'to point out that Heraclitus, Parmenides, and
the Pythagoreans had by no means passed beyond the material-
istic point of view'. Hutton queried two points of scholarship. He questioned the interpretation of Platonic
'ideas' as a form of 'animism' or 'a recrudescence of polytheism', because he believed that Plato wanted the Ideas
of Justice, Beauty and Temperance to be as independent of
God as of man, and he regarded as misleading Pater's
emphasis on Plato an an unsatisfied seeker after truth,
for in Hutton's view Plato was a spiritual moralist of
the highest rank (No. 57). Campbell identified the largest
number of minor 'oversights'. He pointed out that much
of the 'matter' of the book had been common property for
about forty years; that it was incorrect to infer from
isolated passages in the first book of 'The Republic' that
'Art is to be for Art's sake alone, and not for the sake
of life'; that the assessment of Plato's attitude towards
mysticism was inadequate; that Lacedaemon may not have
been the deep and wide dividing line between Dorian and
Ionian characteristics; that some Greek expressions were
incorrect; that Pater may have over-estimated the Puritanism of 'The Republic'; and, finally, that he failed to
capture Plato's spontaneity (No. 59).

Reviewers generally felt that 'Plato and Platonism'
required careful reading. Shorey explained that Pater's
'elaborate diction' would obscure points for some readers.
Ellis pointed out that the book's style was 'loose and
wandering' and that sentences often consisted of nearly
half a page (No. 54). The 'Critic' (1 July 1893) agreed
with this view, but observed that they were 'grammatically
correct' and 'entirely intelligible' (n.s. x, 2). Despite these objections, many readers continued to praise
Pater as 'a master of style'. Campbell described Pater as
a 'poet' and the style of the book as a 'symphony' in
prose. Symons saw his style as 'the most beautiful English
prose' that was being written (No. 58). In his view, Pater
was attempting 'to do with the English language something
of what Goncourt and Verlaine have done with the French',
namely he was seeking strange effects without doing violence to the language.

THE CRITICAL REPUTATION: 1895 TO 1910

Pater's reputation reached its height in the twenty years
after his death. One admirer, John Buchan, wrote in 1909:
'His is undoubtedly the greatest Brasenose name of the
nineteenth century, and it may reasonably be argued that
since Matthew Arnold he is the most distinguished figure

that Oxford has given to the world of letters.' (52)
Pater became a cult figure (Wright, ii, 217) and his admirers vied for membership in the 'little clan' (No. 95)
of disciples.   William Sharp, Campbell Dodgson, G.S.
Street and Lionel Johnson contributed to the mythology
of this cult by propagating the view that he had been ignored by his contemporaries. Johnson, for example, referred to Pater as 'that still obscure great man' (No.
93). His disciples regarded him as a profound thinker,
conscientious scholar, creative critic, sincere humanist
and sound moralist.

The reviewers greeted the posthumous publications with
'mingled pleasure and pain'. William Sharp claimed in
the 'Realm' (25 January 1895) that 'Greek Studies' (1895)
would probably rank with 'Marius' as a work of art (i, 418),
E.E. Hale Jr predicted in the 'Dial' (16 November 1895) that
'Miscellaneous Studies' (1895) would be greeted by a larger audience than any of the works published during his
lifetime (xix, 279) and T.B. Saunders believed that 'Gaston de Latour' (1896) would be met with 'the greatest
gratitude' by all his personal friends (No. 86). Arthur
Symons, however, suspected that Pater would not have con-
sented to the release of these works. In the 'Athenaeum'
(21 September 1901) he protested against the 1901 edition
of 'Essays from "The Guardian"', arguing that the privately
printed edition of 1896 had been offered only 'to the inner
circle of [Pater's] friends' (p. 384). Elsewhere he insisted that the book should not be regarded as 'serious
criticism' at all:

It is certain that the reader will find in it some indications of taste, some perhaps freer passing of judgments,
some valuable side-lights upon the finished work of
which it was never intended to be more than a marginal
note. (No. 94)

Some critics thought that these publications would damage
Pater's reputation. W.M. Ramsay, commenting on 'Greek
Studies', noted: 'It is a doubtful service to the author's
memory to reprint essays resting upon a stage of knowledge
that was perhaps adequate at the time, but is certainly
inadequate now' (No. 77).

Critics were particularly impressed by those studies
which resembled 'imaginary portraits'. A Study of Dionysus, The Myth of Demeter and Persephone and Hippolytus
Veiled, included in 'Greek Studies', together with The
Child in the House, Emerald Uthwart, Apollo in Picardy
and Diaphanéité, included in 'Miscellaneous Studies',
attracted wide attention. Like the writer for the 'Out-

look' (15 January 1896), they hoped that these portraits,
especially the autobiographical ones, would throw some
light on the development of Pater's mind and work (p.
160). C. Milman caught the general impression when she
described The Child in the House and Emerald Uthwart as
images of his own childhood (No. 82). Most reviewers were
impressed by Diaphanéité, which Pater read before the Old
Mortality Society(53) in July of 1864. They thought it
crude and fanciful, but very interesting, because the
definition of that aesthetic nature which treated life
'in the spirit of art' anticipated that 'ideal' nature
which Pater perfected in the Conclusion to 'The Renaissance' and in 'Marius the Epicurean'.
    'Gaston de Latour' was greeted warmly as a companion
piece to 'Marius'. Saunders was not alone in detecting
the same theme in each book, namely 'to show the necessity
of religion', a theme which he felt to be consistent with
Pater's intellectual development in the last years of his
life (No. 86). The chapters on Our Lady's Church (ch. ii),
Suspended Judgment' (ch. v) and The Lower Pantheism (ch.
vii) were isolated for praise by the reviewers. C.W.
Boyd in the 'Spectator' (30 January 1897) spoke of Suspended Judgment as 'one of the most interesting of extant
essays on Montaigne' (lxxviii, 144). Many critics
thought the most attractive feature of the book to be
Pater's 'method of portraiture and scene-painting' (No.
88), reflected, for example, in the vivid description of
Notre Dame de Chartres in the second chapter.
    Pater's 'aesthetic' criticism, which he had defined
in 1886 as 'imaginative criticism: that criticism which
is itself a kind of construction, or creation, as it penetrates through the given literary or artistic product,
into the mental and inner constitution of the producer,
shaping his work' (EG, 29), continued to arouse opposition, especially from critics like Andrew Lang who demanded
strict analysis. Lang found the 'comparative method' wanting in 'Greek Studies' and argued that the Greeks were not
at all like Pater's Greeks (No. 76). As he read the book
he felt himself standing 'in a gallery almost hieratic in
its stately repose, rather chill, full of good things, but
not very interesting, somehow'. Ramsay claimed that 'too
much is evolved from the inner consciousness' (No. 77).
For this reason F.G. Kenyon found some interpretations of
myths and sculpture far-fetched (No. 75). What continued
to appeal to reviewers was Pater's capacity to evoke the
personality behind the book or work of art that he was
discussing (No. 81).
    G.S. Street protested that 'It is too general a habit
to write of Mr Pater as a master of style, and that alone'

(No. 85), but the majority of critics thought of him as a
prose artist with the temperament of a poet. The 'Westminster Review' (January 1896) observed: 'Anything written by the late Mr Walter Pater is well worth reading for
the sake of that delightful critic's style, apart from
the subject matter' (cxlv, 229). R.P. Jacobus called
Pater a Keats in prose in the 'Fortnightly Review' (March
1896, lxv, 384) and the 'Academy' (No. 69) noted that
there were whole pages of 'Gaston de Latour' in which each
sentence seemed 'like a piece of exquisite carving from
the purest marble'. George Saintsbury explained that no
one 'has ever surpassed, and scarcely any one has equalled
Mr Pater in delicate and successful architecture of the
prose-paragraph' (No. 68). Saunders rightly observed that
the style of the later volumes was 'easier and less elaborate' because the art of it was 'more concealed, and
therefore more perfect' (No. 86).

It became evident that there was, as Saintsbury remarked in the 'Bookman' (August 1906), a revival of interest in the author of 'The Renaissance' (xxx, 165). A
number of memorial articles appeared during this period
(see Bibliography), most notably, perhaps, Edmund Gosse's
Walter Pater: A Portrait (December 1894), William Sharp's
Some Personal Reminiscences of Walter Pater (December 1894)
and Arthur Symons's Walter Pater: Some Characteristics
(December 1896). Three extended critical biographies,
which purported to reveal the 'real man' behind the mask,
marked the turning-point in Pater's reputation.

Ferris Greenslet's 'Walter Pater' (London and New
York, 1903) is based on Gosse's essay and an autobiographical reading of Pater's major essays. It is a very
slight, superficial book and leaves the impression that
Pater was essentially a dreamer in possession of a remarkable style.

A.C. Benson's 'Walter Pater' (1906), a more substantial
book, has been called the official biography, for it was
commissioned by Macmillan & Company and sanctioned by
Pater's sisters. It is an immensely readable book, but
is concerned primarily with vindicating Pater against his
detractors, who still viewed him as 'a decadent and a
corruptor of youth'. Pater's personality is really the
central figure, and Benson presents an engaging picture
of him as the Oxford don who lived a singularly ascetic
and placid life and who was always accessible to his
friends. As for the workings of his mind and the development of his aesthetic theories, Benson suspends his judgment. He relied on an autobiographical reading of the
books, quoted from few of Pater's letters and mentioned
few of his friends.

Thomas Wright of Olney regarded Benson's book as 'meagre' and the aim of his two-volume 'Life of Walter Pater' (1907) was to correct the latter's 'principal errors of commission and omission'. In his Preface, Wright identified eight of these, most of which are concerned with biographical facts. For example, he devoted most of the second volume to establishing the view that R.C. Jackson, a brother at St Austin's Priory in Walworth and an intimate associate of Pater's, served as the original upon which the character of Marius was based. His indiscriminate use of anecdotes and hear-say references damned Pater; instead of revealing the genius of 'one of the most brilliant and original writers of the Victorian era', he produced the portrait of a scholar too indolent to get to the foundation of things.

Pater's reputation began to decline about this time. Irving Babbitt (see headnote to No. 100), a Professor of French at Harvard and an influential critic, launched an attack on the 'impressionist' school of criticism. In his article on Impressionist *Versus* Judicial Criticism, (54) Babbitt used the term to signify late nineteenth-century critics like Pater and Saintsbury who appeared to be interested in a book only as it related to their sensibility. Such a critic, in Babbitt's view, never 'judges' a work of art by an impersonal standard; rather, he narrates, as in the case of the Mona Lisa passage, the adventures of his soul among masterpieces.

The lukewarm response to the Library Edition of 1910 confirmed the general belief that Pater would never again be as 'popular' as he had once been. J. Bailey pointed out in the TLS (No. 98) that this edition was not 'brought out for the ordinary member of circulating libraries'. English reviewers generally attempted to find a label which would encompass the whole of his career; Buchan concluded that Pater was 'a humanist, and therefore a moralist' (No. 97), while Bailey concluded that he was essentially a Platonist. They dismissed the old notion that he was an Epicurean and a hedonist. American critics, however, focused their attention on Pater as a critic.

P.E. More argued that Pater was not a proper critic because his first concern was not with the 'right interpretation' of the documents before him. In More's opinion,

He has much to say that is interesting, even persuasive, about the great leaders and movements of the past, but too often his interpretation, when the spell of his manner is broken, will be found essentially perverted. (No. 100)

He examined Pater's major works closely, demonstrated
where he had distorted the facts 'to illustrate and auth-
orize a preconceived theory of life' and defined 'Paterism' as 'the quintessential spirit of Oxford, emptied
of the wholesome intrusions of the world'. Finally, he
concluded that the values espoused in Pater's writings
were 'wrong' and that they were in fact responsible for
Oscar Wilde's misbehaviour.

THE LATER REPUTATION

From about 1910 critical commentaries emphasised the
'aesthetic' nature of Pater's work, especially 'its
remoteness from life, its over-refinement, its interest
in the morbid and the curious, its lack of moral values'.
(55) Pater emerged from Edward Thomas's 'Walter Pater:
A Critical Study' (1913), for example, as a detached
'spectator' of life, whose 'aestheticism' was manifested
in 'his sense of the delicate, drowsy, poisonous, sinister, languid, luxuriant'. Thomas found the quintessence of Pater in the Mona Lisa passage, a prose style
which was sluggish, reticent, uneasy and dispirited, because it lacked a 'masterful impulse'.
    During the 1920s and 1930s Pater's reputation sank to
its nadir as the New Humanists, whose chief spokesmen
included Irving Babbitt, P.E. More and T.S. Eliot (see
headnote to No. 100), dismissed him as a self-indulgent
impressionist and *cul de sac* in Victorian literature.
Their campaign against romanticism culminated in Eliot's
essay on Arnold and Pater, which first appeared in the
'Bookman' (September 1930).
    T.S. Eliot began his attack on Pater in 1919, when in
the essay on 'Hamlet' he posed Pater as an example of the
most dangerous type of critic, a critic whose mind was
naturally of a creative order, but through some weakness
in creative power expressed itself in criticism instead.
(56) In 'The Sacred Wood' (1920) he spoke of Swinburne
as a model critic because 'he was sufficiently interested
in his subject-matter and knew quite enough about it' and
suggested that Pater was one of those critics who were
more 'interested in extracting something from their subject which is not fairly in it'.(57) Ten years later, in
the essay on Arnold and Pater, he claimed that 'The Renaissance' was responsible for some 'untidy lives', because it propagated a confusion between art and life, and
that 'Marius the Epicurean' was 'a hodge-podge of the
learning of the classical don, the impressions of the sensitive holiday visitor to Italy, and a prolonged flirta-

tion with the liturgy'.(58) For Eliot, Pater represented,
even more than Coleridge, 'that inexhaustible discontent,
languor, and homesickness ... the chords of which ring all
through our modern literature' (see Appr, 104).

Since the appearance of Eliot's 1930 essay, and especially since the centenary of Pater's birth, there have
been renewed efforts to rehabilitate Pater as a serious
and original writer of the late Victorian period. In
'The Last Romantics' (1947) Graham Hough examined his
aesthetic philosophy and critical theory and practice and
demonstrated that his triumph was not one of purpose but
temperament. Ian Fletcher has shown in his monograph,
'Walter Pater' (1959), that Pater was not 'a typical
Oxford man', as generations of his transatlantic critics
have thought. In Fletcher's opinion, Pater was 'a self-
explorer' who touched on significant issues of his time
in the process, 'perhaps the first English critic of importance to have the historical sense very profoundly
developed' and 'the most complete, the least trivial,
[symbolical figure] of the aesthetic man'.(59)

That Pater is finally being taken seriously is confirmed
by the fact that more than twice the number of critical
studies have appeared in the last decade than in the previous six.(60) But, as Lawrence Evans has observed, far
too much recent work has been based on 'outright misinfor-
mation' and perspectives still remain confused. Not
enough has been done 'to establish fundamental matters of
fact — of text, canon, and chronology'. It is too convenient to combine the various aspects of Pater's genius
into the category of the 'Scholar-Artist', as Lord David
Cecil has done in 'The Fine Art of Reading' (1957), or
'Humanist', as Richmond Crinkley has done in in 'Walter
Pater: Humanist' (Lexington, 1970). Curiously, Geoffrey
Tillotson's book 'Criticism and the Nineteenth Century'
(1951) still provides the best study of his literary
theory and criticism and Sir Kenneth Clark's Introduction
to the 1961 Fontana edition of 'The Renaissance' offers
one of the best accounts of Pater as an art critic.

Pater's fiction has attracted considerable attention
in recent years and since 1960 the critical trend, among
American scholars especially, has been to show that it has
an imagistic, dramatic or thematic pattern. In 'Religious
Humanism and the Victorian Novel' (1964), U.C. Knoepflmacher has interpreted 'Marius' as an attempt 'to recast
religion' and to present through the medium of fiction a
reconciliation of the new scienticism with the certitude
of the old dispensation. Gerald Monsman has adopted the
most popular approach in 'Pater's Portraits' (Baltimore,
1967); here he has traced the familiar centrifugal-centri-
petal, Dionysiac-Apollonian pattern that informs the por-

traits. Formulas like these, however, tend to be restrictive and to present a distorted picture of Pater as a writer who was preoccupied with mythic systems.

For students of Pater, by far the most valuable works to appear for some time have been Lawrence Evans's highly documented edition of the 'Letters of Walter Pater' (Oxford, 1970) and his chapter on Pater in 'Victorian Prose: A Guide to Research' (New York, 1973). These works, together with the present volume, provide a starting-point for a revaluation of this important writer's achievement.

NOTES

1 Sir Kenneth Clark, Introduction to the Fontana edn (1961) of 'The Renaissance', 11.
2 Humphry Ward, Reminiscences: Brasenose, 1864-1872, 'Brasenose College Quatercentenary Monographs', 2 vols (Oxford, 1909), part XIV, 2(c), 74.
3 'Letters of Dante Gabriel Rossetti' (1965), ed. Oswald Doughty and J.R. Wahl, ii, 765.
4 'Letters of Swinburne' (1959-62), ed. Cecil Y. Lang, ii, 58. Swinburne had recently published Notes on the Designs of the Old Masters at Florence in the 'Fortnightly Review' (July 1868), x, 16-40. For a discussion of the point raised by Rossetti, see William Gaunt, 'The Aesthetic Adventure' (1945), 54.
5 See Edward Manson, Recollections of Walter Pater, 'Oxford Magazine' (7 November 1906), xxv, 61.
6 A Note on Walter Pater. By One Who Knew Him, 'Bookman' (September 1894), vi, 174.
7 Richard Aldington, Introduction to 'Walter Pater: Selected Works' (1948), 13.
8 William Sharp, Some Personal Reminiscences of Walter Pater, 'Atlantic Monthly' (December 1894), lxxiv, 801.
9 'A Note on Walter Pater', 173.
10 See Sharp, op.cit., 812.
11 W.B. Yeats, 'Memoirs' (1972), trans. and ed. Denis Donaghue, 22.
12 Arthur Symons, Walter Pater: Some Characteristics, 'Savoy' (December 1896), iii, 40.
13 The Place of Pater, 'The Eighteen-Eighties' (Cambridge, 1930), ed. Walter de la Mare, 103.
14 Rupert Croft-Cooke, 'Feasting with Panthers' (1967), 187.
15 John Gross, 'The Rise and Fall of the Man of Letters' (1960), 24.
16 Ian Fletcher, 'Walter Pater' (1959), 5.
17 Russell Lynes, The Age of Taste, 'Harper's Magazine'

(October 1950), cci, 60-73.

18 See Is Walter Pater Demoralizing, 'Current Literature' (June 1911), 1, 667-9, and The Alleged Corrupting Influence of Walter Pater, 'Current Literature' (August 1911), li, 213-15.

19 'Journal: 1921-23' (Paris, 1946), 229. For a discussion of Pater's reputation in France between the wars, see A.P. Bertocci, French Criticism and the Pater Problem, 'Boston University Studies in English' (Winter 1955), i, 178-94.

20 See Penrith Goff, Hugo von Hofmannsthal and Walter Pater, 'Comparative Literature Studies' (March 1970), vii, 1-11.

21 See Sharp, op.cit., 813.

22 Edmund Gosse, Walter Pater: A Portrait, 'Contemporary Review' (December 1894), lxvi, 804.

23 Walter Pater, 'Bookman' (August 1906), xxx, 165.

24 Sharp, op.cit., 809. Journalists interpreted 'hedonist' as 'an immoral Greek'. See Aldington, op.cit., 11.

25 Gosse, op.cit., 804.

26 Pater on Style, 'Anglistica' (Copenhagen, 1958), xi, 24-5.

27 'Works and Days: From the Journal of Michael Field' (1933), ed. T. and D.C. Sturge Moore, 119.

28 Sharp, op.cit., 808.

29 Letter of 4 March 1885 in Macmillan & Company Letter Book XLVII. The Macmillan Letter Books (British Museum Add. MSS 55030-55497) are hereafter cited as MLB with appropriate number.

30 A Batch of Memories. XII. Walter Pater, 'Weekend Review' (12 December 1931), 760.

31 Gosse, op.cit., 806.

32 See LWP, 7-8. By this time Pater had published Coleridge's Writings (1866), Winckelmann (1867) and Poems by William Morris (1868) in the 'Westminster Review' and Notes on Leonardo da Vinci (1869), A Fragment on Sandro Botticelli (1870), Pico della Mirandula (1871) and The Poetry of Michelangelo (1871) in the 'Fortnightly Review'. Of the ten essays submitted, the manuscript may have been Luca della Robbia, Aucassin and Nicolette or Joachim du Bellay, which were dated 1872 in the third and later editions of 'The Renaissance'. Pater does not mention the essay on Morris, the last six paragraphs of which virtually became the Conclusion. With justification Lawrence Evans believes that the mysterious manuscript was the first version of The School of Giorgione, which enlarges upon the doctrine expressed in the Preface (LWP, 8n).

33 See Charles Morgan, 'The House of Macmillan: 1843-1943'

(1943), 105.
34 Pater carefully chose the notices which were to be
quoted in the advertisements: the 'Athenaeum' (19
May 1977), the 'Pall Mall Gazette' (24 May 1877) and
the 'Saturday Review' (26 May 1877) each printed ex-
cerpts from the 'Athenaeum' (28 June 1873), the 'Saturday Review' (26 July 1873) and Morley's appreciative
article (No. 5). He discovered a mistake in quoting
Morley's reference to the old and misleading title
and in his fourth notice, that in the 'Pall Mall
Gazette' (31 May 1877), he included extracts from the
'Athenaeum' (28 June 1873) and the 'Saturday Review'
(26 July 1873), which praise his criticism.
35 MLB XXIX.
36 Letter of 2 December 1878 in MLB XXXV.
37 Lawrence Evans, Walter Pater, 'Victorian Prose: A
Guide to Research' (New York, 1973), ed. David J.
De Laura, 327.
38 Sharp, op.cit., 808.
39 Alexander Macmillan acknowledged the receipt of 'The
first chapters — pp. 1-31 of "Marius"' on 9 June 1884
(MLB XLV).
40 MLB XLVI.
41 MLB LX.
42 MLB LVIII.
43 MLB LVII.
44 Arthur Symons, Walter Pater, 'Monthly Review' (September 1906), xxiv, 21-2.
45 MLB LXXIII.
46 MLB LXXXIX.
47 MLB CXXV.
48 Mrs Ward, 'A Writer's Recollections' (1918), 120. See
also W.W. Jackson, 'Ingram Bywater: The Memoir of an
Oxford Scholar' (Oxford, 1917), 77.
49 'The Silence and the Voices of God, with other Sermons'
(1874; 1881 edn), 62.
50 Fletcher, op.cit., 23.
51 Wordsworth was described in The Art of the High Wire:
Pater in Letters as 'by far the most perceptive essay
to appear in [the nineteenth] century; it contains the
seeds of so much that has been later elaborated without
acknowledgement, and resulted, of course, from a co-
incidence of Wordsworth's words and Pater's needs' (TLS,
22 February 1971, 231).
52 Nine Brasenose Worthies, 'Brasenose College Quatercentenary Monographs', part XIV, 2(c), 23.
53 See Gerald Monsman, Old Mortality at Oxford, 'Studies
in Philology' (July 1970), lxvii, 359-89.
54 PMLA (1906), xxi, 687-705.

55 Ruth Child, 'The Aesthetic of Walter Pater' (New York, 1940), 3.
56 'Selected Essays' (1932), 141.
57 'The Sacred Wood' (1920), 24.
58 Arnold and Pater was reprinted as The Place of Pater in 'The Eighteen-Eighties', 93-106.
59 Fletcher, op.cit., 5, 35 and 37.
60 See Evans, Walter Pater, op.cit., 323-59.

Note on the Text

The materials printed in this volume follow the earliest
form of the original texts in all important respects, including the original footnotes. Lengthy extracts from the
works of Pater have been curtailed and passages in the
reviews and articles not directly relevant to the work in
question have been omitted (these alterations are indicated in the headnotes or in the text in square brackets).
Typographical errors in the originals have been silently
corrected and the titles of the books have been put in
quotation marks.

'The Renaissance'
March 1873

1. SIDNEY COLVIN, UNSIGNED REVIEW, 'PALL MALL GAZETTE'

1 March 1873, 11-12

See Introduction, p. 20.

    Sidney Colvin (1845-1927), critic of art and literature, was Slade Professor of Fine Art at Cambridge (1873-85) and Keeper of Paintings and Drawings at the British Museum (1884-1912). Colvin wrote the lives of Landor (1881) and Keats (1887) for the English Men of Letters series and edited the Edinburgh edition of the works of R.L. Stevenson. Although a friend, Pater is not mentioned in his 'Memoirs and Notes of Persons and Places: 1852-1912' (1921).

'The history of art has suffered as much as any other history from trenchant and absolute divisions.' In those words the present writer may be taken as at once ranging himself with other champions who have struck hard of late for the oneness or continuity of history in general, and as indicating the point of view from which he approaches his own subject in particular. He goes on:

> Pagan and Christian art are sometimes hardly opposed, and the Renaissance is represented as a fashion which set in at a definite period. That is the superficial view; the deeper view is that which preserves the identity of European culture. The two are really con-
> tinuous, and there is a sense in which it may be said that the Renaissance was an uninterrupted effort of the Middle Age, that it was ever taking place.

To grasp and hold in this way the notion of the continuity
of the Renaissance requires the dismissal of a good many
ideas from popular currency. Another notion of the Renaissance prevails, representing it as a movement of discon-
tinuity, a movement of aggression and innovation, whereby
Pagan thought and Pagan art were enthroned, and Christian
thought and Christian art supplanted or brought low. It
was from writers of the modern Catholic school in France,
and most of all from the eloquent and comprehensive work
of Rio,(1) that his notion got hold of us. First of all
the decadence — the seventeenth century — had invented
that sharp distinction between the Middle Age, which it
abused, and the Renaissance, which it glorified. Then,
when the Catholic school of our own century arose, the
sharp distinction was turned round upon its inventors,
and we saw the Middle Age glorified, and the Renaissance
abused. The writers in England, who approached with most
enthusiasm the history of art, failed to perceive that the
distinction had been exaggerated from the beginning, and
that, from Frederick the Second to Lorenzo, Middle Age
and Renaissance presented in reality successive phases of
an unbroken movement of the human spirit, a gathering
curiosity about the universe and the past, a gathering
desire to really live, feel, and know. Failing to perceive this, those writers were content to take over the
notions of Rio and the Catholic School, and to enforce
and develop them with new vehemence and acuteness, until
they had got to rule the popular mind. But Mr Pater is
quite right in calling the notions superficial as well
as popular. He himself writes out of a culture too con-
siderate and ripe, and out of reflections too finely
sifted, to let pass anything of the kind. From much
that is well said on this head, up and down his book, we
take these further sentences, as putting, with the most
precision and adequacy, the true view of the matter against
the obsolete view:

> The word Renaissance is now generally used to denote
> not merely that revival of classical antiquity which
> took place in the fifteenth century, and to which the
> word was first applied, but a whole complex movement,
> of which that revival of classical antiquity was but
> one element or symptom. For us the Renaissance is the
> name of a many-sided but yet united movement, in which
> the love of the things of the intellect and the ima-
> gination for their own sake, the desire for a more
> liberal and comely way of conceiving life, make them-
> selves felt, prompting those who experience this desire
> to seek first one and then another means of intellectual

or imaginative enjoyment, and directing them not merely
to the discovery of old and forgotten sources of this
enjoyment, but to divine new sources of it, new experiences, new subjects for poetry, new forms of art.

Starting with this just and comprehensive view of what
the Renaissance means, Mr Pater has gone over a wide field
for episodes, both of art and literature, with which to
illustrate it. He begins early, with one of the Provençal
love pieces, in which there makes itself heard the cry of
human passion calling out for liberty, and in its ardour
slighting alike the threats and promises of the Church.
And he ends, late, with the new stage reached by the study
of antiquity, or man's curiosity about the past, with
Winckelmann in the middle of the last century — a stage
where research and sympathy, scholarship and the artistic
sense, for the first time threw clear light upon each
other, and a vital knowledge of antiquity through its monuments began to emerge without impediment. Between those
two remote points, between the Provençal poet and the German antiquarian, the writer takes the princely scholar
Picus of Mirandula as a representative of what is more commonly called the Renaissance in its encyclopedic guess-
work, and its ambition of finding harmony between conflicting theosophies. He takes the painter Botticelli and
the sculptor Robbia as representatives of it in its introduction into fine art of an unfettered and intimate spirit
of individuality. He takes Michael Angelo and Lionardo da
Vinci as leading representatives of it at its many-sided
consummation, in order to define the impressions he has
received from particular points in the genius of the two
masters. He takes the poet Joachim Du Bellay as representative of it after its dissemination from Italy into
other countries, and especially into France, where from
the time of Lewis XII to the time of Lewis XIII it produced a growth of peculiar and fascinating brilliancy.
Evidently the choice of subjects is fragmentary, and
quite incomplete for any purpose of connected history. But,
as we have pointed out, it is a representative choice, and
if it lacks completeness or the approach to it, possesses
symmetry and a governing idea. Thus, although having the
essay form and essay origin which prevail in contemporary
literature, the book is very remarkable among contemporary
books, not only for the finish and care with which its
essays are severally written, but for its air of deliberate
and polished form upon the whole. If anything, we should
say that Mr Pater was even too great a refiner and polisher
of his work. He has an excellent passage, or indeed more
than one, about those workers who transfuse only a small

part of what they do with themselves at their best —
with their genius or highest powers — and leave the mass
of what they do by comparison ordinary, and like what some
one else might have done. That criticism of Mr Pater's
is not applicable to himself. One feels that he has refined and melted down conscientiously, nay, fastidiously,
until all that is left is matter transfused with his best
powers. The consequence is that one often feels at the end
of one of these essays as if too little had been said, as
if one wanted more. The book is not one for any beginner
to turn to in search of 'information'. The information to
be found in any one of the essays as to the personage who
is its subject will be accurate as far as it goes, but
will only go just far enough to carry the criticism, the
definition of the impression the personage has made upon
the writer individually. That, as Mr Pater in his preface
leads us to expect, will be the main object of the essay.
His idea of the function of the aesthetic critic is a very
distinct idea, the result, it seems, partly of temperament
and partly of reflection upon the nature of things and the
place of aesthetics in life. A temperament acutely sensitive to impressions of art, and subtle differences and
shades in the quality of these impressions, and a philosophy which accepts objects as relative, experience as
everything, the Absolute as a dream — life as a flux, and
consciousness as an incident in the encounter of forces —
these together lead him to value very little the criticism
which works by abstract rules and metaphysical definitions,
and very much the criticism which works by concrete analysis and the precise description of individuals.

> The objects with which aesthetic criticism deals —
> music, poetry, artistic and accomplished forms of
> human life — are receptacles of so many powers or
> forces; they possess, like natural elements, so many
> virtues or qualities.... He who experiences these im-
> pressions strongly, and drives directly at the analysis
> and discrimination of them, need not trouble himself
> with the abstract question what beauty is in itself,
> or its exact relation to truth or experience — meta-
> physical questions as unprofitable as metaphysical
> questions elsewhere.

Whether one allows the general proposition or not, one must
without reserve allow much of what is implied in it. The
analysis and discrimination of impressions, which by another phrase you may call the virtues or qualities of the
things which give the impressions, whether or not it is
the whole of criticism, is certainly a great part of it;

and to be well done it must certainly be done by one who
feels the impressions strongly. By the strength and delicacy of the impressions the present writer feels, by the
pains he has taken completely to realize them to himself,
above all, by the singular and poetical personality with
which they are transfused, he shows himself born for the
task; he seems like a congener of those Florentines of the
fifteenth century in whom he delights, because he thinks it
their characteristic to show

> the impress of a personal quality , a profound expres-
> siveness, what the French call *intimité*; by which is
> meant a subtle sense of originality — the seal on a
> man's work of what is most inward and peculiar in his
> moods and manner of apprehension.

Of course the writer thus setting himself to convey the
impression of what is most inward and peculiar in the moods
of an ancient artist or poet, has a much harder task than
the writer setting himself to give general information
about characters and careers. The former undertaking is
open to much more contradiction than the latter, since the
finest perceptions differ, and every one may find fault with
his neighbour's. For ourselves, the impressions here realized with such careful meditation, and written down with
so refined an art, commend themselves in considerably different degrees. The essay on Michael Angelo, dwelling
chiefly on his poetry, and on the episode of his passion
for Vittoria Colonna, which it describes as 'a page sweet-
ening the volume', 'a charmed and temperate space in Michael
Angelo's life' — this is an essay of very great interest;
but we doubt about the main point it enforces, which is
this: that the true stamp of Michael Angelo, and true type
of the Michael Angelesque, is sweetness together with
strength, or sweetness through strength — *ex forti dulcedo*.(2) It is not a matter which can be argued in a place
like this; but we should rather have said, though there
were undoubtedly moments and flashes of sweetness in
Michael Angelo, his true stamp, speaking generally, was
one not of sweetness at all, but of an energy which has
little to do with that, and much to do with indignation,
menace, and sublimity; we should say that his characteristic expressions were those of a science and power above
other mortals, but an imaginative ambition still trans-
cending that science and power and chafing against their
insufficiency; that is, of sentiments too Titanic, unquiet, and rebellious, to leave much place for those sentiments of love, tranquillity, and tenderness which express themselves in graceful and caressing physical

conditions, such as in art are what we call sweet. Simi-
larly, when we hear how Robbia's system of using low relief,
and copying evanescent expression in his sculpture, is one
means out of many that sculpture has tried for, avoiding a
hard and importunate realism, and how beside it the Greek
means to this end was an ideal abstractness and univer-
sality, and Michael Angelo's means a calculated technical
incompletion and the mystery arising from that; when we
hear this view, we are inclined to say that it is very ingenious and subtle rather than that it unreservedly commends itself. But it is the property of this kind of
writing, when it is thoughtfully done, to suggest even
where it does not illuminate. And on the other hand, we
should say that the accounts of Botticelli and Lionardo
commended themselves signally by their felicity and pene-
tration as well as by their subtlety and poetry; and that
the account of Winckelmann, which is the longest essay in
the book, was completely excellent from beginning to end.

Where all the writing is so close and sifted as here,
it is almost impossible to detach portions or paragraphs
for separate criticism. But in the Winckelmann article
the reader will find most of those well meditated and perfectly expressed views of comparative criticism, and descriptions of various phases of culture in their relations
to each other, which are one of the strengths of the book.
In the articles on Botticelli and Lionardo he will find
most of those passages of delicate poetry and imaginative
charm which are another of its great strengths. For example of the former strength, take the observation that

> *Heiterkeit*, blitheness or repose, and *Allgemeinheit*,(3)
> generality or breadth, are, then, the supreme charac-
> teristic of the Hellenic ideal. But that generality or
> breadth has nothing in common with the lax observation,
> the unlearned thought, the flaccid execution which have
> sometimes claimed superiority in art on the plea of
> being 'broad' or 'general'. Hellenic breadth and gene-
> rality come of a culture minute, severe, constantly
> renewed, rectifying and concentrating its impressions
> into certain pregnant types.

For the former kinds of strength, take the account, which
is too long to quote, of Mona Lisa and her smile; or of
the face of a Madonna of Botticelli's, with 'the white
light on it cast up hard and cheerless from below, as when
snow lies upon the ground, and the children look up with
surprise at the strange whiteness of the ceiling'; or of
the alert sense of outward things possessed by the fif-
teenth-century Italians — 'the alert sense of outward

things which in the pictures of that period fills the
lawns with delicate living creatures, and the hillsides
with pools of water, and the pools of water with flower-
ing reeds'; or this:

> When the shipload of sacred earth from the soil of
> Jerusalem was mingled with the common clay in the Campo
> Santo of Pisa, a new flower grew up from it unlike any
> flower that had been seen before, the anemone with its
> concentric rings of strangely blended colour, still to
> be found by those who search long enough for it in the
> long grass of the Maremma. Just such a strange flower
> was that mythology of the Italian Renaissance which
> grew up from the mixture of two traditions, two sen-
> timents — the sacred and the profane.

We are sensible of quoting to an unusual extent, and
yet of quoting less than we should wish. The fact is that
it is so rare in the literature of the day to find a writer who has not only a style of his own, but a good style,
and not only a good style, but one which he takes care of,
that when such a writer is found the temptation to quote
from him becomes nearly irresistible. It should be apparent by this time that Mr Pater's style is often beautiful,
always intimately his own, and always sedulously taken
care of. The worst that could possibly be said against
it, by a critic having no sympathy with its personal sentiment, would be that it went sometimes to the edge of fancifulness and affectation, or that the poetry of its descriptions and allusions seemed sometimes to cloy by recurrence. The best that could be said of it is something
almost stronger than we like to venture. Or we should say
that no English prose writer of the time had expressed
difficult ideas and inward feelings with so much perfection, address, and purity, or had put more poetical
thoughts or more rhythmical movement into his prose without sacrificing that composure and lenity of manner which
leave it true prose nevertheless. The masterpiece of the
style is the Conclusion, in which the writer expounds
something like a philosophy of life. That philosophy is
not ours. It is a Hedonism — a philosophy of refined
pleasure — which is derived from many sources: from
modern science and the doctrine of relativity; from
Goethe, from Heine, Gautier, and the modern French theorists of art for art's sake; from the sense of life's flux
and instability and the precious things which life may
yield notwithstanding — from all these well transfused
in a personal medium of temperament and reflection, well
purged from technicalities, and cast into a literary

language of faultless lucidity and fitness. But to go with
the writer when he analyzes and discriminates exquisite
impressions is not to go with him when he makes the research of exquisite impressions the true business of a
wise man's life. By all means, let the people whose bent
is art follow art, by all means refine the pleasures of
as many people as possible; but do not tell everybody that
refined pleasure is the one end of life. By refined, they
will understand the most refined they know, and the most
refined they know are gross; and the result will not be
general refinement but general indulgence.

Notes

1 A.F. Rio (1797-1874) wrote 'De la Poésie Chrétienne dans
  son principe, dans sa matière et dans ses formes' (Paris
  1836), which was translated into English as 'The Poetry
  of Christian Art' in 1854.
2 'Out of the strong came forth sweetness' (R, 89).
3 See R, 213. In 'On the Imitation of Greek Art' (1755)
  Winckelmann sums up his teachings about Greek art in the
  phrase: 'noble simplicity and calm grandeur'.

2. J.A. SYMONDS ON PATER

1872, 1873, 1875, 1877

Extracts from 'The Letters of John Addington Symonds'
(1967-9), ed. Herbert M. Schueller and Robert L. Peters.
See Nos 3, 21 and 48.
    Symonds (1840-93), historian, biographer, poet and
critic, contributed to many journals, wrote the lives of
Shelley (1878) and Sir Philip Sidney (1886) for the English
Men of Letters series and 'The Life of Michelangelo Buonar-
roti' (1893) and translated the 'Autobiography of Benvenuto
Cellini' (1888). He is best known for his massive work,
'The Renaissance in Italy' (1875-86).
    Symonds and Pater met early in 1860, but later they fell
into 'a mutual dislike of each other' (Wright, ii, 115).
For a discussion of their rivalry, see No. 70a and Phyllis
Grosskurth, 'John Addington Symonds: A Biography' (1964),
157-73.

(a) From a letter dated 23 October 1872 to Henry Sidgwick

By the way Pater comes out soon with a volume of Essays on
Aesthetics, or some such matter — which I am to review. I
expect the book will be good. (ii, 246)

(b) From a letter dated 20 February 1873 to Henry Graham
Dakyns

You shall have Pater reviewed by me when the Academy comes.
There is a kind of Death clinging to the man, wh[ich] makes
his music (but heavens! how sweet it is!) a little faint &
sickly. His view of life gives me the creeps, as old
women say. I am sure it is a ghastly sham; & that live by
it or not as he may do, his utterance of the theory to the
world has in it a wormy hollow-voiced seductiveness of a
fiend. (ii, 273)

(c) From a letter dated 3 March 1873 to Horatio Forbes
Brown

If you care to do so, correct two misprints on pate 78 of
Pater. Those sonnets are quoted from my translations of
Michael Angelo.(1) In the first sonnet, line 7 *our* should
be *one*, and in the second sonnet line 7 *those* should be
these. It should be well to print *knight* in the last line
of the second sonnet with a large K, since Michael Angelo
designed a pun on the young man's name. (ii, 274-5)

(d) From a letter dated 4 March 1873 to A.C.
Swinburne

What a wonderfully finished piece of artistic work in
criticism Pater has given us! The Style has an indes-
cribable perfume & charm. (ii, 276)

(e) From a letter dated 30 July 1875 to Charlotte
Symonds Green

Pater's article(2) in the Academy on my book is extremely
gratifying. It is the first review wh[ich] has ever
really pleased me of any of my books. What I enjoy is
his appreciation of my aims & sense of what I am about.
Most reviewers are mere blunderbusses charged with blame
or praise, both worthless & alike disregarded by myself.
This is quite another thing. (ii, 377-8).

(f)   From a letter dated 11 November 1877 to Horatio
Forbes Brown

Have you seen an article by Pater in the Oct 'Fortnightly'
on the school of Giorgione?(3)   It is extremely interesting, and if it were not so dogmatic and so contemptuous
towards his brother critics, I should welcome it with more
pleasure as a contribution to the science of aesthetics.
His main point is that contemporary art-critics use poetry
as their standard for judging of the fine arts, and that
they ought to put music in this place.   The argument on
which he founds this view is subtle, and he gets, in the
Venetian school of painting, a seeming support.   But I do
not think it will hold water.   At any rate it is equally
wrong to take Music, as it is to take Poetry, as the standard of all other arts.   I think of sending a critique of
Pater's view to the 'Cornhill',(4) if [Leslie] Stephen will
have it.
    I wonder whether [Roden] Noel has seen this Essay.   It
will make him angry, as Pater says the best Poetry is that
in which the sense is swooning into nonsense.   So it is a
defence of what Noel calls the 'Mesopotamian' theory of
poetry. (ii, 500-1)

Notes

1 Twenty-three Sonnets from Michael Angelo, 'Contemporary
  Review' (September 1872), xx, 505-15.   On p. 77n of
  'The Renaissance' (1873) Pater gives the 'Contemporary
  Review' (September 1872) as the source for these poems,
  but he does not name the translator;   the first sonnet
  is to Vittoria Colonna (Bring Back the Time when Blind
  Desire Ran Free) and the second is to Tommaso Cavalieri
  (Why Should I Seek to East Intense Desire).   In subsequent editions of 'The Renaissance' Pater names the
  translator but does not quote from the poems.
2 Review of 'The Age of the Despots' (1875), in the
  'Academy' (31 July 1875), viii, 105-6.
3 'Fortnightly Review' (October 1877), n.s. xxii, 526-38.
4 Published as Is Music the Type or Measure of all Art?
  in the 'Century Guild Hobby Horse' (January 1888), iii,
  42-51.

3.   J.A. SYMONDS, SIGNED REVIEW, 'ACADEMY'

15 March 1873, iv, 103-5

See Nos 2, 21 and 48.

As Phyllis Grosskurth has observed in 'John Addington Symonds' (1964), Symonds skilfully conceals his antipathy for Pater (see No. 2b) in his ostensibly laudatory review. To his surprise, Pater was not offended by it; in his letter of 24 March 1873 to his sister Charlotte, he wrote: 'I am pleased to hear Pater liked my review. I thought he might think it aigre-doux [bitter-sweet]' ('Letters of John Addington Symonds', ii, 279).

Symonds opens the review by identifying two schools of criticism: the dogmatic (or classical) and the aesthetic (or impressionistic).

... Mr Pater professedly belongs to the second class of critics; his book is a masterpiece of the choicest and most delicate aesthetic criticism. 'What is the peculiar sensation, what is the peculiar quality of pleasure, which his work has the property of exciting in us, and which we cannot get elsewhere?' This question, which Mr Pater asks (p. 40) of Botticelli, strikes the keynote to his critical method. He further explains his purpose in the preface; and each of his eight studies is a wonderfully patient and powerful attempt to do that which is most difficult in criticism, to apprehend for his own mind, and to make manifest to the minds of others, the peculiar *virtue* which gives distinction to the work he has to treat of. In this way the critic becomes himself an artist, a creator. He undertakes at once a higher and more difficult task than the Aristarchus of the schools, who is contented with applying his shallow foot-rule to preconceived opinion. As might be expected, the qualities of Mr Pater's own temperament strongly modify his perceptions. We find in him (to use his own phrase) 'a lover of strange souls'. Nor is he wholly free from the intellectual Sybaritism to which the critics of his school, who feed themselves on beautiful things — '*en exquis amateurs, en humanistes accomplis*'(1) — are liable. Comparatively isolated, indifferent to common tastes and sympathies, careless of maintaining at any cost a vital connection with the universal instincts of humanity, they select what gives them the acutest pleasure, and explain the nature of that pleasure to their readers.

The greatest distinction of this book is that its author has been completely conscious of what he wished to achieve,

and has succeeded in the elaboration of a style perfectly
suited to his matter and the temper of his mind. He has
studied his prose as carefully as poets study their verses,
and has treated criticism as though it were the art of
music. Yet he is no mere rhetorician. The penetrative
force and subtlety of his intellect are everywhere apparent. There is scarcely a superfluous word or a hasty
phrase in the whole volume. Each paragraph, each sentence
is saturated with thought; not with that kind of thought
which Novalis described as a 'dead feeling, a wan, weak
life', but with the very substance of the feeling which
only becomes thought in order that it may receive expression in words. To do justice to such a style either by
quotation or by description is difficult. Yet the following sentences may be extracted as containing in brief
something of the peculiar flavour which gives value to the
book: 'A certain strangeness, something of the blossoming of the aloe, is, indeed, an element in all true
works of art; that they shall excite or surprise us is
indispensable' (p. 62). 'No one ever expressed more truly
than Michel Angelo the notion of inspired sleep, of faces
charged with dreams' (p. 59). 'The spiritualist is satisfied in seeing the sensuous elements escape from his conceptions; his interest grows, as the dyed garment bleaches
in the keener air' (p. 195). 'I suppose nothing brings
the real air of a Tuscan town so vividly to mind as those
pieces of pale blue and white porcelain, by which he is
best known, like fragments of the milky sky itself fallen
into the cool streets and breaking into the darkened
churches' (p. 53). So consummate is Mr Pater's style that
we are surprised to find that he should ever have allowed
himself to repeat the same phrase (pp. 64, 66, 'but only
blank ranges of rock and dim vegetable forms as blank as
they'). In like manner he is so patient and perfect in
his study of picturesque details that we are almost in
spite of ourselves forced to challenge the veracity of his
images. For the most part, he will be found as accurate
as he is subtle. Yet when he speaks (p. 30) of 'that map
or system of the world held as a great target or shield in
the hands of the grey-headed father of all things, in one
of the earlier frescoes of the Campo Santo at Pisa', he
has forgotten that the point of this old picture lies in
the fact that it is *not* the creative Demeurgus, but Christ,
in the prime of manhood, who supports the disc of the universe, with its concentric rings of created beings. Such
minute criticism, however, is mere cavilling.
    The unity of the book, which is made up for the most
part of essays collected from periodicals and polished by
their author, consists in this, that each article treats of

some phase of the Renaissance through a representative
character or work of art. Two are devoted to French literature, and Mr Pater is particularly happy in his exposition of the theory that the renaissance of modern Europe
originated in France. The truth of this theory, which may
easily be exaggerated, is that the renaissance was not a
sudden and violent explosion of the fifteenth century, but
that in all the countries of Europe which possessed the
elements of culture — in southern Spain, in Provence, in
Frederick the Second's Sicily, in the Paris of Abélard, in
the Florence of Boccaccio, and in the Lombardy of the
Paterini heretics — the qualities of renaissance striving
after liberty were discernible within the middle age itself. Of Mr Pater's two French studies, that on Du Bellay,
in whom he sees 'the subtle and delicate sweetness which
belong to a refined and comely decadence', is perhaps the
most interesting. Like Théophile Gautier and like Baudelaire, Mr Pater has a sympathetic feeling for the beauty
of autumn and decay. He is not even insensible to 'what
may be called the fascination of corruption'. This, which
is a very genuine note of his aesthetic temperament, leads
him at times, I think, to make mistakes of criticism. A
notable instance of this is to be found in his interpretation of Botticelli's Madonnas. They are all painted
after one fixed type of beauty — Botticelli, like all
true artists, having selected and assimilated for himself
from the multitudes of forms just that which represented
his peculiar ideal. Mr Pater imagines that in that sad,
languid, sleepy, pallid woman, Botticelli sought to depict
one who, 'though she holds in her hands the "Desire of all
nations", is one of those who are neither for God nor for
his enemies', one to whom the visit of Gabriel brought an
'intolerable honour'. I cannot do justice to the eloquence and grace with which this theory is worked out in
the essay on Sandro Botticelli. But I must suggest that
it ascribes to the painter a far greater amount of sceptical self-consciousness than he was at all likely to have
possessed. However we may explain Botticelli's preference
for that melancholy type of beauty, we must remember that
Lippo Lippi, his master, and Filippino Lippi, his fellow-
student, present us with two other varieties of the same
type, markedly different, it is true, in sentiment from
Botticelli's, but yet like enough to justify the belief
that the type itself was the note of a specific school,
and not the deliberate invention of an antagonist of the
most cherished Catholic tradition. It is far more consistent with Florentine feeling to suppose that in his
Madonna's melancholy Botticelli tried to delineate her
premonition of the coming sword, and not her weariness in

being the mother of the sinless Saviour. A criticism of
Michel Angelo, which is marked by the same subtlety and
originality, may be questioned in like manner as somewhat
over-refined. In the essay on Luca Della Robbia, Mr Pater
defines with much delicacy what are the different methods
by which great sculptors have spiritualized their several
kinds of work. Passing to Michel Angelo, and noticing the
incompleteness of much that he has left, he says: 'Well!
that incompleteness is Michel Angelo's equivalent for colour in sculpture; it is his way of etherealizing pure
form, relieving its hard realism, communicating to it
breath, pulsation, the effect of life.' This is extremely
ingenious, and subjectively it is, perhaps, true: *we* gain
by suggestive ruggedness of much of Michel Angelo's work —
in which it seems as if a soul were escaping from the
stone. But did Michel Angelo really calculate this effect?
That is what is more than doubtful. When he had the time,
the will, the opportunity, he finished with the utmost
polish. His *Moses* and his *Night* — the latter of which he
illustrated by one of his most splendid poems — are
smoothed and rounded and completed in their slightest
curves. And to this perfection of finish his work was
always approximating. That it often fell short may be
explained simply by the facts of his life and the strange
qualities of his temperament.

   In the essay on The Poetry of Michel Angelo Mr Pater
shows the truest sympathy for what has generally been overlooked in this stern master — his sweetness. The analysis of the nature of that sweetness is one of the triumphs
of Mr Pater's criticism. Leonardo da Vinci attracts him
less as an artist merely than as a personality of deep and
splendid fascination. Pico della Mirandola again receives
a separate study, in which we are made to feel with an intensity peculiar to Mr Pater's style, the charm, as of
some melody, which clung about him. The longest essay in
the book is on Winckelmann, which, besides containing a
very interesting sketch of the man, is full of good criticism of the Greek in contrast with the modern spirit.
What is said on p. 195 about the way in which Winckelmann
was privileged to approach Greek art is perfect. As the
book begins with a preface which sets forth the author's
theory of criticism, so it ends with a conclusion in which
he expresses his theory of life. Between the cradle and
the grave we have but a short breathing space. How are we
to use it best by 'getting as many pulsations as possible
into the given time?' Mr Pater's answer is that Art is
after all the most satisfactory pursuit: 'Of this wisdom,
the poetic passion, the desire of beauty, the love of art
for art's sake has most; for art comes to you professing

frankly to give nothing but the highest quality to your
moments as they pass, and simply for those moments' sake.'

Note

1 'as exquisite amateurs, as accomplished humanists'.

4.   JOHN WORDSWORTH ON PATER'S PHILOSOPHY

1873

Extract from a letter dated 17 March 1873 to Pater, from
W.E. Watson's 'Life of Bishop John Wordsworth' (1915),
89-91. See Introduction, p. 22.
    John Wordsworth (1843-1911), ecclesiastic, theologian
and grand-nephew to the poet, was elected to a Fellowship
at Brasenose College in 1867. In the same year he was
ordained and in 1873 he became Chaplain and Tutor of the
College. His book on 'Fragments and Specimens of Early
Latin' (1874) earned him a reputation as one of the best
Latin scholars in Oxford. He subsequently rose to a position of considerable influence. In 1885 he became Bishop
of Salisbury.
    Wordsworth was one of Pater's private pupils for a
single term in his undergraduate career (1861-5).
    He reproaches Pater for the sceptical philosophy of the
Conclusion to 'The Renaissance', which he thinks misleads
weak minds. Pater's reply is missing.

You will, I think, hardly be surprised at my writing to you
in reference to a subject which has been much in my
thoughts of late. I mean your book of studies in the History of the Renaissance. No one can admire more than I do
the beauty of style and the felicity of thought by which
it is distinguished, but I must add that no one can be
more grieved than I am at the conclusions at which you represent yourself as having arrived. I owe so much to you
in time past, and have so much to thank you for as a colleague more recently, that I am very much pained in making
this avowal. But after a perusal of the book I cannot disguise from myself that the concluding pages adequately sum

up the philosophy of the whole; and that that philosophy
is an assertion, that no fixed principles either of religion or morality can be regarded as certain, that the only
thing worth living for is momentary enjoyment and that
probably or certainly the soul dissolves at death into
elements which are destined never to reunite. I believe
you will acknowledge that this is a fair statement of
your position. If it is not, I shall be only too happy
to be disabused of my misconceptions. I am aware that the
concluding pages are, with small exceptions, taken from a
review of Morris's poems published in 1868 in the 'Westminster Review'. But that article was anonymous, whereas
this appears under your own name as a Fellow of Brasenose
and as the mature result of your studies in an important
period of history. If you had not reprinted it with your
name no one would, I presume, have had a right to remon-
strate with you on the subject, but now the case appears
to be different; and I should be faithless to myself and
to the beliefs which I hold, if in the position in which
I find myself as tutor next in standing to yourself I were
to let your book pass without a word. My object in writing is not to attempt argument on these conclusions, nor
simply to let you know the pain they have caused me and I
know also many others. Could you indeed have known the
dangers into which you were likely to lead minds weaker
than your own, you would, I believe, have paused. Could
you have known the grief your words would be to many of
your Oxford contemporaries you might even have found no
ignoble pleasure in refraining from uttering them. But
you may have already weighed these considerations and have
set them aside, and when they are pressed upon you you may
take your stand on your right under the University Tests
Act(1) to teach and publish whatever you please. I must
then, however unwillingly, accept the same ground. The
difference of opinion which you must be well aware has for
some time existed between us must, I fear, become public and
avowed, and it may be my duty to oppose you, I hope always
within the limits of courtesy and moderation, yet openly
and without reserve. It is a painful result to arrive at,
but one which I hope you will not resent as unfair. At
any rate, before it goes any further, I think it right to
let you know my feeling and to ask if you have any reply
to make to my letter. On one practical point perhaps you
will allow me to ask a favour. Would you object to give up
to myself or to the other tutors (if they will take it) your
share in the Divinity Examination in Collections?(2) This
is probably the last time in which the old system will be
in force, and it would be, I confess, a relief to my mind
if you would consent to do so.

Notes

1 This act of 1871 made it no longer obligatory to sign
  the Thirty-nine Articles of the Church of England for
  all university degrees, except divinity.
2 An examination in the Greek text of the New Testament.

5.   JOHN MORLEY ON PATER

1873

Extract from an article entitled Mr Pater's Essays, signed
'Editor', in the 'Fortnightly Review' (April 1873), xix,
469-77. See Introduction, pp. 19 and 22.
   John, Viscount Morley of Blackburn (1838-1923), journalist, biographer, radical politician and statesman. In
1856 Morley won an open scholarship at Lincoln College,
Oxford, then dominated by Mark Pattison (see headnote to
No. 6); disenchanted with the 'intellectual dilapidation'
into which the college had fallen, he left Oxford with
only a pass degree. Morley distinguished himself, however,
as editor of the 'Fortnightly Review' (1867-82), the 'Pall
Mall Gazette' (1880-93) and the English Men of Letters
series, for which he wrote the life of Burke (1867). He
is best remembered as the author of the official biography
of Gladstone (1903).
   F.W. Hirst has printed in 'Early Life and Letters of
John Morley' (1927) the following letter from Morley to
Frederick Harrison:

   I think it very desirable to call attention to any book
   like Pater's, which is likely to quicken public interest
   in the higher sorts of literature. And, moreover, a
   young and unknown writer like him ought to be formally
   introduced to the company by the hired master of cere-
   monies, myself, or another to wit. So pardon my light
   dealing with his transgressions. (i, 240)

   In the opening paragraphs Morley suggests that a sign
'for that general stir of intellectual energy which is now
making itself visible in this country' is 'the rise among
us of a learned, vigorous, and original school of criticism'
On 1 April 1873 Pater wrote to Morley, thanking him for his
'explanation of my ethical point of view, to which I fancy

some readers have given a prominence I did not mean it to
have' (LWP, 14).

... Mr Pater's studies in the history of the Renaissance
and the essay on Winckelmann which he has appropriately
enough attached to them, constitute the most remarkable
example of this younger movement towards a fresh and inner
criticism, and they are in themselves a singular and interesting addition to literature. The subjects are of the
very kind in which we need instruction and guidance, and
there is a moral in the very choice of them. From the
point of view of form and literary composition they are
striking in the highest degree. They introduce to English readers a new and distinguished master in the great
and difficult art of writing prose. Their style is marked
by a flavour at once full and exquisite, by a quality that
mixes richness with delicacy, and a firm coherency with
infinite subtlety. The peril that besets a second-rate
writer who handles a style of this kind lies in the direction of effeminate and flaccid mannerism, and the peril is
especially great when he is dealing with aesthetic subjects;   they tempt to an expansion of feeling, for the expression of which no prose can ever become a proper medium. Mr Pater escapes the danger, first by virtue of his
artistic sense which reveals to him the limits of prose
and gives him spontaneous respect for them, keeping him
well away from all bastard dithyramb, and secondly by virtue of a strain of clear, vigorous, and ordered thought,
which underlies and compacts his analysis of sensuous
impressions. Hence his essays, while abounding in passages of an exquisite and finished loveliness that recall
the completeness of perfected verse, are saved by a marked
gravity and reserve from any taint of the sin of random
poetical expatiation and lyric effusion. Mr Pater's style
is far too singular in its excellence not to contain the
germs of possible excess in some later day. All excellent
style does so;   if it is of a large and noble eloquence,
like Burke's or Bossuet's,(1) it holds the seeds of turgid-
ity;   if it is racy and generously imaginative, it may
easily degenerate into vulgarity or weedy rankness or the
grotesque;   if it is of a severe and chastened elevation,
it is apt to fall over, and substitute aetherialised
phrase for real and robust ideas. And so subtlety and
love of minor tones may lead a writer who is not in constant and rigorous discipline, into affectation and a certain mawkishness. Meantime we trust to Mr Pater's intellectual firmness, to his literary conscience and scrupu-

losity, and above all to his reserve. This fine reserve,
besides the negative merit of suppressing misplaced effusion, has a positive effect of its own, an effect of subtle
and penetrating suggestiveness that but for the sobriety
and balance of the general colour would leave one with half
weird, unsatisfied, unreal impressions. Thus at the close
of the beautiful piece on Joachim du Bellay, after giving
us the song which is the writer's title to commemoration,
Mr Pater justly says that nearly all the pleasure of it 'is
in the surprise at the happy and dexterous way in which a
thing slight in itself is handled', and then concludes
generally:

> One seems to hear the measured falling of the fans with
> a child's pleasure on coming across the incident for the
> first time in one of those great barns of Du Bellay's
> own country, La Beauce, the granary of France. A sud-
> den light transfigures a trivial thing, a weather-vane,
> a wind-mill, a winnowing flail, the dirt in the barn-
> door; a moment, — and the thing has vanished, be-
> cause it was pure effect; but it leaves a relish be-
> hind it, a longing that the accident may happen again.

This brief sentence is the happiest summary of criticism,
leaving the reader with the key, and leaving him, too,
with a desire to use it and explore what further may be
locked up in verse or picture. This is the manner of Mr
Pater's criticism throughout. The same passage illustrates another of its qualities. It is concrete and positive, not metaphysical; a record or suggestion of impressions, not an analysis of their ultimate composition, nor
an abstract search for the law of their effects.

> The more you come to understand what imaginative colour-
> ing really is, that *all colour is no mere delightful
> quality of outward things, but a spirit upon them by
> which they become expressive to the spirit*, the better
> you will like this peculiar quality of colour (p. 48).

How full at once of suggestion, and of explanation, yet
without that parade of speculative and technical apparatus,
which has made most art criticism, especially among ourselves, so little nourishing, so little real or lifelike.
'What is important,' as Mr Pater says in words that define
his own method and position, 'is not that the critic should
possess a correct abstract definition of beauty, but a certain kind of temperament, the power of being deeply moved
by the presence of beautiful objects. He will remember
that beauty exists in many forms. And often,' he continues,

'it will require great nicety to disengage this virtue
from the commoner elements with which it may be found in
combination.' It is probably this keen susceptibility to
minute suggestions that underlies the writer's care for
the lesser stars in the great firmament, his love for bits
of work other than the gigantic or sublime, the attraction
to him of hints of beauty and faintly marked traces of
exquisite peculiarity, rather than the noon-day splendour
of master works. We can suppose that the simplicity of
some Gregorian chant would please him better than a great
Beethoven symphony, and that the church at Gernerode or
St. Cunibert's at Cologne would give him more heartfelt
delight than the glories of the great Cölner Dom itself.
After all anybody may be stirred by the sublime or the
superb. We can well afford to welcome to literature one
of the less common spirits, gifted with a sense for the
dimmer beauties, and to whom the more distant tones are
audible and harmonious. Such gifts are extraordinarily
welcome to our own literature, which rich as it is in
magnificent as in sweet and homely productions, is anything but rich in work marked by subtlety of aesthetic
vision. If Mr Pater continues to remember that it is
exactly in the region of man's gifts where he most needs
caution and self-discipline, lest the fatal law of excess
turn his strength into his weakness, we may expect from
him delight and instruction of the rarest kind.

In one or two places there is perhaps to be noticed a
tinge of obscurity, or at least of doubtfulness of meaning,
the result of a refining of thought into excess of tenuity.
It is so difficult a thing rigorously to put aside as taken
for granted all commonplace impression and obvious phrase,
and only to seize what is the inner virtue of the matter,
without going beyond the sight and grasp of plainer men.
We have one man of genius who is as great a master of subtle
insight into character, as Mr Pater is of analysis of beautiful impressions; Mr Meredith, like Mr Pater, is not always easy to follow, and for the same reason. After all
the plain men are at least as much in fault as those who
touch them with perplexity. This fault, however, in Mr
Pater's case, if it is really there, and not merely a fancy
of my own, is only to be found in the essay on Winckelmann,
which is the earliest of the compositions in the volume;
and so we may suppose that it is a fault of which the
writer has already cured himself. We may, perhaps, also
venture to notice the occasional appearance of a very minor
defect, which is far too common in all contemporary writing
and conversation, but which jars more than usually in so
considerable a stylist as Mr Pater; I mean the use of
German and French phrases, like *intimité*,(2) *Allgemeinheit*,

Heiterkeit,(3) and the rest.   It seems just now to be peculiarly the duty of a writer who respects his own language,
and has the honourable aspiration of maintaining its purity,
strength, and comprehensiveness, carefully to resist every
temptation to introduce a single foreign word into his
prose upon any pretext whatever.   Even quotations from foreign writers ought, as I presume to think, to be given in
English, and not in French, German, Greek, Italian, excepting of course quotations in verse, and of these the good
prose writer is naturally most sparing in any language.
   Concreteness, prevented from running to unprofitable
amplitude of description alike by the reserve of the writer's style, and by the subtlety of the only impressions
which he thinks worth recording, is connected with a prime
characteristic of Mr Pater's work, its constant association of art with the actual moods and purposes of men in
life.   He redeems beautiful production in all its kinds
from the arid bondage of their technicalities, and unfolds
its significance in relation to human culture and the perplexities of human destiny.   This is to make art veritably
fruitful, and criticism too.   His criticism is endowed with
strength and substance by the abundance of intellectual
ideas which have come to him from the union of careful
cultivation with an original individuality, and these intellectual ideas are grouped in an unsystematic way round
a distinct theory of life and its purport, which thus in
the manner we pointed out at first gives colour and meaning to all Mr Pater has to say about the special objects
of his study.   This theory is worth attention.   The exponent of it sees only the fluid elements in life, only its
brevity and the inevitable abyss that lies at the end of
our path.

   We have an interval and then our place knows us no more.
   Some spend their interval in listlessness, some in high
   passions, the wisest in art and song.   For our one chance
   is in expanding that interval, in getting as many pulsations as possible into the given time.   High passions
   give one this quickened sense of life, ecstasy and sorrow of love, political or religious enthusiasm, or 'the
   enthusiasm of humanity'.   Only, be sure that it does
   yield you this fruit of a quickened multiplied consciousness.   Of this wisdom, the poetic passion, the
   desire of beauty, the love of art for art's sake has
   most;   for art comes to you professing frankly to give
   nothing but the highest quality to your moments as they
   pass and simply for those moments' sake (p. 212).

Of course this neither is, nor is meant to be, a complete

scheme for wise living and wise dying. The Hedonist, and
this is what Mr Pater must be called by those who like to
affix labels, holds just the same maxims with reference to
the bulk of human conduct, the homespun substance of our
days, as are held by other people in their senses. He
knows perfectly well that the commonplace virtues of honesty, industry, punctuality, and the like, are the conditions of material prosperity, and moral integrity. Here
he stands on the same ground as the rest of the world. He
takes all that for granted, with or without regret that
these limitations should be imposed by inexorable circumstance upon the capacity of human nature for fine delight
in the passing moments. He has no design of interfering
with the minor or major morals of the world, but only of
dealing with what we may perhaps call the accentuating portion of life. In the majority of their daily actions a
Catholic, a Protestant, a Positivist, are indistinguishable
from one another; just as they are indistinguishable in
the clothes they wear. It is the accentuating parts of
conduct and belief that reveal their differences, and this
is obviously of the most extreme importance, — less in its
effect upon commonplace external morality which can take
care of itself on independent grounds, than in its influence over the spiritual drift of the believer's life. It
is what remains for a man seriously to do or feel, over and
above earning his living and respecting the laws. What is
to give significance and worth to his life, after comply-
ing with the conditions essential to its maintenance and
outward order? A great many people in all times, perhaps
the most, give a practical answer to the question by ignoring it, and living unaccented lives of dullness or frivolity. A great many others find an answer in devotion to
divine mysteries, which round the purpose of their lives
and light the weariness of mechanical days. The writer
of the essays before us answers it as we have seen, and
there is now a numerous sect among cultivated people who
accept his answer and act upon it. So far as we know,
there never was seen before in this country so distinct an
attempt to bring the aesthetical element closely and vividly round daily life. It has an exaggerated side. Dutch
farmhouses are systematically swept by brokers, that the
vulgarity of ormolu may be replaced by delft, and nankin,
and magic bits of oriental blue and white. There is an
orthodoxy in wall-papers, and you may commit the unpardonable sin in discordant window-curtains. Members of the
sect are as solicitous about the right in tables and the
correct in legs of chairs, as members of another sect are
careful about the cut of chasuble or dalmatica. Bric-a-
brac rises to the level of religions, and the whirligig of

time is bringing us back to fetishism and the worship of
little domestic gods, not seldom bleak and uncouth.
   In all this, notwithstanding its exaggeration, there is
something to be glad of. It is the excess of a reaction,
in itself very wholesome, against the vulgar luxury of
commonplace decoration, and implies a certain appreciation
of the permanent principles of beautiful ornament. But
there is something deeper than this underneath, at least
in the minds of the vigorous leaders of the movement, and
in such men as Mr Pater, just as there was something deeper
than the puerilities of the fussier and sillier sort of
ritualists in the mind of Mr Ward or Dr Newman. Indeed,
this more recent pagan movement is one more wave of the
great current of reactionary force which the Oxford movement first released. It is infinitely less powerful,
among other reasons because it only appeals to persons with
some culture, but it is equally a protest against the mechanical and graceless formalism of the modern era, equally
an attempt to find a substitute for a narrow popular creed
in a return upon the older manifestations of the human
spirit, and equally a craving for the infusion of something
harmonious and beautiful about the bare lines of daily
living. Since the first powerful attempt to revive a gracious spirituality in the country by a renovation of sac-
ramentalism, science has come. The Newmanite generation in
Oxford was followed by a generation who were formed on Mr
Mill's Logic and Grote's Greece. The aesthetic spirits
were no longer able to find rest in a system associated
with theology. Then Mr Ruskin came, and the Pre-Raphaelite
painters, and Mr Swinburne, and Mr Morris, and now lastly
a critic like Mr Pater, all with faces averted from theology, most of them indeed blessed with a simple and happy
unconsciousness of the very existence of the conventional
gods. Many of them are as indifferent to the conventional
aims and phrases of politics and philanthropy as they are
to things called heavenly. Mr Ruskin indeed, as we all
know, has plunged chivalrously into the difficult career of
the social reconstructor, but hardly with a success that
any man can call considerable. And Mr Swinburne, like that
most powerful of all French poets whom he calls master, has
always shown a generous ardour in the greater human causes.
But here is Mr Pater courageously saying that the love of
art for art's sake has most of the true wisdom that makes
life full. The fact that such a saying is possible in the
mouth of an able and shrewd-witted man of wide culture and
knowledge, and that a serious writer should thus raise
aesthetic interest to the throne lately filled by religion,
only shows how void the old theologies have become.

And if such a doctrine fails of their inspiring earnestness and gravity, at the same time it escapes their cramp-
ing narrowness. It is pregnant with intellectual play and
expansion, and it is this intellectual play and expansion
that we require, before the social changes craved by so
many can fully ripen. It is assuredly good for us to possess such a school. There is no reason to be afraid of
their taking too firm a hold, or occupying too much ground,
to the detriment of energetic social action in the country.
We have suffered more from the excessive absorption of national interest in theological strife and the futilities
of political faction, than we are at all likely to suffer
from the devotion of a few men of special impulses to the
subjects where those impulses will tell with most effect.
The prodigious block of our philistinism needs to have wed-
ges driven in at many points, and even then they will be
all too few. Sincere and disinterested work by competent
hands upon exactly such subjects as Mr Pater has chosen,
real yet detached from the clamour of to-day, is one of the
first among the many fertilising agents that the time demands. To excite people's interests in numerous fields, to
persuade them of the worth of other activity than material
and political activity, is to make life more various, and
to give the many different aptitudes of men an ampler
chance of finding themselves.

Politics and the acquisition of wealth do not constitute
the only peril to the growth of culture in England. The
specialism of physical science threatens dangers of a new
kind. On this side too we need protection for other than
scientific manifestations of intellectual activity and
fruitfulness. Only on condition of this spacious and manifold energizing in diverse directions, can we hope in our
time for that directly effective social action which some
of us think calculated to give a higher quality to the
moments as they pass than art and song, just because it is
not 'simply for those moments' sake'. For after all, the
Heraclitean word which Mr Pater has expounded with such
singular attractiveness both of phrase and sentiment only
represents one aspect of the great world. If all is very
fluid, yet in another way how stable it all is. Our globe
is whirling through space like a speck of dust borne on a
mighty wind, yet to us it is solid and fixed. And so with
our lives and all that compasses them. Seen in reference
to the long aeons, they are as sparks that glow for an indivisible moment of time, and then sink into darkness, but
for ourselves the months are threads which we may work
into a stout and durable web.

Notes

1 Jacques Benigne Bossuet (1627-1704), French Roman Catholic prelate, tutor to the dauphin and Bishop of Meaux,
  was renowned as a pulpit orator.
2 See p. 51.
3 See p. 52.

6. MRS PATTISON, UNSIGNED REVIEW, 'WESTMINSTER REVIEW'

April 1873, n.s.   xliii, 639-41

See No. 32 and Introduction, pp. 8 and 20.
   Emilia Frances Strong (1840-1904), writer and historian
of French art. Emilia distinguished herself as a scholar
at Oxford and made the acquaintance of the leading profes-
sors and personalities of the day. In 1861 she married
one of them, the Reverend Mark Pattison (1813-84), the Rec-
tor of Lincoln College, and thereupon became the centre of
a circle of liberal thinkers. In 1885 she married Sir
Charles Wentworth Dilke (1843-1911), the brilliant politician and author. Pater praised her book, 'The Renaissance
of Art in France' (1879) as 'a work of great taste and
learning' (R, 157n).
   For a discussion of her historical bias and critical
severity, see Benson, 37-8, and Wright, i, 252-4.

'Studies in the History of the Renaissance' is the title of
a volume of essays (several of which have already appeared
in print) recently published by Mr Walter Pater, Fellow of
Brasenose College, Oxford. The title is misleading. The
historical element is precisely that which is wanting, and
its absence makes the weak place of the whole book. The
contents embrace a wide field. The names of Pico della
Mirandula, of Botticelli, of Michael Angelo, of Joachim du
Bellay, standing at the head of the respective chapters,
will be a sufficient indication of its variety as well as
extent. But the work is in no wise a contribution to the
history of the Renaissance. For instead of approaching his
subject, whether Art or Literature, by the true scientific
method, through the life of the time of which it was an
outcome, Mr Pater prefers in each instance to detach it

wholly from its surroundings, to suspend it isolated before
him, as if it were indeed a kind of air-plant independent
of ordinary sources of nourishment. The consequence is that
he loses a great deal of the meaning of the very objects
which he regards most intently. This is especially noticeable when he passes from the examination of fragments to
deal with the period as a whole. Take for instance the
passages of general criticism with which the first essay
opens. Mr Pater writes of the Renaissance as if it were a
kind of sentimental revolution having no relation to the
conditions of the actual world. Whilst he discriminates or
characterizes with great delicacy of touch the sentiment of
the Renaissance, he does not let us know that it was precisely as the expression of vital changes in human society
that this sentiment is so pregnant for us with weighty
meaning. Thus we miss the sense of the connexion subsist-
ing between art and literature and the other forms of which
they are the outward expression, and feel as if we were wandering in a world of unsubstantial dreams. We do not feel
that the writer has that intimate possession of his subject
in its essence and entirety which alone can convey to us
the impression of reality. The hold upon the art of the
day becomes uncertain because the grasp of life of the day
is ill-assured. This it is which destroys for us much of
the charm of a charming book, a book which shows a touch of
real genius. Mr Pater possesses to a remarkable degree an
unusual power of recognising and finely discriminating delicate differences of sentiment. He can detect with singular
subtlety the shades of tremulous variation which have been
embodied in throbbing pulsations of colour, in doubtful
turns of line, in veiled words; he can not only do this,
but he can match them for us in words, in the choice of
which he is often so brilliantly accurate that they gleam
upon the page with the radiance of jewels. In this respect
these studies of the sentiment of the Renaissance have a
real critical value. But they are not history, nor are
they even to be relied on for accurate statement of simple
matters of fact. For instance, Mr Pater tells the old
legend of how Leonardo da Vinci, when a boy, was allowed
by his master, Verrocchio, to paint an Angel for him in the
left hand corner of a Baptism of Christ which Verrocchio
was executing for the brethren of Vallombrosa, and how
Verrocchio turned away when it was finished as one stunned,
seeing the pupil had surpassed the master.(1) This story
has long been exploded as having no foundation, nor even
verisimilitude, and the angel, which may still be seen at
Florence, shows not a trace of special beauty nor even a
sign that it had been touched by a different hand to that
which painted the rest of the picture. Yet Mr Pater

actually calls the figure 'a space of sunlight in the cold
laboured old picture'. And again, Mr Pater is quite mistaken in supposing that

> M Arsène Houssaye, gather together all that is known
> about Leonardo in an easily accessible form, has done
> for the third of the three great masters what Grimm
> has done for Michael Angelo, and Passavant long since,
> for Raffaelle. Antiquarianism has no more to do.(2)

M Houssaye's book is a mere romance of no scientific pretensions whatever.

Notes

1 Pater's source (see R, 102) is Giorgio Vasari (1511-74),
  who tells this story in 'Lives of the Artists' (1550 and
  1568).
2 This passage was removed from the second and subsequent
  editions.
  Arsène Houssaye (1815-96), French novelist and art critic, wrote 'Léonard de Vinci' (Paris, 1869). Hermann
  Friedrich Grimm (1828-1901), German art critic, teacher
  and novelist, wrote 'Das Leben Michelangelos' (Hanover,
  1860-3), which was translated by F.E. Bunnètt (2 vols,
  1865). John David Passavant (1787-1861), German painter
  and scholar, is best known for his three-volume 'Rafael
  von Urbino und sein Vater Giovanni Santi' (Leipzig, 1839).

7. Z: MODERN CYRENAICISM, 'EXAMINER'

12 April 1873, 381-2

The article which prompted John Morley's letter to the
editor of this periodical, dated 19 April 1873:

> The writer of the article on Modern Cyrenaicism in the
> last number of the 'Examiner' says that I pass an 'ex-
> travagant eulogium' on Mr Pater's 'theory of life'.
> On the contrary, in the paper in question, I very ob-
> stinately repudiated it. The writer has also put into
> my mouth about half a page, setting forth this theory,
> which is not mine at all, but Mr Pater's. Surely one

has a claim to be protected against critical violences
of this degree. (p. 410)

The reviewer hints at a slight acquaintance with Pater.

Mr Pater, of Brasenose College, Oxford, has written a
volume of remarkably able essays upon the Renaissance, and
Mr John Morley has devoted an article to it in the 'Fortnightly Review'. What seems most to attract Mr Morley is
Mr Pater's theory of life.

[Quotes from No. 5: 'This theory is worth attention' to
'simply for those moments' sake'.]

And again — 'Here is Mr Pater courageously saying that the
love of art for art's sake has most of the true wisdom that
makes life full'. The fact delights Mr Morley immensely.
He and Mr Pater are not at one upon many points, and probably have less in common than even Mr Morley supposes. But
then Mr Pater says, or rather implies, in his own exquisite
way, that, 'Little as life is, it yet is all we have'. He
echoes Mr Swinburne's view of unhappy man:

   He weaves and is clothed with derision,
   Sows and he shall not reap,
   His life is a watch or a vision,
   Between a sleep or a sleep.(1)

   'Have you,' says Box to Cox, 'a strawberry mark upon
your left arm?' 'No, I have not.' 'Then,' is the prompt
reply, 'you are my long lost brother.' And so Mr Morley,
finding that Mr Pater, a fellow of a College, and an educated man, holds ideas that are logically incompatible with
Christianity, makes as much to-do as if he had found Osiris,
and begs us, showman like, to walk up and look at the gentleman whose theory of life is that the best thing to do is to
squeeze in the maximum of pulsations between birth and
death, and that the best way to do this is to study art for
its own sake.
   Now it is very commendable, no doubt, in a young and
able writer to hold beliefs that are logically incompatible
with any creed short of atheism. But so many young and
able writers do this nowadays, and have done it in all
ages and at all times, that we must be content to take Mr
Pater's theory of life by itself and so to ask whether it
is worth the extravagant eulogium Mr Morley passes on it.

'The old theologies' have become 'void' no doubt. No one
questions that. But we are not on that account bound to
accept with thankfulness the first substitute that is
offered us for them. Mr Pater's theory has at any rate the
merit of clearness. All that we have is life, and we owe
it to ourselves to make life as happy as possible. To
effect this, we must crowd into it the greatest possible
amount of the best possible pleasure. And the best possible pleasure is that derived from the contemplation of
the beautiful. Such is the gospel according to Mr Pater,
and Mr Morley makes an admirable Ali to Mr Pater's Moham-
med. To do him justice he is very careful to explain that
theories such as these have reference only to 'the accentuating portions' of our life; that they do not affect the
'homespun substance of our days', or 'the common-place
virtues of honesty, industry, punctuality, and the like'.
We must not suppose Mr Pater to say that an hour with the
Elgin marbles atones for a life mis-spent, or to wish to
elevate a profligate and selfish old peer who buys
Coreggios to the dignity of a saint. No one who knows Mr
Pater, as all Oxford men of this generation do know him,
would ever accuse him of saying anything of the sort. His
theory leaves our common-place duties where they were. It
simply refers to that portion of our lives which is our
own.

   But the objection to it is that it is nothing new. It
is simply the old story of Cyrenaicism over again. Mr
Pater narrows life down to the 'watch between a sleep and
a sleep'; the Cyrenaics narrowed it to the moment. Memories and hopes Aristippus(2) refused to estimate. What
we possess, he taught us, is that which now *is*; that
which now is, is the moment; and the pleasure of the
moment — the μονόχρονος ἡδονὴ — is all that man has.
What the difference is between Mr Pater and Aristippus we
leave to Mr Morley to point out. The great founder of the
Cyrenaic sect was, as every schoolboy knows, better than
his creed; and we would have, in all probability, accepted
with delight the theory that it is art, after all, which
yields the best and fullest μονόχρονος ἡδονὴ, or — to use
the modern equivalent — 'pulsation'. Indeed, Aristippus
indignantly repudiated the assertion that his philosophy,
logically carried out, throned delirious debauchery in the
seat of virtue; nor have we any wish to accuse Mr Pater
of even remotely favouring the vulgar doctrine that 'life
is all beer and skittles'. The true objection to these
Hedonistic theories is not quite so much upon the surface
as this.

   Get your self-contained pleasure, cried Aristippus; get
your 'pulsation', cries Mr Pater. Yet, but we surely need

a criterion of 'pulsations'. The housemaid who revels in
the sensation novels of the 'London Journal' holds with
Mr Pater — only less consciously — that it is its pulsations that make life worth the living; and the question
is whether the pulsation philosophy is not as fully realised by the housemaid with her Miss Braddon,(3) as by Mr
Pater with his Winckelmann; whether it is not, after all,
the philosophy of the parodist of 'Guy Livingstone'(4) with
his exquisite 'O! let us all go and be dissolute heavy
dragoons'.

It is easy to see how this is Cyrenaicism — for
Cyrenaicism it is which Mr Pater preaches — is the moral
philosophy of scepticism. Scepticism denies the possibility of reducing life to an organic whole; and its
moral philosophy, denying the possibility of a criterion,
bids us seize the minute, and make the best of it. Life,
said Aristippus, is so dull, so dreary, so stupid, that I
prefer to lie on the seashore watching the gulls overhead,
and throwing pebbles into the waves. And in a similar
spirit Mr Pater, apostle of the artistic apotheosis of
lotus-eating, finds life so dull and hopeless, and in a
word 'Philistine', that he prefers to wile his moments
away with the joys of shape, and sound, and colour. 'We
are all going to Heaven,' said Gainsborough as he died,
'and Van Dyke is among the company.' Here was a 'pulsation', indeed, fully making up for all that before it might
have rendered a long life joyless.

Strange as it may seem, Cyrenaicism and Monasticism are
essentially one. Mr Pater wandering through a picture gallery is the exact antitype of the eremite singing his hymn
of praise among the rocks. 'Hora novissima tempora pessima
sunt,' says St Bernard, and deduces the moral 'vigilemus';
(5) and from the same premises Mr Pater deduces the moral,
Let us worship Beauty with all our heart, and all our soul,
and all our strength; and as for our neighbour — why the
homespun portion of our days takes sufficient care of itself. Sufficient for daily life is the daily morality
thereof. What is strange is not the theory itself, but
the manner in which it recurs, and the various forms that
it takes. It is an endeavour to stand aloof from the
world and the things thereof, and to lead the life philosophic. And its error is, as has over and over again been
shown, that the life philosophic presupposes philosophy;
that philosophy presupposes the criterion of truth, or in
other words of good; and that for a man who possesses the
criterion of good and is able by its aid to organise his
life, it were not only absurd but, worse than absurd,
wicked to withdraw from life and to leave the world to itself. The philosopher, as Plato says, is bound if only in

self-defence to take his part in active life.

Thus, then, Cyrenaicism is an attempt to lead the life philosophic, coupled with a denial of the possibility of philosophy. Such a creed is in itself a contradiction. Mr Tennyson is nearer the mark when he says, 'Hold thou the Good, define it well', and denounces the philosophy which, losing sight of the Good, stoops to become 'procuress to the Lords of Hell'.(6) It is a myth, no doubt, that Nero, being in want of a new 'pulsation', 'put Rome on fire and fiddled to the flames'. But Mr Plimsoll with his griev- ance, Lord Shaftesbury in spite of himself, Miss Rye with her schemes of emigration, Mr MacGregor with his industrial schools, Mr Spurgeon with his orphanage — these, and those like these, have a truer theory of life, and are thus bet- ter philosophers than any number of Paters with any amount of 'pulsations'. The very word itself recalls Mr Harold Skimpole. If utilitarianism had no value of its own, it would yet be valuable as a protest against this new 'lilies of the field' theory of life and its duties. Mr Ruskin is as fond of art and gets as many 'pulsations' out of it as most men. We should like to know his opinion of Mr Pater and of Mr Pater's critic.(7)

The writer of this article knows, as all who know Oxford know, that Pater is an industrious, energetic, self-sacri- ficing College tutor, and that his theories about life are the relaxation of a life sternly devoted to duty. This must be mentioned lest an attack upon a theory should ap- pear to be what it is not, an attack upon a man. Nor, as far as the theory itself is concerned, does any one deny or wish to deny their value to the 'pulsations' yielded by art? All that we humbly assert is that the doctrine that 'the love of art for art's sake has most of the true wisdom that makes life full' is far from new, and very far indeed from true.

Notes

1 'Atalanta in Calydon' (1865), 11. 357-60.
2 Greek philosopher (c.435 - c.356 BC), pupil of Socrates.
3 Mary Elizabeth Braddon (1837-1915), author of some eighty romantic novels.
4 A novel (1857) by G.A. Lawrence (1827-76)
5 From 'De Contemptu Mundi' (1145). These lines have been translated by S.A.W. Duffield (1867) as: 'These are the latter times, these are not better times: Let us stand waiting.'
6 'In Memoriam' (1850), liii, 13-16.
7 In 'The Life and Work of John Ruskin' (1893), W.G.

Collingwood observes that in the 'Ariadne' lectures
Ruskin 'quoted with appreciation the passage from the
Venus Anadyomene from Mr Pater's "Studies in the Renaissance" just published' (ii, 137).   E.T. Cook and Alexander Wedderburn, editors of 'The Works of John Ruskin'
(1903-12), point out that 'This does not appear in the
lectures as published' (XXII, xxxviin).

8.   F.G. STEPHENS, UNSIGNED REVIEW, 'ATHENAEUM'

28 June 1873, 828-9

Frederick George Stephens (1828-1907) was a student at the
Royal College when, along with James Collinson, Holman
Hunt, J.E. Millais, D.G. Rossetti, W.M. Rossetti and
Thomas Woolner, he became one of the original members of
the Pre-Raphaelite Brotherhood in 1848.   He later abandoned
painting and became the art critic (1860-1901) for the
'Athenaeum'.

We confess to a feeling of dislike for books which, like
Mr Pater's, deal with the aesthetics of painting, sculpture, and architecture.   Those concerning architecture are
the least objectionable, because it is the least like a
fine art of the three.   The more we know about the other
two the stronger grows our conviction that aesthetic discourses leave the subject much where it was before.   He
must have but crude notions of painting and sculpture who
has not rid himself of the idea that they are matters for
scientific analysis in any but their most superficial
aspects.
    We took up Mr Pater's book with reluctance, and a
strong sense of duty;   we put it down with relief, not
unmixed with satisfaction, for we soon found the author
to possess clear notions of what he is about.   Mr Pater
disclaims anything like transcendental criticism.

    'What is this song or picture, this engaging person-
    ality, presented in life or in a book, to me?   What
    effect does it really produce on me?   Does it give me
    pleasure?   How is my nature modified by its pressure
    or under its influence?'   The answers to these ques-

tions are the original facts with which the aesthetic
critic has to do;   and, as in the study of light, of
morals, of number, one must realize such primary data
for oneself, or not at all.   And he who experiences
these impressions strongly, and drives directly at the
analysis and discrimination of them, need not trouble
himself with the abstract question, what beauty is in
itself, or its exact relation to truth or experience, —
metaphysical questions, as unprofitable as metaphysical
questions elsewhere.   He may pass them all by as being,
answerable or not, of no interest to him.

Here and there we come upon passages in this book which
are inexplicable.   For example, he says that to the critic
'all periods, types, and schools of taste, are in themselves equal'.   On the other hand, Mr Pater has a sound and
comprehensive, though rather confused and irregular, conception of the more important phenomena connected with the
progress of and changes in the arts, their history and
movements.   His theory of the Renaissance is a good one.
It is not, of course, new to students, but it is by no
means commonly known to writers of essays.   This theory
sets the true Renaissance back in time as far as the day
of Abelard, and names Paris as its birth-place, but goes
a little too far in accepting what is called 'love' as its
vivifying power.   Those who know say with one voice that
the fifteenth century, for the fine arts at least, was,
with some individual exceptions, but the commencement of
the decline and ruin of the true Renaissance.   In its
real beginning, this marvellous movement — probably the
most wonderful that has affected the minds of men — was
subject to discipline;   its continuation was impossible
without that;   and when discipline, or the restraints
of the artistic conscience, lost their power, the outcome
was splendid indeed for awhile, but the inheritance of Art
was squandered.   There are some who complain that, as she
had done before under the Romans, Italy, at this later
time, seized on the hard-won inheritance of design, and
spent it in riotous living.   However this may be, it is
certain, as Mr Pater knows, and tells his readers: that
the Renaissance did not begin in Italy.   'This outbreak
of the human spirit may be traced far into the middle age
itself.'   Of course it may; for it is beyond doubt that,
long before the Italian sculptors confounded the limits
of their art with those of painting, — long before the
glass-painters produced preposterous transparencies, which
showed at once their ignorance of Art and their contempt
for its logic, there were men labouring in France and England whose works attest that nothing truer in sculpture,

and very little that was half so loyally beautiful, had
been known since Greece declined; works like the portals
of Auxerre, which remain unsurpassed, or even approached,
unless by Flaxman.(1) It is the same with regard to
glass-painting, except that the antetype and model were
at Le Mans and elsewhere in France. Mr Pater has not the
courage of these convictions, if he has yet gained the
convictions themselves; and we think he has not yet done
so, for he speaks of the new vitality of the twelfth and
thirteenth centuries as a 'Renaissance within the limits of
the middle age itself, — a brilliant, but in part abortive, effort to do for human life and the human mind what
was afterwards done in the fifteenth' century. Now the
later period, as Mr Pater probably knows, in no respect
did, nor was capable of doing, anything like what the
earlier centuries began, and almost achieved. What is
popularly called the Renaissance, i.e., the introduction of
classic (more strictly to say, corrupted Roman arts) learning and art, was so far from being the true Renaissance,
that it was to this introduction more than to anything else
that the strangling of the true new life was due. The
child of the new birth was overlaid by its 'classic'
nurses, and there was an end of it. The fact is, the true
Renaissance aimed at something else than enjoying itself
in this life, which is what the later ages seemed created
for, an aim, of which they reaped the inevitable results.
It is true that Mr Pater recognizes and appreciates in a
high degree the fine character of the true Renaissance, as
his essay, Aucassin and Nicolette, shows; but he does not
seem, to us, sufficiently affected by its nobler qualities,
and, above all, by the splendor of its achievements in the
fine arts, to say nothing of poetry. What is called the
renaissance in painting was really a new thing altogether,
not capable of being brought into the same category with
anything that remained, or even appears to have had being
in earlier ages of our era, or in antiquity.

The essays which constitute this book are delightful
reading; they possess a geniality and an elegance of
thought, fancy, and diction, which are rare indeed in themselves, but rarer still in combination, as they are here,
with considerable learning and acumen. There is no parade
of learning in these pages: a rapid reader might not hesitate to say that between the covers not a single sign appeared of more than common study or of recondite knowledge; nevertheless, the power of writing on such a subject as the later Renaissance in the comprehensive, yet
exact and singularly appreciative, manner of Mr Pater, is
proof of unusual accomplishments, and no small share of
original power. Few essays that we have read are equal to

that on Sandro Botticelli; nor is the little treatise on
Luca della Robbia inferior in appreciation either of the
art of the sculptor or his work. We mention these essays
as examples of what may be found in this book. There are,
besides papers on The Poetry of Michael Angelo, L. Da
Vinci, a first-rate analysis, another on Joachim du Bellay,
and two more. All will be read with pleasure by those who
have paid attention to the subjects. To others they may
be, so to say, keys to new regions of thought.

Note

1 John Flaxman (1755-1826), the eminent sculptor. His
  lectures on sculpture (read before the Royal Academy)
  were published in 1829.

9. W.J. STILLMAN, UNSIGNED REVIEW, 'NATION'

9 October 1873, xvii, 243-4

See Introduction, pp. 20 and 21.
   William James Stillman (1828-1901), American artist,
journalist and diplomat, co-founded the 'Crayon', which reprinted a considerable portion of Ruskin's work. Stillman
settled in England and married Marie Spartali (1844-1927),
the Greek-born painter and model who frequently sat for
Burne-Jones. In 1876 he became the Special Correspondent
and in 1884 the Rome Correspondent of 'The Times'. The
Stillmans probably met Pater at the home of the Robinsons.
Stillman and Pater were candidates for the Oxford Slade
Professorship left vacant by Ruskin (VLL, 178).

Mr Pater, in a book which on the whole deserves the epithet
fascinating, shows a power of expression and a subtlety of
analysis which at first reading disposed us to admit him
to a place among the best critics; but when we return to
study out the meaning unfolded and measure our acquisitions, we find we must change the word. Much is enfolded
and much is told that is admirable in telling, but not so
much of the theme as of Mr Pater himself; of him we obtain a very distinct and pleasing notion in general, but

of his nominal subject we hardly know more than before we
read his 'Studies'. The author is too much of an artist
to be a good critic, and hardly attempts to disguise the
fact that he is more interested in the perfection of his
own style than in the mysteries of the art on which his
studies are based. In fact, he sets out with a fallacy
which shows clearly enough that 'diletto' rather than 'cog-
nosco'(1) is the root of his thinking.

> Such discussions [on beauty in the abstract, etc.] help
> us very little to enjoy what has been well done in art
> or poetry, to discriminate between what is more and
> what is less excellent in them, or to use words like
> beauty, excellence, art, or poetry with more meaning
> than they would otherwise have. Beauty, like all other
> qualities presented to human experience, is relative,
> and the definition of it becomes unmeaning and useless
> in proportion to its abstractness. To define beauty,
> not in the most abstract, but in the most concrete
> terms possible, not to find a universal formula for
> it, but the formula which expresses most adequately
> this or that special manifestation of it, is the aim
> of the true student of aesthetics.

And having thus broadly stated his creed, which is that of
most dilettanti, viz., that there is no standard, that
there are no fundamental principles in art, but simply
recognitions of personal sympathies and expressions of
personal delights, he goes on to define with a logic not
so successful as his rhetoric what the aesthetic critic
has to do with.
    The simple fact is that for want of definitions, for-
mulas, abstract terms, and all those precise and 'metaphysical' distinctions which our author holds in defiance,
if not in abhorrence, the criticism of art is all afloat —
is in effect nothing but the unreasoning and generally un-
reasonable expression of individual preferences or tastes,
which may to-day be adopted as the standard from the personal prestige of the holder and to-morrow be rejected
because another has supplanted him; and in this field he
is king who has most power of persuasion, not he who has
most reason. The habitual critic is simply a dilettante
with more or less experience of art, with a set of rules
which are pure assumption, and which contribute in no
degree to establish taste on a sounder basis. What is
wanted to render criticism a science and make even dilettantism certain and progressive, is a thorough nomencla-
ture of art and definition of all its qualities in the
abstract; and a declaration that any such attainments

are either hopeless or useless, or in any degree inap-
plicable, is a confession of individual incapacity to
attain to or make use of them.

To assert that art and beauty have not laws capable of
rigid definition, and as rigid application to all cases
which can ever come under them, is equivalent to asserting
that there is no such thing as beauty, and that art is
whatever any one chooses to call it. Art, speaking in
the distinctive sense of that term in which it is used
when considered in reference to the expression of an ideal,
is purely and only the metrical, rhythmical, harmonic (what
the Greeks termed musical, pertaining to any of the Muses),
or concordant expression of emotion, whether it be in
poetry, painting, music, dancing, or any other conceivable
way of opening the soul to influences above and beyond it;
and to say that any of the arts thereby evolved is incapable of as absolute analysis and as abstract definition as music or color, is to confess a voluntary and
factitious limit to the powers of the human intellect. The
arts are but different forms of the same thing, and the
analogies are so absolute and coherent that to have analyzed one is to have shown the way to analyze the whole.

It is true that in the moment of the enjoyment of any
art-expression the analysis is, if not impossible, at
least destructive of the completeness of the enjoyment,
except to highly trained and peculiarly fitted minds; and
the recognition of this half-truth is what Mr Pater, like
almost all dilettante critics, means by his statement.
The absolute definition and embodiment in laws (not rules)
of the principles which lie at the root of art is not only
possible, but as indispensable to its complete and final
development as the laws which govern the heavenly bodies
are to the calculation of eclipses. It does not follow
that art can be evoked by knowledge or application of
rules, but that it cannot be fully understood and most
effectively cultivated without that knowledge and application.

Mr Pater takes with the word *renaissance* a liberty
which, though very common, is historically and logically
inadmissible. The word does not mean a revival, but a new
birth, and was applied to a phase of art which its votaries
believed to be the re-creation of Greek art. Its proper
and technical meaning is in the resumption of classical
forms of art-expression, as seen in Raphael's later work,
Michael Angelo, and the indefinite horde who followed,
amongst whom we notice most commonly Poussin, etc., etc. —
an art which, far from being a new birth or even a revival,
was, in its substitution of the borrowed and imitated
themes which it effected, in reality the decay of art —

that inevitable decay which accompanies the substitution
of a reflected and imitative enthusiasm for genuine emotions which compel their own rhythmical expression and
develop their own forms. If the term 'renaissance' is in
any way applicable to Italian art, it belongs to Giotto,
who first went frankly to the original springs of art, the
pure beauty of nature; but it is very doubtful if there
was ever any suspense or renaissance in art, since when
it subsided in one form it broke out in another, and the
spirit was always the same, and immortal. A peculiar
national temperament develops one form; change the nature of its emotions and the form of the art changes; but
so long as there is genuine and lofty emotion, there will
be art, be there schools or no schools. Nature is herself
the great mistress — not, as the German critics have it,
external and material nature, but the universal human-
divine nature, in which are born and nourished every aspiration and emotion the embodiment of which becomes art.

The 'Studies' have the coherence which might be expected from separate essays on kindred topics, but written
without any central thought; they are full of thought and
suggestion, and abound in evidence of culture and accomplishment, but they must be taken not as a book, but each
on its distinct merits. The last on Winckelmann is perhaps one of the completest expressions of the dilettante
view of that celebrated art-writer which we can expect to
have. It takes Winckelmann's side of Winckelmann, who
was an art-critic in the sense that German painters are
idealists when they *try* to be ideal, who confounded artifice with art, the form of things with their substance,
and, like all worshippers of the renaissance, died in the
worship of form and accident, not of substance and law.
He was a narrow-minded man, whose nature was only open to
reflected (and hence artificial) emotions, and the rigid
forms of Greek art appealed to his narrow side — the
nature which was the source of Greek art he had no eye
for. He sought for the secret of the perfection of that
art in a hypothetical and visionary physical perfection
amongst the Greeks instead of where it really was, in the
serene and exalted character of the Greek intellect,
healthy and happy, full of sublime passions, with a remarkable freedom from sensuality, with a tranquil faith, and
lives singularly free from what we may call worldly ambitions. If the whole known *répertoire* of Greek sculpture
were alive and walking amongst us to-day, we should no
more develop great sculptors than we do, because the
temper in which that was conceived and born does not exist
in modern times. This Winckelmann and his followers do
not comprehend; they do not see that all the copying and

imitation of antique statues which doomsday will permit
will no more make an artist than the study of Greek hexa-
meters will make another Homer. Art that looks back
ceases to be art, and becomes artifice; a renaissance
that is the renewal of dead forms is not a new birth, it
is a galvanic resuscitation; and the modern sympathy
(like Winckelmann's) with the Renaissance so-called, is
but a morbid abhorrence of life and health, and fondness
for death and artifice.

But we must not leave Mr Pater with our differences
alone adjusted. Differ in opinion with him we must, and
continually, yet with profound respect for his opinion.
The essay on Pico Della Mirandola is so full of genuine
appreciation, so complete, so comprehensive, that, without having previous knowledge of Mirandola, one feels that,
if living, he would say that Mr Pater has told him better
than he could have told himself. And generally the essays
on literary themes are better than those on artistic (using the
word in its narrow, common sense), for the simple reason
that without being to a certain extent an artist it is
absolutely impossible to be a comprehensive critic of art.
In poetry, Mr Pater is one of the cognoscenti; in painting, as we have said, only a dilettante. His conception
of literary qualities seems clear and definite, but that
of pictorial character evasive and indefinite, like a
picture drawn by an untrained talent, with a vague, un-
incisive touch. But in whichever theme, his power, individuality, and charm of style are such as to make his book
one of the best acquisitions which art-literature has made
of late.

Note

1 Pleasure rather than knowledge.

10. MRS OLIPHANT, UNSIGNED REVIEW, 'BLACKWOOD'S MAGAZINE'

November 1873, cxiv, 604-9

See No. 45 and Introduction, pp. 9, 19 and 20.
Margaret Wilson Oliphant (1828-97), Scottish critic,
literary historian, novelist of considerable stature and
regular contributor to the magazine, is chiefly known for

her history of Blackwood's publishing house and for her
books dealing with provincial English life in the nineteenth century. Her best novels are the 'Chronicles of
Carlingford', issued anonymously between 1863 and 1876.
    Preceding this extract was her review of Colvin's book,
'Children in Italian and English Design' (1872).

We cannot speak with the same praise of Mr Pater's pretentious volume as we have done of the graceful criticism,
poetic and fanciful as his subject, of Mr Colvin. Both,
perhaps, may be taken in their different ways as good
specimens of the productions of a class removed from ordinary mankind by that ultra-culture and academical contemplation of the world as a place chiefly occupied by
other beings equally cultured and refined, which — perhaps by natural reaction against the too boisterous
vitality of young life in these learned shades — forms
an inner circle of Illuminati   in almost every university;
and very different from those poor but daring adventurers
of literature who cultivated the Muses on a little oatmeal,
worship attenuated and refined adumbrations of Art, Philosophy, and Thought, amid all the collected prettiness of
modern-antique decoration, putting up their delicate
atheisms, like their old china, on velvet shelves and conspicuous brackets to meet the eye. We beg Mr Sidney
Colvin's pardon if we do him injustice in this classification, for he has given us a charming little book, such
as, indeed, the ordinary mass of readers will put aside,
bewildered, as so much trifling — but which will be acceptable and delightful to the smaller class, of which
alone, probably, he thought in writing it. But Mr Pater's
volume, though there are bits of very pretty writing in it,
and here and there a saying which is worth quoting, is full
of so much 'windy suspiration of forced breath', and
solemn assumption of an oracular importance, that the
critic scarcely knows whether to laugh or frown at the
loftiness of the intention. Whether art-criticism could
ever be made interesting to the common mind is a question
which it is difficult to decide. We think it very doubtful;
though, indeed, the perverse and fantastic but always
graceful and attractive philosophisings about art with
which Mr Ruskin has made the world acquainted of late
years have attained a great popularity — a popularity of
which perhaps Mr Pater, who is not a Ruskin, is one of the
results. The pretensions of the lesser, however, are quite
as exalted as those of the greater writer. Mr Pater sets
the 'aesthetic critic' at once before us, in full possession

of his high office, standing, as it were, a mediator
between art and the world.

[Quotes Preface: 'What is this song or picture' to 'under
its influence?']

Thus it is in furtherance of the grand pursuit of self-
culture that he writes, treating all the great art and
artists of the past, and all the centuries of men, as
chiefly important and attractive in their relations to
that Me who is the centre of the *dilettante's* world. That
class of pious persons who call themselves Evangelical
have passionately taken up the same view, and have had to
bear much abuse on account of their determined effort to
save the souls of their Me at all hazards — an attempt
which has been characterised as the last horror of spiritual selfishness by many an indignant critic; yet self-
culture claims all the sympathy of most of these critics,
and is set forth here as the highest of aims, as it is
also set forth in many a finer and more important work. We
do not, we fear, understand the distinction. Let us have
fair-play; High Intellectualism and Low Churchism are in
this point so entirely at one, that their agreement merits
full recognition. To ourselves, the idea of regarding
Michael Angelo or Leonardo, or even Botticelli, a lesser
name, as only interesting in so far as we can get something out of them, is as revolting as it would be to apply
the same rule to our living friends, whom generally we are
fond of in exactly an inverse ratio, liking those best to
whom we give most, instead of receiving. The world is
bad enough, we suppose, but it would be considerably worse
were this highest, lofty, superior principle to be put in
practical operation. Mr Pater, however, has after all a
better definition of a critic to give us. When he describes his special function as that of identifying the
special excellence of each artist's work, and separating
this highest soul and meaning of art from the earthly
elements in which it is so often enveloped, we understand
and sympathise in his view; and his application of this
theory to the case of Wordsworth is very felicitous — and
while magnifying, not unjustly, the critic's office, gives
us a real perception of its value to all less careful and
studious readers.

Take, for instance, the writings of Wordsworth — the
heat of his genius, entering into the substance of his
work, has crystallised a part, but only a part, of it;
and in that great mass of verse, there is much that
might well be forgotten. But scattered up and down it,

sometimes fusing and transforming entire compositions,
like the 'Stanzas on Resolution and Independence', and
the ode on the 'Recollections of Childhood', sometimes
as if at random turning a fine crystal here and there
in a matter it does not wholly search through and transform, we have the action of his unique incommunicable
faculty, that strange mystical sense of a life in
natural things, and of man's life as a part of nature,
drawing strength and colour and character from local
influences, from the hills and streams, and natural
sights and sounds. Well, that is *virtue*, the active
principle in Wordsworth's poetry; and thus the function
of the critic of Wordsworth is to trace that active
principle, to disengage it, to mark the degree in which
it penetrates his verse.

This is extremely well said, and with much insight and
fine perception. Very different, however, is that fantastic criticism which, taking for its subject the works of
Sandro Botticelli, a painter whose pictures have become
more generally known to the ordinary English public during
recent years by the late exhibitions of the old masters in
Burlington House, fixes upon this simple-minded artist of
an early age, on whom the questionings of a perturbed nineteenth century had certainly never dawned, a meaning oddly
characteristic of the conventional over-refinement of the
present day. It is something like the curious trick by
which Mr Kingsley, in his 'Saint's Tragedy',(1) converted
Elizabeth of Hungary, in her undoubting medieval faith,
into a perplexed young Churchwoman of 1835 or so, torn to
pieces between the reasonings of nature and a new-taught
conviction of the excellence of absolute obedience. Mr
Pater finds in the old painter's reverential, pathetic
angel-faces, and wistful, thoughtful Madonnas, a sentiment
of dislike and repulsion from the divine mystery placed
among them, such as, we think we may venture to say, never
entered into the most advanced imagination within two or
three hundred years of Botticelli's time, and was as alien
to the spirit of a medieval Italian, as it is perfectly
consistent with that of a delicate Oxford Don in the latter
half of the nineteenth century. Sheer determination to con-
fer upon this primitive teacher some 'unique faculty',
which no one else has divined, and to find out for him a
special virtue which shall act upon Mr Pater's Me in a distinct and recognisable way, lies, it is apparent, at the
bottom of this complacent suggestion. Botticelli's angel-
faces, as all students of art will recollect, are of an
intensely serious type — countenances blurred as with weeping, the tears momentarily arrested till their praise or

rapt contemplation shall be over. Even while they fiddle
they are ready to weep; and the Virgin abstractedly holding her divine Child in the midst, is as sadly conscious of
the sword which is to pierce her own heart also as they
are. But it is not necessary to be a student of art to
perceive the curious artificial fancifulness of Mr Pater's
criticism.

Hardly any collection of note is without one of these
circular pictures into which the attendant angels de-
press their heads so naïvely. Perhaps you have sometimes wondered why those peevish-looking Madonnas, con-
formed to no acknowledged or obvious type of beauty,
attract you more and more, and often come back to you
when the Sistine Madonna and the virgins of Fra Angelico
are forgotten. At first, contrasting them with those,
you may have thought that there was even something in
them mean and abject, for the abstract lines of the face
have little nobleness, and the colour is wan. For with
Botticelli, she too, though she holds in her hands the
'Desire of all nations', is one of those who is neither
for God nor for His enemies; and her choice is on her
face. The white light on it is cast up hard and cheerless from below, as when snow lies upon the ground, and
the children look up with surprise at the strange whiteness of the ceiling. Her trouble is in the very caress
of the mysterious child, whose gaze is always far from
her, and who has already that sweet look of devotion
which men have never been able altogether to love, and
which makes the born saint an object almost of suspicion to his earthly brethren. Once, indeed, he guides
her hand to transcribe in a book the words of her exaltation, the *Ave*, and the *Magnificat*, and the *Gaude Maria*,
and the young angels, glad to rouse her for a moment from
her dejection, are eager to hold the inkhorn and support
the book; but the pen almost drops from her hand, and
the high cold words have no meaning for her, and her
true children are those others, in the midst of whom,
in her rude home, the intolerable honour came to her,
with that look of wistful inquiry on their irregular
faces which you see in startled animals.

This is surely the very madness of fantastic modernism
trying to foist its own refinements into the primitive mind
and age used to no such wire-drawing. The same mixture of
sense and nonsense, of real discrimination and downright
want of understanding, runs through the whole book. On one
page we have a really fine description of Da Vinci's
Gioconda, — that strange face, with its sidelong smile and

sinister sweetness, which seems to have haunted the great
Leonardo, thrusting itself into almost all his pictures;
while on another our author drops into absolute abtuseness,
explaining the sublime group, often repeated, to which
Italian sentiment has given the name of Pietá, as an embodiment of pity, the 'pity of all mothers over all dead
sons', — the still more abstract pity of philosophical
observers over death in general!

On this point Mr Pater elaborately explains to us how
Italian painters must have 'leant over' the 'lifeless
body', studying it in its first solemnity and quiet; and
how, following it perhaps one stage further, and dwelling
for a moment on the point where all that transitory dignity broke up, and discerning with no clearness a new
body, they paused just in time, and abstained with a sentiment of profound pity. We doubt very much if any man with
a human soul in him, painter or otherwise, ever contemplated a fellow-creature dead with this perfectly calm and
abstract sentiment; but there is a curious dulness of apprehension which is quite startling, in the mind which can
take this superficial feeling as exposing all that is to be
found in Michael Angelo's Pietá. What can be said to such
a conception? It seems to argue some fundamental incom-
petence — some impotency of the mind and imagination
against which all manner of remonstrance might beat in vain.

The conclusion of this very artificial book has a curious kind of human interest in it, as showing what Greek —
not the language but the tone of mind and condition of
thought, taken up a thousand years or so too late, on the
top of a long heritage of other thoughts and conditions —
may bring Oxford to. Poor, young, too rich, too clever,
too dull, too refined souls! Greekness, if we may use such
a word, developed far down here in the centuries — with
that uneasy consciousness of a long spell of Christianity
lying between, of which the most Hellenic mind cannot di-
vest itself — is as different a thing from the real light-
hearted Greek, in its own time and generation, as is the
armour of a masquerade from the rude coats of mail in which
our forefathers hacked and hewed at each other. It is hard
to accept as quite serious the grandiloquent description
of life as set forth by the writer in the closing pages,
which is half pitiful, half amusing, in its earnest self-
persuasion, and attempt to look and feel as if so many
fine-sounding words must be true.

[Quotes the last three paragraphs of the Conclusion from
'The science of philosophy' to 'for those moments' sake'.
In the Library Edition, the quotation begins 'The service
of philosophy'.]

With this wonderful moral we may well close our remarks
upon Mr Pater's curious bit of philosophy and criticism.
Its conscious grandeur will probably tempt the grave reader to a smile — and we are not afraid that this elegant
materialism will strike many minds as a desirable view of
life; but it evidently sounds very fine and original, as
over-strained conventionality often does to the writer.
The book is *rococo* from beginning to end, — in its new
version of that coarse old refrain of the Epicureans' gay
despair, 'Let us eat and drink, for to-morrow we die' —
as well as in its prettiness of phrase and graceful but
far-fetched fancies. The writer reminds us of Stothard's
(2) big-headed babe peering at a butterfly on a flower,
with sage imaginations, doubtless, of new meaning in its
painted wings, who is represented in one of the charming
vignettes which Mr Colvin recalls to our recollection. To
weight this purely decorative piece of work with a pompous
confession of faith at the end, is about as bad taste —
and rather less cognate to the matter — as the Athanasian
Creed would be appended to a work on Christian art. It is
just this curious mingling, however, of bad taste and conventional originality, with much that is really graceful
and attractive, which gives to art the characteristics
which are embodied in the term *rococo*. And we are obliged
to add, that though Mr Colvin's book is infinitely simpler
and better in aim than the other, both of these pretty
productions are exotic — things conceived in a limited
atmosphere, comprehensible only in a narrow sphere, and,
by the very peculiarities of their being, betraying the
decay among us of all true and loving art. If art were
alive and vigorous in this world, its enthusiasts would
have something better to do than to deck its dim altars
with such ephemeral wreaths of evanescent flowers.

Notes

1·Charles Kingsley (1819-75), clergyman, novelist and
   poet, published this work in 1848.
2 Thomas Stothard (1775-1834), the celebrated painter and
   illustrator, executed some 5,000 designs for magazines
   and books.

11.   GEORGE ELIOT ON PATER

1873

Extract from a letter dated 5 November 1873 to John Blackwood, in 'The George Eliot Letters' (1954-6), ed. Gordon
S. Haight, vi, 455.
    George Eliot (1819-80) first met Pater at a dinner
party given by her friends the Pattisons (see headnote to
No. 6) on 27 May 1870. Pater admired her novels, particularly 'Romola' (Wright, ii, 180). Haight notes in
'George Eliot: A Biography' (Oxford, 1968) that she became a 'staunch' friend of Benjamin Jowett, but developed
'a strong aversion' towards Pater (p. 428).

I agreed very warmly with the remarks made by your contributor this month on Mr Pater's book,(1) which seems to
me quite poisonous in its false principles of criticism
and false conceptions of life.

Note

1 See No. 10

12.   W.J. COURTHOPE: MODERN CRITICISM, 'QUARTERLY REVIEW'

July 1874, cxxxvii, 389-415

See No. 51 and Introduction, pp. 4 and 21.
    William John Courthope (1842-1917), civil servant, poet
and critic. His chief works are the last five volumes of
the standard edition of Pope's works (1871-89), the volume
on Addison (1884) in the English Men of Letters series and
'The History of English Poetry' (1895-1910). From 1895
to 1900 he was Professor of Poetry at Oxford. Courthope,
Symonds (a close friend of his) and Pater were contestants
for the professorship in 1877. See Phyllis Grosskurth,
'John Addington Symonds' (1964), 168-73.

Courthope argues that, through the influence of Wordsworth and Arnold, modern criticism (or 'culture' as the
latter called it) is mere sophistry, a matter of individual feeling rather than of judgment, and that this emphasis on the cultivation of individual perceptions 'results in a science of style'.

... As culture has turned poetry into criticism so does
it transform criticism into poetry. Aristotle blamed the
Sophists for making prose poetical, observing acutely that
those who wrote in this manner sought to conceal the
poverty of their thought by the showiness of their style.
(1) Poetical prose, however, introduced by Mr Ruskin and
Mr Carlyle, has made rapid advances in England. The following extract from Mr Pater's criticism on Leonardo da
Vinci's picture 'La Gioconda' is a good specimen of this
epicene style:

[Quotes Leonardo da Vinci: 'The presence that so strangely
rose beside the waters' to 'the sins of the Borgias'.]

Now all this is plain, downright, unmistakable poetry.
The picture is made the thesis which serves to display
the writer's extensive reading and the finery of his style.
Of reasoning in the ordinary sense there is positively
none. 'The eyelids are a little weary,' therefore it is
quite plain that 'all the ends of the earth are come upon
her head.' The beauty is different from the Greek type.
What then can be more obvious than that this particular
face expresses the whole experience of mankind between the
age of Phidias and Leonardo? The lady appears to Mr Pater
to have a somewhat sensual expression. A fact which fully
warrants a critical rhetorician in concluding that she is
an unconscious incarnation of all the vices which he has
found preserved in the literature of the Renaissance.
Judgments of this kind, we are told, are the result of
'penetrative sympathy' or 'perceptive insight'. It may
be so; we cannot say that the qualities Mr Pater discovers
in this picture are not to be found there. What we can say
is that, as the reasoning in the above passage assumes a
knowledge in the critic of motives which are beyond the
reach of evidence, there is no justification for calling
that criticism which is in fact pure romance. In some
cases we may go farther, and show that the freemasonry
acquired by perpetual reading, uncorrected by actual observation, is really of a kind to weaken that acute saga-
city which is necessary for a judge. For instance, by an

error precisely resembling Winckelmann's absurd overesti-
mate of Raphael Mengs,(2) a critic of such natural good
sense and sound judgment as Mr Symonds, whose book(3) we
have classed with Mr Pater's at the head of our article,
has been induced to assert that an execrable American
scribbler, one Walt Whitman, is the true representative
of Greek life in the nineteenth century. A hundred other
instances might be quoted to prove how critics who reject
the natural standards of common sense in favour of private
perceptions derived from books are made the dupes of
quackery and imposture. Everywhere we see examples to
confirm the truth of Milton's reproach:

> The man who reads
> Incessantly, and to his reading brings not
> A spirit and judgment equal or superior
> (And what he brings why need he elsewhere seek?),
> Uncertain and unsettled still remains.
> Deep versed in books, but shallow in himself,
> Crude or intoxicate, collecting toys
> And trifles for choice matters, worth a sponge,
> As children gathering pebbles by the shore.(4)

Notes

1 Aristotle's 'Rhetoric', III, i, 9.
2 The German historical and portrait painter and critic
  (1728-79). He met Winckelmann in 1755 and was influenced by the latter's theories.
3 'Studies of the Greek Poets' (1873).
4 'Paradise Regained', iv, 321-30.

13.   BISHOP OF OXFORD ON SCEPTICISM

1875

Extract from a pamphlet entitled 'A Charge Delivered to
the Diocese of Oxford' (1875), 13-16. See Introduction,
p.22.
   John Fielder Mackarness (1820-89) was Bishop of Oxford
from 1870 to 1888. He matriculated at Merton College and
was elected (30 June 1844) to a Fellowship at Exeter
College, which he vacated in 1846 after receiving prefer-

ment in the Church. On the recommendation of Gladstone he
was appointed to the See of Oxford and consecrated bishop
on 25 January 1870.
    The address was delivered at his second visitation in
the Cathedral Church of Christ on 20 April 1875. Not
unexpectedly, it attacks the Conclusion to 'The Renaissance' as a subversive influence on Oxford youth.

... It were well if the progress of unbelief were confined
to that agricultural population, of which this Diocese
chiefly consists. The city, in which we are gathered together for the opening on this Visitation, presents another
aspect of the same unhappy tendency of the time. Our
Cathedral is so intimately, though accidentally, connected
with the academical life of the foremost University in
England, that we cannot, on such an occasion, omit all
notice of the unbelief with which our educated classes are
leavened continually more and more. To speak the simple
truth, a considerable number of Graduates who hold office
in the University, or Fellowships in the Colleges, have
ceased to be Christians in anything but name; — in some
cases, even the name is repudiated, when arguments based
upon its retention are pressed. It is not only that text-
books in some branches of study are recognised, which
assume a disbelief of Christian doctrine, and that some
lecturers hint, or express, their own rejection of it; —
there is a reserve on the part of Christian teachers in
commending to their pupils the truths they believe.
Thirty years ago the ablest and most highly esteemed of
Oxford Tutors took it for granted, in their ethical teaching, that Christianity furnished the only certain standard
in morals, and were accustomed to correct the shortcomings
of other systems by its rule: Christians are expected to
forget the existence of such an authority, when they cross
the threshold of their lecture-rooms, now. The historical
facts of Christianity fare no better than its precepts:
deference to scientific criticism (whatever that may mean),
forbids them to be taken for true. I make no mention here
of the removal of tests and statutory guarantees for orthodoxy,(1) because I do not ascribe the progress of unbelief
to their abolition; nor do I hold that their absence requires, or justifies, the tacit understanding I have described. As one of those who voted in Parliament for the
abolition of such academical tests, I am entitled to recall
the claim of right then made to preserve for ourselves
the freedom of opinion which was about to be conceded to
others. There is no reason why those who have advocated

the largest opening of our Universities to students of
all creeds, or of none, should abstain from vindicating
with all courtesy, but with manly and loyal frankness,
the spiritual supremacy of their own holy faith. For
want, it may be, of such frankness on the part of those who
should guide them, too many of the younger students
go miserably astray. Of these, some, indeed, have grave
and sad perplexities, for which no compassion can be too
tender, no sympathy too gentle. Others jest over their
doubts, and chuckle at the thought that they can laugh at
what their elders believed. With self-complacency, which
would be amusing if the subject were less serious, they
dispose of religion, natural or revealed, with the airy
phrase they have borrowed from the latest sceptical Review.
Ignorant of the Scriptures they reject, but glad to be rid
of the restraint which the Divine precepts impose, they
wander this way or that, as materialism on one side, or
some new phase of philosophy on the other, seem to offer an
escape. The practical result of this education is a selfishness of character far from attractive. Learners in the
school of unbelief have been taught that it is folly to
disturb themselves for the sake of others: they have lost
all motive for serious action: self-restraint and self-
sacrifice are discovered to be 'mere moral babble'; it is,
at the best, an amiable weakness to do good. Human life
is but the interval, longer or shorter, which condemned
mortals have to pass before they die.

> Our one chance [it is said] is in expanding that inter-
> val, in getting as many pulsations as possible into the
> given time.... Not the fruit of experience, but exper-
> ience itself is the end.... The Theory, or idea, or
> system, which requires of us the sacrifice of any part
> of this experience, in consideration of some interest,
> into which we cannot enter, or some abstract morality
> we have not identified with ourselves, or what is only
> conventional, has no real claim upon us.

So sceptics teach:- can you wonder that some who played
an honourable part in Oxford life a generation since, refuse to let their sons imbibe lessons so alien from the
lore they learned? Can you wonder that to young men who
have imbibed this teaching the Cross is an offence, and
the notion of a vocation to preach it an unintelligible
craze?...

Note

1 See p. 63n.

14.   SARAH WISTER ON PATER

1875

Extract from a signed article entitled Pater, Rio, and
Burckhardt, in 'North American Review' (July 1875), cxxi,
156-71.   See Introduction, pp. 19-21.
    Sarah Wister (1835-1908), pianist and linguist, was the
daughter of Pierce Butler (a wealthy Georgian planter) and
Fanny Kemble (the famous Shakespearian actress) and the
wife of Dr Owen Wister of Philadelphia and a close friend
of Henry James.   She wrote unsigned articles for the
'Atlantic Monthly' and edited 'Selections from the Prose
and Poetry of Alfred de Musset' (1872).   Her son, Owen
Wister (1860-1938), became well known for his novel 'The
Virginians' (1902).
    In the earlier part of her article she claims: 'Since
Ruskin set the example of a literary man erecting himself
into a dictator on questions of art, we have been subjected
to a fearful tyranny in aesthetics.'

... We think we recognize in Mr Pater ... one of the new
Mahomets, although he has not yet bared his scimitar and
proclaimed himself monarch as well as prophet.   He lacks
two capital qualifications for such a mission, — originality and earnestness;   yet he has already votaries, and,
seeking for the secret of his influence, we are inclined
to think that it lies primarily in the subjects of which
he treats, names and themes which are incantations in
themselves, whose very sound possesses a magic which nothing can dispel;   secondly, in his treatment of them, and
this is a snare.   He has the peculiar eloquence which goes
with insobriety of style, and all the charm and force which
can be snatched by breaking rules.   Still, the effects of
this lawlessness are by no means always happy.   The spell
would also be more potent for many readers, if the author
were not so palpably intoxicated by it himself;   sometimes
his ear seems to be tickled by a single word, which he

repeats in every imaginable combination; thus we have
'comely clerks', 'comely decadence', 'comely gestures',
'comely divinities', 'comely ways of conceiving life';
then it is 'sweetness', *ad nauseam*; sometimes a whole
phrase repeated verbatim, like the burden of a ballad.
Now this trick of iteration may be pardoned in an old
gentleman like Mr Carlyle, but it certainly suggests dot-
age. He coins like a true despot, and uses words without
italics which are not English, such as 'débris' and 'cult',
— to whatever language that may belong, — and gives us
such parts of speech as 'siderealized'. And why does he
talk about Pico della Mirandula, whom all modern Europe
knows as Mirandola? This is mere affectation; but when
he speaks of the Pitti Palace and the Sistine Chapel as
'the Pitti' and 'the Sistine', it is a bad habit, and has
a taint of vulgarity. A graver fault than these is his
inaccuracy; for instance, in support of a theory he
alleges that the Greek goddesses were always childless;
he cannot be ignorant of the beautiful Juno suckling a
babe in the Pio Clementino Museum of the Vatican, not to
speak of the common subject of Venus and Cupid. Elsewhere there is a trifling detail which strongly marks his
preference for effect over exactness; he gives a minute
and poetical description of Raphael's great frescos known
as the Debate on the Sacrament and Parnassus, speaking of
them as companion pieces designed to illustrate respectively orthodoxy of doctrine and orthodoxy of taste. Now
these compositions are in no sense whatever companions;
they differ in shape, size, and position; if the *Disputa*
have a companion, it is the famous School of Athens.

To pass to the more agreeable task of pointing out
merits, Mr Pater has a most unusual gift of conveying half-
defined emotions, modulations of feeling, shades of
thought; rare fineness of perception, an aerial grace and
delicacy of touch; an exquisite felicity of epithet, of
description, of presenting lovely images to the mind; his
prose is sometimes as fraught with the unspeakable as
music itself, although never with the highest rapture; in
these twin talents of calling up the seen and the unseen
must lie much of his fascination. A more tangible quality, though one seldom brought into service, is his power
of giving to his theories — and some few of those about
art are perfectly sound — the clearness of chiselled
marble. It is true that they are mainly borrowed, but he
makes good use of them occasionally. An example of this is
his remarks on the proper limits of sculpture (p. 188), or
a still finer passage concerning the influence of external
conditions on religion (p. 171):

[Quotes Winckelmann: 'Greek art, when we first catch sight of it' to 'one of the gravest functions of religious criticism'.]

Having called attention to these beauties, of which the above are by no means the only examples, there is no help for it but to go back to fault-finding. The volume is a collection of essays chiefly on matters of art in one form or another. It is curious that having much of the dogmatism, inaccuracy, fancifulness, love of paradox, and arbitrariness of Ruskin, Mr Pater's purpose should be the glorification of that period or movement, as one may consider it, which has called forth the former's most eloquent denunciations.(1) Movement we must say, since our author removes the landmarks and limits of his subject so completely as to leave no means of bounding it. Thus we have a quarrel with him at the outset, for we deny the right to wrest a term of long-established and universally accepted significance from its conventional meaning and give it a wider, perhaps a broader, but at the same time a looser and less accurate application, so that it ceases to be the aid that all such general terms are meant to be. The word Renaissance has been used technically to express an epoch, a fact, an intellectual phase, and a social condition. To use it as Mr Pater does is as though a writer on ecclesiastical history should persist in including in the term Reformation the Albigenses, Waldenses, iconoclast emperors, or whatever resistance to hierarchical authority has arisen in Christendom from apostolic days down; or as though the historian of England should begin the Revolution with the meeting at Runnymede, or the downfall of Ethelred the Unready. The review of this movement leads Mr Pater to touch upon some of the gravest preoccupations of the human mind; he always does so with the air of one who is trifling with his subject; there is no earnestness in his manner; he never goes to the root of the question, he never sounds the soul of the inquirer; he talks about 'religions', but he knows nothing of religion; fallacies bloom about his path; he never forgets that he is a *dilettante*; he shrinks from no assertion however unfounded, and has no hesitation in contradicting himself a few pages later. In his preface he says that, to the critic, 'all periods, types, schools of taste, are in themselves equal.... "The ages are all equal", says William Blake, "but genius is always above its age."' This is very well for Blake, the *pictor ignotus*:(2) but the ages have been notoriously unequal, or why do we hear of the age of Pericles, the Augustan age, the *Cinquecento*, the Elizabethan era, the *Grand Siècle*? And genius is not above its

age, but above its fellow-men, for the the heirs of immortal fame posterity has seldom done more than confirm
the verdict of their own century. And are we to believe
that Mr Pater really esteems the school of taste which
produced Mansard and Lemercier equal to that which brought
forth Arnolfo and the Pisani? His definition of the critic's function, to discern and detach from the mass of an
author's works the pure ore, the fine crystals of his
genius, which make its intrinsic and distinctive value, is
true and well put; but what are we to think of his own
critical capacity when in that very passage he classes
Byron with Goethe as artist or workman?

The first examples given of that revival of classical
feeling which common consent has assigned to the fifteenth
and sixteenth centuries, but which Mr Pater wishes to
trace back to the dark ages, is a poetical story in Provençal of the latter half of the thirteenth century, or
even later; there is no proof extant of an older deriva-
tion, and at that time Dante had come, besides the con-
stellation of lesser lights who preceded him, whom Mr D.G.
Rossetti(3) has made known to us. This date is the fact;
the shadowy possibilities of an earlier origin are not sufficient to make this story serve as proof of a return towards Hellenism in the eleventh century; moreover those
very possibilities indicate, not a Greek, but an Arabic
source. Mr Pater gives no complete or consecutive account
of this tale or the literature of which it is a sample; we
are not told the story; the selections are few and scanty,
though so full of beauty, grace, and quaintness as to make
us long for more; his method throughout is like humming
bits of a tune to one's self. Reduce chapter first to its
substance and what remains is about this: that in a certain book there is a story which Mr Pater thinks very
pretty, and which confirms, to his mind, certain notions
of his own. For a clear conception of either the story or
the subject which it illustrates we must look for it in
M Fauriel's 'History of Provençal Poetry'.(4)

From the thirteenth century Mr Pater leaps lightly into
the fifteenth, where his first point is: 'The attempt made
by certain Italian scholars to reconcile Christianity with
the religion of ancient Greece'. It may be doubted whether
they did so seriously and in good faith. The men who carried the parallel furthest really cared for myth more than
for truth; the best Christians among the humanists did not
bother themselves with such amalgamation, but kept their
religion and their philosophy in different phials. Pico
della Mirandola, whom Mr Pater selects as the type of
these experimentalists, was of an earnest and ardent nature, and less interested in any one form of human belief

than in a general scheme which should include all that
men had known and learned, — the science and wisdom of
the obsolete scholiasts, of the Arabic and Jewish teachers,
as well as of the heathen sages. The impression left by
Mr Pater's description of Pico, a youth of the most extraordinary endowments and erudition even in that age of pro-
digies, is of something between a wax-figure and a sleep-
walker; a single sentence of his own gives us at once
more sense of reality and a more ideal conception of him:

> 'In the midst of the world I have placed thee,' says
> the Creator, 'that thou mayest the better survey it
> and all that it contains. I have made thee a creature
> neither all heavenly nor all earthly, neither purely
> immortal nor mortal, that thou mayest shape and subdue
> thyself unhindered; thou canst degrade thyself to a
> beast and regenerate thyself to a godlike being. The
> brutes bring with them from the womb what is to be
> theirs; the higher spirits are from the beginning
> what they are to remain throughout eternity. Thou
> alone hast development, a power of voluntary growth;
> thou hast within thee the germs of universal life.'

'The fifteenth century was an impassioned age,' proceeds Mr Pater, 'so ardent and serious in its pursuit of
art that it consecrated everything with which art has to
do, as a religious object.... It was too serious to play
with a religion.' This is far from true; it better describes the general temper of the previous century; there
was an intense and impassioned strain in the fifteenth
which found expression in many ways, but the age was willing to play with its own religion in architecture, in
painting, in literary academies, in actual life. It was
no age of shams, yet a tinge of artifice had become apparent long before it drew to a close. In the latter half
of this century, according to M Rio,(5) letters and the
arts had begun to decline and degenerate in Florence, yet
there were still some chosen spirits who understood the
ideal aspirations of their predecessors and were found
worthy to continue the unfinished work of Fra Angelico
in the Vatican. With them were associated the leaders of
the Umbrian school, — that school, to quote the same
orthodox authority, which was imbued with the purest traditions, brought up under the shadow of the sanctuary at
Assisi, rich in the frescos of Cimabue and Giotto, where
the painters elevated their genius by the contact of popular piety and monastic fervor. At the head of this band
was Sandro Botticelli. Of this master's tendencies, Mr
Pater gives us the following metaphysical summary:

[Quotes Sandro Botticelli: 'What Dante scorns' to 'the
complexion of humanity'.]

Then follow descriptions of several of his most noted
pictures, in which we are told of the 'peevish-looking
Madonnas', who wish they had been let alone in their
humble homes among the gypsy brood who are their true
children.   It is impossible to argue such a subject by
pitting description against description;   but let any one
who has seen and studied them recall the circular picture
of the Uffizi where the child guides the mother's pen, and
that in the Louvre where he lays his little hand against
her face with unutterable love and compassion, yet with a
natural baby action which every mother knows, and let them
decide whether Mr Pater has not gone very far out of his
way to find a meaning for Botticelli's painting which is
foreign to it.   There is indeed a faltering, a fainting in
his Madonnas, as if the burden laid upon them were too
heavy to bear, the cup too bitter to drink, but they are
sweetness and weakness personified;   not their trouble,
but their comfort is the caress of the babe whose tender
childish sympathy is blended with the sustaining calm of
divine foreknowledge.   Botticelli's Madonnas may not be
reciting the *Magnificat* or the *Gaude Maria*, but they are
ready to say with drooping head, '*Ecce ancilla Domini*;   be
it unto me according to thy word.'(6)   He possesses to a
singular degree the gift granted to the real masters of
that day of making us feel their own personal and peculiar
sentiment regarding a subject, however conventional the
treatment or crude the execution, so that it affects us
as it affected them.   Mr Pater analyzes it well in speaking of Luca della Robbia:

[Quotes Luca della Robbia: 'His work possesses' to 'its
highest degree of intensity'.]

   Before we reach the essay on Michael Angelo's poetry
which forms one of Mr Pater's studies, we have met (p. 57)
with the statement that the unfinished condition of many of
Michael Angelo's greatest statues was 'his way of etherealizing pure form', that 'this incompleteness is Michael
Angelo's equivalent for color in sculpture'.   If the author's object be to astonish us by this paradox, we are
certainly astonished, but such a mode of producing effect
is too much akin to that of a child who hides to jump out
and cry 'Booh!'   After we have once been startled in this
way the trick fails, and we laugh or shrug our shoulders.
Even those who have never seen the original statues can
judge of the value of the interpretation when they learn

that the only unfinished portion of the David is a very
small bit among the locks of the hair, and in the Dawn,
the toes of one foot. Our next surprise is the ascription of 'sweetness' to Michael Angelo as an essential element of his ascendency. Most people would, indeed, be
'puzzled' (p. 63) if asked to define wherein that sweetness resides, and equally so to point it out in Victor
Hugo, to whom Mr Pater compares Michael Angelo in this particular; the instance chosen to illustrate it in the
former, of the butterfly alighting on the blood-stained
barricade(7) being merely a Frenchman's theatrical delight
in violent contrasts. Of Michael Angelo's *tenderness*, the
deep well whence flows all that softens his severity and
makes his tremendous sublimity tolerable to weaker humanity,
we hear not a word. Nor of those strange spheres, unvisi-
ted by any other mortal, where he dwelt apart among the
grand beings whom he has depicted, — that mighty world
with its mighty race, Titans, or demi-gods, or stupendous
avatars, incorporations of great primordial and moral
forces, standing, reposing, or stalking about in their own
immensurate realm.

Mr Pater closes his chapter on Michael Angelo with a
sort of monody on the Medicean chapel, where are the tombs
of Lorenzo and Giuliano with their slumberous guardians.

[Quotes The Poetry of Michelangelo: 'The titles assigned
traditionally' to 'a feather in the wind'.]

He who can stand in the silent precincts of those awful
presences, those solemn genii of the mysterious border-
land between Life and Death, the Known and the Unknown,
talking of them as if they were airy sylphs or shapeless
phantasms, however full of fancy he may be, lacks imagination, enthusiasm, feeling for the power and magnitude
of what is real, wholly lacks the capacity to lose himself in the genius even of the greatest.

The essay upon Leonardo da Vinci is far above any which
precedes it, because the subject legitimately affords
scope for speculation and paradox. The most general and
ordinary reading of it must needs abound in guesses and
half-expressed meanings, and Mr Pater's fantastic pen
finds here fit material for exquisite elaboration and
overlaying with mystical embroidery. If the way to perfection be 'through a series of disgusts' (p. 95), one
may fancy that at one period of Leonardo's career every
picture was a step on the road, such repulsion lurks
within the subtle inscrutability of his faces; they may
stimulate the curiosity, but while we wonder whether this
enigmatical personage, here called St John the Baptist,

there Bacchus, anon the Madonna, again Herodias's daughter,
be man or woman, faun or human, angel or demon, we feel
that to understand might be to loathe. When Mr Pater has
said that it is 'by a certain mystery in his work, and
something enigmatical beyond the usual measure of great
men, that he fascinates, or perhaps half repels'; that
'his type of beauty is so exotic that it fascinates a larger number than it delights, and seems more than that of
any other artist to reflect ideas and views and some scheme
of the world within'; that by the study of Nature and her
occult relations 'he learned the art of going deep, of
tracking the sources of expression to their subtlest re-
treats'; and — by way of summing up — 'curiosity and
the desire of beauty, — these are the two elementary
forces in Leonardo's genius'; he has perhaps given us as
distinct a conception of Leonardo's genius as words alone
can convey. Yet some common-place and common-sense might
have been useful in the analysis even of this subject. We
should not have had Mr Pater's eloquent lucubrations about
Mona Lisa, for instance; and why does he feel compelled
to translate this accepted title and call her Lady Lisa?
But neither should we have had such an opinion as he gives
of the Last Supper, by which Leonardo is most widely
known, — that immortal work of which some common reproduction is the treasure of many a humble home, where the
painter's name is a household word with simple souls who
never heard of La Gioconda; that work whose power and
pathos and living truth have triumphed over anachronisms
in treatment, the ravages of accident, the falsifications
of restorers, fixing, as our author himself says, the type
of Christ for all succeeding generations.

[Quotes Leonardo da Vinci: 'Vasari pretends that the central head was never finished' to 'spirits which have not
flesh and bones'.]

This is all that Mr Pater finds to say of that work which
has made real to us Christ in his most human aspect; of
that act which still, after nearly two thousand years,
whenever it is commemorated has the power to move us to
our inmost soul, and draw tears of tenderness from the
purest springs of feeling, as for one long lost but ever
beloved; the sole act which for all time to come established a bond of earthly fellowship between the Saviour and
mankind; which can bring all unborn generations during the
brief rite as near their Friend and Master as those who
walked with him daily upon earth. In fine, had Mr Pater
been more occupied with his subject than himself, he would
have given us, instead of *silhouettes* on cobwebs, a vivid,

full-face portrait of Leonardo's personality, about which
there is no mystery or secret, — daring rider, graceful
dancer, sweet singer, skilful engineer, peerless painter,
chemist, caricaturist, mechanician, poet, courtier, hand-
somest of human beings, the most concrete and consummate
illustration of that many-sided and glowing fifteenth century about which Mr Pater seems bent on weaving veils of
mist and moonlight.

The notice of Joachim du Bellay is in one way the best
chapter in the book, giving the author opportunity for his
dainty and delicate fingering, his light strokes of meta-
phor and suggestion, the short, airy, discursive flights,
which he loves, and from which he alights for a moment on
cathedral-spires, palace-pinnacles, and tree-tops, on the
horizon of his subject, often just at the vanishing-
point. But if one wishes for the gist rather than the
pollen-dust of the matter, it is given by Ste Beuve in the
last volume of his 'Nouveaux Lundis'.(8)

Of the peculiar metaphysical and ethical views of which
Mr Pater occasionally gives us glimpses, we have yet said
nothing. He stands aloof, in an attitude of superfine
separateness, whence he critically and dispassionately surveys the world of morals. The most striking instance of
this is his way of looking at Winckelmann's apostasy, confessedly the result of interested motives; he considers
it the consistent act of a man who is true to the key-note
of his nature, who obeys his highest instinct, which, in
Winckelmann was the artistic. We admit that frequent and
careful reading has still left us in doubt as to Mr Pater's
meaning in certain passages, and we shrink from incurring
the charge of stupidity, which we ourselves have sometimes
sharply brought against critics who cannot discriminate
between an author's real opinions and his temporary assumption of the opinions of others. But throughout this last
essay, and the conclusion, Mr Pater lays himself open to
the charge of being a heathen, or of trying to be one; for
no Englishman of the present day can become a genuine
heathen, any more than he could become a Jew or a Mussul-
man; even Mr Swinburne has only succeeded in being godless.
Page 181 he writes as follows:

[Quotes Winckelmann: 'The Temper of the antique world' to
'youth still read with life in its grave'.]

We can extract no meaning from all this, except that the
only compensation Christianity has given mankind for Greek
paganism is in that the resurrection of the body immor-
talizes materialism. 'The form in which one age of the
world chose "the better part"', — does he really mean

that men may choose 'the better part' in any form which
seems good to themselves?   Is there no such thing as calling the worse the better, and that bread which satisfieth
not?   What became of the uncomely and unlovely ones in such
a world as this?   Where was the comfort of the feeble and
the deformed, — 'the disgraced', as the beauty-loving
Italians call them still, — of the unsuccessful, the unhappy?   They were not pointed to one whose visage was so
marred more than any man;   *that* earth was an earth for the
beautiful and the beloved, but not for others, and there
was no different heaven for them to raise their eyes to.
He says that 'the mystical art of the Christian middle
age is always struggling to express thoughts beyond itself';   and in this respect compares Fra Angelico's *Coro-
nation of the Virgin* with 'the many-headed gods of the
East, the orientalized Ephesian Diana with its numerous
breasts ... overcharged symbols, a means of hinting at an
idea which art cannot adequately express, which still remains in the world of shadows'.   So the best that mediaeval
genius and piety have produced is to be likened to the
monstrous idols of barbarous nations!   'Such forms of art
are inadequate to the matter they clothe;   they remain
ever below its level.'   Ay, but how they lift the soul and
intellect to regions which cannot be expressed?   *there* is
the key to the language which cannot be translated into
common speech;   *there* dwell the truths which can only be
shown in types, — but the language is not a whisper, those
truths not shadows.

[Quotes passages from Winckelmann: 'The broad characteristic of all religions' to 'is confined to a few'.]

Could this assertion be proclaimed to the world in intelligent terms, hundreds of thousands of fervent voices would
deny it from the profoundest recesses of their soul.   It
is not the prescience of homesickness for this groaning
earth, this travailing creation, which makes life sombre
and sad;   it is the sense of exile, the intimations of a
former and a future state to which we truly belong;   the
dim consciousness of a task to be done, a race to be run,
a fight to be fought, a term to be fulfilled, a probation
to be endured, which is at once the bane and the balm of
mortal existence.   It is towards this better country that
all Christendom is yearning, is tending;   it is the voice
of this yearning which finds utterance in such hymns as,
'Jerusalem the golden', and 'I would not live alway', for
multitudes who cannot clothe their aspirations in words of
their own.   And all this is so old, — so old, — that it
seems strange there should be need to say it again;   but

old as it is, it is not worn out, for it is true. Mr
Pater goes on elaborating rather than expanding his idea,
talking about the 'pagan sentiment', and the 'pagan sadness', and the forms they have taken in various European
countries, ignoring the trite fact that just where religion
has retained most of the old heathen element in creed and
ceremonial, is where the material, the finite prevails, and
where men are most gay and child-like; while it is where
the level of religious life *has* been changed and raised,
that the seriousness, the sadness, if he will, is to be
found, because the sense of banishment, the longing for the
real home is deeper; but there, too, is the serener and
the loftier cheer. When he styles the Roman Catholic ritual a 'sad mechanic exercise', one is almost irritated by
his perversity and love of paradox. Yet, notwithstanding
the evident contradiction, he will have it that whatever
of calm or joyousness was left in the religious life of
Christendom was a remnant of paganism or a revival of art.
'Even in the worship of sorrow the native blitheness of
art asserted itself' (p. 199). Why not acknowledge that,
to the exalted religious perception, the eternal sun becomes visible behind the clouds, that the clear shining of
perfect day transfuses the mists of earth? He insists on
the '*grayness* of the ideal or spiritual world', as compared
with the rich colors of the sensuous; he has never lifted
his eyes to the sun-illumined blue of the purest ideal, the
highest spiritual life, nor beheld the snowy ranges of
sublimest abstract thought and principle flushed with the
warm feelings of humanity and benevolence, fiery with
patriotism, with the martyr-spirit, with all intense enthusiasms; he has not rejoiced in the rainbow tints of
hope, the glow of faith, the deep-hued ardor of adoration.
Once more let him speak for himself (p. 210):

[Quotes the Conclusion: 'The service of philosophy' to
'simply for those moments' sake'.]

So ends the book. The last two chapters have little in
common with the rest, beyond that of being within the same
covers. The preceding essays form a separate part, of
which the result is inconclusive and insubstantial; the
theories of art are Winckelman's, the theories of life are
Goethe's; but Mr Pater has passed them through his own peculiar medium, and we are left with only the fine-spun
sieve and a residuum of filmy impressions. Compared with
the latter portion of the book, Mr Ruskin's most incoherent
utterances are worthy of respect, for he at least is always in earnest, and never talks of art with its high aspirations and profound convictions as a pastime, or of life

with its solemn issues, its rapture and its anguish, as a
play or a picture-gallery where the wise man lounges in
cold-blooded dilettanteism, reckoning his emotions by
clock and thermometer. These concluding chapters have at
least this merit; they are definite and tangible as to
what they attempt to express; it is for the reader to
judge whether that be true, wholesome, even sensible, or
false, foolish, and pernicious....

Notes

1 Ruskin frequently attacked the Renaissance as a worldly,
   pagan epoch. He argued in the third volume (1856) of
   'Modern Painters' that in the Gothic period art was employed for the display of religious facts, while in the
   Renaissance religious facts were employed for the display
   of art.
2 Unknown painter.
3 I.e. 'The Early Italian Poets' (1861), re-titled 'Dante
   and his Circle' (1874).
4 Claude Fauriel (1772–1844), French historian and critic,
   published the 'History of Provençal Poetry' (Paris,
   1846), one of the source-books for Aesthetic Poetry
   (1868).
5 See p. 54n.
6 See Luke i, 38.
7 In 'Les Misérables' (1862).
8 Charles Augustin Sainte-Beuve (1804–69), French critic,
   poet, and novelist, became famous for his Monday critical articles, some of which were published in thirteen
   volumes as 'Nouveaux Lundis' (1863–70).

15. UNSIGNED NOTICE, 'ART-JOURNAL'

1877, xvi, 288

We are not surprised to see a new edition of Mr Walter
Pater's book on the Art and Poetry of the Renaissance issue
from the press, for it is pleasant and instructive reading,
yet one withal to be appreciated only by those who will
take the trouble to think, and that studiously, while they
read. This is called a 'revised' edition, but we find
little difference, and none of importance, between it and

its predecessor, except that the concluding chapter — a
few pages of general reflections — is now omitted, for
what reason is not explained. Its absence in no degree
lessens the value of the work, yet it might well have
been retained. We can but repeat what we said of the book
when reviewing it four years ago,(1) that this 'small but
most interesting volume leaves on the mind a striking impression of the mental impulses that worked out through
various channels the great movement of the Renaissance'.

Note

1 'Art-Journal' (1873), xii, 160.

16. HAVELOCK ELLIS ON CRITICISM

1885

Extract from a signed article entitled The Present Position
of English Criticism, in 'Time' (December 1885), xiii, 669-
78. See Introduction, pp. 3-4.

   Henry Havelock Ellis (1859-1939), social critic, essayist, editor and pioneer in the study of sex. He saw the
search for scientific truth as a source of artistic satisfaction and chose the study of sex as his life work. He
began the Mermaid series of dramatists contemporary with
Shakespeare and edited the Contemporary Science series
(1889-1915). His publications include 'Studies in the
Psychology of Sex' (1897-1928) and 'The Dance of Life'
(1923). Symonds collaborated with him in the writing of
'Sexual Inversion', the first volume of the 'Psychology of
Sex'.

   Ellis surveys the critical works by F.W.H. Myers, Theodore Watts, A.C. Swinburne, William Sharp, Walter Pater
and J.A. Symonds. He observes that Matthew Arnold exercised a bad influence on English criticism;   in defining
criticism as 'a disinterested endeavour to learn and pro-
pagate the best that is known and thought in the world',
Arnold made it catholic and sympathetic, 'but a little too
literary and too artificial'. Rather than grasping what
is 'really essential and significant in the artistic product before him', he moralised and invented catchwords,
which he repeated in varying tones of voice in an attempt

to give them new meanings. Though not a critic of the first order, Pater is to be applauded for extracting the 'quintessence' of his subject.

In 'My Life' (1940) Ellis noted that he had underestimated Pater as a critic in this article.

... Narrowness of range marks some of our best critics. Mr Pater, if he has nothing else in common with Burroughs, (1) is a true critic within an almost equally narrow range, and with a similar synthetic method. Mr Burroughs' range is that of large, virile, Catholic, sweet-blooded things; he is half on the side of Emerson, but altogether on the side of Rabelais, of Shakspere, of Whitman. Mr Pater is not, indeed, on the side of 'Zoroaster and the saints'; but there is no room in his heart for the things that Mr Burroughs loves. For him there is nothing so good in the world as the soft, spiritual aroma — telling, as nothing else tells, of the very quintessence of the Renaissance itself — that exhales from Della Robbia ware, or the long-lost impossible Platonism of Mirandola, or certain subtle and evanescent aspects of Botticelli's art. To find how the flavour of these things may be most exquisitely tasted, there is nothing so well worth seeking as that. Even in 'Marius' the 'new Cyrenaicism' in reality rules to the end. Joachim du Bellay is too fragile to bear the touch of analytic criticism, but certainly it would be impossible to do more for him than Mr Pater has done by his synthetic method. For Mr Pater the objects with which aesthetic criticism deals are 'the receptacles of so many powers or forces' which he wishes to seize in the most complete manner; they are, as it were, plants from each of which he wishes to extract its own peculiar alkaloid or volatile oil. For him 'the picture, the landscape, the engaging personality in life or in a book, "La Gioconda", the hills of Carrara, Pico of Mirandola, are valuable for their virtues, as we say in speaking of a herb, a wine, a gem; for the property each has of affecting one with a special impression of pleasure'. This was an ingenious and almost scientific theory of criticism, and had not Mr Pater seemed to swoon by the way over the subtle perfumes he had evoked, he might, one thinks, have gone far.

If, however, the area which Mr Pater occupies with his herbs, and gems, and wines is small, however choice, that is but saying that he is not a critic of the first order, and that critics of the first order are rare. With so definite, and apparently fruitful a method, one might have

thought that all things were possible for Mr Pater. But
a fairly catholic critic like Sainte-Beuve(2) — for with
all his cynical caution Sainte-Beuve was catholic —
rarely has a definite method, a method to which he adheres.
However it may be in the future, the critic, in his largest
development, hitherto has been a highly-evolved and complex
personality, whose judgments have proceeded from the almost
spontaneous reaction of his own nature with the things with
which he has come in contact; and so long as that is the
case, the main point is to ascertain the exact weight and
quality of the factor which the critic himself brings. In
that way, while we shall still be nothing less than infinitely removed from the realisation of so primitive a conception of the critic's function as Matthew Arnold's, —
'to see the thing as in itself it really is', — can we
only at present truly attain a sound criticism. Mr J.A.
Symonds, among English critics, possesses, I think unquestionably, the most marked catholicity. He has not, like
Mr Pater, the advantage or disadvantage of a definite
method. He lives and moves in 'the free atmosphere of art,
which is nature permeated by emotion'. This allows him
at once a large scope, both for analytic criticism and for
mere description....

Notes

1 John Burroughs (1837-1921), the American naturalist,
  honoured his friend with the publication of 'Notes on
  Walt Whitman: Poet and Person' (1867).
2 See p. 108n.

17. UNSIGNED REVIEW, 'OXFORD MAGAZINE'

16 October 1889, viii, 13

Significant for the claim that Pater had already secured a
permanent place in English letters — as a stylist.

If we have been somewhat tardy in acknowledging the third
edition of Mr Pater's 'Renaissance', it is certainly not
for any lack of appreciation. Mr Pater is by this time

independent of reviewers, and if at the first onset he did
not find his public, he may now at any rate claim to have
made it. The new edition of the 'Renaissance' differs from
its predecessor in two points. In the first place, it contains an essay on the School of Giorgione, the opening
paragraphs of which embody in a very beautiful and perfect
form Mr Pater's philosophy of art. In the second place, it
contains the conclusion, discredited for its avowal of
Cyrenaicism in the first edition, discarded in the second,
and now reinstated and remodelled in the third. If in the
School of Giorgione Mr Pater has given us his philosophy
of art, in the conclusion he has given us his philosophy
of life. Let the concluding sentence be its epitome:

[Quotes from the Conclusion: 'Of this wisdom' to 'simply
for those moments' sake'.]

How far such a philosophy will satisfy human needs is a
question which need not here be raised. Although we respect an art critic for giving us his scheme of life, we
read him for his art, and not for his scheme. We turn to
the 'Renaissance' that we may share in the deep and loving
insight of a subtle critic, that we may learn something of
beauty's secret from a man who has spent his years in
acquiring it.

'Marius the Epicurean'
March 1885

18. WILLIAM SHARP, UNSIGNED REVIEW, 'ATHENAEUM'

28 February 1885, 271-3

Reprinted in 'Papers Critical and Reminiscent' (1912),
229-40. See No. 40 and Introduction, pp. 10 and 25.

William Sharp (1855-1905), Scottish poet, critic, editor
and anthologist, wrote the lives of D.G. Rossetti (1882),
Shelley (1887), Heine (1888) and Browning (1890); a number
of volumes of poetry and romances; and (from 1893) 'mystical' prose and verse under the pseudonym 'Fiona Macleod'.
He became the art critic for the 'Glasgow Herald' in 1884.

Sharp met Pater at a dinner party given by the Robinsons
(see Introduction, p. 2) early in 1882. He got to know
Pater extremely well and sensed the anxiety fantasies that
troubled him. After 1885 Sharp spent considerable time
abroad and saw less of Pater.

Sharp printed two premature reviews of 'Marius': this
and the piece in 'Time' (March 1885), n.s. i, 341-54. It
is probable that Pater solicited both. On 1 March 1885 he
wrote to Sharp:

> I have read your article in The Athenaeum with very
> real pleasure; feeling criticism, at once so indepen-
> dent and so sympathetic, to be a reward for all the
> long labours the book has cost me. You seem to me to
> have struck a note of criticism not merely pleasant but
> judicious; and there are one or two important points —
> literary ones — on which you have said precisely what
> I should have wished, and thought it important for me,
> to have said....

As regards the ethical drift of Marius, I should like
to talk to you, if you were here. I *did* mean it to be
more anti-Epicurean than it has struck you as being. In
one way however I am glad that you have mistaken me a
little on this point, as I had some fears that I might
seem to be pleading for a formal thesis, or 'parti pris'.
Be assured how cheering your praise — praise from so
genuine and accomplished a fellow-workman — has been to
me. Such recognition is especially a help to one whose
work is so exclusively personal and solitary as the kind
of literary work, which I feel I can do best, must be.
(LWP, 58-9)

... In our own day the chief English exponent of the central doctrine of Epicurus is Mr Walter Pater, and though
his new 'Cyrenaicism' is manifest throughout the well-
known 'Studies of the Renaissance', and especially in the
famous epilogue, it is to be discerned more distinctively
and in more strictly philosophic garb in one or two of
those uncollected essays of his which have attracted only
less attention than those in his volume — especially in
his acute and sympathetic dissertation upon Wordsworth.
Now, however, Mr Pater publishes the fruit of his long
contemplatious on the problem of how to make the most of
life for the benefit of all who care to feast on it, to
become wiser or to turn away dissatisfied from that 'To-
day' 'which has outlasted so many tomorrows', as the translator of the 'Rubáiyát' says.
In these two volumes Mr Pater writes an imaginary biography of a young man, brought up in the pagan religion
and in strictly Roman grooves of thought, who in the reign
of the last of the Antonines passes through a variety of
mental and spiritual experiences, comes into contact with
Marcus Aurelius himself, and finally makes acquaintance
with the new religion which had been brought out of the
mysterious East by one Paul, who on his westward way had
astonished even the Athenian sceptics by his dissertation
On the Unknown God. It is but a brief acquaintance, however, for by a strange irony he, the accomplished Epicurean, dies an obscure death among ignorant peasant adher-
ents of the new faith, and thus attains to honours of martyrdom, the significance of which he would not have understood even if he had foreknown all that was to happen after
the last breath had passed away from his lips.

[Detailed summary of plot omitted.]

It is open to doubt if it has been Pater's intention to offer an apology for the higher Epicureanism: possibly he has merely endeavoured to trace the development of a cultured mind in a period that bears no slight resemblance to our own — development from belief in a venerable inherited creed to the adoption of a strictly worldly philosophy, a philosophy of how to make the most of life, the latter yielding in turn to spiritual weariness and even hopelessness; relieved, perchance, not by vision of any ultimate individual good, but by a somewhat broader view of the future of humanity than had formerly been entertained. On the other hand, there are, at any rate, some pages here and there in these two volumes which unmistakably express the personal opinions of the author, and these, conjointly with portions of Mr Pater's other published writings, constitute sufficient basis for the assumption that he does, indeed, recognize the teaching of Epicurus as — in its quintessential doctrine — not unworthy, even in these days of manifold *isms*, of serious consideration as a practical philosophy of life. Of course, no one can be better aware that this teaching in its entirety is antagonistic to the attainment of wide culture; but as this antagonism is more the result of the ancient philosopher's own idiosyncrasy than the logical outcome of his philosophy of sensation as the means of knowledge and of self-satisfaction as the end of life, Mr Pater may well be willing to join hands with him so far.

If, however, it has been his intention to demonstrate the futility of either Epicurean or Stoic philosophy, and to show that Christianity is alone in any sense really responsive to man's deepest aspirations, then he has been only very partially successful. Indubitably he has in 'Marius' skilfully, and without precipitation, disclosed the lees that abide in the bottom of the cup that contains the mellow wine of the wisdom of Epicurus; but at most he only vaguely suggests that in its place, if we care to partake thereof, there is a draught of more vivifying essence, of more estimable flavour — yet of the permanency of whose subtle regenerative quality he can say, as he knows, nothing.

In a word, the mental history of Marius the Epicurean will hardly help any one in the same plight as was Marius himself after all his years of careful introspection, anxious thought, and vague expectancy. There is no real transition, on the part of the latter, from refined and in some points greatly modified Epicureanism to Christianity; nor, even if he had not, with strange irony of circumstance, perished so untimely, is it in the least degree likely that he would ever have become an actual convert to the new

faith. He would have found it impossible to reconcile two
teachings so really antagonistic — or, rather, so really
distinct — as that of the pagan philosopher and that of
the new God. His first conversion took place when, still
a youth undisturbed in his reverence for and belief in the
ancient religion of Rome, he hearkened with keenly receptive ears to the lessons of the young priest of the Temple
of Æsculapius; as for a second conversion, does it ever
really take place, or even seem as if it might have taken
place if death had not intervened?

In impassioned contemplation, Mr Pater says in that
essay on Wordsworth already referred to, lies the true
moral significance of art and poetry. But the passion
must arise out of intensity of insight and be no mere mystical emotion; with this writer, as with the Marius of
whom he tells, there is a keen appreciation 'of the poetic
beauty of mere clearness of mind — the actually aesthetic
charm of a cold austerity of thought; as if the kinship of
that to the clearness of physical light were something more
than a figure of speech'.

There is no living writer who excels Mr Pater in grace
of style. He does not indulge in passages of sustained
eloquence, but every word he writes is calculated to be
the best word in that place, to have its full signification brought out. Here and there, of course, there are
passages of exceptional beauty; but fine as these are,
Mr Pater's special faculty for verbal expression is more
noticeable in his occasional use of certain words which in
his mouth, so to speak, act like a charm. While he is the
most rhythmical of English prose-writers, his is the music
of the viola rather than of the violin.

It is no joyous evangel that Mr Pater proclaims in these
two volumes, albeit it clearly infers the possibility of
many joyous experiences. Everything that is is evanescent. The darkness beyond is still darkness for us; hence
it is that these joys, these exhilarating flashes of insight and moments of vivid pleasurable emotion, are enhanced, 'like the glow of summer itself', by the thought
of their brevity. Consciously or unconsciously, there is
in all that he has written a strain of that partly sad,
partly genuinely contentful resignation of the great Aurelius which found fullest expression in these words:

Sayest thou, 'I have not played five acts'. True!
but in human life three acts only make sometimes a
complete play. That is the composer's business, not
thine. Retire with a good will; for that too hath,
perchance, a good will which dismisseth thee from thy
part.(1)

Note

1 'Meditations of Marcus Aurelius', xii, 36.

19.   UNSIGNED REVIEW, 'PALL MALL GAZETTE'

18 March 1885, 4-5

A book which is entirely unlike other books has in that
fact a certain claim to respect, independent of any other
merits which it may possess; for the faults of other
books (that is to say, of books in general) are numerous
and common, and by its mere unlikeness a book which is
unlike them escapes these faults. Mr Pater's new book,
published twelve years after his first, and after a silence
rarely broken of late even by essays in periodicals, is as
unlike its companions on the shelves as may well be.   In
the first place it defies classification. There is a
thread of narrative running through it, and certain proper
names recur. Yet it has nothing in common with the usual
dreary 'classical story', and indeed can hardly be called
a story at all. Marius, a long descended and fairly
wealthy Roman of the time of the later Antonines, is
brought up as a fatherless boy in Northern Etruria, at a
country villa, where the strict old Roman life is observed;
goes to school in the neighbouring town, and falls under
the influence of a brilliant freedman's son, named Flavian; loses his mother, and sets out for Rome, making on
the way the acquaintance of a youthful knight, Cornelius;
is presented to the Emperor Marcus Aurelius, and serves
him in some literary capacity and otherwise; meets Apuleius and Lucian; adopts for a time the philosophy of
Cyrene, with its *monochronos hedone*,(1) its theory of the
indifference of things, and the wisdom of experiencing and
enjoying them with a mixture of self-indulgence and self-
restraint; falls in with the Christian worship, and without being exactly converted is strongly impressed by its
dignity, repose, and soothing influence on the mind and
feelings; is arrested as a Christian in the recrudescence
of persecution towards the end of the reign of Aurelius;
sacrifices himself for his friend Cornelius; and dies of
the plague, not unhouseled or unaneled. This is a précis
of almost all the main action in the volumes, though there
are some episodes — a visit to the hill temple of

AEsculapius, an interview with Faustina, a dinner at
Tusculum, a scene in the Amphitheatre.   It is so far from
being an ill service to Mr Pater to give it in this fashion
that the book would perhaps be improved by an 'argument' of
a somewhat similar and slightly more extended kind.

Its five hundred pages, however (there are scarcely so
many in the two volumes, for the paper is of the finest and
stoutest), are far, very far, from being ill filled, despite the lack of story for those who read for the story. In
some of Mr Pater's essays, printed after the appearance of
his first volume, timid people thought they discerned an
undue elaboration (in the direction of ornament and preciousness) of the singularly beautiful style which the
author had attained in the 'Studies of the Renaissance'.
These persons ought to be reassured by the style of 'Marius
the Epicurean', just as others who were alarmed by Mr
Pater's apolausticism (to use university slang) will be reassured also.   With a beauty of phrase hardly inferior, if
inferior at all, to that of the famous, or should be famous, passage on Monna Lisa which has been for a dozen
years the delight of all who care for English style, there
is in 'Marius the Epicurean' a gravity of thought and tone
which almost amounts to severity.   The extraordinary quietness of which Mr Pater has the secret also reappears here
to the full;   the fulness of colour which is somehow never
staring, the brilliancy which never dazzles.   Whether the
matter, whose form receives and deserves such high praise,
will attract much attention from many readers, is another
question, and one which cannot be so confidently discussed.
It has been said that Mr Pater's themes are mostly grave,
and even the frequent and exquisite descriptive passages
which are scattered about the book may not fully sweeten to
a generation avid of personality and movement the constant
discussion of rather abstruse problems of life, the reasonings on fragmentary and half-understood Greek philosophies,
the careful descriptions of ceremonial observances, the
disquisitions on the moods of men in that twilight of the
Old World which has been so often compared to our own
times.   Some people will say that Mr Pater preaches, and
though his preaching ought to be wholly inoffensive to any
reasonable person, it does not follow that it will be so.
One point deserving especial notice and commendation — a
point in which the writer's careful and long-matured scholarship on the one hand and his mastery of English style
on the other come very happily together — is the use he
has made of the literature of his period.   He has drawn,
of course, on Marcus himself, but that excellent Emperor
has been much written about of late, and is comparatively
hackneyed.   Far more interesting are his dealings with

three writers, little read (at least in the original) by
any but scholars nowadays, though the works of all three
are among the most peculiar and precious legacies of
ancient letters. The notion of ascribing the exquisite
'Pervigilium Veneris',(2) the crown and flower of all anonymous poetry, to the boy-poet Flavian on his deathbed is
ingenious in itself; and Mr Pater has worked it out with
all his power of description, and with a singularly pathetic effect. His remarks on the style of Apuleius (another
eccentric writer who has the faculty of turning almost all
his admirers into devotees) are remarkably happy as criticism, and the shortened paraphrase of the ever-welcome
Cupid and Psyche legend which he gives is a worthy exercise for his pen. Not less happy is the similar paraphrase or rather translation in part which he gives of the
Hermotimus of Lucian, a translation worked very neatly into harmony with the text. This is so good that we only
wish Mr Pater would follow it up with more versions of the
Samosatene. There are, indeed, few writers whose lovers
would less willingly lose the original language, for
Lucian's Greek is a thing apart, which whoso has once tasted is as a lotus-eater. But if any one can give something
of an equivalent charm in English (we do not say of the
same charm, for the ways of the men are different), it is
Mr Pater.

This review is desultory. It would not be fair to add
'but the book is much more desultory than the review', to
parody a writer whom Lucian naturally suggests. But the
fact is that 'Marius the Epicurean' is a book to read and
re-read, rather than to analyse or criticise, unless space
could be given for analysis and criticism at very great
length. It would be easy to write a theme on Cyrenaicism
or an essay on that side of Christianity which most attracted Marius, but our readers would not much thank us.
Enough has been said to show those who are likely to appreciate the book what unusual matter for appreciation
they have within reach.

Notes

1 Pleasure of the moment.
2 A Latin poem of ninety-three lines (in throchaic tetra-
   meters) of unknown authorship and date.

20.   J.M. GRAY, SIGNED REVIEW, 'ACADEMY'

21 March 1885, xxvii, 197-9

The first of two reviews. The second, in the Edinburgh
'Courant', 4 April 1885, 3, is reprinted in 'John Miller
Gray: Memoir and Remains' (1895), ed. J. Balfour Paul and
W.R. Macdonald, iii, 3-9. See Introduction, pp. 22, 23 and 25.
    John Miller Gray (1850-94), art critic and first curator
of the Scottish National Gallery, contributed regularly to
the 'Academy' and the Edinburgh 'Courant'. Through Frederick Wedmore (1844-1921), art critic and mutual friend,
Gray met Pater in Oxford about 1 June 1878 (LWP, 31n). The
two became close acquaintances and Gray sent Pater articles
for his opinion. Gray reviewed The Child in the House in
the 'Academy' (17 August 1878), xiv, 166.
    Pater probably solicited the review (see Introduction,
p. 11).   On 24 March 1885 Pater wrote:

It gives me extreme pleasure to know from your generous
article on it in the 'Academy' that my new book has not
disappointed you - one of the most valued of my readers.
Of three or four very friendly recognitions of my work,
yours is the most complete, and it is a great encouragement to me to receive a criticism so kindly in what is
itself so graceful a piece of writing.(LWP, 59)

One is strongly reminded in this book of Mr Pater's — the
most important and sustained work that he has yet offered
to the public — of an earlier fragment, of The Child in
the House, which he contributed some six years ago to 'Macmillan's Magazine', and which has not yet been republished.
In The Child in the House, in the young Florian Deleal, we
find the initial sketch — truly a 'finished' one — for
this portrait of 'Marius the Epicurean'. The sketch, as is
the way with artists, is altered, expanded, traced in fuller detail in the picture; yet, substantially, the personality portrayed is the same, though changed in aspect, by
this or that new disposition of light or shadow, by this or
the other new environment of time and circumstance, which,
in our 'each and all' of things, modifies and alters the
subject. Florian was an English child. The career of his
soul was followed no further than the period of early
youth. The things that moulded him were, of course, no
formal philosophies — nothing in the remotest degree doc-

trinal — but only the unconsciously received impressions
of external things, impinging, moment by moment, upon his
original and sensitive nature — these and the instruc-
tions of his elders, which also were received in a child-
like, and so unconscious, way. The career of Marius, on
the other hand, is detailed in fullest circumstance from
childhood to death in early manhood, and the record deals
not only with the influences received passively by the
open mind of childhood, and their effects, but also, with
the conscious acceptance and consequent operation of various systems of belief — of one and the other accepted
form of philosophy.

[Summary of plot omitted.]

With comparatively little action, with hardly any display
of the more ordinary human emotions — with, for instance,
scarcely a reference in it to sexual love, the book never
fails of interest. It is attractive through the author's
vivid sense of beauty, through his constant mode of throwing even the processes of thought into a concrete and pictured form. Its personalities seem not quite the historical Stoic Aurelius, hardly the possibly historical Epicurean Marius: they are raised a little, refined on a
little, set on a somewhat higher plane than that of mere
actuality. They come to us with a certain sense of
strangeness: homely touches, here or there, make us recognise their human nearness; yet their treatment is as far
removed as it could well be from the crude realism that is
so commonly substituted for delicate artistry, and the cry
for which is one of the most unreasoning of the cants of
our time.
   The exposition of Epicureanism which these 'sensations
and ideas' of Marius present is more complete than any the
author has hitherto given; fuller, also, of 'gentleness
and sweet reasonableness', more fairly perceptive of the
difficulties and weaknesses of a philosophy which mani-
festly is a scheme of things that possesses the strongest
personal attractions for the writer, and the most serious
claims, in his view, to be considered as a guide towards a
right practice of life. He admits that a career ordered
with the aim of making each moment rich, many-coloured,
and full of exquisite experiences, is open to the constant
dread, to the final certainty, that the last of all these
moments may come, must come; and surely it can be no perfect philosophy which leaves its followers liable to be
startled by each possible chance of every day, by every
falling stone that grazes their heel, and which permits
their whole life to be shadowed with the terror of its

certain end. We have no due prominence given to the fact
that this delicate Epicureanism is possible only to the
few, and that even they at any moment may be prevented by
disease or mischance from participation in it; nor does
the author lay sufficient stress upon the dangers that beset such a life: the temptation to seclude one's self in
some lovely 'palace of art', regardless of surrounding
misery — a danger from which Marius was saved mainly by
the exceptionally sweet admixture in him of the original
constituents of his nature. Again, the favourite doctrines
of the book — that the means, not the end, is the main
thing, that life should be a jealous calculation of loss
and gain, so that each moment may yield its utmost, its
most refined, product — do these not smite on the very
face the highest life of man? Can all this preoccupation
with self have any absorbing place in a right human life?
Is it not in quite another fashion that the chosen spirits
of the race have lived, with a fine unconsciousness which
hungered and thirsted after righteousness itself, and not
after any exquisite moments that righteousness might bring
either now or in the future? And surely an absorption in
some high and impersonal aim, the kindling of a man's
whole soul and effort towards it, delivers him, as nothing
else in the world can, from the fear of death, so that, as
Lord Bacon says, when his end comes, he is like one smitten
down 'in hot blood', in the fervour of battle; he falls,
yet feels no wound.

No, the Epicureanism which finds such calm and delicate
exposition in the book can be no permanent dwelling-place
of the human spirit. It may, indeed, afford a healthful
corrective to many crude and unlovely tendencies of modern
thought. In a mood of wise eclecticism we may receive much
from it, may linger for a while in its charmed and golden,
though enervating air; but if we would preserve our spiritual health we must press onwards, and breathe the more bracing atmosphere of sterner upland places.

As we should expect from the philosophy of the book,
which is so constantly occupied with the concrete, the
visible, the tangible, its descriptions of men, of landscape, are especially varied and beautiful. For instance
of this we may turn to the chapter which describes the
feast given in honour of Apuleius: a very Tadema(1) in its
perfection of finish, in its legitimate and artist-like use
of archaeological knowledge for the purposes of mere present beauty; a Tadema, too, in its delighted preoccupation
with the lovely details of precious objects of still-life,
with the 'togas of altogether lost hue and texture', the
'crystal cups darkened with old wine', and the 'dusky fires
of the rare twelve-petalled roses'.

As an example of the pregnant brevity with which Mr
Pater can reproduce a landscape, we may take the following — a view from the house of Cecilia, the Christian
widow of Rome:

> The orchard or meadow through which their path lay, was
> already grey in the dewy twilight, though the western
> sky, in which the greater stars were visible, was still
> afloat with ruddy splendour, *seeming to repress by con-
> trast the colouring of all earthly things, yet with the
> sense of a great richness lingering in their shadows.*

And the landscape is always linked — as nature, to be
intimate and touching, must ever be — with humanity. The
passage continues:

> Just then the voices of the singers, a 'voice of joy
> and health', concentrated themselves, with a solemn anti-
> strophic movement, into an evening, or 'candle' hymn —
> *the hymn of the kindling of the lamp.* It was like the
> evening itself, its hopes and fears, and the stars shin-
> ing in the midst of it, made audible.

Before closing, a word should be said as to the style of
the book — a style of perfectly finished beauty, full of
an exquisite restraint, and, after all, the only fitting
and adequate expression of the exactest thinking. The
author's style is like that of his own Fronto, in whose lectures, he says, 'subtle unexpected meanings were brought out
by familiar words'. It is so easy and apparently unlaboured
in its flow that it seems like mere spontaneous talk — only
become strangely select, as though ordered, by some happy
chance, with uncommon sweetness. The wise labour that has
been spent upon the book has effaced all marks of labour;
but, undoubtedly, each sentence has been often touched by
the file which, to use an expression that the author is
fond of repeating, adds more than value for each particle
of gold which it removes. As we read the pages characterised by such unfailing fitness of phrase, finished from
their first to their final line with a flawless perfection
which one demands in the brief lyric of a master, but
hardly looks for in a prose work of extended length, we
find far more than the justification of the author's long
cessation from slighter literary efforts — a continued
silence which has been felt, at least by some lovers of
sweet and sifted English, as nothing less than a real personal loss.

Note

1 Sir Lawrence Alma-Tadema (1836-1912), a Dutch painter,
  settled in London in 1873. He became a remarkable social
  and financial success.

21. J.A. SYMONDS ON PATER

1885

Extracts from 'The Letters of John Addington Symonds'
(1967-9), ed. Herbert M. Schueller and Robert L. Peters.
See Nos 2, 3 and 48.

(a) From a letter dated 30 March 1885 to Mary Robinson

Mr Pater's 'Marius' will of course be read by me — I hope
in a gondola. My brain is so badly made that I cannot
easily bear the sustained monotonous refinement in his
style. To that exquisite instrument of expression I daresay that I shall do justice in the languor & the largeness
of the lagoons — better than I can in this eager air of
mountains, where everything is jagged & up & down & horr-
ibly *natural*.
    I cannot sympathize with Pater's theory of life; & as
this book seems to give it elaborate utterance, I do not
want to study it in discordant circumstances: — for I
want at least to respect it. But I have always thought it
the theory of one who has not lived & loved — of a Pagan,
not a Papal soprano [castrato]. (iii, 41-2)

(b) From a letter dated 5 April 1885 to Henry Sidgwick

'Marius' I have not read. I suppose I must. But I shrink
from approaching Pater's style, which has a peculiarly dis-
agreeable effect upon my nerves — like the presence of a
civet cat. Still, I believe I must read it. (iii, 43)

(c) From a letter dated 20 May 1885 to Mrs R.L. Stevenson

What do you think of 'Marius the Epicurean'? I wish I could
talk to both of you about that book & some others. (iii, 48)

22.   UNSIGNED NOTICE, 'THE TIMES'

9 April 1885, 3

See Introduction, pp. 3 and 23.

'Marius the Epicurean' may be briefly defined as fine writing and hard reading. Loving and careful labour has been
clearly bestowed upon it; the file has been freely used,
and this philosophical and historical novel of the later
Empire is the fruit of wide reading and deep research. We
should be unjust and ungrateful to Mr Pater if we did not
say that there is much in 'Marius' which is admirable and
enjoyable. We are carried along in spite of ourselves by
vivid and enchanting descriptions of old Roman life and
manners and scenery. A delicate and poetical fancy revives
the pictures of the past, and the men of the age, who were
to leave their mark on their times, are reproduced with
subtle touches and a satisfactory semblance of vitality.
The conflicting systems of philosophy are brilliantly analyzed by a sympathetic and intelligent student; the beauties, the deformities, and the degradations of the old
pagan religion are indicated with truth as well as with
poetry; as they are happily contrasted with the regenerat-
ing influences of the new Christian faith of charity and
self-sacrifice. Yet, with its undeniable beauties and
merits, the book is aesthetic rather than artistic. Everything, from the speculations of the philosophers to the
lights on the landscapes and the mountain cities, is regarded and treated from the aesthetical point of view. If
we dared to apply the principles of commonplace criticism
to any piece of workmanship so refined and transcendental,
we should say that Mr Pater has missed brilliant opportunities, if he has not, indeed, deliberately thrown them
away. Had he condescended to the concrete or the dramatic
he must often have impressed us most forcibly. We may take
as an example of what we mean the presentation of his philosophical hero to Marcus Aurelius. As it is, the scene is
a painful one, and we are made to feel something of the
majesty of the great Emperor and of the awe with which the
intellectual neophyte introduced himself to the godlike
presence. But in place of our attention being concentrated on the leading actors in the scene, it is almost per-
versely distracted and diverted. Mr Pater turns aside to
describe the rooms and their decorations, the Empress

Faustina, with the rumours circulated to her disadvantage,
the imperial children, and Fronto, their venerable tutor,
as to whom we are favoured with a biographical and literary sketch. Everything written as to all and each of
these is excellent, only we feel that it is sadly out of
place. So the whole of the story, if story it may be
called, is made up of a loose series of episodes and of
digressions more or less irrelevant, though we are bound to
say that in respect of many of these digressions the author
could hardly help himself when he had once selected his
subject. Guiding his readers in their ignorance over unfamiliar ground, he was compelled to inform and educate
them as he led them along. Nineteen out of twenty know
little of the old pagan philosophy, while the twentieth,
who might possibly be a philosophical student, had never
pictured to himself the Italy of Marcus Aurelius, so that
the story with its explanation, the incidents with their
illustrations, the musings and their commentaries, are
continually running on parallel lines.

To the great majority of readers the charm of the book
will be in those pictures of life and scenery to which we
have alluded. Mr Pater's cultivated fancy has reconstruc-
ted old buildings, from the dilapidated country house of
the impoverished country gentleman to the temples of Imperial Rome, and the palace of the Caesars on the Pala-
tine. He seizes admiringly on the decay of the Roman
power to paint the sad beauties of desolation encroaching
on the cultivated fields, and already casting its shadows
over the Maremma and the Roman Campagna. He revels in the
weeds among the *tesserae*(1) of the pavements, in the mosses
creeping over the rifts in the ruined walls, as in the
crumbling convictions of the ancient faith, and the indolence that was demoralising the once sturdy labourers.
That faith, though it was yielding to scepticism in the
towns, still flourished in remote country districts with
something of its earlier vitality.

[Summary of plot omitted.]

We have objected to the irrelevancies in which Mr Pater
indulges; yet some of these in themselves are the most
charming passages in the volumes. Nothing, for example,
can be more graceful than the romantic version of the loves
of Psyche and Cupid, freely translated from Apuleius. Nothing can be more admirable as an eloquent illustration of
character, as a presentment of the higher intellectual
thought of the time, than the discourses of the Emperor
Marcus Aurelius. But what please us the most, after all,
are some of those graceful and graphic descriptions of

scenery we have praised already, and we can hardly give a
better idea of the book than by concluding our notice with
one or two of these taken at random. For their sparkle is
cast broadcast over the pages, and all are gems in their
way. This is the sketch of 'White Nights', the farmhouse
which Marius had inherited from his father:

[Quotes ch. i: 'The traveller descending from the slopes
of Luna' to 'the scent of the new-mown hay along all the
passages of the house'.]

Here is the Rome of the dying paganism and decaying Empire,
as the young Epicurean saw it for the first time:

[Quotes ch. xi: 'And at no period of its history' to
'though the bird had built freely among them'.]

Note

1 Square paving stones.

23. MRS HUMPHRY WARD, SIGNED REVIEW, 'MACMILLAN'S
MAGAZINE'

May 1885, lii, 132-9

See Introduction, pp. 23-5.
   Mary Augusta Ward (1851-1920), eminent novelist and hu-
manitarian, was the granddaughter of Thomas Arnold of Rugby,
niece of Matthew Arnold, aunt of the Huxleys and grandmother of the Trevelyans. She was born in Tasmania and
settled with her family in Oxford (1865), where she met
Benjamin Jowett, and Pater and his sisters. In 1872 she
married T. Humphry Ward (1845-1926), one of Pater's first
pupils and later Fellow and Tutor (1869-81) of Brasenose
College. The Wards moved to London in 1881, where Humphry
joined the staff of 'The Times' (often writing art criticism). Mary wrote thirty books; the most famous was her
novel about the crisis of doubt, 'Robert Elsmere' (1888),
which Pater reviewed in the 'Guardian' (EG, 55-70). For
her reminiscences of the Paters, see her book, 'A Writer's
Recollections' (1918), 120-5.

Mrs Ward is quick to see that 'Marius' is not simply an imaginative re-creation of second-century Antonine Rome but a subtle investigation of the problem of doubt in Victorian England. On 2 June 1885 Pater wrote:

> I have read your paper on Marius in 'Macmillan', and cannot help sending a few lines to tell you how much it has pleased me. To be really understood by a critic at once so accomplished and so generous as yourself, is a real reward for all one's labours. When one has taken pains about a piece of work, it is certainly pleasant to have a criticism upon it which is itself so graceful and painstaking.
>   Coming from one who, like yourself, has really mastered those matters, the objects you have urged, are also full of import and interest to me. The chief of them, I feel I must try to deal with before very long. Meantime, my sincere thanks for all your care for my work: I can only hope it has not taken too much time from your own varied and admirable literary work.(LWP, 60-1)

In spite of the numerous revisions to the third edition (1892), Pater never adequately dealt with her objections (LWP, 61n). For evidence of their continuing differences of opinion on the problem of faith, see his review of 'Robert Elsmere'.

This is a book which has long been expected with interest by a certain circle of readers. The 'Studies in the History of the Renaissance', which Mr Pater published twelve years ago, made a distinct mark in modern literary history. They excited as much antipathy as admiration, perhaps; they were the object of many denunciations, and, like some heretical treatise of the second or third century, received definite episcopal reprimand;(1) but at the same time they rose well above the crowd of books, and produced the effect which rightly belongs to all the heartfelt individual utterance of literature. The utterance might be distasteful, but it represented an intellectual mood by no means within everybody's reach, a mood which was the result of high culture working on a sensitive and plastic nature, and of which the expression had the force as well as some of the narrowness of passion. The object of the book was to reproduce, as vividly as possible, certain 'special unique impressions of pleasure', made on an individual mind by various beautiful things in art and literature, to

'disengage the virtue of a picture, a landscape, a fair
personality in life or in a book', so as to pass on the
experience of the author to the reader intact, and as it
were still warm with feeling and emotion. Such was the
programme laid down in the preface to the 'Studies', while
at the close of the book its general principles found
still more bold and eloquent expression in sentences which
were much quoted, and scandalised many to whom the rest of
the book remained altogether unknown.

[Quotes from the Conclusion to 'The Renaissance': 'The
service of philosophy' to 'the given time'.]

Here was the characteristic note of the book. Mr Pater,
indeed, was careful to explain that among 'high passions'
he reckoned all the great motives, political, religious, or
scientific, of mankind, and that what he asked was simply
that life under whatever banner should be lived strenu-
ously and not listlessly, with ardour and not with apathy.
Still it was felt that the foundation of it all was in the
true sense epicurean. 'Do good and be good', he seemed to
say:

   learn and know, for one end only — the end of a rich
   experience. All other systems are delusive; this only
   justifies itself perpetually. Choose and refine your
   experience; cultivate and enlarge your receptive faculties, and make life yield you its best. There is no
   other system of living which at once commends itself to
   the reason and satisfies the feeling.

Since this remarkable exposition of what he himself in
his later book calls 'a new Cyrenaicism', Mr Pater has published a certain number of scattered essays, on Greek and
English subjects, of which the latter at least have showed
a steadily widening and developing power. The masterly
essay on Wordsworth, which appeared in the 'Fortnightly
Review', some years after the 'Studies', must have taken
some innocent Wordsworthians by surprise. The austere
and yet tender feeling of the whole, the suggestiveness
and pregnancy of treatment, the deep sympathy it showed
for the peasant life and the peasant sorrows, and a sort
of bracing mountain-breath in it, revealed new qualities
in the man whose name in certain quarters had become un-
reasonably synonymous with a mere effeminate philosophy of
pleasure. The two English studies which followed the
Wordsworth, one on 'Measure for Measure', the other on
Charles Lamb, though less intrinsically weighty, perhaps,
had even higher artistic merit, while in the articles on

the Demeter myth, Mr Pater employed extraordinary resources
of style with results which were not wholly adequate to the
delicate labour spent upon them. Then came an attempt in a
totally new direction — the curious story The Child in the
House, of which a fragment appeared in 'Macmillan' in the
course of 1879. The author never finished it; nor is the
fact to be seriously regretted. The disguise furnished by
the story for the autobiographical matter, of which it was
obviously composed, was not a particularly happy one; above
all, it was not disguise enough. Some form of presentation
more impersonal, more remote from actual life was needed,
before the writer's thought could allow itself fair play.
Such a form has now been found in the story of 'Marius the
Epicurean'.

[Summary of plot omitted.]

   Those who know Mr Pater's work will hardly need to be
told with what delicacy and beauty he has worked out the
theme of 'Marius'. The style has its drawbacks, but even
in those passages of it which suffer most from a certain
looseness and confusion of plan, elements of distinction
and musical refinement are never wanting, while at its best
the fascination of it is irresistible. There are some half-
dozen scenes, which in their own way are unrivalled, where
both thought and expression are elaborated with a sort of
loving, lingering care, while yet the general impression is
one of subdued and measured charm, of a fastidious self-
control in the writer, leading to a singular gentleness and
purity of presentation. Then to the beauty of style, which
springs from his own highly-trained faculty, Mr Pater has
added all that classical culture could supply in the way of
adorning and enrichment. The translations from the literature, both Greek and Latin, of the time, in which the book
abounds, are in themselves evidence of brilliant literary
capacity; the version of Cupid and Psyche especially is a
masterpiece. And there is also added to the charm of style,
and deftly handled learning, a tenderness of feeling, a
tone of reverence for human affections, and pity for the
tragedy of human weakness worthy of George Eliot; so that
the book is rich in attractiveness for those who are content to take it simply as it is offered them, and to lose
themselves in the feelings and speculations of the hero,
without a too curious inquiry into the general meaning of
it all, or into the relation of the motives and impressions
described to the motives and impressions of the nineteenth
century.
   Most of those, however, who have already fallen under Mr
Pater's spell will certainly approach the book differently.

They will see in it a wonderfully delicate and faithful
reflection of the workings of a real mind, and that a mind
of the nineteenth century, and not of the second. The indirect way in which the mental processes which are the
subject of the book are presented to us, is but one more
illustration of an English characteristic. As a nation we
are not fond of direct 'confessions'. All our autobiographical literature, compared to the French or German,
has a touch of dryness and reserve. It is in books like
'Sartor Resartus', or 'The Nemesis of Faith', 'Alton
Locke', or 'Marius', rather than in the avowed specimens
of self-revelation which the time has produced, that the
future student of the nineteenth century will have to look
for what is deepest, most intimate, and most real in its
personal experience. In the case of those natures whose
spiritual experience is richest and most original, there is
with us, coupled with the natural tendency to expression, a
natural tendency to disguise. We want to describe for
others the spiritual things which have delighted or admon-
ished ourselves, but we shrink from a too great realism of
method. English feeling, at its best and subtlest, has
almost always something elusive in it, something which re-
sents a spectator, and only moves at ease when it has succeeded in interposing some light screen or some obvious
mask between it and the public.

No one can fail to catch the autobiographical note of
'Marius' who will compare the present book with its predecessors. Marius, in fact, as a young man, starts in
life on the principles expressed in the concluding pages
of the 'Studies'. While still a student at Pisa, he reads
Heraclitus and Aristippus, and resigns himself to the
teaching of these old Greek masters. From Heraclitus, or
from his school, he learns the doctrine of the 'subjectivity of knowledge', according to which 'the momentary sensible apprehension of the individual is the only standard
of what is or is not'; while from Aristippus he learns
how to cultivate and refine sensation, and how to make the
philosophy of pleasure minister to the most delicate needs
of the spiritual and intellectual life.

[Quotes ch. viii: 'How reassuring' to 'as we stand so
briefly in its presence'.]

In this frame of mind Marius goes up to Rome, makes
acquaintance with Marcus Aurelius, and is brought across
the Stoical philosophy then engaged upon that great effort
for the conquest of the Roman world, which was to be apparently defeated by the success of Christianity, and to
find its ultimate fruition, as Renan(2) points out, in the

great system of Roman law, of which it influenced the
development, and through which it has taken a partial
possession of modern life.   The effect of this contact
with Stoicism on the flexible mind of Marius, is to lead
to a certain modification of his main point of view; and
in the remarkable chapter called Second Thoughts, Mr Pater
describes, in the person of Marius, what is evidently the
main development of the mind which produced the 'Studies
in the History of the Renaissance'.   In the first place
there is an apology for the 'philosophy of moments', an
explanation of its naturalness, its inevitableness, so to
speak, at the outset of certain intellectual careers.

> We may note [says Marius's biographer] as Marius could
> hardly have done, that that new Cyrenaicism of his is
> ever the characteristic philosophy of youth — one of
> those subjective and partial ideals, based on vivid,
> because limited, apprehension of the truth of one as-
> pect of experience — in this case of the beauty of
> the world and the brevity of man's life in it — of
> which it may be said that it is the special vocation
> of the young to express them.

Such a youthful fanaticism,

> just because it seems to call on one to make the sacri-
> fice, accompanied by a vivid sensation of power and
> will, of what others value — the sacrifice of some con-
> viction, or doctrine, or supposed first principle — for
> the sake of that clear-eyed intellectual integrity or
> consistency, which is like spotless bodily cleanliness
> and nicety, or scrupulous personal honour, — has for
> the mind of the youthful student, when he first comes
> to appreciate it, itself the fascination of an ideal.

> All sorts of incidents and influences tend in youth to
> develop the Cyrenaic theory.   The changes of the seasons,
> 'the new poem in every spring', 'life in modern London
> even, in the heavy glory of summer', 'the workshops of the
> artist' with all their suggestions of beauty and refine-
> ment — all these quicken the covetousness of the artistic
> temperament, its eagerness to seize 'the highly-coloured
> moments which are to pass away so quickly', and the satis-
> faction of a natural passion becomes for a time a reasoned
> principle of action.
> But after a while the glamour of youth dies away, and
> a man begins to see that a system which has only the wor-
> ship and pursuit of 'exquisite moments' to recommend as a
> rule of life, leaves three-fourths of life untouched.

Mankind has never been content to spend itself on a worship of 'moments', or in a pursuit of fugitive impressions
as such. Rather, with a tenacious and pathetic faith, it
has sought for continuity, for what lasts and binds, and
can be handed on from soul to soul. It has tried to fix
and distil the essence of innumerable impressions in one
great tradition — the ethical tradition — which is at
once the product and the condition of human life. To live
in the mere pursuit of sensations, however refined, is to
live outside this tradition, so far as is possible, and
therefore outside the broad main stream of human history.
And more than this. As the stream is strong and tyrannous
and fills a large bed, the wandering epicurean, bent on an
unfettered quest of sensations, may well find himself
brought into hostile and disastrous contact with it, and
may recognise, when too late, his own puniness, and the
strength and masterfulness of the great currents and tendencies of things. The individual bent on claiming 'an
entire personal liberty of heart and mind — liberty above
all from conventional answers to first questions', finds
all round him 'a venerable system of sentiment and ideas,
widely extended in time and place, actually in a kind of
impregnable possession of human life', and discovers that
by isolating himself from it, he is cutting himself off
from a great wealth of human experience, from a great possible increase of intellectual 'colour, variety, and relief', which might be gained by attaching himself to it.
  Mr Pater, it will be observed, still speaks of morals as
it were in terms of aesthetics. His hero advances, or partially advances, from the aesthetic to the ethical standpoint, not because of any 'conventional first principles'
on which morals may depend for their sanction, but because
of the enriched experience, the 'quickened sympathies'
which are to be gained from the advance. Practically,
the same motive power is at work in the second stage as
in the first. But as the sphere of its operation enlarges,
it tends to coalesce and join hands with other powers,
starting from very different bases. The worship of beauty,
carried far enough, tends to transform itself into a passion moral in essence and in aim.

  For the variety of men's possible reflections on their
  experience, as of that experience itself, is not really
  as great as it seems. All the highest spirits, from
  whatever contrasted points they may have started, will
  yet be found to entertain in their moral consciousness,
  as actually realised, much the same kind of company.

One feels as though one were reading another 'Palace of

Art' with a difference! Here, in Mr Pater's system, the
soul ceases to live solitary in the midst of a dainty
world of its own choice, not because it is overtaken by
any crushing conviction of sin and ruin in so doing, but
because it learns to recognise that such a worship of
beauty defeats its own ends, that by opening the windows
of its palace to the outside light and air, and placing the
life within under the common human law, it really increases
its own chances of beautiful impressions, of 'exquisite
moments'. To put it in the language of the present book,
'Marius saw that he would be but an inconsistent Cyrenaic —
mistaken in his estimate of values, of loss and gain, and
untrue to the well-considered economy of life which he had
brought to Rome with him — that some drops of the great
cup would fall to the ground' — if he did not make the
concession of a 'voluntary curtailment of liberty' to the
ancient and wonderful order actually in possession of the
world, if he did not purchase by a willing self-control,
participation in that rich store of crystallised feeling
represented by the world's moral beliefs.

Still, although the fundamental argument is really the
same as that on which Mr Pater based a general view of life
twelve years ago, the practical advance in position shown
by the present book is considerable. 'That theory, or
idea, or system', said the writer of the 'Studies', in
1873, 'which requires of us the sacrifice of any part of
experience in consideration of some interest into which we
cannot enter, or some abstract morality we have not identified with ourselves, or what is only conventional, has
no real claim upon us'. Now the legitimacy and necessity
of some such sacrifice is admitted; for evidently the one
mental process, in spite of the indirectness of its presentation, is but a continuation of the other. 'Marius'
carries on the train of reflection begun by the 'Studies',
and the upshot of the whole so far is a utilitarian or
Epicurean theory of morals. For, stripped of its poetical
dress, the ethical argument of 'Marius' is essentially
utilitarian. After protesting against the curtailment of
experience in favour of 'some abstract morality we have
not identified with ourselves', Mr Pater now presents
obedience to this same morality as desirable, not because
of any absolute virtue or authority inherent in it, but
because practically obedience is a source of pleasure and
quickened faculty to the individual.

There is nothing new, of course, in such an argument,
though Mr Pater's presentation of it is full of individuality and fresh suggestions. But what makes the great
psychological interest of the book, while it constitutes
what seems to us its principal intellectual weakness, is

the further application of this Epicurean principle of an
aesthetic loss and gain not only to morals, but to religion. We have described the way in which Mr Pater handles
the claim of the moral system of the civilised world upon
a mind in search of beauty. His treatment of the claim of
religion on a similar order of mind is precisely the same
in tone and general plan. Just as adhesion to the accepted
moral order enriches and beautifies the experience of the
individual, and so gives a greater savour and attractiveness to life, so acquiescence in the religious order, which
a man finds about him, opens for him opportunities of feeling and sensation which would otherwise be denied him, provides him with a fresh series of 'exquisite moments', and
brings him generally within the range of an influence
soothing and refining, by virtue partly of its venerable-
ness, its source in an immemorial past, partly of the wealth
of beautiful human experience which has gone, age after age,
to the strengthening of it. From the contention in the
chapter, Second Thoughts, that Cyrenaicism disobeyed its
own principles, and neglected means of spiritual and intellectual joy which it might have utilised, by its contempt
for all the established forms of ancient religion; — from
the expressions used in reference to Marius's first contact with Christianity, when the new faith appealed, 'according to the unchangeable law of his character, to the
eye, the visual faculty of mind — '; from the constant
dwelling on the blitheness, and brightness, and sweetness
of Christian feeling, on the poetry of Christian rites, and
on the way in which the pathos of the Christian story
seemed to make all this visible morality, death itself,
more beautiful than any fantastic dream of old mythology
had ever hoped to make it; — and lastly, from the persistent intellectual detachment of Marius, a detachment maintained apparently through a long subsequent experience of
Christianity, and which makes him realise when he is com-
promised with the government, that for him martyrdom — to
the Christian, 'the overpowering act of testimony that
Heaven had come down among men', — would be but a common
execution; from all these different indications, and from
the melancholy beauty of the death-scene, we gather a
theory of religious philosophy, which is much commoner
among us than most of us think, but which has never been
expressed so fully or so attractively as in the story of
'Marius'.

> Submit [it seems to say] to the religious order about
> you, accept the common beliefs, or at least behave as
> if you accepted them, and live habitually in the atmos-
> phere of feeling and sensation which they have engen-

dered and still engender; surrender your feeling,
while still maintaining the intellectual citadel intact; pray, weep, dream with the majority while you
think with the elect; only so will you obtain from
life all it has to give, its most delicate flavour,
its subtlest aroma.

Such an appeal has an extraordinary force with a certain
order of minds. Probably as time goes we shall see a larger and larger response to it on the part of modern society.
But with another order of minds in whom the religious need
is not less strong, it has not, and never will have, any
chance of success, for they regard it as involving the be-
trayal of a worship dearer to them than the worship of
beauty or consolation, and the surrender of something more
precious to them than any of those delicate emotional joys,
which feeling, divorced from truth, from the sense of reality, has to offer. All existing religions have issued from
the sense of reality, from a perception of some truth; certain facts or supposed facts of sense or spirit have lain
at the root of them. It is surely a degradation of all
religion to say to its advocates,

> Your facts are no facts; our sense of reality is op-
> posed to them; but for the sake of beauty, the charm,
> the consolation to be got out of the intricate system
> you have built upon this chimerical basis, we are ready
> to give up to you all we can — our sympathy, our si-
> lence, our ready co-operation in all your lovely and
> soothing rites and practices, hoping thereby to cheat
> life of some of its pains, and to brighten some of its
> darkness with dreams fairer even than those which
> Æsculapius inspired in his votaries.

It is useful and salutary to compare with such a temper
as this, a temper like Clough's — that mood of heroic
submission to the limitations of life and mind which inspired all his verse, that determination of his to seek no
personal ease or relief at the expense of truth, and to
put no fairy tales knowingly into the place which belongs
to realities. How full his work is of religious yearning
and religious passion, and yet how eloquent of a religious
fear lest the mind should hold its 'dread communion' with
the unseen 'source of all our light and life', 'in ways
unworthy Thee', — how instinct at times with an almost
superhuman repudiation of the mere personal need!

It fortifies my soul to know
That, though I perish, Truth is so;

That, howsoe'er I stray and range,
Whate'er I do, Thou dost not change.
I steadier step when I recall
That, if I slip, Thou dost not fall.(3)

Here is one 'counsel of perfection', and a nobler one,
as we hold it, than the 'counsel' which Mr Pater has embodied as a main drift or moral in the story of Marius.
But with this protest our fault-finding comes to an end.

There are many other minor points in the book which
would repay discussion. Has it done justice to the complexities either of the Roman world or of Christianity in
the second century? In fairness to Marcus Aurelius and
the pagan world, ought there not to have been some hint
of that aspect of the Christian question which leads Renan
to apply to the position of the Christian in a pagan city
the analogy of that of 'a Protestant missionary in a
Spanish town where Catholicism is very strong, preaching
against the saints, the Virgin, and processions?' Would
it not have been well, as an accompaniment to the exquisite picture of primitive Christian life, to have given us
some glimpse into the strange excitements and agitations
of Christian thought in the second century? As far as
Marius is concerned, the different currents of Christian
speculation at the time might hardly have existed. Then
again, is there not a little humour wanting, which, according to the facts, ought to have been there, in such a
description as that lovely one, of the temple and rites of
AEsculapius? But these questions we can only throw out
for the reader of 'Marius' to ponder if he will. However
they may be answered, the value and delightfulness of the
book remain. It is so full of exquisite work, of thought
fresh from heart and brain, that when the reader has made
all his reservations, and steadily refused his adhesion to
this or that appeal which it contains, he will come back
with fresh delight to the passages and descriptions and
reveries in which a poetical and meditative nature has
poured out a wealth of imaginative reflection. Two pieces
especially he will lay by in the store-house of memory —
the 'pagan death' of Flavian, the half-Christian death of
Marius. Let us give a last satisfaction to the feelings
of admiration stirred in us by a remarkable book by quoting the beautiful concluding paragraph which describes how
the sensitive soul of Marius passes from the world it had
sought so early to understand and enjoy:

[Quotes ch. xxviii: 'Then, as before' to 'a kind of
sacrament with plenary grace'.]

Notes

1 See No. 13.
2 Ernest Renan (1823-92), French critic and scholar, was
  the author of the 'Life of Jesus' (1863) and the 'History
  of the Origins of Christianity' (1866-81).
3 Poem entitled It Fortifies My Soul to Know.

24.   UNSIGNED NOTICE, 'HARPER'S NEW MONTHLY MAGAZINE'

May 1885, lxx, 972-3

See Introduction, pp. 5, 22 and 23.

Much the most important and characteristic work of pure
literature published this month, indeed the most essentially literary work of recent date, is Mr W.H. Pater's
'Marius the Epicurean'. For more than ten years, Mr Pater
has reposed on the laurels, perhaps one should say the
myrtles, of his 'Studies of the Renaissance'. That remarkable volume, so much praised and so much blamed,
showed Mr Pater to possess a rhetoric and a view of life
all his own. Whatever ideas the so-called 'Aesthetic
movement' had to boast were extracted from 'Studies of the
Renaissance', and from Mr Ruskin's various and not very
consistent remarks on all things. It might be, and was,
objected to Mr Pater's early book, that his view of life
was narrow, was touched, in spite of so-called 'Hedonism'
or advocacy of pleasure, with the deepest gloom, and was
stated in language always carefully selected and personal,
but somewhat too 'precious' and somewhat too exclamatory.
We do not think that the latter accusation, at all events,
can be brought against the style of 'Marius the Epicurean'.
Mr Pater, while writing about Apuleius, one of the characters of his new apologue, defends a more or less 'precious'
manner of writing, as at all events better than the hasty,
slovenly composition of hack scribblers. Better it is,
certainly, and indisputably better, but there is a point
at which research becomes too manifest, and is apt to fret
the reader. While far less florid than certain passages
of 'Studies of the Renaissance', the manner of 'Marius' is
not without the defects of its qualities. Certain adjec-

tives, such as 'firm' (applied to the unbroken summer weather and morning atmosphere), such as 'bland', 'dainty',
with a few others, recur frequently. They and their chosen
companions among adjectives go a considerable way towards
producing the effects at which Mr Pater aims, but their
'repeated air' may not improbably irritate as many readers
as they charm. The length of many of Mr Pater's periods,
too, may bewilder some of his audience. He is often, one
might say always, writing about moods and sensations which
are very unusual. His subject is difficult; the involu-
tions of his sentences do not make his sense more easy to
grasp by a hurrying modern generation. But it is not easy
to speak too highly of the conscientious care which has
presided over the production of 'Marius the Epicurean'.
As a student of the age of Marcus Aurelius, the age of the
Antonines, Mr Pater shows wide and deeply attentive reading.
Probably he has discovered the secret of the thought of that
time, of an age whose best minds were learned, contemplative
and dissatisfied, wearied of imperial mastery, of imperial
luxury, seeking here and there for a sign, and allured by
the hope of somehow making the very best, in a high sense,
of this life. This period of human thought Mr Pater examines on all sides, we may say, except two. He writes
little, if at all, about the life of the people, the cob-
blers and parasites, the traders, the starveling Greeks and
Syrians, the untaught peasants, the idle beggar population
of Rome and of rural Italy. He does, indeed, show us, in
a few large lines, the origins of the change to modern
Italy, the lonely spaces which malaria was beginning to
touch, driving the country folk into the towns, the first
breath of ruin blowing on weedy overgrown walls, and towers
that were never to be restored to their trim and massive
strength. But, on the whole, the popular life is outside
his view. The people he cares for are all 'seekers after
a city', whether the universal city of Stoicism, or the New
Jerusalem of Christianity. On the fringe of the religious
or speculative world we catch glimpses of a fashionable
restless crowd, women like the ladies who now run after
Esoteric Buddhism, Socialism, Psychical Research, sentimental philanthropy. We are admitted to hear a discourse
by the old philosopher Fronto, the master of Marcus Aurelius, himself, as it were, a popular preacher. The audience, lightly and easily moved, would have been glad (had
it been a charity sermon) to 'make a collection', so Mr
Pater hints. This is one of the very rare touches of
humour in his book, for the humorous no less than the
popular aspect of human existence is wholly neglected in
this picture of old Rome. Yet Mr Pater had many excellent
opportunities to relieve the grave austerity of his labours.

He introduces Lucian among his characters, Lucian, the
most modern of the ancients, the Voltaire and the Rabelais
of the classical world, the contented mocker, the *persi-
fleur*,(1) the most diverting of all writers who have
sought fun, and found it, in burlesquing an out-worn mythology. But Lucian only appears in one of his moods of
gravity, to hold a serious Platonic dialogue with a young
student. It is curious, too, that Mr Pater, writing about
the emotional and intellectual life of a young man, says
nothing about what a young man's fancy 'lightly turns to',
according to the author of 'Locksley Hall'. Marius the
Epicurean, in short, is never in love. Now 'it was not
in nature there should not be kissing', as the jolly piper
says in Clough's 'Bothy'. If Marius had only fallen in
love he would have been much less absorbed in himself, in
taking long views of life, in weighing and balancing the
philosophy of the Cyrenaics, and in accommodating it to
the inherited morality and commonsense of the world. But
we suppose that, if Marius had fallen in love, there would
not have been this long tale of a subjective and contemplative life to tell. Mr Pater would have lost his topic,
and Marius, in ceasing to be a prig, would have become the
hero of a novel. The narrative of his brooding existence
is an apologue, or a parable, or a study, or a sermon, not
a romance: there is no young woman in it, and the hero
does not even lose his heart to Faustina, as a French hero
certainly would have done. The book is as 'inward', almost,
as the letters of Senancour, but it has the advantage of
containing many admirable pictures of human manners and
occupations in an age little known to any one but the professional student. In these pictures of old Roman life
the rapid general reader will find his pleasure and reward, for we can hardly expect him not to skip the reveries
and spiritual sensations (which are not 'sensational') of
Marius. He will like the studies of the ancient rural religion of Italy, the services and rites paid to ancestral
ghosts, and garden gods. He will like the beautiful description, grave as sculpture, yet glowing with subdued
colour, of a rustic temple of Aesculapius, in the hills.
Very different is this from the sketch of such a temple,
and such 'faith-healing', in the 'Plutus' of Aristophanes.
Then we have the school-days of Marius, and the strange
death-bed of his friend Flavian, dying in the very act of
composing the beautiful Pervigilium Veneris. The portrait
of Marcus Aurelius, the admirably delicate sketch of Faustina, the enigmatic empress, are certain to allure, and
there is an extraordinary contrast between a Roman dinner-
party (less noisy than the supper of Petronius) and a
scene in the family vault of a Christian family, or the

beautiful description of the celebration of the Eucharist.
Just when the loveliness of the early Christian services,
and the happiness of the early Church, are winning Marius
(always through his aesthetic consciousness) he dies, an
unreclaimed epicurean, indeed, but in circumstances which
win for him the name and fame of a Christian martyr. We
are not led to think, however, that Marius would ever have
left the old gods, formally, or even have stood the tor-
ments of the persecutors. He was, indeed, *felix opportu-
nitate mortis.*(2) Perhaps one cannot pretend to much
sympathy with this rather too open-minded and indifferent
young man. His whole view of life was the view suggested
to an unimpassioned and sceptical, but not heartless, nature, by the visible aspects of the world. He hated
cruelty, he loved order, intellectual and spiritual, because he naturally hated what was ugly, and liked what
was beautiful. Almost, but not quite, he possessed the
εὐφνία(3) of the born saint of Pluto. But he lacked the
power of losing himself in other people, he lacked spontaneity and charm, and, in a miraculous manner, and to a
wonderful extent, Marius the Epicurean lacked humour. So
his creator has been pleased to design him, in one of the
most remarkable, and to the right reader, one of the most
interesting books of the decade.

Notes

1 Chaffer.
2 Happy to have a chance to die.
3 Serenity.

25. JULIA WEDGWOOD, SIGNED REVIEW, 'CONTEMPORARY REVIEW'

May 1885, xlvii, 750-1

See Introduction, p. 23.
    Frances Julia Wedgwood (1833-1913), author, was a des-
cendant of Josiah Wedgwood and a niece of Charles Darwin.
She frequently contributed (1870-99) to the 'Contemporary
Review' and reprinted a number of her articles on literary
topics in 'Nineteenth Century Teachers' (1909). She is
perhaps best remembered for her 'Life of John Wesley'
(1870).

She reviews 'Vernon Lee's' (see headnote to No. 66)
'Miss Brown' (1884), a novel denouncing the new paganism,
with 'Marius', an espousal of the 'aesthetic character',
because both books 'paint the confused condition of thought
in our day better than any sermon'.

... Vernon Lee and Mr Pater are kindred spirits, and their
works follow without any change of key-note, while some
of our remarks on the first novel apply to both. We
should have welcomed the amount of thought in either more
gladly as an essay than as a novel. 'Marius the Epicurean'
is more satisfactory as a literary work than 'Miss Brown',
although, on the other hand, the development of an aesthetic character in the age of the Antonines is a more arduous
theme for the average novel-reader than any similar picture
taken from contemporary life, and 'Marius' has even less
incident than 'Miss Brown' has. The interest is, in our
view, too purely intellectual for that of a novel. But
there is, in the delicate, fastidious appropriateness of
the style, in the easy flow of a set of descriptions (we
can hardly call it a narrative), in which every page reveals learning and not a line demands effort, in the faint,
soft, pure colouring of the whole, like a picture by
Albert Moore,(1) a peculiar charm, which will be felt, we
should imagine, by a few readers in more than one generation, though we do not expect it will ever be felt by
many. As a picture of thought under Marcus Aurelius, it
strikes the present writer (conscious, however, of inadequacy in making the remark) as wanting in grasp; and
surely to make the Epicurean a central figure in an age of
Stoicism was to choose a position from which the more obvious characteristics of the time were cast into the
shade, nor do all the references to Lucretius strike us
as happy. What appears to have attracted Mr Pater is a
certain resemblance of that age to our own, which has
struck others who have studied it. The faith of the past
was fading, the faith of the future had not as yet reached
a point where it strongly influenced the thought of the
world, the allusions which we find to it in literature are
slight and scarce, and its own records can scarcely be
called literary. There was a mystic yearning after some
harmonizing truth lying beneath the decaying creeds of
the age which prepared the way for all that was deepest
in the path of Christ, although it perhaps somewhat opposed that impulse by which Christianity conquered the
world; and there was a profound sense of blank and empti-
ness, a gaze of longing turned back to the past, a weary

sigh, a feeling of the littleness of life, such as we are
accustomed to fancy a peculiarly modern feeling; in some
form it may have existed in every age, but the form which
it then took seems often to mirror the life of our own.
Mr Pater, at any rate, seems to us to find his interest in
that intellectual exercise afforded by the translation of
the feelings of one age into the dialect of another. We
read of 'the religion of Numa' in the age of Marcus Aurelius, and we think of the contemporaries of John Henry
Newman; we watch the fading of this antiquarian piety, and
we think of such characters as that revealed to us in the
'Memoirs'(2) of Mark Pattison. When the Voltaire of the
age appears upon the scene we are somewhat disappointed;
and yet it is an actual dialogue which (if our memory
serves) is reproduced in substance from Lucian. Apuleius
reproduces, if not any distinct individuality of modern
life, at least much of its vague mysticism, but his literary gem seems to us a little out of place here. The picture of the faith which was new then, and is old now,
though it suggests no modern counterpart separate from itself, yet seems to recall the problems of our day as the
morning recalls the evening twilight. We are left somewhat puzzled as to the impression meant to be conveyed of
Christianity, which the hero does not embrace, but in supposed martyrdom for which he dies, and which 'seems to
define what he might require of the powers, whatsoever
they might be, that had brought him into the world to make
him not unhappy in it'. He is impressed by the image of
'a young man giving up, one by one, the greatest gifts,
parting with himself and that deep and divine serenity of
his own mind, yet from the midst of his distress crying
out upon the greatness of his success, as if foreseeing
this very worship'; yet this impression is no dominant
influence in his nature, and we are left to understand,
apparently, that he stood aloof from the faith that impressed his imagination as from some rightful lord of a
part in his nature that made a claim upon the whole. The
gospel of culture will not blend with any other gospel;
we are only surprised to find that it leaves so large a
space for a possible rival.

Notes

1 Albert Joseph Moore (1841-93) executed decorative work
  for theatres and churches.
2 Edited by Mrs Pattison (No. 6) in 1885.

26.   G.E. WOODBERRY, UNSIGNED REVIEW, 'NATION'

10 September 1885, xli, 219-21

Reprinted in 'Makers of Literature' (New York, 1900).
See No. 34 and Introduction, pp. 24 and 25.

George Edward Woodberry (1855-1930), American poet,
critic and educator, studied method in history and biography under Henry Adams and aesthetics under C.E. Norton
(see headnote to No. 27) at Harvard. He frequently contributed (1876-91) to the 'Atlantic Monthly' and the
'Nation', published a biography of Edgar Allan Poe (1885)
and was Professor of Literature at Columbia University
from 1891 to 1904.

Along with R.H. Stoddard, Bayard Taylor, G.H. Boker,
T.B. Aldrich, E.C. Stedman and H.W. Mabie, Woodberry was
a member of a 'band' of critics known as the 'defenders of
Ideality'. L.C. Moulton (No. 47) was associated with the
group. In literature they championed the Platonic tradition of Poe and Emerson, equating Beauty with Truth. They
thought that literature was 'not a thing to be known
merely like science, but to be lived'. See Introduction,
p. 26.

The heart of this work lies in its thought about the ideal,
and it is in the nature of all such thought to make a
peculiar demand upon the reader. Its wisdom is felt to be,
as it were, sacerdotal, and requires a conscious preparation of mind in him who would know of it; its vision is
supernal, and disclosed only when some spiritual illumination has been sent before. So runs a Platonic doctrine of
election and grace that has been held as rigorously in
literature as in theology. This aristocracy of idealism —
its exclusiveness, its jealousy of any intrusion of the
common and worldly within the company it keeps, its sense
of a preciousness, as of sacred things, within itself — is
incorporate in every fibre of Mr Pater's work; and he
makes the demand natural to it, not only implicitly by an
unrelaxing use of such aesthetic and intellectual elements
as appeal exclusively to the subtlest faculties of appreciation in their highest development, but explicitly also
by the character of his hero. Marius, before he became an
Epicurean, was moulded for his fate; his creator demanded
an exceptional nature for the aesthetic ideal to react upon
in a noble way, and so Marius was born in the upland farm

among the fair mountains to the north of Pisa, and was
possessed from boyhood of the devout seriousness, the mood
of trustful waiting for the god's coming, which is exacted
in all profound idealism. *'Favete linguis!*(1) With the
lad Marius there was a devout effort to complete this impressive outward silence by that inward tacitness of mind
esteemed so important by religious Romans in the performance of their sacred functions'. Marius was born one of
the choice natures in whom the heavenly powers are well
pleased; and emphasis must be given to this circumstance
because it follows that the ideal life which he lived,
deeply meditated though it is, is really an individual
one. Marius is not typical, nor even illustrative in any
broad way of the practice of aesthetic morals; and yet,
since he is not national, nor local, nor historic, in his
essential self, since he is more than an enlightened
philosopher and yet less than the enlightened Christian,
since his personality approaches the elect souls of other
ages, other sentiments and devotions, and yet is without
any real contact with them, he is typical and illustrative perhaps of something that might be. This confusedness
of impression springs from the fact that Mr Pater, while he
imagines in Italy, always thinks in London; he has modernized his hero, has Anglicized him, indeed, and nevertheless
has not really taken him out of the second century. It was
a bold thing to attempt. It was necessary for his purposes as an evangelist of ideal living, and perhaps within
the range of moral teaching it is successful; but the way
in which it was done is a main point of interest.

A Roman Epicurean, one suspects, was not unlike the pro-
verbial Italianated Englishman. The native incompatibility
between the distinctive Roman temperament and the light-
hearted gayety of Greek sensuousness was similar to that
between the English and the Italian character in the later
times; the perfection of Marius by a Greek ideal, therefore, may run parallel with English culture under southern
influences. There was, too, in Roman character a trait or
two which brings it near to qualities that lie at the base
of our own stock. Even in the Italian landscape there are
northern notes such as Mr Pater mentions when Marius, in
his walks to the coast, sees 'the marsh with the dwarf
roses and wild lavender, the abandoned boat, the ruined
floodgates, the flock of wild birds', and has an especial
relish for all that. We are told, also, that 'poetic
souls in old Italy felt, hardly less strongly than the
English, the pleasures of winter, of the hearth, with the
very dead warm in its generous heat, keeping the young
myrtles in flower, though the hail is beating hard without'. This note of Marius's home-life and the love he had

for it, with his particular regard for 'Domiduca, the goddess who watches over one's safe coming home', and with the
ideal of maternity that grew up in his memory of home —
this peculiarly English note is struck in the opening and
is dominant at the end.   Certain other characteristics
ally this Etrurian boy with that nobler strain of English
blood, the Puritan strain as it was in Spenser.   His instinctive seriousness, his scrupulosity of conscience, his
inheritance of a certain sombreness from the stock that
adorned the Etruscan funeral urns, his attachment to
places and awe of some of them as sacred by the touch of
a divine power, his sense of invisible enemies about his
path, his rigorous self-discipline in preparation for certain hereditary sacred offices, a deadly earnestness at
times — as when he gazes so fixedly on the rigid corpse
of his friend Flavian — such are some of the traits that
define his nature as essentially rather northern than
southern, and provide a ground of special sympathy and
understanding to us.

The second device by which Marius is modernized is by
giving to him a power which, for him who runs as he reads,
makes the character incredible.   He is said to be affected
sometimes in a way the opposite of the common experience
which many have who, on seeing a new place, seem to have
been there before: Marius feels, in the most marked of his
experiences, something that shall be — he has always a
prescience.   Thus, in the cadence of Flavian's verses he
hears the music of the Latin hymnology;   in the sight of
his second friend, Cornelius, who displays and puts on his
armor of a Roman knight in the dusty sunshine of the shut-
tered country-house, he foresees the Christian chivalry;
in the faces and groups of the worshippers in Cecilia's
house he discerns the serene light and streaming joy of
Giotto's and of Dante's vision, and looks on the Madonna
and the Child that Raphael first painted.   In all this
there seems an unreality;   in the Puritan Roman, the Cyrenaic Christian, there is a sense almost of conscious artifice, as if one were being befooled.   And yet, as for those
northern notes of landscape, custom, and character, scholarship can give chapter and verse for them;   and as for the
gift of prescience — well, if it were impossible for
Marius to have it, in a sufficient measure at least, then
the theory of ideal living which he held to was at fault.
And this Marius, so constituted, his creator places in an
Italy over which the romantic desolation, which we know,
was laying its charm of dreamful decay, and in a Rome
which, then as now, was the huddled deposit of religions.

The intellectual conviction on which Marius conducted
his life was simple and common enough, as must be the case

with every theory capable of being made a principle of
living. The world is what we think it, and our part in
existence is the fleeting moment of present consciousness.
What shall be done with this moment? Economize it, said
Marius, in dissent from the Stoic who said, 'Contemn it.'
Economize it; make the most of the phenomena that arise
in it, and see, so far as it depends on you, that these
phenomena, both of sensation and idea, as they arise, are
the most valuable possible to the moment; and so your experience — in other words, your life — will be the fullest and most refined. Above all, do not forget the main
thing in this doctrine of economy, which is that the worth
of experience depends not on what it is at the moment in
its detached and transitory phase, but what it will prove
in memory when it takes its place permanently and in relation to the whole life. In such a scheme, receptivity, the
most alert and varied powers of taking in impressions, is
the one aim of cultivation. Here, too, much depended on
the nature of Marius, this time on the side of his southern endowment. An impressibility through sensation was his
gift, his talent; and especially he was susceptible to
what the eye takes in: he was one of those who are 'made
perfect by the love of visible beauty'. This is the point
of union of his life with the aesthetic ideal, and makes
the story of it a pathway through scenes of loveliness
not unlike, in a certain mild beauty, the frescoes on ancient walls. The narrative is pictorial, almost to the
point of decoration, and moves always with an outlook on
some fair sight. From the landscape of the villa where
Marius was born — among those delightful Etrurian hills
whence one looks to the marble drifts of Carrara gleaming
above olive and chestnut slopes, and gazes off through the
purple sea-valley of Venus's Port, that noblest gateway of
the descending sun — to the last throttling earthquake
morning, a beautiful visible world is about us, and exercises its attractiveness both in nature and in humanity.
The one end of Marius was to appropriate all this, to
choose the best of sensation and its most nearly connected
emotions, and to live in that. To do this involves a
secondary talent, a gift of insight, a power to perceive
relative values, which in reality means a faculty of moral
discrimination; and just here one may easily fail to see
whence Marius derived this.

Why was it, for example, that he, being so attached to
sensation and the emotions that cling closest to it, rejected voluptuousness, with all its forms of beauty and
joyfulness, as a thing essentially not beautiful nor joy-
ful? What was it that kept him, the comrade of Flavian,
who represents the pagan surrender to this life, pure —

so pure, indeed, that with his visionary sense he foresaw in chastity an ideal that was to be, and foreknew its supreme beauty? A mere interpreter of character, an analyst, would say, that Marius obeyed in these choices his own nature — that Puritan nature whose compulsion is always strong. He venerated his own soul and cherished its early instincts, and this was his salvation. But one might also give another explanation, which would seem more harmonious with the purpose of the author; one might say that what is moral is in its outward manifestation so clothed with beauty, visible beauty, that the man who looks for beauty only, the noblest, the ideal beauty, will find therewith the highest, the ideal good. It is essential to such a seeker that he shall look with his own eyes and be frank with himself, shall 'look straight out' and acknowledge what he sees; and this Marius does, thereby prefiguring in a way and practically making that 'return to nature' which is the continually recurring necessity of all sincerity. If virtue does in fact wear this outward loveliness — and who would deny it? — why may not the lover of beauty have truly seen the new and springing forms of goodness, recognized them, and taken their promise into his life? In other words, was not that prescience of Marius merely a power of clear and honest seeing of the elements of beauty and ugliness there before him?

That this is Mr Pater's view of the matter is indicated most definitely by the contrast which he continually insists on between Marcus Aurelius and Marius, and which he brings out clearly in the attitude of these two toward the gladiatorial shows. In the amphitheatre Marius is conscious of the Emperor, the strenuous Stoic, as 'eternally his inferior on the question of righteousness'. The young Epicurean has a 'decisive conscience on sight' which is indubitable — that conscience which, in its condemnation of the great sin of an age, is the touchstone of the select few in it, which makes them on the side of the future and aware of its excellence to be, when 'not to have been, by instinctive election, on the right side was to have failed in life'. Aurelius, we are told, made the great mistake: *Vale, anima infeticissima!*(2) is the last word of our author to him on the eve of the persecutions. And the reason is, that the Stoic was truly blind; he had paltered with his senses until they lied to him or spoke not at all. Marius saw the deformity of the evil, and, while rejecting it as something he might not see and live, chose the good by its beauty, and so selected in the midst of that Roman corruption the Christian elements in whose excellence the Church would triumph and be made fair.

There may be some surprise in perceiving in the evangel
of aestheticism a morality of this height, a concentration
of attention on the beauty of austerity, an exaltation of
a noble Puritanism toward which the Cyrenaic ideal may
lead. When this is understood, however, one finds it
natural enough that the pervading tone of this history of
an ideal life is really religious; idealism, when it is
living, cannot be otherwise than essentially religious.
Nevertheless, it is a bold thing to put the question, as
Mr Pater implicitly does, whether an attention to the beautiful, to visible beauty, may not only be equivalent to
moral discrimination and a safeguard of virtue, but also
a mode of solving these ultimate religious questions of
deity and man's relation to it. Marius does arrive at an
intimation, perhaps a faith, that a protective divine companionship goes beside him, and at an emotion of gratitude
to that All-Father.

Two points only, in this wide branch of the speculation,
can be dwelt on now. He says toward the end that he thinks
he has failed in love; and here he touches on one weakness
of his ideal, for it is only by love, as he perceives, that
any reconciliation between the lover of beauty and the mul-
titudinous pitiful pain which is so large a part of the
objective universe can be obtained. The second weakness is
perhaps greater. In his ideal there is both doubt and
isolation; the subjective element in his knowledge, the
exclusive reliance on his own impressions, the fact that
in metaphysical belief the world is only his world and in
actual living the experience is individual — all this
holds in it a basis of ultimate incertitude. True and
real for him it no doubt is, but is that, indeed, the necessary limit of knowledge and life? In effect, too, his
creed is Protestant; independently of the necessary element of doubt in it, it has the isolating force inevitable
to the believer who will accept only the results of his
own examination by exercise of private judgment. This
position is unsatisfactory; and he seems to allow the rationality of that principle of authority by which an individual life obtains correction for its idiosyncrasies, can-
cels the personal error, and at the same time lets in upon
itself the flood of the total experience of humanity summed
up and defined in the whole body of the elect. Though
stated here in terms of the Stoical philosophy, this is
the Catholic conclusion. Or, if Marius does not quite as-
sent to this, he does accept it in a half-hearted way as an
hypothesis which is worth making since it reunites him to
mankind. There is, it may be observed, a tendency toward
Catholicism throughout the religious speculation. Another

note of it, for example, is the attraction felt by Marius
in the ritual of worship as the perfection of that cere-
monialism to which in his boyish worship of the old gods
he was devoutly trained.

After all, at the end one still states the promises of
this aesthetic ideal, even when working on so unusual a
nature as Marius's, interrogatively. Marius's life does
not set it forth with convincing power. For one thing, it
is not a vital life, but a painted one; and there is an
inconsequence in the series of pictures — they do not
seem to follow one another by any iron necessity. It
would be foolish to complain that a life avowedly only receptive and contemplative of the beautiful is inactive.
Marius does nothing except at the end. Yet, within such
limits, one never sees how beauty affected Marius or developed his soul, and though he is said to have got much
from companionship, one sees love operative in him very
seldom, and then it is a very silent and unexpressed love.
He repeats his own epitaph — *tristem neminem fecit*(3) —
and it was true; but all his life seems negative, and continually one asks, How did he really live? and gets no
answer. His whole life was a *meditatio mortis*(4) — that
is all that is told us.

A sense of failure, or rather of incompleteness, oppresses one when he lays down the volumes. Even granting that
the success Marius is said to have achieved — one is never
quite sure that he did — by that exquisite appreciation of
beauty and impassioned contemplation of its ideal forms,
was, in fact, his, yet of what worth was it — what did it
mean to either God or man? The northern idealist, the
Puritan, cannot dispense with some serviceableness as essential to any high living. We would not push the point
too far, however. Independently of all that has been said,
any one who cares to think on counsels of perfection for
man's life will find profound and original thought about
the ideal elements still at hand in modern days for use,
and many wise reflections, sown along these pages. It is
a rare work, and not carelessly to be read. Some exquisiteness of taste, some delight in scholarship, some knowledge
of what is best worth knowing in the historic expressions
of man's aspiration, and, above all, that 'inward tacitness
of mind' the reader must bring to its perusal. What of it?
Have we not the highest authority for casting our pearls
where Circe's herd cannot come?

Notes

1 'Listen all in silence': Horace, 'Odes',III, i, 1.

2 Good bye, most unhappy soul.
3 He did not make anybody unhappy.
4 Meditation on death.

27. C.E. NORTON ON PATER

1886

Extract from a letter dated 30 January 1886 to G.E. Woodberry (see headnote to No. 26), from the 'Letters of Charles
Eliot Norton' (Boston and New York, 1913), ed. Sara Norton
and M.A. De Wolfe Howe, ii, 175.
   Norton (1827-1908), influential teacher and man of letters, was joint editor (1864-8) of the 'North American
Review', one of the founders of the 'Nation' and Professor
of the History of Art at Harvard (1875-98). He visited
Europe often and made the acquaintance of most of the prominent literary figures of the day, including John Ruskin,
John Stuart Mill, G.H. Lewes and George Eliot.

I shall send back the poem(1) to-day, or Monday, together
with 'Marius'. I am very much obliged to you for this book,
but on the whole you think more highly of it than I. The
first half of it deserves your praise better than the last.
There is an affectation, a *préciosité* in it, that sometimes
takes from its worth the one thing needful, — sincerity of
feeling.

Note

1 My County.

28. GEORGE MOORE ON PATER

1888

Extract from 'Confessions of a Young Man' (1888: Ebury

edn, 1937), 139-41. See Introduction, p. 2.

George Augustus Moore (1852-1933), the Anglo-Irish poet,
critic, novelist and playwright. He defended the impressionist movement in painting and the naturalist movement
in literature. Moore admired Pater's 'genius' for making
'everything read as if it were autobiographical'.

Moore met Pater at the home of Mary Robinson in the
summer of 1885, but, in spite of his belief that he
had a gift for intimacy, Moore failed to secure Pater's
friendship and confidence. For his impressionistic account
of their disappointing relationship, see Avowals. VI.
Walter Pater, 'Pall Mall Magazine' (August 1904), xxxiii,
527-33, which forms the basis for chapters ix to xi of
'Avowals' (1919). He wearies of Pater's reticence and the
two men became estranged after the publication of the 'Confessions', a copy of which he sent to Pater. Pater read
the book with some delight, but, as he observed in his
letter of 4 March 1888, found much of it provocative and
cynical (see LWP, 81).

... this book is not a course of literature, and I will
tarry no longer with mere criticism, but go direct to the
book to which I owe the last temple in my soul — 'Marius
the Epicurean'. Well I remember when I read the opening
lines, and how they came upon me sweetly as the flowing
breath of a bright spring. I knew that I was awakened a
fourth time, that a fourth vision of life was to be given
to me. Shelley had revealed to me the unimagined skies
where the spirit sings of light and grace; Gautier had
shown me how extravagantly beautiful is the visible world
and how divine is the rage of the flesh; and with Balzac
I had descended circle by circle into the nether world of
the soul, and watched its afflictions. Then there were
minor awakenings. Zola had enchanted me with decoration
and inebriated me with theory; Flaubert had astonished
with the wonderful delicacy and subtlety of his workmanship; Goncourt's brilliant adjectival effects had capti-
vated me for a time, but all these impulses were crumbling
into dust, these aspirations were etiolated, sickly as
faces grown old in gaslight.

I had not thought of the simple and unaffected joy of
the heart of natural things; the colour of the open air,
the many forms of the country, the birds flying — that
one making for the sea; the abandoned boat, the dwarf
roses and wild lavender; nor had I thought of the beauty
of mildness in life, and how by a certain avoidance of the

wilfully passionate, and the surely ugly, we may secure an
aspect of temporal life which is abiding and soul-sufficing.
A new dawn was in my brain, fresh and fair, full of wide
temples and studious hours, and the lurking fragrance of
incense; that such a vision of life was possible I had no
suspicion, and it came upon me almost with the same
strength, almost as intensely, as that divine song of the
flesh, 'Mademoiselle de Maupin'.

In my mind, these books will be always intimately associated; and when a few adventitious points of difference
are forgotten, it is interesting to note how firm is the
alliance, and how cognate and co-equal the sympathies of
which it is based; the same glad worship of the visible
world, and the same incurable belief that the beauty of
material things is sufficient for all the needs of life.
Mr Pater can join hands with Gautier in saying — *je trouve
la terre aussi belle que le ciel, et je pense que la correction de la forme est la vertu.*(1) And I too am of
their company — in this at least I too love the great
pagan world, its bloodshed, its slaves, its injustice, its
loathing of all that is feeble.

But 'Marius the Epicurean' was more to me than a mere
emotional influence, precious and rare though that may be,
for this book was the first in English prose I had come
across that procured for me any genuine pleasure in the
language itself, in the combination of words for silver or
gold chime, and unconventional cadence, and for all those
lurking half-meanings, and that evanescent suggestion,
like the odour of dead roses, that words retain to the
last of other times and elder usage. Until I read 'Marius'
the English language (English prose) was to me what French
must be to the majority of English readers. I read for the
sense and that was all; the language itself seemed to me
coarse and plain, and awoke in me neither aesthetic emotion nor even interest. 'Marius' was the stepping-stone
that carried me across the channel into the genius of my
own tongue. The translation was not too abrupt; I found
a constant and careful invocation of meaning that was a
little aside of the common comprehension, and also a sweet
depravity of ear for unexpected falls of phrase, and of eye
for the less observed depths of colours, which although new
was a sort of sequel to the education I had chosen, and a
continuance of it in a foreign, but not wholly unfamiliar
medium; and having saturated myself with Pater, the passage in De Quincey was easy. He, too, was a Latin in
manner and in temper of mind; but he was truly English,
and through him I passed to the study of the Elizabethan
dramatists, the real literature of my race, and washed myself clean of France....

Note

1 I find the earth as beautiful as the sky, and I consider
  that the correction of form is virtue.

29.   ERNEST DOWSON ON PATER

1889, 1890, 1892

Extracts from the 'Letters of Ernest Dowson' (1967), ed.
Desmond Flower and Henry Maas.

   Ernest Christopher Dowson (1867-1900), representative
poet of the 1890s and member of what W.B. Yeats called
'The Tragic Generation'. He was a prominent member of
the Rhymers' Club and published 'Verses' (1896), containing the widely anthologised poem Cynara, which has the famous refrain 'I have been faithful to thee, Cynara! in my
fashion'.

(a)   From a letter dated 3 January 1889 to Arthur Moore

[Zola] reminds me — or rather this episode [in 'Le Reve'
(1888),where 'Monsignore brings the extreme unction to the
girl who is supposed to be dying'] reminds me — (excuse
this desultory criticism) of Pater — a strange conjunction
but it is so. I suppose it is the superficial resemblance
of incident to the last few pages of 'Marius'. It is a
pity bye the bye that Pater can not write a *real* novel. If
he had the force of concentration necessary it would be a
book unsurpassed & not surpassable. I am thankful for the
two of them — but should like them hugely rolled into
one. You must read the 'extreme unction' pages even if you
cannot stomach the whole. The purifying of the separate
orifices of sensation with the consecrated oils strikes me
as an excessively fine notion.(1) I think if I have a
death-bed (wh I don't desire) I must be reconciled to Rome
for the sake of that piece of ritual. It seems to me the
most fitting exit for the epicurean — after all one *is*
chiefly that — & one would procure it — (it seems essentially pagan) without undue compromise or affectation of a
belief in 'a sort of a something somewhere', simply as an
exquisite sensation, & for the sensation's sake. (Pp. 21-2)

(b) From a letter dated 28 March 1890 to Arthur Moore

M Aurelius' optimism — wh certainly had no 'secret of
cheerfulness' in it reduces itself to that at last — to
the very blankest Pessimism — the impression which Pater's
epicureanism leaves on you is very much the same.

> For there is a certain grief in things as they are, in
> man as he has come to be, as he certainly is, over &
> above those griefs of circumstances which are in a
> measure removable — an inexplicable short-coming or
> misadventure on the part of nature itself — death and
> old age as it must needs be, and that watching of their
> approach, which makes every stage of life like a dying
> over & over again.(2)

No there is no 'secret of cheerfulness' in Pater. (Pp. 144-
5)

(c) From a letter dated 31 March 1890 to Arthur Moore

The XVIIIth Cent has a complacency of demeanour which is
merely good breeding: Johnson & Swift & Sterne let the
cat out of the bag. And as for now, the two people considered, I suppose, sanest, Browning and Meredith, — ! —
What an absurdity! As for Pater & Newman — the two
greatest men of the century, surely? I doubt if even
British suburban criticism could discover much health or
sanity in them! (P. 146)

(d) From a postcard (postmarked 17 December 1892) to
William Theodore Peters

I envy you your meeting with Pater: the finest artist now
with us, & from all accounts the most wonderful in his
personality. (P. 257)

Notes

1 Dowson had this passage in mind when he wrote the poem
  'Extreme Unction' (1893).
2 ME, ii, 181-2.

30. RICHARD LE GALLIENNE ON PATER

1892

Review of the third edition, in 'Retrospective Reviews:
A Literary Log' (New York, 1896), i, 174-81. See Nos 53
and 62 and Introduction, pp. 3 and 9.

Richard Thomas Le Gallienne (1866-1947), the Liverpool-
born poet, belletrist and legendary 'golden boy' of the
1890s. He was literary critic for the London 'Star' (writing under the pseudonym of 'Logroller'), a member of the
Rhymers' Club and literary adviser to the Bodley Head, the
publishing firm of Elkin Matthews (1851-1921) and John Lane
(1854-1925), founders of the 'Yellow Book'.

Le Gallienne greatly admired Pater and met him in October 1892 at an Oxford dinner party given by C.H.O. Daniel
(1836-1919), Fellow and later Provost of Worcester College,
Oxford, and founder of one of the most famous private
presses of late Victorian England. See 'The Romantic
'Nineties' (1926), 74-9, and On Re-Reading Walter Pater,
'North American Review' (February 1912), cxcv, 214-24.

Le Gallienne believed that 'Criticism is the Art of
Praise' and that 'Praise is more important than judgment.'
This review is characteristically 'charming' and mannered.

THE BOOK BEAUTIFUL

'Marius the Epicurean' is preeminently that for many of us.
Perhaps no book since 'Sartor Resartus' has been read with
such a sense of awakening, and indeed it may be said that
it has, in some needed measure, modified the influence of
'Sartor', with its sublime factory gospel of work. For
the imperative 'Do!' of Carlyle it substitutes the gentle
pleading 'Be!' 'Be ye perfect!' The culture of the individual in a well-ordered unity, body, soul, and spirit: that
is its message. But not a selfish culture. 'He must satisfy, with a kind of sacred equity, he must be very cautious
not to be wanting to the claims of others, in their joys
and calamities.' That was one of the earliest axioms
Marius took with him on his progress from the primitive
religion of his fathers, through Epicureanism, to that
final mood of his mind in which the careful justice of such
an axiom was being deepened by the warmer sentiment of a
Christian pity. What that mood quite was we are left a
little in doubt — as how else could it be in regard to a

complex being such as Marius? His experience of life had
been too various, too humanising, for him to become the
bondsman of any mere dogma; though in the formulae of
Christianity, the earlier, unmonastic Christianity, he had,
perhaps, come nearest to finding the formulae which most
expressed his own gentle individuality — if formulae
must be!

Some people will have nothing of Mr Pater. One has
heard them say that he is all manner and no matter. A
strange doctrine, for certainly it seemed to some of us,
when first we read 'Marius' with glowing heart, that it
was full indeed of burning matters. It seemed that no
'spiritual pastor' had so harmonised the claims of body
and soul, so wondrously captured for us those fine elusive
moods of which we are hardly aware till we recognise them
in another; and that no one had written more movingly of
friendship, of goodness, of beauty, or of death — great
matters as we thought. It is true that Mr Pater's manner
is occasionally a little too priestlike in its extreme,
its maiden-like fastidiousness. But even so, such fastidiousness comes but of his sincerity towards his meaning.
It is instructive to remember what he writes of Flavian:

> His dilettantism, his assiduous preoccupation with what
> might seem but the details of mere form or manner, was,
> after all, bent upon the function of bringing to the
> surface, sincerely, and in their integrity, certain
> strong personal intuitions, certain visions or appre-
> hensions of things as being, with important results,
> in this way rather than that.

To this sincerity the revisions in the present edition
bear almost painful witness. One had looked forward to
them with some eagerness, for one might well feel that Mr
Pater could hardly have 'completely revised' his 'golden
book' without revealing in the process some new secrets of
perfection. I proposed to myself the task of collating the
two versions; but that is a task for leisure, and my leisure has not been equal to it, nor, I must add, my austerity. For the task soon began to resemble the numbering
of the golden hairs on a beloved head. One kept continually forgetting the collation to luxuriate in the pleasure
of mere reading. So presently I fell to lazily dipping
and comparing here and there, at various well-remembered
pages. Besides, devotion even to a master must be kept
within bounds, if we are not to make him and ourselves
ludicrous; to register his every trivial change in prosody or punctuation, after the manner of some editors,
'were', as Polonius wisely said, 'nothing but to waste
night, day, and time'.

And so far as I have examined, the majority of Mr Pater's
emendations are merely matters of prosody and punctuation,
though such as they are, they are numberless. We are sometimes sententiously reminded that, though we seem the same
person as we did seven years ago, there is actually not a
molecule of us which has not been replaced. Was it not
Cowley who ingeniously excused his inconstancy on this Heraclitean principle, though he found it convenient to say
five years?

My *Members*, then, the *Father Members* were,
From whence *These* take their birth, which now are here,
If, then, this *Body* love what th' other did,
'Twere *Incest*, which by Nature is forbid.(1)

Such a complete minute change of texture seems to have overtaken Mr Pater's 'Marius' since its first publication in
1885 — exactly, you will remark, seven years ago. Comparing the old text with the present, one is reminded of
an ant-hill, the busy units of which are changing every
moment, but the total impression to the eye remaining the
same. One recalls, too, that passage in Mr Pater's exposition of the Heraclitean doctrine of the eternal flux:
'It was as if, recognising perpetual motion as the law of
Nature, Marius identified his own way of life cordially
with it, throwing himself into the stream, as we say: he,
too, must maintain a harmony with that soul of motion in
things, by a constantly renewed mobility of character.'
Strange dilemma of the artist, that while seeking perfection even his ideal of perfection must be changing.
On every page one finds minute changes in punctuation.
Colons replace semi-colons, commas fall out altogether,
and Mr Pater seems to have endeavoured to cure himself of
his fondness for the parenthetic dash. With none of his
disciples' contempt of the unlearned reader, he has translated one or two Latin quotations which had escaped translation in the other editions — not obviously, as to hurt the
susceptibilities of that unlearned reader, but by a graceful repetition, as though merely for emphasis. There is
sometimes quite a homely touch in Mr Pater's writing, very
winning; and one may refer here to his scrupulous care,
when possible, to express his thought in simple English.
He never uses a word foreign to the language, unless the
idea is foreign also. The reader will remember that in
one or two instances the chapter headings were simply two
or three lines from Pliny, the Vulgate, and in one case a
line from Rousseau. These Mr Pater has now retained as
mottoes, but in most cases replaced them as chapter headings by English titles — not always successful. In one

case, at least, he would seem to have carried his complacency towards the merely English reader to a somewhat grotesque result; for, surely, Change of Air is an oddly un-
dignified, unsuggestive title for the beautiful chapter
describing Marius's sojourn at the temple of Æsculapius
among the hills. How much more fit in every way was the
Dilexi decorem domus tuae;(2) and few readers who care to
read Mr Pater at all are so unlearned as not now and again
to appreciate the beauty, the decorative beauty, of a sprig
of Latin such as that. Chap iv of part i is now described
as The Tree of Knowledge, and chapter vii appears as A
Pagan End instead of the original and more impressive
title of Pagan Death. In part ii, the journey to Rome
(chap x) is hardly distinctly suggested by On the Way. In
part iii, there are two changes for the better, chap xvii
is now inscribed *Beata Urbs*, instead of merely bearing the
quotation Many Prophets and Kings, etc., and chap xix,
The Will as Vision. In part iv chap xxiii, is now entitled
Divine Service, and chap xxvi, The Martyrs. In all the
instances except Change of Air and On the Way the emendations have been improvements. Perhaps they were really too
trifling to record; but, after all, as the old story goes,
it is the trifles that make perfection, and perfection is
no trifle.

It is, however, with more anxious expectancy that one
turns to certain passages in the text, passages which to
some of us, coming as that copy of Apuleius came to the
young Flavian, in a 'fortunate' moment, have been real
watchwords of our lives, as many a line in Browning or
Carlyle has been. Such to me were: 'He must be very cautious not to be wanting to the claims of others, in their
joys and calamities'; 'not pleasure, but fulness, completeness of life generally'; 'to be absolutely virgin
towards a direct and concrete experience'; and lastly,
towards the close of the wonderful chapter on the gladiatorial games:

Yes! what was wanting was the heart that would make it
impossible to witness all this; and the future would
be with the forces that could begat a heart like that.
His favourite philosophy had said, Trust the eye: strive
to be right always regarding the concrete experience:
Never falsify your impressions. And its sanction had
been at least effective here, in saying, It is what I
may not see! Surely, evil was a real thing; and the
wise man wanting in the sense of it, where not to have
been, by instinctive election, on the right side, was
to have failed in life.

One goes to the new edition, prepared to resent any
changes in such passages as these, in the same spirit in
which we resent 'the revised version' of any great familiar
thing. We feel that any essential change must be impossible, and all the more resent any merely vexatious change
of phrase, clashing as it does with our old sacred familiarity. In every one of the passages cited, Mr Pater, in
some such vexatious way, offends against our cherished
remembrance of his words. In no instance does there seem
to have been any real need of alteration, and except in
the case of 'his *favourite* philosophy', in the last passage, for 'his *chosen* philosophy' there is nothing characteristic in the changes. In the first sentence we have
for 'not to be wanting to' 'lest he be found wanting to',
and 'not pleasure, but a general completeness of life' is
the new and certainly closer form of the second aphorism,
though one misses the effect of the word 'fulness'. But
the third, most helpful, phrase is now rendered unquotable
by its being made to depend on the conclusion of another
sentence: '... the impressions of an experience, concrete
and direct, to be absolutely virgin towards such experience ...'. There is certainly no gain here, but a distinct loss of force.

If the examples cited may be taken as fairly representative of Mr Pater's revisions, one may feel comfortable that
'Marius' remains much as it was, though one has all the
more reason to fear the possibility of Mr Pater's, so to
say, being overcome by a grammatical affection of the
nerves, which, if encouraged, will not allow either him or
his readers any peace. Had changes been necessary to bring
his text nearer to his meaning, one must have borne them;
but that sentence after sentence should be pulled about to
satisfy, not the instinct of expression, but a morbid desire of punctuation, is not bearable. Yet, after all, however many septennial changes overtake 'Marius', it cannot
well be robbed of its high beauty, of its deep humanity.
It will still remain one of the most convincing expressions of the inherent priesthood of man, whatever be the
new last word of presumptuous biologists, or its mistaken
application by sensualists, who, as of old, take the name
of Epicurus in vain, and who in spite of its central doctrine, 'not pleasure, but a general completeness of life',
dare to quote its authority for a life of foolish *in*completeness, a mere cultivation of certain detached appetites.

Mr Pater has not failed to impress his reader with that
danger of misapplication. Who can ever forget the closing
passage in 'The Renaissance': 'To burn always with this
hard, gem-like flame, to maintain this ecstasy, is success
in life'? But again: 'Only be sure it is passion — that

it does yield you this fruit of a quickened, multiplied
consciousness.' *Only be sure it is passion!* It is a
haunting cry, hard to forget; and only those who have
forgotten it have read Mr Pater to their undoing.

Notes

1 From Inconstancy, 'The Mistress: or Several Copies of
  Love-Verses' (1668), by A. Cowley (1618-67).
2 I loved the beauty of thy house.

'Imaginary Portraits'
May 1887

31.   OSCAR WILDE, UNSIGNED REVIEW, 'PALL MALL GAZETTE'

11 June 1887, 2-3

Reprinted in 'Reviews' (1908), 172-5. See No. 50 and
Introduction, pp. 28 and 29.
    Oscar Fingal O'Flahertie Wills Wilde (1854-1900), Irish
poet, critic, dramatist and wit. When he left Oxford in
1878 he was already known as the champion of the Aesthetic
Movement and the creed of 'art for art's sake'.
    Wilde first met Pater at Oxford in the Michaelmas term
of 1877, remained one of his most devoted disciples and
frequently acknowledged his artistic indebtedness to him.
At his first trial, as reported by H. Montgomery Hyde in
'The Trials of Oscar Wilde' (1948), he spoke (3 April
1895) of Pater as 'the only critic of the century whose
opinion I set high' (p. 124). In his letter dated January-
March of 1897 to Lord Alfred Douglas he wrote: 'I remember
during my first term at Oxford reading ... Pater's "Renaissance" — that book which has had such a strange influence
over my life.' See 'Letters of Oscar Wilde' (1962), ed.
Rupert Hart-Davis, 471. Their cordial relations may have
been dampened by Pater's unsympathetic review of 'The
Picture of Dorian Gray' (1891) in the 'Bookman' (November
1891), i, 59-60. It is widely believed that Pater regarded
Wilde as one of the 'young men' misled by the Conclusion to
'The Renaissance'.
    The review is an apprentice piece and shows Wilde in the
role of a conventional reviewer with little hint of his
characteristic later style.

To convey ideas through the medium of images has always
been the aim of those who are artists as well as thinkers
in literature, and it is to a desire to give a sensuous
environment to intellectual concepts that we owe Mr Pater's
last volume. For these Imaginary, or, as we would prefer
to call them, Imaginative Portraits of his, form a series
of philosophic studies, in which the philosophy is tempered by personality, and the thought shown under varying
conditions of mood and manner, the very permanence of each
principle gaining something from the change and colour of
the life through which it finds expression. The most fascinating of all these pictures is undoubtedly that of
Sebastian Van Storck. The account of Watteau is perhaps
a little too fanciful, and the description of him as one
who was 'always a seeker after something in the world that
is there in no satisfying measure, or not at all', seems
to us more applicable to him who saw Monna Lisa sitting
among the rocks than to the gay and debonnair *peintre des
fêtes galantes*.(1) But Sebastian, the grave young Dutch
philosopher, is charmingly drawn. From the first glimpse
we get of him, skating over the watermeadows with his plume
of squirrel's tail and his fur muff, in all the modest
pleasantness of boyhood, down to his strange death in the
desolate house amid the sands of the Helder, we seem to
see him, to know him, almost to hear the low music of his
voice. He is a dreamer, as the common phrase goes, and
yet he is practical in this sense, that his theorems shape
life for him, directly. Early in youth he is stirred by a
fine saying of Spinoza, and sets himself to realize the
ideal of an intellectual disinterestedness, separating
himself more and more from the transient world of sensation, accident, and even affection, till what is finite
and relative becomes of no interest to him, and he feels
that as Nature is but a thought of his, so he himself is
but a passing thought of God. This conception, of the
power of a mere metaphysical abstraction over the mind of
one so fortunately endowed for the reception of the sensible world, is exceedingly delightful, and Mr Pater has
never written a more subtle psychological study, the fact
that Sebastian dies in an attempt to save the life of a
little child giving to the whole story a touch of poignant
pathos and sad irony.
  Denys L'Auxerrois is suggested by a figure found, or
said to be found, on some old tapestries at Auxerre, the
figure of 'a flaxen and flowery creature, sometimes well-
nigh naked among the vine-leaves, sometimes muffled in
skins against the cold, sometimes in the dress of a monk',
but always with a strong impress of real character and
incident from the veritable streets of the town itself.

From this strange design Mr Pater has fashioned a curious
medieval myth of the return of Dionysus among men, a myth
steeped in colour and passion and old romance, full of
wonder and full of worship, Denys himself being half animal and half god, making the whole world mad with a new
ecstasy of living, stirring the artists simply by his
visible presence, drawing the marvel of music from reed
and pipe, and slain at last in a stage play by those who
had loved him. In its rich affluence of imagery this
story is like a picture by Mantegna, and indeed Mantegna
might have suggested the description of the pageant in
which Denys rides upon a gaily-painted chariot, in soft
silken raiment and, for head dress, a strange elephant
scalp with gilded tusks.

If Denys L'Auxerrois symbolizes the passion of the
senses, and Sebastian Van Storck the philosophic passion,
as they certainly seem to do, though no mere formula or
definition can adequately express the freedom and variety
of the life that they portray, the passion for the imaginative world of art is the basis of the story of Duke Carl
of Rosenmold. Duke Carl is not unlike the late King of
Bavaria, in his love of France, his admiration for the
Grand Monarque, and his fantastic desire to amaze and to
bewilder, but the resemblance is possibly only a chance
one. In fact Mr Pater's young hero is the precursor of
the *Aufklärung*(2) of the last century, the German precursor
of Herder, and Lessing, and Goethe himself, and finds the
forms of art ready to his hand without any national spirit
to fill them, or make them vital and responsive. He too
dies, trampled to death by the soldiers of the country he
so much admired, on the night of his marriage with a peasant girl, the very failure of his life lending him a certain melancholy grace and dramatic interest.

On the whole, then, this is a singularly attractive book.
Mr Pater is an intellectual impressionist. He does not
weary us with any definite doctrine, or seek to suit life
to any formal creed. He is always looking for exquisite
moments, and, when he has found them, he analyzes them
with delicate and delightful art, and then passes on, often
to the opposite pole of thought or feeling, knowing that
every mood has its own quality and charm, and is justified
by its mere existence. He has taken the sensationalism of
Greek philosophy, and made it a new method of art criticism.
As for his style, it is curiously ascetic. Now and then we
come across phrases with a strange sensuousness of expression, as when he tells us how Denys L'Auxerrois, on his return from a long journey, 'ate flesh for the first time,
tearing the hot, red morsels with his delicate fingers in
a kind of wild greed', but such passages are rare.

Asceticism is the keynote of Mr Pater's prose; at times it
is almost too severe in its self-control, and makes us long
for a little more freedom. For indeed, the danger of such
prose as his is that it is apt to become somewhat laborious.
Here and there one is tempted to say of Mr Pater that he is
'a seeker after something in language that is there in no
satisfying measure, or not at all'. The continual preoccu-
pation with phrase and epithet has its drawbacks as well as
its virtues. And yet, when all is said, what wonderful
prose it is, with its subtle preferences, its fastidious
purity, its rejection of what is common or ordinary! Mr
Pater has the true spirit of selection, the true tact of
omission. If he be not among the greatest prose-writers of
our literature he is at least our greatest artist in prose;
and though it may be admitted that the best style is that
which seems an unconscious result rather than a conscious
aim, still in these latter days, when violent rhetoric does
duty for eloquence, and vulgarity usurps the name of nature, we should be grateful for a style that deliberately
aims at perfection of form, that seeks to produce its
effect by artistic means, and that sets before itself an
ideal of grave and chastened beauty.

Notes

1 Painter of 'gay entertainments'.
2 Enlightenment.

32. LADY DILKE, UNSIGNED REVIEW, 'ATHENAEUM'

25 June 1887, 824-5

See No. 6 and Introduction, pp.28-9.Significant for its recognition of the autobiographical impulse in Pater's writings (compare No. 23) and its warmer response.

In Mr Pater's volume of 'Imaginary Portraits' his eclectic
philosophy of sensation has once more been turned to account in a fashion intensely personal and attractive. 'Marius the Epicurean' demonstrated the absence in the author
of that dramatic instinct which can create and vivify

various conceptions of character. The deepest interest of
that graceful story arose not from the portrayal of some
imagined Marius, but from the picture given of what Mr
Pater thought he himself would have been like had he started life under the same conditions as his Latin double.
'Marius the Epicurean' was, we repeat, a vision of Mr
Pater by himself — a subjective analysis of that which he
would have been and felt and thought had he lived in the
crisis of the great transition from old things to new — a
dream abruptly broken, inconsequent, incomplete, but lovely
in its very inefficiency, in its purposeless phases and
hasty end. And here, again, in other 'imaginary portraits',
we have other presentments of Mr Pater's self, now masquerading delicately in the flowered sacque of Watteau's girl
friend (for of Watteau himself there is no image); now
greedily gallant in the joy of life as Denys l'Auxerrois —
type of that after-living of the classic day into the Middle
Age which carried with it an atmosphere of witchery, rousing
ultimate suspicion and wrath in the Christian witnesses of
its irresistible charm; now enamoured of a high and stain-
less learning as the comely young Dutch philosopher Sebastian van Storck, and again demanding a combination of the
choicest pleasures of taste and fancy and experience in the
person of Duke Carl of Rosenmold.

Each of these images of himself which Mr Pater sees in
the mirror of past days trembles, breaks up, disappears
abruptly! No gentle fading, no even passing onwards to
conclusion and some final accomplishment of fate; as soon
as he catches sight of the state of mind which would have
been born in him of life in such or such an hour he drops
the glass. It is enough! Now the very incompleteness of
these portraits, or rather that which would be incompleteness if we had to look on them as portrayals of any others
than Mr Pater himself, adds to the reality of their char-
acterization as pictures of states of his own mind, and increases the interest with which we read in them moods of
the inmost soul of one amongst ourselves, and one of no
mean order — moods in which are rendered some of the most
interesting currents of the thought of the day.

The consciousness of the wider training and further outlook which fall to the lot of us, the heirs of all the ages,
if it has bred in the coarser fibres a brutal certainty of
judgment and light of appraisement of all things not to be
measured by the yard of sense, has engendered in minds of
a different mould a great hesitancy, due to the very vast-
ness of their inherited possessions — a hesitancy which
seems to paralyze the happy putting forth of their powers
in an hour which lacks that simplicity of affirmation and
denial necessary to work out its issues in matters other

than practical. Such as these, therefore, retire on themselves and on the stored riches of the past — these at least they may enjoy; but here, too, the problem of life seems insoluble. So Marius and Sebastian pass away in the hour of their blossoming, and the girl in her journal declares that her friend has sought in life that which is not there, and the golden age returns with Denys only to find the world afraid to take its share in it, and the new gospel of revolution sweeps Duke Carl before it in the hour of his pleasure. Thus in every page the answer to the unspoken question is evaded, and it is because on this point, as on many others, we find in these pages the reflection of one of the most intellectual phases of the modern mind, that Mr Pater's 'Imaginary Portraits' should be read by all lovers of psychological problems, and not only by those who value him for the pleasantness and choiceness of his language.

33. E. PRICE, UNSIGNED REVIEW, 'SPECTATOR'

16 July 1887, 1x, 966-7

See Introduction, pp. 27-9.
    Probably by Eleanor Catharine Price, the novelist who appears in the British Museum Catalogue and also in the 'Literary Yearbook' for 1916, 1920 and 1922. She published many books, including 'Only One' (1874), 'In the Lion's Mouth' (1894), 'The Queen's Man' (1905) and 'Cardinal de Richelieu' (1912).

In reading or reviewing a book of Mr Pater's, it is well to bear in mind Mr Pater's own definition of the aim of aesthetic criticism, with one of the objects of which, 'artistic and accomplished forms of human life', this new book deals:

[Quotes the Preface to 'The Renaissance': 'The aesthetic critic, then, regards all the objects' to 'this special impression of beauty or pleasure'.]

In these books, then, with their wonderful charm of style, and often of thought too, we are to look for impressions, not convictions. The aesthetic heathenism of 'Studies in

the Renaissance', with all its so-called Hellenism, its
'exquisite faintness', its 'worship of the body', its
'morality which is all sympathy', and so forth, is hardly
to be found, it is true, in the grave dignity of 'Marius';
and the signs of it in 'Imaginary Portraits' are few and
far between. Mr Pater's 'impressions' have become more
natural, more honest, and have almost entirely lost what
one might have called their affectation. His style is
always beautiful in its quietness; his colours, faint as
ever, are clearer and purer than of old; we can now read
his books without longing to dash cold water over them and
ourselves, and to call Dr Johnson to the rescue.

On the whole, 'Imaginary Portraits', though not equal
to 'Marius' in power and charm, will certainly not dis-
credit Mr Pater's name as a writer and a critic. The 'portraits' are four in number, and it does not seem at first
as if they could all lay claim to being imaginary, for the
first name on the list is Watteau. We are not able to discover that the other three originals of these 'portraits'
ever really existed; they seem to be types; and in the
illustration of these, many meanings and fancies are suggested, more than a reviewer can venture to attempt finding out.

The portrait of A Prince of Court Painters is painted,
and most exquisitely, in the journal of a woman of his
native town, Valenciennes, whose hopeless, lifelong affection for him is tenderly touched, for she paints her own
portrait as well as that of Antony Watteau. The few facts
known of Watteau's life are expanded into this beautiful
sketch, which to us has more charm, though perhaps less
power, than any other in the book. The 'dark-haired
youth', with 'large, unquiet eyes', goes away to seek his
fortune in Paris in 1702, leaving his old father and mother
in their dull stone house. Often, in the following years,
he comes back to Valenciennes, and this friend of his
youth, the daughter of the sculptor who encouraged his
early taste for art, keeps a sort of journal of his advance, his ambitions, his achievements. The new manner of
painting puzzles her very much, till in one of Antony's
visits he 'has taken it into his kind head to paint and
decorate our chief *salon*'. And then the old, dark, heavy
room becomes dainty, aerial, pale-rose, four spaces of it
to be filled with 'fantasies' of the Four Seasons. New
arm-chairs of Antony's devising are to come from Paris:

> Our old silver candlesticks look well on the chimney-
> piece. Odd, faint-coloured flowers fill coquettishly
> the little empty spaces here and there, like ghosts of
> nosegays left by visitors long ago, which paled thus,

sympathetically, at the decease of their old owners....
He has completed the ovals — the Four Seasons. Oh!
the summer-like grace, the freedom and softness of the
'Summer', — a hayfield such as we visited to-day, but
boundless, and with touches of level Italian architecture in the hot, white, elusive distance, and wreaths
of flowers, fairy hayrakes and the like, suspended from
tree to tree, with that wonderful lightness which is
one of the charms of his work. I can understand
through this, at last, what it is he enjoys, what he
selects by preference from all that various world we
pass our lives in.

As time goes on, with a sad heart, Antony's friend understands him and his work better and better. He is restless,
melancholy, scornful, discontented, in the midst of all
his fashion and fame; yet these things are necessary, they
are everything to him. Her own poor likeness which he began, he leaves unfinished; yet she finds some satisfaction in a theory of her own, that Antony 'paints that
delicate life of Paris so excellently, with so much spirit,
partly because, after all, he looks down upon it or despises it'. All the journal is equally charming; and one
almost feels like a barbarian in suggesting that no French-
woman of 1717 would have been capable of it. Such prophet
criticism as this, for instance:

> And at last one has actual sight of his work — what
> it is. He has brought with him certain long-cherished
> designs to finish here in quiet, as he protests he has
> never finished before. That charming *noblesse*, — can
> it be really so distinguished to the minutest point, so
> naturally aristocratic? Half in masquerade, playing
> the drawing-room or garden comedy of life, these per-
> sons have upon them, not less than the landscape he
> composes, and among the accidents of which they group
> themselves with such a perfect fittingness, a certain
> light we should seek for in vain upon anything real.
> For their framework they have around them a veritable
> architecture — a tree architecture — of which those
> moss-grown balusters, *termes*, statues, fountains, are
> really but accessories. Only, as I gaze upon those
> windless afternoons, I find myself always saying to
> myself involuntarily, 'The evening will be a wet one.'
> The storm is always brooding through the massy splen-
> dour of the trees, above those sun-dried glades or
> lawns, where delicate children may be trusted thinly
> clad; and the secular trees themselves will hardly
> outlast another generation.

Denys l'Auxerrois is the most striking of these pictures; the most characteristic, the most adorned with
touches in Mr Pater's own peculiar style. He is here on
his favourite Renaissance ground; but it is the early
Renaissance of the thirteenth century, of which he has already written in his earlier essay on Aucassin and Nicolette. Denys, the strange, unearthly being, flashes into
the solemn life of old Auxerre like an incarnation of some
long-forgotten pagan deity, — Dionysus, we guess from his
name, from the great vintage of the time, from the discovery of the Roman wine-flask, which seems to begin a
sort of golden age at Auxerre. He takes the part of the
Wine-God, too, in a morality acted in the Cathedral square.
'A flaxen and flowery creature', he leads the youth of
Auxerre into this new golden age of theirs. There are a
few wonderful years of luxuriant fruits and flowers and
perpetual summer, during which Denys, unaccountable, mysterious, often disappearing, is known as an unrivalled
gardener,

> keeping a stall in the great Cathedral square for the
> sale of melons and pomegranates, all manner of seeds
> and flowers, honey also, wax tapers, sweetmeats hot
> from the frying-pan, rough home-made pots and pans from
> the little pottery in the wood, loaves baked by the
> aged woman in whose house he lived.... He had lived on
> spring water and fruit.... It was on his sudden return
> after a long journey ... that he ate flesh for the
> first time, tearing the hot, red morsels with his deli-
> cate fingers in a sort of wild greed.

We quote this last as a characteristic touch; the sensation
or impression that it produces, is perhaps not exactly pleasurable! Also the list of things that Denys brings back to
his stall from that long journey, — 'Seeds of marvellous
new flowers, creatures wild and tame, new pottery painted in
raw gaudy tints, the skins of animals, meats fried with un-
heard-of condiments.' On the whole, it is a remarkable al-
legory, more striking in this way, possibly, than the author
meant. Nothing but weariness and disgust comes of it all;
the gold becomes dim, frost and sunless days return; 'mysterious, dark rains prevailed throughout the summer'. Denys,
suspected of witchcraft, takes refuge with the monks St
Germain, works at the unfinished cathedral, invents and
builds an organ. Then comes the tragic close, proving, let
us hope, that the reign of pagan gods on the earth is over.
Whether Denys has really left traces of himself in stained
glass and old tapestries at Auxerre, is a question we cannot answer; we have no clue to where imagination ends, and
fact begins.

Sebastian van Storck is a young Dutch philosopher of
the seventeenth century, whose portrait Van Ostade(1) is
supposed to have painted as a boy. Most people will
think Sebastian less interesting than any of his three
companions; still, in the telling of his story, there is
a power of a very remarkable kind. It is in what one may
call Mr Pater's later manner, the manner of the philosophical part of 'Marius'. Sebastian is a sort of hero, his
life is a kind of sacrifice; only, like other creatures
without passion or affection, he is quite as ready to
sacrifice others as himself. Cold, stoic, ungracious, entirely intellectual, it is yet no surprise that he gave up
his life to save the life of a child; and this although,
'making the Infinite his beginning and his end, Sebastian
had come to think all definite forms of being, the warm
pressure of life, the cry of humanity itself, no more than
a troublesome irritation of the surface of the one absolute mind, a passing vexatious thought or uneasy dream
there, at its height of petulant importunity in the eager
human creature'. Sebastian is, of course, a type of the
intellectual movement in Holland at that time, soon after
her struggle with Spain, a movement coloured by the nature
of her people and the character of her landscape.
    Duke Carl of Rosenmold is a figure standing in the Ger-
man dawn of the early eighteenth century, one of those
fore-runners whom Goethe recognised, 'and understood that
there had been a thousand others, looking forward to a new
era in German literature with the desire which is in some
sort a "forecast of capacity", awakening each other to the
permanent reality of a poetic ideal in human life, slowly
forming that public consciousness to which Goethe actually
addressed himself'. To us, Carl, bringing his 'Apolline
Aurora' to Rosenmold in the French fashion of the day,
with Dresden china and yellow satin, a 'rococo seventeenth-
century imitation of the true Renaissance', is the least
attractive and least interesting portrait of the four; yet
there is a great deal of curious originality in the sad
story of the young Duke.
    The book leaves upon our mind a vague sensation of
pleasure, and a stronger sensation of a very great want.
These 'portraits' have no background. There is not even
a curtain between them and the infinite dreariness of
space, without hope and without religion. From its very
quietness, which makes it so great an advance on 'The Renaissance', it is the saddest book that Mr Pater has yet
written.

Note

1 Adriaen van Ostade (1610-84), the Dutch painter, painted
  almost every subject except marine pictures. His favourite subjects include smoking dens, taverns in which low
  types, aroused by wine and food, freely indulge in sensual pleasure.

34. G.E. WOODBERRY, UNSIGNED REVIEW, 'NATION'

28 July 1887, xlv, 78-9

See No. 26 and Introduction, pp. 27 and 28.

The four studies that make up this volume portray rather
the times in which the scene of them is laid than the individuals who figure in them. In fact, they present certain
historical phases of culture, moods of the human spirit.
That subtle appreciation and the infinite number of small
touches in the rendering of what he sees, which lie at the
heart of Mr Pater's literary individuality and give to his
style its extraordinary distinction, lift the book out of
the range of the common, and set it apart as unique with
his other work, to the refined thoughtfulness of which we
have heretofore endeavored to do some justice. But it does
not in all respects reach the level of that stronger and
richer, though not more elaborated, work; and the four
studies, as between themselves, have very different degrees
of success. One of them deals with the French taste of the
early eighteenth century and the personal relation of
Antony Watteau to it; a second sets forth the Bacchic and
grotesque and physically morbid aspects of mediaevalism at
the first gleam of the Renaissance in a kind of moral fable
of one Denys L'Auxerrois — a literary attempt at a new
Donatello,(1) and not so far below Hawthorne's as to fall
into the incredible or the absurd; the third brings together in the person and circumstances of Sebastian Van
Storck the curious contrast developed in the Low Countries
of Spinozism with Dutch burgomasters' wives, the genre
painters, and the practical struggle inch by inch for the
ground to stand on; the fourth pictures in Duke Carl of
Rosenmold a predecessor of Goethe in the passion for an

illumination of Germany, much — to compare great things
with small — as Browning found in Sordello a predecessor
of Dante. These four points in the history of culture are
all interesting, with fine backgrounds of color and of
thought, and such as one would call 'subjects made to his
hand', were it not that Pater in a sense always creates
his subject.

The first of these is so much the most highly finished
and clearly made out as to leave the others far behind.
It is in the main a criticism on Antony Watteau, told by
means of extracts from the journal of a woman who knew and
loved him from the opening of his genius, and in whose
family he received his encouragement; but it is directly
a criticism of Watteau's temperament rather than his works,
and indirectly a view of the whole real meaning of that
age as seen through art. It is all very simple, however.
Only two lights are thrown on the painter — one, which
shows him ironically indifferent to the luminous gayety in
depicting which he was so easily master; the other, which
reveals the impatient jealousy of genius in the presence
of that talent which by industry comes so nigh to the same
perfection. There is praise enough of his works — excellent, discriminating, definite praise. The sum of his
doings Pater gives apparently in this extract:

[Quotes A Prince of Court Painters: 'Himself really of the
old time' to 'the height of a Corneille'.]

Perhaps it is too much to ask that criticism so subtle
as this should be accepted; it is almost too perfectly
plausible. But it is enough if it be understood. One
cannot condense Pater's work, however, or give impression
of its structural completeness, of its endless charm of
detail, by bringing the traditional brick in the shape of
a paragraph. Of the minor touches, nevertheless, let us
spare space to mention the beautiful old age of Monseigneur
le Prince de Cambrai, seen by a sidelight of the narrative,
the most dramatic vividness of the chance introduction of
the story of 'Manon Lescaut',(2) then a new book, the imaginative pathos of the incident of the bird lost among the
cathedral arches where it will beat its life out helplessly,
and the glimpse of the Revolution to come which he affords
us when, looking on some of Watteau's designs, the writer
says:

Only as I gaze upon those windless afternoons I find
myself always saying to myself involuntarily, 'The
evening will be a wet one.' The storm is always brooding through the massy splendor of the trees, above

those sun-dried glades or lawns where delicate children
may be trusted thinly clad;   and the secular trees themselves will hardly outlast another generation.

None of the remaining three studies approach measurably
near this of Watteau either in power or subtlety or purity.
The new Donatello, as we named him above, or Denys L'Auxerrois, as Pater calls him, is a child of nature whose being
gradually passes under the cloud of humanity, whose
achievement is the building of the first organ, and whose
death is a kind of martyrdom, a being torn limb from limb
by the populace, who have perceived and come to fear and
hate the daimonic power in his genius.   The legend is perhaps too obviously managed, and too much is crowded into
it for a single impersonation.   The opening landscape is
possibly the best of it.
    So, in the next study (the contrast of the Low Dutch
life with Spinozism in Sebastian Van Storck, who 'abne-
gates' the fat and homely comforts, and endeavors to put
himself in the way of absorption into the absolute), the
landscape is the one thing successfully treated — 'the
standing force of pathos' existing in the very conditions
of life where man is 'like a navigator when the sea was
risen, like a shipwrecked mariner when it was retired'.
And that this was true so long ago as Pliny's time seems
to cast a deeper misery upon the land.   In the personal
part of the story and in the thought history of it, the
author is out of his own field.   The heavy grossness of
the circumstances and the incongruousness of the intellectual parts with the scene are too difficult matters for
his hand — in the mass at least, for there are felicities
in the detail.
    In the last study, likewise, one finds lack of that sub-
stance in the midst of picturesqueness to which Pater has
accustomed us, and the picturesqueness itself is of a somewhat rubbishy kind.   The time was rubbishy, possibly the
author would say in comment on the criticism;   and it is of
interest to observe that he sets up a defence for those
poor people who go into raptures and enthusiasms over
third-rate things:

The higher informing capacity, if it exist within, will
mould an unpromising matter to it itself;   will realize
itself by selection and the preference of the better
in what is bad or indifferent, asserting its prerogative
under the most unlikely conditions.

Carl, he says, made 'a really heroic effort of mind at a
disadvantage', and put into his enthusiasm for Louis XIV

and the aesthetic achievements of that age what young
France had felt for Francis I and Da Vinci. This is of
great comfort to the aesthetic class that has no access to
the best and greatest, yet must feel strongly. To us,
unfortunately, the essay in which it occurs seems to belong to the grade of Louis XIV rather than of Francis I,
and too clearly within hailing distance of Pater's feminine disciple, Vernon Lee.(3) When a man's best is as
good as Pater's *noblesse oblige* — he must keep to it.

Notes

1 Donatello is a character in Nathaniel Hawthorne's allegorical romance, 'The Marble Faun' (1860), which was
  issued in England under the title of 'Transformation'.
2 A famous novel by Abbé Prévost, published in 1731.
3 See No. 66.

35.   ARTHUR SYMONS, SIGNED REVIEW, 'TIME'

August 1887, n.s. vi, 157-62

See Nos 42, 58 and 94 and Introduction, pp. 28 and 29.
   Arthur Symons (1865-1945), poet, translator and major
critic, was the spokesman for the Decadent Movement (see
No. 58) and the chief interpreter of the French Symbolists.
He was a member of the Rhymers' Club; contributor to the
'Yellow Book'; editor of the 'Savoy'; and author of several volumes of verse, in addition to the influential book
on 'The Symbolist Movement in Literature' (1899).
   As a young man Symons idolised Pater and was delighted
to discover the latter's favourable review of his first
book, 'An Introduction to the Study of Browning' (1886),
in the 'Guardian' (9 November 1887). See EG, 41-51. They
met in London on 7 August 1888, after almost two years'
correspondence. Symons overcame Pater's native reserve
and the two were close friends until about two years before
Pater's death. In Symons Pater found a genuine disciple
and he used his influence with Macmillan & Company to publish 'Days and Nights' (1889), which is dedicated 'To
Walter Pater in all gratitude'. Symons expressed his admiration for Pater in a number of reminiscent articles,
some of which were collected in 'A Study of Walter Pater'
(1932).

This review is an enthusiastic defence of Pater's prose style and a perceptive assessment of 'Imaginary Portraits'. Symons replies to the common criticism that Pater had not made his characters 'come alive' (see No. 32).   On 9 August 1887 Pater wrote to Symons:

> Accept my sincere thanks for ... so kindly sending me your article in 'Time', which I have read carefully and on the whole with much pleasure. It strikes me as the work of a really critical mind and a well-skilled pen, and I feel grateful for it. (LWP, 75)

For it is with the delicacies of fine literature espe-cially, its gradations of expression, its fine judgment, its pure sense of words, of vocabulary, — things, alas! dying out in the English literature of the present, to-gether with the appreciation of them in our literature of the past, — that his literary mission is chiefly concerned.(1)

These words, applied by Mr Pater to Charles Lamb, might very reasonably be spoken of Mr Pater himself. His care has always been of the 'delicacies of fine literature', alike in others and himself. As a critic, in that unique volume of 'Studies in the Renaissance', and in the scattered essays on poets and painters, he has selected for analysis only those types of artistic character in which 'delicacy', an exquisite fineness, is the prevailing feature; or if, as with Michel Angelo, he has been drawn towards some more rugged personality, some more massive, less finished art, it has been less from sym-pathy with these more obvious qualities of ruggedness and strength, than because he has divined the sweetness lying at the heart of the strength - *ex forti dulcedo*.(2) Leonardo da Vinci, Charles Lamb, Joachim du Bellay, Giorgione: in every one something not merely frank and broad, a large straight-forward talent, but in one direction or another a refinement upon refinement, a choice and exotic exquisiteness, a subtle and *recherché*(3) beauty; something which it requires an ef-fort to disengage, and which appeals for its perfect appre-ciation to a public within the public, — people who take their aesthetic pleasures consciously, deliberately, criti-cally, as amateurs take their wine. And not as a critic only, judging others, but in his own person as a writer, both of critical and of imaginative work, Mr Pater shows his preoccu-pation with the 'delicacies of fine literature'. He expends as much labour over his prose as Lord Tennyson gives to his poetry. Nothing is left to inspiration; like Baudelaire, he would better nature; and he would certainly reject a 'fine careless rapture', if one came to him. It is all goldsmith's work as he has told us; mosaic-work, we might say for a

change; and he has wrought in the spirit of the craftsmen
of olden days, with laborious delight.
    The development of Mr Pater's style is interesting to
observe. The 'Studies', though written at different periods, tend towards one ideal, and are the product, mentally,
of a single period. Taken on its own formal merits, that
book is the most beautiful book of prose in our literature.
It is a book to be read, as Lamb or Shelley speaks somewhere
of doing, with 'shouts of delight'; or perhaps rather with
a delight silent and continuous, for it is all finished and
perfect, and it rings everywhere flawless as a bell. From
beginning to end there is not a hasty sentence, a cadence
not considered, not prepared, a word thrown on the page at
random. Anything like eloquence, anything of rhetoric or
display, is not to be found in it. Like Baudelaire, Mr
Pater has '*rêvé le miracle d'une prose poétique, musicale
sans rhythme et sans rime*';(4) and, like Baudelaire, he has
affected his miracle without any violent aids or thefts
from the proper domain to poetry. An almost oppressive
quiet — a quietness which seems to breathe of an atmosphere heavy with tropical flowers — broods over these
pages; a subdued light shadows them; they depend for
their charm on no contrasts, epigrams, paradoxes, sudden
twists and turns, thunder-claps, summersaults of diction,
lyric raptures. The most felicitous touches come we know
not whence — 'a breath, a flame in the doorway, a feather
in the wind', — effects produced by the cunning employment of the simplest words, words which take suddenly a
new colour and sound, and reveal undreamt-of properties.
In this book of the 'Studies', prose seemed to have conquered a new province. So difficult is it, however, to
avoid the defects of our qualities, that it was feared
lest Mr Pater's mastery over colour and sound in words
should lead him too far; lest, as it has been cruelly
said, he should 'swoon by the way over the subtle perfumes
he has evoked'. And perhaps some of the essays, wonderfully beautiful as they are, which followed the publication of that volume, might have seemed a little to confirm
the fear. But when at last, after twelve years, I think,
Mr Pater's second work appeared, it was found, probably to
the surprise of many people, that alike in style and in
thought the progress had been, not in the direction of
licence, of over-sumptuous richness, but towards a somewhat chill asceticism, a restraint sometimes almost painful. The goldsmith, adding more value, as he thought, for
every trace of gold that he removed, might seem to some to
have scraped a little too assiduously. And in this third
book, coming after an interval of only three years, we find
the same self-restraint, perhaps grown still more fastidious,

and the same self-conscious artistry that has ruled from
the first.

Writers who have paid particular attention to style have
often been accused of caring little *what* they say, knowing
how beautifully they can say anything. The accusation has
generally been unjust, though the writers themselves have
frequently given occasion to it by speaking rashly on the
subject. The merit more than any other which distinguishes
Mr Pater's prose, though it is not the merit most on the
surface, is the attention to, and perfection of, the *ensemble*. Under the soft and musical phrases an inexorable
chain of logic hides itself, sometimes only too well. Link
is added silently but faultlessly to link; the argument
marches, carrying you with it, while you fancy you are only
listening to the music with which it keeps step. You can
take an essay to pieces, and you will find that it is constructed with mathematical precision; every piece can be
taken out and replaced in order. I do not know any contemporary writer who observes the logical requirements so
scrupulously, who conducts an argument so steadily from
deliberate point to point   towards a determined goal. And
what I have said about the essays may be applied, with
slight changes, to the imaginative work — to 'Marius the
Epicurean', and to these 'Imaginary Portraits'. With the
construction of 'Marius', when viewed as a whole, I do not
know that it is possible to be quite satisfied; it is too
much a mere sequence of scenes and of moods; but certainly
each of these many sections has an admirable *ensemble* of
its own. The 'Imaginary Portraits', much shorter, are
placed, arranged, developed with an art which of its kind
is quite flawless; I am not sure that they do not show Mr
Pater's combined imaginative and artistic faculties at
their point of most perfect fusion.

The term Portrait is very happily given to these four
studies in narrative form. Not merely is each a portrait,
in the looser sense of the term, of a single soul, but it
is a *portrait*, in the literal sense, a picture painted with
a brush. So microscopic a brush only a Meissonnier(5) could
wield. The touches which go to form the portrait are so
fine that it is difficult to see quite how much they do
and mean, until, the end being reached, the whole picture
starts out before you. The result of Mr Pater's method is
so charming that we have no right, I think, to complain that
he gives us just, and only, what he does. At the same time
it is quite obvious that neither Watteau, nor Denys, nor
Sebastian, nor Duke Carl really lives, in so much as a
finger-tip, with actual imaginative life; they are all
ghosts, names, puppets of an artist and a philosopher who
has evoked or constructed them for his purpose, but has not

been able, or has not wished, to endow them with flesh
and blood, with the breath of life. 'Mr Pater thinks only
with the front of his brain,' said one day a lady who has
written the most profoundly *human* book that has come into
our literature for many years; and the criticism implied
in the phrase is perfectly just. He has indeed an almost
complete lack of passion, of emotion, of any directly
humanising instinct; at least he admits nothing of the
kind in his work, or only in so faint a form that it never
gets so far as our hearts; and there can be no doubt, I
suppose, that the greatest literature, other things being
equal, is that which represents the most of 'life immense
in passion, pulse, and power'. But putting aside the
Shakespeares and Michel Angelos, there is exquisite delight to be obtained, no doubt on a much lower plane, from
the Gautiers and Albert Moores — serene artists who seek
only beauty, and to whom any emotional disturbance is a
mere distraction and a trouble. I do not think we have
any right to turn from these men, to be dissatisfied with
what they give us; for the aim they have reached at and
attained is a perfectly legitimate one, and we show ourselves narrow, *borné*, if we refuse to see it.

   Mr Pater, then, has not given in these four portraits,
any more than in 'Marius the Epicurean', proof that he
possesses the genuine dramatic power of creating characters which shall live and move and have a being independent
of their creator; at the same time he cannot be said to
have fallen short in his aim, for it is not this precisely
that he has tried to do. What he has done, and what he has
doubtless intended to do, is to give a concrete form to
abstract ideas; to represent certain types of character,
to trace certain developments, in the picturesque and attractive way of narrative. Each, also, with perhaps one
exception, is the study of a soul, or rather of a consciousness; such a study as one might make, granted certain gifts and cultures, by simply looking within, and pro-
jecting now this now that side of oneself on an exterior
plane. I do not mean to say that I attribute the philosophical theories of Sebastian van Storck, or the artistic
ideals of Duke Carl of Rosenmold, to Mr Pater himself. I
only mean that the attitude of mind, the outlook, in the
most general sense, is always limited and directed in a
certain way, giving one always the picture of a delicate,
subtle, aspiring, unsatisfied personality, open to all
impressions, living chiefly by sensations, little anxious
to reap any or much of the rich harvest of its intangible
but keenly possessed gains; a personality withdrawn from
action, which it despises or dreads, solitary with its
ideals, in the circle of its 'exquisite moments', in the

Palace of Art, where it is never quite at rest. It is
somewhat such a soul, I have thought, as that which
Browning has traced in 'Sordello'; indeed, when reading
'Marius the Epicurean', I was struck with a certain resemblance between those two exquisite books, and a little of
the same feeling comes up again when reading some of the
'Imaginary Portraits'. Had that other Imaginary Portrait,
The Child in the House, published nine years ago in 'Macmillan's Magazine', appeared, as we had every reason to
suppose it would, in company with the four later portraits,
the likeness would have again been apparent, for the childhood of Florian Deleal in the old house with its wonderful
garden, carries us back, almost unconsciously, to the childhood of that other imaginative boy in the castle and gardens
of Goito.

Personally, for one deals here only in impressions, it
seems to me that the most wonderful of the four portraits
in this new book is the poem, for it is really a poem,
named Denys l'Auxerrois. This is not the study of a soul,
it is the study of a myth — a translation, in which one
hardly knows whether most to admire the learning, the ingenuity, or the real imagination, of the strangest myth of
the Greeks, that 'Pagan after-thought' of Dionysus Zagreus,
into the conditions of mediaeval life. It is a poem in
prose, and in prose so coloured, so modulated, that one can
scarcely feel as if the rhythm of actual metre could add to
its charm. And what a variety of every sort of poetic
richness does it contain! It has even the *suggestiveness*
of poetry, that most volatile and unseizable property, of
which prose has so rarely been able to possess itself. And
all this without any sort of approach to that rhapsodic
manner which mimicks the cadences of verse without becoming verse, and is neither verse nor prose, but a hateful
and impotent hermaphrodite. The style of Denys l'Auxerrois has a subdued heat and veiled richness of colour,
which contrasts very strikingly with the silvery-grey coolness of A Prince of Court Painters, the chill, more leaden
grey of Sebastian van Storck, though it has a certain affinity, perhaps, with the more variously-tinted canvas of
Duke Carl of Rosenmold. Watteau, Sebastian, Carl — unsatisfied seekers, all of them, this after an artistic ideal
of impossible perfection, that after a chill and barren
ideal of philosophic thinking and living, that other after
yet another ideal, unattainable to him in his period, of
life '*im Ganzen, Guten, Schönen*',(6) a beautiful and effective culture. The story of each is a tragedy, ending in
every case with an actual physical severance of bodily
existence, always with some subtly ironic effect, as if
Fate 'struck them gracefully, cutting off their young

histories with a catastrophic dash'. The mirror is held
up to Watteau while he struggles desperately or vaguely
forward, snatching now this now that closely-held secret
of art; then, with a stroke, it is broken, and he sinks
out of sight, into a narrow grave of mere red earth. The
mirror is held up to Sebastian as he moves deliberately,
coldly onward in the midst of a warm life which has so
little attraction for him, freeing himself one by one from
all the obstructions to a clear philosophic equilibrium;
and the mirror is broken, with a like suddenness, and the
seeker disappears from our sight — to find, perhaps,
what he has sought. It is held up to Duke Carl, the seeker
after the satisfying things of art and experience, the dilettante in material and spiritual enjoyment, the experi-
menter on life; and again it is broken, with an almost
terrifying shock, just as he is come to a certain rash
crisis — is it a step upward or downward? a step certainly
towards the concrete, towards a possible material felicity;
and Duke Carl disappears obscurely, with his beggar-queen,
under the hoofs of an indifferent army, crushing him out in
the dark like a mere worm or beetle.

   Just so, it will be remembered, was Marius left at the
end of the beautiful book of his sensations and ideas;
dying ambiguously, half, or altogether, or not at all a
Christian, and buried by humble people with Christian
rites, as a martyr: 'for martyrdom, as the Church had
always said, was a kind of sacrament with plenary grace'.
Just so we take leave of the child Florian, at the crisis
of a great change, with his foot on the long road leading who knows whitherward? It is evident that to Mr Pater
there is a particular charm in this abrupt finish, this
sudden displacement and descent, as through one of those
oubliettes(7) of the Middle Ages, of the human figure
walking forward so uncertainly, yet with no suspicion of
any such prompt solving of the *grand Peut-être*.(8) Again
like Sordello! In truth, Mr Pater is no moralist, and
alike as an artist and as a thinker, he feels called upon
to draw no moral, to deduce no consequences, from the fail-
ures or successes he has chronicled to a certain culminating
point. 'There is the portrait,' he seems to say; 'all I
have been writing is but as so many touches toward that
single visible outline: there is the portrait!'

Notes

1 In The Character of the Humourist: Charles Lamb, 'Fortnightly Review' (October 1878), n.s. xxiv, 466-74, and
  included in 'Appreciations' (1889).

2 See p. 54n.
3 'a taste for the *bizarre*' (R, 110).
4 'Dreamed the miracle of a poetic prose, musical without
  rhythm and without rhyme'.
5 Jean Louis Ernest Meissonnier (1815-91), French painter,
  etcher, lithographer and sculptor, was famous for his
  highly finished paintings of the Napoleonic campaigns.
6 From Goethe's poem, 'General Confessions': 'To live in
  totality, goodness, beauty, and determination' (11. 34-5).
7 Secret dungeon with entrance only by trap door.
8 Grand possibility. See EG, 68.

36. SELWYN IMAGE ON PATER'S VIRTUES

1888

Signed article entitled Two Critical Notices: Mr Pater's
'Imaginary Portraits', in the 'Century Guild Hobby Horse'
(January 1888), iii, 14-18.
    Selwyn Image (1849-1930), poet and artist, was co-
founder of the Church and Stage Guild and associated with
Arthur Macmurdo (1851-1942) in the production of the
'Hobby Horse'. He was a disciple of Ruskin and became
the Slade Professor of Fine Art at Oxford (1910-16). Image
is best remembered for his stained-glass and book designs.
    He probably met Pater through a mutual friend, Herbert
Horne (1864-1916), architect, writer, connoisseur and editor (1887-91) of the 'Hobby Horse'.
    Image's article may best be described as 'charming' and
suggestive — in the 'appreciative' tradition of the period.

Whenever there is announced a new book or a new article by
Mr Pater, we know that there is indeed a good thing in
store for us. For Mr Pater has this almost unique distinction amongst contemporary writers, that he publishes
very little. In sixteen years he has given us three books,
his 'Studies in the Renaissance', his 'Marius the Epicurean',
and now a few months ago his 'Imaginary Portraits': while
even his contributions during this time to the Magazines
make but a little list. Yet Mr Pater is acknowledged by all
sincere admirers of the Art of Literature to be one of its
finest living English representatives; for the quality of

his work is always first-rate. And what is it that makes
it first-rate? What makes it almost a certainty for us,
that when we take up any writing of his, we shall find in
it first-rate thought, and a first-rate style? It is of
course primarily Mr Pater's natural 'incommunicable'
ability. But then there have been surely people not less
able than he, who have yet been immeasurably less certain, who have so often fallen below their proper standard
and disappointed us. Yet, they have lacked self-restraint,
they have been in a hurry, they have forgotten the necessity of what spiritual writers call 'Recollection'. Mr
Pater does not forget it, he is extraordinarily self-res-
trained, he is never in a hurry: and so it comes to pass,
in the second place, that his writing is almost unfail-
ingly of the first order.

How admirable are these virtues in Mr Pater, how much
better the world of Art would be in every branch supposing our best artists even practised them more devotedly,
we need scarcely that any one should tell us. It took
God six days, says the old tradition, to create the world:
at the close of each day He pondered over its production:
on the seventh He rested wholly from His labours. The
meditation, the leisure, the pauses of self-criticism
which characterized the Divine Workman, are indispensable
for all fine work. Even when that curse of curses, the
consideration of how we can make an income quickly, is out
of the way, it is not in itself reason enough for production, that a man has something within him that he can produce: for the world is not benefited by production, but
only by the production of what is fine. After all, in the
life even of a man whom Nature has created for an artist,
there are many common, human, hourly interests and activities besides those which are artistic: and the golden
rule is this, that he should give us the work of his particular, differentiating inspiration, his artistic inspiration that is, only when he is able with accurate self-criticism to pronounce it the production of a fine mood,
transmitted to us with the utmost care and skill of which
he is capable. Now these moods, even in the greatest
geniuses, are not permanent, or to be had at the beckon-
ing; while for this care and skill there is required an
abundance of time; and for the self-criticism, which is
finally to pronounce judgment, there is required scarcely
less: so that, in the nature of the case, no artist can
give us much work of that quality, which alone justifies
him completely in giving us any. The first thing that I
have to say about Mr Pater to his exceeding honour is, that
in a singular degree he has recognized this, and been
strong enough from the first to submit himself.

I am afraid that the title with which this little article
commences may prove misleading: for I have been asked not
to write a criticism of the 'Imaginary Portraits', but to
take these merely as a felicitous occasion on which to call
attention to some characteristics of Mr Pater's work. And
even this much I am to do more in the way of suggestion,
and for temporary notice, than anything else; since we are
promised later on in the 'Hobby Horse' a careful study of
this admirable artist's purposes and methods from a writer
whose insight into them is more searching, and whose judgment will be more complete, than is any present insight or
judgment of mine.(1)

Now let me mention the second thing that I would notice
about Mr Pater, the subtlety of his thoughts and of their
expression. He does not come to us then with elaborately
finished theories, and clear-cut facts which are to illustrate and establish them. He does not offer us anything
which we can lay hold of at the moment, and store away
neatly squared and packed in our memories. He is essentially a seeker, a seeker after life's secrets, a seeker
who is conscious of the mysteries which lie deep and everywhere around us, and in the discovery of which to the reverent and delicate spirit will be found the finest moments
of existence. And in this perpetual search of his after
the hidden life he takes us step by step along with him.
To those who are contented with the satisfaction of our immediate and surface needs, who never dream indeed of anything beyond, it is a search that is unutterably wearisome,
it irritates, it actually seems to us affected and even
nonsensical. Well, if that is our feeling, we had better
keep a long way off from Mr Pater; for to 'the average
sensual man' he speaks certainly and always in a tongue unknown. Even in the first of these 'Imaginary Portraits',
which under the title of A Prince of Court Painters gives
us a study of Watteau's life and aims, and is of all the
four Portraits much the most simple and generally touching,
even here this perpetual striving in the painter to get
behind things, to be never contented till he is drinking
at their sources of the world's beauty and best interests,
to lay hands on and capture the very spirit of the moment
as it passes by, meets us at every turn, with its consequent and inevitable accompaniment of much weariness, and
dissatisfaction, and failure. And if this is so with the
first of these Portraits, it is so still more with the
remaining three, with Denys l'Auxerrois, Sebastian van
Storck, and Duke Carl of Rosenmold. In each of these
studies we have a different character set indeed in dif-
fering surroundings, yet alike in this fundamental point,
that they all seek passionately to be delivered out of the

captivity which keeps us contented with the world's ways
and aims, with even its refined ways and aims; for the
rare secret is beyond even the best of these appearances.
Is it? Is it at all events to be found in indifference
to them? Here is the penalty such spirits have to pay for
their delicate instincts, that at times they are over-
whelmed by a sense not of failure, that is endurable, but
of pursuing and only caring to pursue, what may be indeed
a phantom. Mr Pater ends his essay upon Watteau with the
following sentence: one might write it as an inscription
for the whole book, as an inscription for every spirit,
that has been touched with the fine madness of mysticism:
'He has been a sick man all his life. He was always a
seeker after something in the world that is there in no
satisfying measure, or not at all.'

The treatment of such subjects as are in these 'Imaginary Portraits' by a writer, who is himself entirely and at
all times in sympathy with them, involves, one hardly
needs to be reminded, much subtlety of language. A simple
thought, or a fact, if we are once master of them, should
shape themselves under our hand into expressions not less
simple: when in such cases there is not this simplicity
of expression, we are conscious of an inappropriateness;
and it comes, we know, either from a want of mastery over
our subject, or from a want of art in our writing, or at
best from some fancy for affectations. But Mr Pater's
characteristic thoughts are not in the nature of them
simple, and it is not with facts, as we commonly use that
word, that he largely concerned himself. How, for instance,
is it possible to express an emotion with the firm, clear
words and the completeness, which express with ease and
adequately a scientific fact or an intellectual conception? In the world of mysteries, which underlies the
world of our common and surface experience, we are in the
presence of things so delicate, so evanescent, so personal,
so partially revealed, as to permit their true lineaments,
significance, and indeed sometimes their existence, to be
by ourselves even little more than suspected; and to
cause that any efforts, which we make to let others share
them with us, shall be for the most part by hints and
symbols. True, we can deny the existence of such a world:
but supposing that it does exist, there is no wonder, at
all events, though the regret and irritation may be immense, if we cannot experience and communicate it readily
out of hand, or communicate it at all, perhaps, with ade-
quateness.

There is one more thing to which I would call attention
before finishing this notice. Mr Pater's method is not to
advertise the amount and accuracy of his knowledge by fact

heaped upon fact, reference heaped upon reference. A
careless, or ignorant, or unsympathetic reader may pass
from end to end of his writings, and never recognize the
knowledge and the realization of knowledge, which underlie
them, but which are never suffered to parade themselves.
Perhaps it would be impossible to compare two writers more
unlike one another than Mr Pater and Lord Macaulay: but
their comparison for a moment is singularly to the point,
in order to illustrate what I am here saying. Lord
Macaulay was a man who had accumulated in his mind a store
of facts that was astounding: and there they are on every
page of his brilliant essays thrown in our faces, as it
were, sentence after sentence. How the man must have
read! we cry: and what a memory! But of Mr Pater's reading we do not think; he gets himself too completely out
of the way; it is only by and by, when we come to criticize what we have been reading, that the sense of how much
must have gone to produce these admirably full and accurate
impressions, these slight but significant hints, these
deeply searching judgments or suggestions, begins to dawn
on us. I must not, however, be tempted into quotations at
all, nor into references either outside the 'Imaginary
Portraits'. Even here I will be content with two. Let
anybody turn then and read on pages 53 and 54 the description of the town and Cathedral of Troyes; and on pages 111
and 112 the description of the Catholic Religion as it presented itself to the mind of Sebastian van Storck. It is
hard, as I look over the volume, not to copy these two
passages out, and several other passages as well, some of
them even more significant, perhaps, and fascinating. But
an artist in Literature is not to be judged by extracts,
any more than an artist in Painting is to be judged by a
few inches cut here and there from his canvas. It is the
whole effect of Mr Pater's work upon you that is the thing:
it is that which justifies me, I am very sure, in speaking
of him as I have here spoken.

Note

1 The article to which Image refers is probably that by
  Lionel Johnson (No. 46).

37.   UNSIGNED NOTICE, 'OXFORD MAGAZINE'

25 January 1888, vi, 181-2

Little but praise can be said of this book. The author's
name is a guarantee for the extreme beauty of the style,
and those vignettes of portraiture are precisely the kind
of work best suited to that style. 'Marius the Epicurean',
in spite of its intricate beauty of workmanship, perhaps
because of it, can hardly escape the charge of dullness;
but the portrait of Watteau with which this short gallery
opens is as good as anything that Mr Pater has given us.
It has real pathos — that drop of human blood so much
more valuable than the writer's fine gold. The restless
craving of a successful artist is finely depicted; the
style seems to move with Watteau's own grace, and the
writer of the journal which tells the story touches us
more deeply than we can at first admit to ourselves.
'Sebastian Van Storck' is to our mind the least successful
portrait in the book. The subject is in himself too cold
to interest successfully. A young man who rejects an unaffected and *bourgeoise* maiden through love of the Absolute is not so interesting as he is rare. Also, though
the criticism seems a trifle ungenerous, Art seems to be
dragged in by the heels — a process only less reprehen-
sible than expelling Nature with a pitchfork, the crime of
Sebastian Van Storck. The information on pp. 103, 104 is
surely superfluous. The Hondecoeters, for instance, might
have been allowed to come to dinner without visiting the
hen-roost beforehand, even though it were only for hints
towards a new 'Concert of Birds'.
    Duke Carl of Rosenmold and Denys l'Auxerrois are both
fine portraits — the former more human, the latter a
picture of Dionysus transferred to the scenery of old
France. But in all these the finish of style is the same:
the finish of detail, the nicety with which the author
catches and reflects whatever is beautiful in a past age,
the very sound of the sentences, — all these prove Mr
Pater at his best. In a newspaper age this book, with its
handsome margin, rich paper, and writing beautiful for
writing's sake, will be prized by too few.

38. GEORGE STURT ON PATER

1890, 1892

Extracts from 'The Journals of George Sturt: 1890-1927
(Cambridge, 1967), ed. E.D. Mackerness. See Introduction,
pp. 26-7.
   George Sturt (1863-1927), writer under the pseudonym of
George Bourne, worked (from 1855) at a firm of wheelwrights
at Farnham, where his ancestors had worked since 1706. He
is best known for his book 'The Wheelwright's Shop' (1923).

(a) From his journal (on the theme of 'the education of
one's soul to a greater sensitiveness'), dated 22 November
1890

It is the natural process of development in artistic work,
when any beauty is discovered, to make the most of it; and
I can well understand Etty,(1) overpowered with the beauty
he dared to paint, carrying it to the verge of repletion.
But when the grosser forms of beauty are acknowledged,
taste begins to discriminate, and demands in the drawing of
an arm for instance not only the bold sweep of the muscles,
but those delicate curves as well, which tremble between
the convex and concave, eluding the eye which can only be
positive that they are not straight. And so there grows
up a fine sense that rejects all exaggeration, and finds
the truest beauty and most perfect strength in a kind of
fastidious temperance, rounded in by that border-line,
delicate as the bloom on a ripe plum, to be within which
would be too little, and to overstep which would be too
much. It is an austerity without severity, which it takes
years to at all appreciate: but once recognised, it is
seen to be the truest good, serene as a perfect summer day.
In literature, I know nothing that comes so near this standard, as Walter Pater's 'Marius the Epicurean'. But a
comparison of Carlyle's tempest storm with the restrained
passion of Thoreau's 'Plea for Captain John Brown'(2) will
indicate the superior force of conviction that the more
temperate art carries with it. (i, 80)

(b) From his journal, dated 18 January 1892

My desire for writing remains, though tempered still by
weakness of energy.... At dinner I scanned through

Swinburne's 'Poems and Ballads' (First Series); but not
with appreciation. I merely wished to know how Swinburne
treated the erotic subjects which William Morris handles
with such cleanly strength. My judgment may be as yet
dull; but Swinburne seems to write merely by force of
intellect, as if by artificial energy, with spontaneous
life. The book gave me not the smallest pleasure, but
only an unsteadiness of brain, like water whose ruffled
surface receives no image of aught that surrounds it. For
recalling calm, there could hardly have been found a book
more effective than the next I took up, — Walter Pater's
'Imaginary Portraits'. The cool quiet, as of grey but
limpid weather, that Pater spreads over his work was almost too soothing. It was scarce possible for myself to
write anything that would not seem unworthy, in the atmosphere of such masterly work. (i, 174)

(c) From his journal, dated 26 January 1892

I don't understand why I should still be so feeble, almost
a week after the sickness that lately kept me indoors. But
whatever may be the reason, the little walk this afternoon,
though not more than two miles, was enough to make me quite
tired, by the time I got back home. I have been fit for
very little since: and indeed have done nothing, except to
read the third of Pater's 'Imaginary Portraits' — Sebastian
van Storck. It may have been owing to my fatigue that I
grew weary of this fine piece of writing, whose measured
stateliness became oppressive towards the end. (i, 178)

(b) From his journal, dated 12 June 1892

I had really supposed that my thoughts on the materials of
literature might prove new, except perhaps for some hazy
occasional guess of dim instinct, now analysed. But to-
day, reading the essay on Botticelli in Pater's 'Renaissance', I found it written down, as though everybody knew
it, how Poetry is concerned with sentiment and story,
rather than with the sensuous forms and colours of painting. Here is the sentence: 'He' (i.e. Botticelli) 'is before all things a poetical painter, blending the charm of
story and sentiment, the medium of the art of poetry, with
the charm of line and colour, the medium of abstract
painting.'(3) 1870 is the date of the essay: at least so
early was the principle recognised: my secret was babbled
two-and-twenty years ago....
     For my own part, I find that I grow less and less able
to begin a novel which promises to excite me, with suspense
to its close, or with strong emotions of sympathy or repug-

nance for its characters. For this cause 'Diana of the
Crossways' and 'The Egoist' also distressed me greatly on
the first reading: I enjoyed them far better when I read
them again, in this last spring. It is doubtful, though,
if there be in 'Harry Richmond' so much beauty, lovable
for its own sake, as that which fills the other two books.
'Few artists,' writes Pater, 'not Goethe or Byron even,
work quite cleanly, casting off all débris, and leaving
us only what the heat of their imagination has fused and
transformed.'(4) (i, 197-8)

(e)   From his journal, dated 13 June 1892

The excitement which I disapprove of in Art, is that which
substitutes itself for the pleasure of receiving impressions;   that which makes us hurry through the present
situation, in order to unriddle it in the next. It produces a kind of *coma*, — a suspended animation — in the
faculties: deeply restful, and so, useful to them, if they
are wearied;   but inartistic for that very reason, that the
faculties are lulled to sleep....
     These essays of Pater's, dealing chiefly with Italian
painters, have one noteworthy characteristic. In each of
them the endeavour is made, to spell the hidden meaning
in the artists' work: to distil from them, by a kind of
chemistry of criticism, the philosophy, sentiment, or belief, which found their way into them from the Artist's
Personality. Judging from Pater's point of view, one
might almost suppose that these men, — Robbia, Botticelli,
Michaelangelo — painted with the purpose of teaching us, —
of instilling us with their own peculiar spirit: and that
to them, line and colour were of small value, compared
with the lessons which line and colour would convey. Even
so far is the essential painting and sculpture ignored.
Necessarily: for what can a writer say, about beauty of
hue and of form? His medium of language is almost useless
for such an end: he must deal rather with the thoughts
and sentiments which accompany the visual. It looks almost as though Pater were unaware that he was dealing with
a matter of quite secondary interest in these men's work:
he appears to think that this acute insight into peculiarities of manner has shown him the real kernel of the matter.
It has really shown him (so far as one can tell) little
enough of the sensuous beauty in this Renaissance work, but
only a hypothetical state of mind, which appears to account
for some of that work's peculiarities.
     I said 'the real kernel of the matter'; of course, if I
deny that Pater has actually arrived at it, I am open to
just criticism. Possibly he has found what he looked for: —

that mental condition which produced this phase of the
Renaissance. It must however be remembered, that this is
to study Art with the Historian's eyes, not with the
Artist's. So a biographer will read a poem, not for its
own beauty, but for the insight it gives him into the poet's
mind. He reads *between* the lines; making the poem itself
of secondary importance to his study. Now, if this kind of
interest is the only kind to be found in Renaissance work,
it is obvious that an artist may pass it by, leaving it to
the Historian, and the Antiquary. But if it contain aught
valuable to the Artist, that value must be *not* in its
subtle associations or indications of temperament, but in
its own sensuous beauty, apart from all other considerations. How, then, should an artist criticise it? Not historically, or with any allowance made for era or temperament; but from the absolutely modern standpoint, comparing
it with the ideally best. And all art must be treated in
this eclectic way; because Art is not a thing that was, but
a thing that *is*; depending on its power of attracting us,
of arousing our powers of appreciation, and providing them
with pleasant food.

And judging past work in this modern spirit, may not an
artist widen his field of observation; obtaining from the
more extended experience a more perfect abstraction of
beauty, and an ideal that shall be more enduring, than was
possible for them to attain who had only the experience of
their own life, and their own vacuity, to study from?

But such criticism, — that of the painter, I mean, —
cannot be made in language. Walter Pater has chosen for
his work perhaps the only part of the subject that was
open to the literary artist: and he has done it most artistically. Whether his conclusions are reliable or not is
another question. I incline to think them not only hypothetical explanations, but unsatisfactory. It is a curious
thing, for instance, if death were a subject of so deep a
sentiment, to the men of the Renaissance; that time when
Life, as Symonds points out, was assuming an interest so
many-coloured and so absorbing. But to Pater these works
of art convey that meaning which he expresses: and seeing
that it arouses us with the pleasure it gives and the charm
it casts over us, (to adapt his studied English) — seeing
that it exhibits a lovely strangeness, strange in its suggestions and lovely in its expression, it may well be
classed as a work of very elaborate art. (i, 199-200)

(f) From his journal, dated 6 July 1892

The immediate question is, What ought, or should a perfect
work of Art be?

And (as Pater has shown) the answer is, the choice handling of a choice subject-matter. I think we are got wrong,
— modern writers are especially wrong — in neglecting the
second element. Probably, the subject matter should be
submitted to as rigorous an appreciation as are the forms
in which it should be presented. As these are carefully
selected, every word, every note, every speck of colour
coming up to be weighed against others, — so subjects too
should be put on their trial before the artist. (i, 201-2)

(g) From his journal, dated 15 September 1892

If I were asked to point out the man who seems to me the
best exponent of the principles I have lately been evolving for myself, I should have little hesitation in pointing to Walter Pater. One would say of him that he is perfectly sane, — that he never loses his conscious self-
hood, or is carried away by any emotion: and further, that
recognising his senses as the channels of experience, he
of all men has taken control of experience, and made it
yield honey to his senses.
    And yet it is worth noting, how completely he has
yielded to the bias of his own temperament, until its
gratification has become a passion to the man whose philosophy should override all passion. I can think of but few
things to compare with his creative work, — 'Imaginary
Portraits' and 'Marius the Epicurean'; — they seem
unique, and perfect as works of art. But these character
pictures present after all only one order of character,
which one might suppose to be Pater's own seen in various
lights. Marius, Watteau, (and the Diarist who wrote
Watteau), Sebastian van Storck, — they are all men of
that refined and contemplative habit which one attributes
to Pater himself.... Nowhere in Pater's work have I found
any attempt to 'appreciate' any other kind of life, or to
find satisfaction in the modern and commonplace. It is
evident that in his eyes these grovel: often they must
disgust him, at the best he finds them dull and uninterest-
ing.
    The other living master of English prose, — Stevenson —
is entirely different from this. Somewhere he has confessed
himself a 'faddling hedonist'; but he is probably too canny
a Scot to give himself away to a theory. Like Thoreau, he
prefers always to have his life *with an undefined edge* in
front of him, — always to have the privilege of choice, un-
biased by conviction or principle. This may be the fundamental difference between his habits and Pater's. Stevenson too can at times yield to the impulse of emotion (if I
have formed a correct idea — without having seen it — of

his defence of Father Damien):(5) and yet it is incon-
ceivable that he should ever give the reins over to passion's handling.... But especially I would note how, unlike Pater, he seems in his creative work (apart from
his essays) never to give one a hint of his own bias. He
too, like the other, judges ('appreciates') and chooses;
is wholly artistic therefore. But the things he chooses
are modern, common-place, — often squalid or at least
sordid. All is grist that comes to his mill, — the stupid, the illiterate, the mean and grasping, above all,
the ordinary average man, — all, except perhaps the very
characters that delight Pater: these contemplative souls
seem to find no responsive attraction in Stevenson. His
people have an active full-blooded urge to be doing: and
this is what Stevenson likes: — one can tell it in his
essay on Thoreau,(6) written with a kind of itching of the
fingers to set the man at work.
    Here then are two great artists, whose art seems limited
by personal bias, — who are therefore, to that extent, un-
artistic (???). The one ultra refined, solitary, avoiding society with a student's aversion; the other refined
too, but boisterous withal, — hail fellow well met with
every common or ordinary mortal, finding this sort infinitely amusing and their very dullness delicious: but
with a kind of distaste for the solitary student, at least
as a subject for his art.
    If this criticism be tenable, then we may assume that
either would be a greater artist, if he could contain and
appreciate the bias of the other. That is to say, that
temperament *may* be a hindrance to art, and the man who has
his own under the control of his consciousness is truly
the great or 'world artist'.(7) (i, 209-11)

Notes

1 William Etty (1787-1849), painter from York, is remembered for his studies of the nude, which reflect great
  sheen and sensuosity.
2 Henry David Thoreau (1817-62) delivered a 'Plea for
  Captain John Brown' in the Concord Town Hall on 30 October 1859.
3 Quoted from Sandro Botticelli (R, 52).
4 See R, x-xi.
5 'Father Damien. An Open Letter to the Reverend Dr Hyde
  of Honolulu' (1890).
6 Henry David Thoreau: His Character and Opinions first
  appeared in the 'Cornhill Magazine' (June 1880); it
  was reprinted in 'Familiar Studies of Men and Books' (1882).
7 I.e. Dante, Chaucer, Shakespeare, Milton, Victor Hugo
  and others.

'Appreciations'
November 1889

39. CLEMENT SHORTER, UNSIGNED REVIEW, 'STAR'

21 November 1889, 4

See Introduction, p. 11.
     Clement Shorter (1857-1926), journalist, biographer and
art critic, wrote (from 1888) a Books and Bookmen column
for the 'Star' and was editor from 1890 of the 'Illustrated
London News'. As a journalist he influenced the pictorial
press. Shorter published substantial studies of the
Brontës, George Barrow and Samuel Johnson.
     Pater probably solicited the review. It contains a pic-
ture of Pater from an engraving based on an early photo-
graph, probably taken c. 1870.

In one of his most pleasant books Mr Henry James says of a
man that he had appreciation, but no productive power. Now,
no one will say of Mr Walter Pater that he has no productive
power. His 'Marius the Epicurean' and his 'Renaissance' are
surely literature in the best sense. But to have 'appreciation' is not given to every man of high power. Wordsworth
and Carlyle, for example, had little enough of it. And so
one takes up Mr Walter Pater's volume with additional zest
because of its attractive title. Some of his essays we have
read before, two of them we possess in Ward's 'English
Poets', but all are so illuminating, and yet so sympathetic that one delights to read them again. This sympathy is
best shown, perhaps, in such essays as those on Lamb, Wordsworth, and Coleridge, and the luminousness in the essays on
'Measure for Measure' and 'Love's Labour's Lost'. All

194

boast a style which, if now and again a little over-ela-
borated, is, on the whole, well-nigh perfect. Mr Pater
gives us here an Essay on Style, and his book might have
been called 'An Essay on Style: with Illustrations'. For
who among our moderns has written with so much delicacy
and finish. The right vocabulary, he tells us, is of most
importance for a translator; more important than anything
else. And Mr Pater always has the right vocabulary.

40. WILLIAM SHARP, UNSIGNED REVIEW, 'GLASGOW HERALD'

28 November 1889, 9

See No. 18. Possibly solicited by Pater. Sharp also reviewed 'Greek Studies' (see Introduction, p. 36). On 3
December 1889 Pater wrote to Sharp:

> Sincere thanks! I read yesterday, with great pleasure,
> in the 'Glasgow Herald', the so appreciative criticism
> of my 'Appreciations', by so excellent a critic as
> yourself. (LWP, 104)

Admirers of Mr Walter Pater's work — and they are constantly increasing in numbers — have, doubtless, for the most
part, been aware of the essays on literary and artistic
subjects which he has published in magazines from time to
time. Each of these was distinguished by such rare grace
of style and subtlety of critical insight that, even in
the mass of periodical literature, they stood out in bold
relief. It has long been the hope of the readers of these,
or some of these studies, that the author would issue them
again, with such rearrangement as might be necessary, in
book form, and this he has now done in so far as the essays
on literary subjects are concerned. But it would be very
misleading to allow the inference that 'Appreciations' is
a volume composed simply of reprints. True, more than two
thirds of it has appeared in print before, but this re-
issued matter has been so carefully revised and frequently
so amplified, and, moreover, was originally published at
times wide apart, varying, indeed, from 1865 to 1889, that,
even if for no other reason, the present volume would have
to be regarded otherwise than as a mere representment of

old materials. But, as it happens, the book is as essentially one work as though the separate essays were but
sectional parts for the reader's convenience: a unity of
aim animates it throughout; a continuity of thought and
method links essay to essay as much as sentence to sentence. There is, it will be unnecessary to add for those
who already know Mr Pater's writings, infinite charm in
these 'Appreciations' — the charm of an exquisitely refined style, of a thoroughly trained critical faculty, of
an exceptionally acute and delicate insight. To many this
volume will seem to contain the wisest and most significant *urbana scripta*(1) of its accomplished author, and this
we may say while unforgetful of the 'Studies in the Renaissance', a book that has exercised a far deeper influence
for good among the younger writers of the day than is commonly realised, and of that austere romance of mental and
spiritual development in that 'Victorian Era' of the past,
the period of Marcus Aurelius, 'Marius the Epicurean'. Of
the essays included in the present volume, the following,
at any rate, have in some form already appeared:- The
acute and truly critical 'appreciation' of Wordsworth was
first issued, if we remember rightly, in the 'Fortnightly
Review' in the days of Mr John Morley's editorship. That
of Coleridge, one of the most delightful of all, was in
part contributed to the 'Westminster Review', more than
20 years ago: another portion of it appeared as the Introduction to Coleridge in Ward's 'English Poets', whence also
comes the short but peculiarly discriminative study of
Rossetti as a poet. The studies of Charles Lamb, Shakespeare's Kings, 'Measure for Measure', and 'Love's Labour's
Lost' have already appealed to us in the 'Fortnightly' and
elsewhere. Then there is the study which for many readers
will be the most important in the book, the exquisitely
artistic but yet simple and practical essay on Style, in
itself ample inducement towards purchase of 'Appreciations'.
In addition, there are two suggestive new papers, one dealing with Aesthetic Poetry, and the other, called simply
Postscript, occupied with some very judicious and timely
words on the much-vexed feud between classicism and romanticism, with special stress on the fact that the genuine
artist need concern himself little about either 'ism',
time being the sole arbiter in this respect. It would be
difficult to overpraise some of the essays, in particular
(among those which deal with individuals) those upon Wordsworth and Coleridge. How remarkably true, and yet how
lucidly concise, is, for example, this concluding estimate
of Dante Gabriel Rossetti, though we may quote first a few
prior words —

[Quotes Dante Gabriel Rossetti: 'With him, indeed, as in
some revival of the old mythopoeic age' to 'one of Love's
lovers'.]

These passages occur early or midway in the essay; here is
the conclusion alluded to:

> But poetry, at all times, exercises two distinct func-
> tions: it may reveal, it may unveil to every eye, the
> ideal aspects of common things ... or it may actually
> add to the number of motives, poetic and uncommon in
> themselves, by the imaginative creation of things that
> are ideal from their very birth. Rossetti did some-
> thing, something excellent, of the former kind; but
> his characteristic, his really revealing work, lay in
> the adding to poetry of fresh poetic material, of a
> new order of phenomena, in the creation of a new ideal.

How fine, again, this of Coleridge in his later years:

[Quotes Coleridge: 'De Quincey said of him' to 'which is
not of the breeze'.]

We would now draw special attention to certain passages in
the Wordsworth essay, but find adequate quotation imprac-
ticable, save at a length which exigencies of space pro-
hibit. How fine this, moreover, from the study of Charles
Lamb, and how human the sentiment pervading it from the
outset to its grandiose close:

[Quotes the concluding paragraph from Charles Lamb: 'He
felt the genius of places' to 'bleached stone steeples'.]

It is from the essay on Style, however, that one could
gather the greatest number of quotable passages and sentences. Mr Pater has the faculty of enunciating truisms
in such collocations as to make them fresh and insistent,
but withal adding to them just that touch of refined
thought which gives all he says such a happy individuality.

> Truth! [he exclaims] there can be no merit, no craft at
> all, without that! and, further, all beauty is in the
> long run only *fineness* of truth, or what we call ex-
> pression, the finer accommodation of speech to that
> vision within.

Although in the deepest sense form and matter are inseparable, the two are often referred to as distinct, as of
course in a superficial sense they are. It seems an ill

courtesy to conclude a notice of such a book with just one
of those hackneyed phrases which the author so seriously
deprecates, yet when one is anxious to say that no one
with any heed to our best contemporary literature, no one
in particular who would learn, will care to be without this
book, what can one do but adopt the stereotyped phraseology,
and hope that the worthiness of the intention may excuse
literary bad manners!

Note

1 Urbanities.

41. UNSIGNED REVIEW, 'PALL MALL GAZETTE'

10 December 1889, xlix, 3

See Introduction, pp. 29 and 30.

In our little band of critics, Mr Walter Pater certainly
deserves an eminent, if not a pre-eminent, place. He is
less arbitrary, one may almost say less whimsical, than
Mr Arnold; with all Mr Swinburne's subtlety of perception
he combines an adequate psychology, and a just insight
into the essence and function of literature as a whole.
There is no fear of his becoming, as a recent critic of
criticism puts it, 'a specialist in verbiage, a kind of
artistic Talmudist, living in a world of word-begotten
thoughts, the mere spectra of ideas'. He knows how to
bring his individual judgments into relation with larger
laws, and, without any pedantry of system, is the least
empirical of English aestheticians. The critic, he says,
should be 'the Interpreter of the House Beautiful'; and
that he is in very deed. The present volume contains some
of his finest work, belonging to various periods. Part
of the long paper on Coleridge dates from 1865; the essay
on Aesthetic Poetry was written in 1868 while yet 'The
Earthly Paradise' was incomplete; 'Wordsworth' is fifteen
years old, 'Charles Lamb' eleven, 'Sir Thomas Browne' only
three. The last is to our mind the least satisfactory.
It contains admirable work, but is a trifle diffuse and

rambling. The Wordsworth and Lamb are probably the best
things in the book, abounding in essential and what may be
called cosmic critical truths — general statements, that
is to say, which bring into order and co-relation a number
of particular facts. But we shall not attempt an arrangement of Mr Pater's essays in any order of merit. That
were to prove ourselves blind to one great merit which
pervades them all: the absence of arbitrary and more or
less odious comparisons. Mr Pater's studies are strictly
appreciations, not depreciations. He does not rob Peter
to pay Paul; nor does he attempt, by a nice arrangement
of epithets and superlatives, to establish a hard and fast
gradation of achievement in the works of Paul himself. Mr
Pater is very chary of superlatives. He is the Interpreter
of the House Beautiful, not an examiner assigning plus and
minus marks in the great Immortality Tripos.

How comes it, one would like to know, that the act of
writing about style tends to play havoc with the style of
the writer? Mr Stevenson's essay on style, published some
time ago in the 'Contemporary Review',(1) was probably the
worst piece of writing he ever put his name to. Mr John
M. Robertson, in his 'Essays towards a Critical Method',
(2) has a paper on Science in Criticism, mainly concerned
of course with style, which would be luminous — if it
were not obscure. And now Mr Pater, with some excellent
things to say on style, contrives to say some of them with
curious infelicity. We do not, on the whole, admire Mr
Pater's style so fervently as some people. It has distinction and delicacy, but it lacks vivacity, and, worse
than that, it is not always absolutely clear. Mr Pater's
sedateness verges upon solemnity. Urbane and even insinuating as his discourses are, one feels now and then an
impish longing to play some practical joke on this bland
imperturbability, in the hope of extorting from it either
a smile or a frown. Humour has its legitimate place in
criticism; for if it be not true that who drives fat oxen
must himself be fat, it is certain that the critic of
humourists must himself be something of a humourist. We
cannot but regard this monotony of mood, this total absence
of buoyancy or sparkle, as a serious limitation in Mr
Pater's style. It makes us yearn at times for the elaborate wit of Mr Lowell(3) or even the allusive flippancy of
Mr Lang.(4) In support of our second and graver accusation let us quote the following sentence from the essay
on Style:

The true distinction between prose and poetry he [Words-
worth] regarded as the almost technical or accidental
one of the absence or presence of metrical beauty, or,

say! metrical restraint; and for him the opposition
came to be between verse and prose of course — you
can't scan Wordsworth's prose: but, as the essential
dichotomy in this matter, between imaginative and unimaginative writing, parallel to De Quincey's distinction between 'the literature of power and the literature of knowledge', in the former of which the composer
gives us not fact, but his peculiar sense of fact,
whether past or present, or prospective, it may be, as
often in oratory.

Now, frankly, reader, have you more than a faint glimmer of
the meaning of this wounded snake of a sentence? Don't you
want to try back, to unravel it, laboriously tracing out
the logical structure, the process and opposition of ideas?
And this, though perhaps an extreme, is very far from being
a solitary, case. Again and again, one has to re-read a
sentence in order to make quite sure of its meaning. In
one or two instances, we have at first suspected that the
printer must have made havoc of the text; our faith in
his accuracy being undermined at the outset by the quaint
misprint of 'Malony' for 'Malory'. Further study has in
almost all cases exonerated the compositor, at Mr Pater's
expense. For there is surely something amiss when a fairly
attentive reader keeps on stumbling and having to try back.
We happened to take up a book of Jules Lemaître's(5) immediately after finishing this essay on Style, and the
sensation was that of skating on smooth ice immediately
after having struggled through an obstacle-race. Yet M.
Lemaître is not at all incapable of expressing complex and
subtle ideas.

Notes

1 On Style in Literature: its Technical Elements, 'Contemporary Review' (April 1885), xlvii, 548-61.
2 John Mackinnon Robertson (1856-1933), critic and politician, published this work in 1889.
3 James Russell Lowell (1819-91), poet and essayist, succeeded Longfellow as Professor of Belles-lettres at Harvard
  in 1855.
4 See No. 76.
5 See p. 380n.

42. ARTHUR SYMONS, UNSIGNED REVIEW, 'ATHENAEUM'

14 December 1889, 813-4

See Nos 35 and 58 and Introduction, pp. 30 and 32. Possibly
solicited by Pater. Symons traces the influence of the art
and poetry of the Pre-Raphaelites on Pater's criticism and
stresses his achievement as the triumph of a unique temperament (see No. 48b).

It is now sixteen years since Mr Pater's first and, until
now, only volume of criticism appeared — the 'Studies in
the History of the Renaissance', as it was called. Entirely
individual, the spontaneous outcome of a rare temperament,
it had many affinities with the poetic and pictorial art of
Rossetti, Mr Swinburne, and Mr Burne Jones, just then exciting special curiosity, and seems to have been taken as
the critical manifesto of the so-called 'aesthetic' school.
And, indeed, it may be very well compared, as artistic
prose, with the poetry of Rossetti — as fine, as careful,
as new a thing as that, and with something of the same exotic odour about it — a savour, in the case, of French soil,
a Watteau grace and lightness. Here was criticism as a
fine art, in prose which one lingered over as over poetry —
modulated prose which made the splendours of Mr Ruskin seem
exaggerated, and by the side of which the neatness of
Matthew Arnold looked finikin, the orchestration of Carlyle
sounded strident. The subject-matter of the book was as
novel to most English readers as its form. By its way of
proposing it, it made criticism something it had never precisely been before.

[Quotes the Preface to 'The Renaissance': 'The aesthetic
critic' to 'a special, a unique, impression of pleasure'.]

Such, briefly were the principles underlying the singularly
subtle valuations of Leonardo, Botticelli, Joachim du Bellay,
and the others who made up this first volume of criticism;
such, still, are the principles underlying the second
volume, itself composed at many periods, which in its collected form comes to us to-day, under the title of 'Appreciations' — a word occurring very often in the essays, and
used, evidently, in the sense of the French *appréciation*, a
weighing, a valuing, more even than in the general English
sense of valuing highly. It is appropriate, however, in

that sense too, from a quality of the criticism about which we shall have something to say later.

We have quoted from the preface to the 'Renaissance' volume a statement of Mr Pater's ideal in criticism, and that statement may be supplemented by another, to be found in the essay on Wordsworth — perhaps the finest of Mr Pater's critical essays:

> What special sense does Wordsworth exercise, and what instincts does he satisfy? What are the subjects and the motives which in him excite the imaginative faculty? What are the qualities in things and persons which he values, the impression and sense of which he can convey to others, in an extraordinary way?

Such an ideal is far enough from the old theory, not yet extinct, which may be stated in the words of Edgar Poe, who tells us that,

> while the critic is *permitted* to play, at times, the part of the mere commentator — while he is *allowed*, by way of merely *interesting* his readers, to put in the fairest light the merits of his author — his *legitimate* task is still in pointing out and analysing defects, and showing how the work might have been improved, to aid the general cause of letters, without undue heed of the individual literary men.(1)

Poe energetically protests against the more merciful (and how infinitely more fruitful!) principles of Goethe, who held that what it concerns us to know about a work or a writer are the merits, not the defects, of man or thing. Mr Pater certainly carries this theory to its furthest possible limits, and may almost be said never, except by implication, to condemn anything. But then the force of this implication is immense, testifying to a fastidiousness far in excess of that shown by the more generally unfavourable critics. Is it necessary to *say* that one dislikes a thing? It is possible to ignore it, and Mr Pater ignores all that does not come up to his very exacting standard, contenting himself with writing about the residue. And here there is a curious point to note. 'It was thus,' we are told of Gaston de Latour in one of the chapters of that beautiful First Book, as one supposes, of a romance as yet unfinished — 'it was thus Gaston understood the poetry of Ronsard, *generously expanding it to the full measure of its intention.*' That is precisely what Mr Pater does in his criticisms, in which one might almost say there is as much creation as criticism. He has a quite unique faculty of seeing, through all the imperfections which must encumber all moral endeavour,

the perfect work, the work as the artist saw it, as he
strove to make it, as he failed, in his measure, quite
adequately to achieve it. Disengaging the better from
the baser elements, he seizes thus upon what is fundamental, getting at the true root of the matter, and leaving
all the rest out of the question. The essay on Wordsworth is certainly the very best example of this, for it
has fallen to the lot of Wordsworth to suffer more than
most at the hands of interpreters. Here, at last, is a
critic who can see in him 'a poet somewhat bolder and more
passionate than might at first sight be supposed, but not
too bold for true poetical taste; an unimpassioned writer,
you might sometimes fancy, yet thinking the chief aim, in
life and art alike, to be a certain deep emotion'; one
whose 'words are themselves thought and feeling'; 'a
master, an expert, in the art of impassioned contemplation'.
Often in one vivid phrase one is brought to realize a
whole temperament or artistic procedure. Of Rossetti, for
instance, and the surcharged intensity of his style, how
revealing are these words: 'To him life is a crisis at
every moment'. Take again this passage, from the singularly beautiful essay on Charles Lamb:

[Quotes Charles Lamb: 'The writings of Charles Lamb are
an excellent illustration' to 'till the end of days'.]

Reading these essays, one feels, over and over again, if
Lamb and Wordsworth, if Shakspeare, if Sir Thomas Browne,
could come to life again and read what has here been written about them, would they not say: 'Here is a man who
understands just what I meant to do, what was almost too
deep in me for expression, and would have, I knew, to be
divined — who sees what is best in my work, just where I
felt it was best?' With this writer criticism means sympathy, and sympathy with him is a key that opens all locks.
Is not this sympathy, it was asked on the publication of
the Renaissance studies, after all somewhat limited? No
one can think that after reading the first and the last
essay in the present volume. The one, an Essay on Style,
coming with all the authority of so fine a master of it,
and the other, a discussion of the question of what is
classical and what romantic in literature, show, both of
them, a remarkable breadth and catholicity. One cannot but
think, indeed, that Mr Pater's outlook is larger to-day
than it was sixteen years ago; or perhaps he has only
given utterance to what was really latent from the first.
The tendency, certainly, in his style has been towards
emancipation, breadth, 'naturalness', just in the same way
as Rossetti's style developed in the period between the

composition of the earlier and the later sonnets. In both
cases there is something lost, something to regret. In
the later style of Mr Pater there is less sensuousness,
a severer ordering and ornament, more of what he calls
'*mind* in style', more freedom also; and if we get no more
passages like that one on Monna Lisa, like other perfect
pages of the earlier book, we get passages like this, in
which there is an organ note unheard till now:

[Quotes Style: 'It is on the quality of the matter it informs' to 'the great structure of human life'.]

There, in an essay on style, really practical and full
of good counsel, is an illustration of one kind of method
in style, the

long-contending, victoriously intricate sentence ... the
sort of sentence in which, if you look closely, you can
see much contrivance, much adjustment, to bring a highly qualified matter into compass at one view.

Elsewhere we may find illustrations of the 'blithe, crisp
sentence, decisive as a child's expression of its needs ...
the sentence, born with the integrity of a single word'.
Indeed, it might be profitable to go over the volume, finding at every step some admirable example of quality after
quality of good style, pointed out in that introductory
essay. In his study of Charles Lamb, Mr Pater speaks of
'the student of literature as a fine art'. That is what
he himself is; but he is more than that. He is a critic
who has made a fine art of criticism itself. His criticism — abounding in the close and strenuous qualities of
really earnest judgment, grappling with his subject as if
there were nothing to do but that, the 'fine writing' in it
being largely mere conscientiousness in providing a subtle
and delicate matter with words as subtle and delicate —
is, in effect, written with as scrupulous a care, with as
much artistic finish, as any imaginative work whatever —
being indeed, in a sense in which, perhaps, no other critical work is, imaginative work itself.

Note

1 From Critics and Criticism, which first appeared in
  'Graham's Magazine' (January 1850), after Poe's death.

43. WILLIAM WATSON, SIGNED REVIEW, 'ACADEMY'

21 December 1889, xxxvi, 399-400

See Introduction, pp. 29, 31 and 32.
   Sir William Watson (1858-1935) gained overnight fame
for his poem on Wordsworth, published in 1890. Two years
later he was chosen to write the official elegy on Tennyson, which appeared under the title 'Lachrymae Musarum'
(1892). Watson received some support as a candidate for
the Poet Laureateship when the office fell vacant in 1892,
1913 and 1930, but was passed over on each occasion.
   Pater was delighted with Watson's pronouncements on him
as a critic and writer, for he enclosed a clipping of the
review in his letter dated 24 December 1889 to Herbert
Horne (see Introduction, p. 10).

To the essays here grouped under one cover their author
has given a general title which, in the case of a writer
accustomed as Mr Pater is to employ words with a jealously
scholastic regard to their exact signification, might mean
simply estimates, favourable or otherwise — valuations,
pricings — but which apparently is to be understood here
as used in the popular sense that implies above all else
admiration and sympathy. In this sense the title is happily chosen, and the reader who approaches this volume of
'appreciations' in a spirit other than appreciative is
not a person whose mental attitude can be recommended for
imitation. It is noteworthy that in these studies, where
the critical posture is invariably one of extreme modesty
— the writer contentedly sitting at the feet of his
Gamaliels and reverently transmitting to us the essence
of their utterances with such elucidatory comment as he
may think needful — it is noteworthy that by virtue of
this very humility and apparent self-repression he attains
to something like kinship and equality with the masters
whom it is his ambition simply to understand and report.
He says of Charles Lamb — and we may with equal truth
say it of himself —

   To feel strongly the charm of some poet, or essayist,
   or painter, and then to interpret that charm, to convey it to others — he seeming to himself but to hand
   on to others, in mere humble ministration, that of which
   for them he is really the creator — this is the way of
   his criticism.

There was a time when some of Mr Pater's qualities of
style almost threatened to crystallise into mannerisms;
and even after such noble writing as was to be found, for
instance, in the papers on Lionardo and Giorgione, he was
capable of relapsing into the mere honeyed effeminacy that
made readers with virile tastes turn away from Florian
Deleal. He and English literature are to be congratulated
upon his having left all this behind him and chastened his
style into something which, while for fastidiousness it is
perhaps unparalleled, is also full of real, though very
quiet, strength — strength that is not combative but pre-
hensile, the strength of a steady grasp, never of a blow.
Once only in these pages does he impress us at all unpleasantly as speaking with the falsetto of a school and the
accent of an epoch; and that is in the paper on Aesthetic
Poetry, where, conformably to the matter under discussion,
the manner seems in places somewhat fantastic — where,
though the hand is the hand of Mr Pater, the voice is —
well, a mingling of the voices of two or three singers
prominent in the latter-day choir.

The opening paper, on Style — in reality concerning
itself rather with diction, or with artifices of prose composition, than with that abstract effect, that air and carriage, which the word 'style' has almost insensibly come to
stand for — is perhaps for this reason a little disappointing. Yet it is full of excellent touches, examples of Mr
Pater's gift of saying what is emphatically the right
thing with unerring precision of phrase. Could the specific differences of two related words be better illustrated
than in such a sentence as the following? 'Blake, in the
last century, is an instance of preponderating soul, em-
barrassed, at a loss, in an era of preponderating mind.'
Or what could be more salutary in a literary period like
the present than this admonition? 'It is good in the criticism of verse to look for those hard, logical, quasi-
prosaic excellences which that, too, has or needs.' But
it is when we pass to the 'Appreciations' properly so-
called that we find Mr Pater at his best. Could anything
be finer than such a phrase as Wordsworth's 'mountain atmosphere of mind'? or truer than the ascription to that
poet of the power of

conveying to the consciousness of the reader abstract
and elementary impressions — silence, darkness, absolute motionlessness; or, again, the whole complex sentiment of a particular place, the abstract expression
of desolation in the long white road, of peacefulness
in a particular folding of the hills.

And what magic of expression when, with fine insight, he notes in Wordsworth

> the sudden passage from lowly thoughts and places to the majestic forms of philosophical imagination, the play of these forms over a world so different, enlarging so strangely the bounds of its humble churchyards, and breaking such a wild light on the graves of christened children.

Mr Pater finds Coleridge's 'chief offence' as a philosophical writer to lie in 'an excess of seriousness', the want of 'a certain shade of unconcern, the perfect manner of the eighteenth century'. It is doubtful whether he does not for once exaggerate when he declares Coleridge to be the typical 'flower of the *ennuyé*',(1) the mouthpiece of the modern *Weltschmerz*,(2) 'more than Childe Harold, more than Werther,(3) more than René'(4) himself'. Dreamer as he was, Coleridge's eager interest not only in metaphysics and literature, but in such mundane matters as politics, together with his notorious activity as a personal propagandist, zealous to impress his views upon every man, woman, and child who came within reach of the irrepressible tongue, seem to place him at some distance from the Obermann family. Unlike that weary and dejected race, he was essentially an enthusiast, pursuing knowledge, as Hazlitt says of him, 'with outstretched hands and winged speed'. Up to the very last he was to Wordsworth 'the Rapt One'; and his religious creed, whatever abstract value we may attach to it now, at least saved him from the philosophy of the school of despair.

I think Mr Pater is at his very best — which is only another way of saying that he is wholly delightful — in the paper on Sir Thomas Browne, that strange great writer to whom, as his latest critic happily says, 'the whole world was a museum'. Perhaps the author of the 'Hydriotaphia'(5) has received no such entirely sympathetic, and at the same time discriminative, treatment as here. Mr Pater really renders him for us, conveying to us the finest inflexions of his voice as if by some eclectic telephone, which dropped out the harsher notes but suffered no rich cadence to be lost in transmission. Once or twice he lets his own style be tinged for a moment with his author's. We feel this in such a clause as 'a tardiness and reluctancy in the circumstances of dissolution'. He is speaking of one, a friend of Sir Thomas Browne's, who, in the course of a lingering death, seemed sensibly to anticipate the hereafter; and though the image of life as a stream flowing into eternity's ocean is trite enough, what a novel and

poetic turn Mr Pater gives it! 'The infinite future had
invaded this life perceptibly to the senses, *like an ocean
felt far inland up a tidal river*.'

The Shakspere studies are none the worse for being anything but ponderous, and are marked by the delicately luminous perception which shares with Mr Pater's exquisite
style the distinction of being his chief value as a writer.
In 'Richard II' he finds the leading *motif* to be 'the irony
of kingship — average human nature, flung with wonderfully pathetic effect into the vortex of great events'.
Though reverent enough, he is no prostrate idolator at the
Stratford shrine; and it is refreshing to hear him speak
of 'the tiresome German superstition ... which challenged
us to a dogmatic faith in the plenary verbal inspiration
of every one of Shakspere's clowns'.

The faults of Mr Pater's book are few and slight, but
the fallen nature of the reviewer drives him to find one or
two if he cannot invent them. Mr Pater's vocabulary being
really very rich and various, he does himself some injustice by letting a chance epithet, such as 'blithe', get
the upper hand. Then his religiously accurate and anti-
popular use of certain words, such as 'complexion' and
'mortified', is, perhaps, academic to the verge of pedantry.
At all events it raises the question whether, since language is after all but a set of arbitrary symbols which the
people have fashioned and have, therefore, some right to
refashion, such correctness is worth purchasing at the
price of strangeness, real or apparent. To touch upon a
quite different matter, I think Mr Pater lays himself open
to animadversion when, in his interesting postscript, he
derives even the more extreme developments of the romantic
spirit from the desire of beauty plus the passion of curiosity. Surely it might, with at least equal plausibility,
be argued that the very contrary is nearer the truth, as
regards the latter of these two alleged constituents of
romanticism. Is it not rather the absence of true curiosity — a deficient interest in the astonishing realities
around us — that makes us go out of our way to invent the
grotesque, the mostrous, the impossible, substituting the
bizarre wardrobe of fancy for the infinitely wilder attire
of fact?

But perhaps it is churlish to speak of anything but the
charm and power of a volume so eminent in both, so rich in
beauty, so wide in the circuit of its judgments — a volume
which shows Mr Pater finally victorious over certain temptations to mere daintiness once jeopardising a noble grace
of diction; and which must further consolidate its author's
fame as one of the most catholic of living critics, and beyond rivalry the subtlest artist in contemporary English
prose.

Notes

1 Boredom.
2 World-weariness.
3 Protagonist of 'The Sorrows of Young Werther' (1774; 1787) by Goethe (1749-1832).
4 Protagonist of 'René' (1802) by François René Chateaubriand (1768-1848).
5 A treatise published in 1658.

44. C.L. GRAVES, UNSIGNED REVIEW, 'SPECTATOR'

21 December 1889, 887-8

See Introduction, pp.10, 31 and 32.
    Charles Larcom Graves (1856-1944), Irish writer, editor and music enthusiast. He joined the staff of the 'Spectator' in 1894 and was Assistant Editor from 1899 to 1917. He was also on the staff of 'Punch' throughout 1902-36, serving as Assistant Editor from 1928. Graves's publications include 'Life and Letters of Alexander Macmillan' (1910) and 'Mr Punch's History of the Great War (1919).
    Pater possibly had Graves's review in mind when he suppressed Aesthetic Poetry from the second and subsequent editions of 'Appreciations'.

Approaching Mr Pater's new volume not without a certain misgiving as to our ability to do justice to a writer whose mannerism has sometimes moved us to impatience, we are free to confess that its perusal has given us a great deal more pleasure than we expected. There are certain passages — notably in the essay on Aesthetic Poetry — in which Mr Pater, without intending it, almost persuades the plain person to be a Philistine. But this essay was written in 1868, and in his later work we observe far more of that self-restraint and 'frugal closeness' of style which in his opening chapter he declares to be so essential to scholarly writing. Not only is his diction less exuberant, but his criticism is riper, sounder, and more manly. We are surprised — we had well-nigh said, delighted — to find Mr Pater applauding the frank outspokenness of Doctor Johnson at the expense of the modern German commentators on

Shakespeare. His essay on Rossetti, while eminently sympathetic, strikes us as singularly just. For example,
after noting the strange and almost grotesque lengths to
which Rossetti's delight in concrete definitions led him,
and his excessive indulgence in personification, Mr Pater
continues:

> Poetry as a *mania* — one of Plato's two higher forms of
> 'divine' mania — has, in all its species, a mere in-
> sanity incidental to it, the 'defect of its quality',
> into which it may lapse in its moment of weakness; and
> the insanity which follows a vivid poetic anthropomor-
> phism like that of Rossetti may be noted here and there
> in his work, in a forced and almost grotesque material-
> ising of abstractions, as Dante also became at times a
> mere subject of the scholastic realism of the Middle Age.

Another excellent point about these essays is the extreme
aptness of the quotations. Mr Pater quotes sparingly, but
with true artistic choice. Thus, in the essay on Shakespeare's English Kings, he illustrates very happily Shakespeare's conception of war, in which 'the pity of it' always
comes as an afterthought to the poet's admiration for the
grandiose aspects of martial life. Mr Pater has not only
a sure instinct for things intrinsically beautiful in literature, but he is also very adroit in citing passages to
illustrate his own meaning. To take one example, after
dwelling with approval on Flaubert's extraordinary loyalty
to his art, and the unwearied persistence with which he
laboured to fit the right word to the meaning, Mr Pater
illuminates, as it were, his version of the old maxim,
χαλεπὰ τὰ καλά,(1) with this happy image from one of Flaubert's own letters, which expresses so vividly and painfully the discouragement which all conscientious artists
must occasionally feel: 'I am like a man whose ear is true
but who plays falsely on the violin: his fingers refuse to
reproduce precisely those sounds of which he has the inward
sense.' These words of Flaubert's remind us, however, that
Mr Pater is hardly to be congratulated on *his* employment
of musical imagery. In the essay on Shakespeare's English
Kings, to which we have already alluded, occurs a simili-
tude the appropriateness of which no musician would admit.
The writer has been saying that Richard finally attains
contentment in the merely passive recognition of superior
strength, and continues: 'As in some sweet anthem of
Handel, the sufferer, who put finger to organ under the utmost pressure of mental conflict, extracts a kind of peace
at last from the mere skill with which he sets his distress
to music.' Such indulgence in the luxury of grief is, we

think, entirely alien from the whole spirit of Handel's
robust genius. But Mr Pater is evidently enamoured of the
comparison, for he recurs to it a couple of pages lower
down, in a passage worded with curious laxity for so studied a writer:

> Like some melodiously contending anthem of Handel's,
> I said, of Richard's meek 'undoing' of himself in the
> mirror-scene; and, in fact, the play of 'Richard II'
> does, like a musical composition, possess a certain
> concentration of all its parts, a simple continuity,
> an evenness of execution, which are rare in the great
> dramatist.

Unlucky, again, is the musical allusion in the sentence
where Mr Pater speaks of prose literature as 'the characteristic art of the nineteenth century, as others, thinking of its triumphs since the youth of Bach, have assigned
that place to music'. If Mr Pater had said Hucbald,(2) we
should not have quarrelled with him; but to regard a
colossus like Bach as representative of the infancy of
music, is indeed a strange solecism.
   The prefatory essay on Style amounts in its sum to a
well-reasoned plea for eclecticism, and the note struck
here is repeated in the postscript on Classicism and Romanticism. There he declares that the scholar of the future
will admit that the style of the nineteenth century was
justified by necessity, — 'a style very different, alike
from the baldness of an impossible "Queen Anne" revival,
and an incorrect, incondite exuberance, after the mode of
Elizabeth'. The literary artist, who must inevitably be a
scholar, will find the laws of language not a restriction,
but an opportunity. They will brace rather than hamper
him. But he must beget a vocabulary of his own; he must
expand and purify the elements of his language, and restore the finer edge of words still in use. Viewed in the
light of a practical experiment on these lines, it cannot
be said that these essays are wholly successful. The very
title of the book — 'Appreciations' — is a case in point,
and, to us at least, the effort to acclimatise a Gallicism
smacks of affectation. Again, to any one who has ever
glanced at a cookery-book, the word to 'clarify' is saturated with culinary associations. Mr Pater has endeavoured
to restore to it its finer edge by applying the term 'clari-
fying' to somebody's soul; but we fear that his gallant
effort will prove abortive. Soyer and Francatelli(3) are
not to be robbed of their own. What we care least about
in the Patristic school is its foppery of phrase, 'the
fancy', as its chief puts it, 'so many of us have for an

exquisite and curious skill in the use of words', and
which occasionally degenerates into a sort of fantastic
rhapsodising, — as, for example, when Mr Pater describes
the Provençal poetry:

> Here under this strange complex of conditions, as in
> some medicated air, exotic flowers of sentiment expand,
> among people of a remote and unaccustomed beauty, som-
> nambulistic, frail, androgynous, the light almost shin-
> ing through them.

This is not the work of a man of letters, but a 'stylist',
— to use a base coinage which has at least the merit of
suggesting artificiality and affectation.

The 'appreciation' of Wordsworth is, we think, excellent, and full of acute remarks. 'There was in Wordsworth's character,' writes Mr Pater, 'a certain contentment, a sort of inborn religious placidity, seldom found
united with a sensibility so mobile as his, which was
favourable to the quiet, habitual observation of inanimate,
or imperfectly animate, existence.' 'To read one of his
longer pastoral poems for the first time, is like a day
spent in a new country: the memory is crowded for a while
with its precise and vivid incidents.' Later on, Mr Pater
insists with much force that man's close connection with
natural objects, so far from degrading him in Wordsworth's
eyes by emphasising the physical connection of our nature
with the actual lime and clay of the soil, rather tended
to the dignity of human nature, because they tended to
tranquillise it. 'By raising nature to the level of human
thought, he gives it power and expression: he subdues man
to the level of human nature, and gives him thereby a certain breadth and coolness and solemnity.' It was because
he saw man as a part of Nature that Wordsworth was able to
appreciate passion in the lowly.

> He chooses to depict people from humble life, because,
> being nearer to Nature than others, they are on the
> whole more impassioned, certainly more direct in their
> expression of passion, than other men: it is for this
> direct expression of passion that he values their
> humble words.

'What he values most [in scenes of pastoral life] is the
almost elementary expression of elementary feelings.'
Finally, Mr Pater regards Wordsworth's poetry as a continual protest against the predominance of machinery in
our existence — i.e., the conception of means and ends —
the end-in-itself with the poet being 'impassioned con-

templation'. In the study of Coleridge, Mr Pater's
faculty of quotation is again most happily exhibited.
There is an interesting passage in which Wordsworth and
Coleridge are contrasted, from which we may be allowed to
take the following paragraph:

[Quotes Coleridge: 'Wordsworth's flawless temperament' to
'the transcendental schools of Germany'.]

Mr Pater is at his best in what he says of Coleridge's
superlative skill in handling the supernatural, compared
with which 'the too palpable intruders from a spiritual
world in almost all ghost literature, in Scott and Shakespeare even, have a kind of crudity or coarseness'. The
estimate of Charles Lamb which follows is, but for one or
two slightly 'precious' paragraphs, an excellent piece of
sympathetic criticism. In the character as well as in
the writings of Lamb, one may see, according to Mr Pater,
a visible interpretation and instance of the distinction
between wit and humour. Mr Pater dwells on Lamb's lifelong sacrifice, the ever-present undercurrent of tragedy
beneath his cheerful exterior, his modesty, and his disinterested devotion to literature pure and simple, pointing out with great truth that his detachment from the
theories of the time, combined with his immediate contact
with what was real, have given to his work an exceptional
enduringness. Mr Pater's habitual pensiveness as a critic, and the autumnal tone of his work, make this tribute
to Charles Lamb all the more remarkable. In the books and
domestic correspondence of Sir Thomas Browne, Mr Pater has
found another thoroughly congenial subject on which he discourses in a long and thoughtful paper. But, on the whole,
the best and most penetrating criticism in the volume is
contained in the short postscript on Classicism and Romanticism. Mr Pater is scrupulously fair to the advocates
of either school, and while he holds Stendhal's views to
be more suggestive, admits the greater reasonableness of
Sainte-Beuve. Again, though holding France to be — whether in the old Provençal poetry or the prose of this century — the best and truest representative of the Romantic
temper, he regrets its antinomian *bizarrerie*,(4) the malign
element which mars its beauty. Finally, after declaring
his conviction that both elements are united in perfect
art, he defines it to be the proper aim and problem of
modern literary art

  to induce order upon the contorted, proportionless
  accumulation of our knowledge and experience, our
  science and history, our hopes and disillusions, and

in effecting this, to do consciously what has been done
hitherto too unconsciously, to write our English language as the Latins wrote theirs, as the French write,
as scholars should write.

'Consciously', — there is where the danger resides, for
consciousness so often degenerates into self-consciousness.
We have read these essays with a great deal of pleasure,
which would have been further enhanced could we but rid
ourselves of the occasional impression, — we admit that
it is only occasional, — that the author was thinking less
of what he wanted to say than of the effect that his periods would produce on his audience.

Notes

1 Things which are noble are different.
2 Hucbald (c. 840-930): a Flemish monk and musical theorist.
  What has been preserved of his musical work is confined
  to the treatise entitled 'De harmonica institutione'.
3 Alexis Soyer (1809-58) and Charles Francatelli (1805-76)
  were celebrated London cooks (both were chefs at the
  Reform Club).
4 Peculiarity

45. MRS OLIPHANT, UNSIGNED REVIEW, 'BLACKWOOD'S MAGAZINE'

January 1890, cxlvii, 140-5

See No. 10 and Introduction, p. 31. Mrs Oliphant recalls
her attack on Pater's interpretation of Botticelli's
Madonnas in 1873 and commends him for his recantation.

... we have here a specimen of a critic who is of the most
cultured and esoteric type; one of those who demands a
special audience, and almost a special education in order
to understand and enter into the strain of thought which
is almost too superfine for human nature's daily food. We
remember our own first startling encounter with this refiner of refined gold, in one of his early efforts, when
he described the Madonna of one of Botticelli's pictures

(a master just discovered, so to speak, by a new generation of connoisseurs, and rising into notoriety through
their judicious exertions), as accepting her divine mother-
hood with angry reluctance, and writing her Magnificat
sullenly with rebellion in her heart. The idea was so
remarkable, that we have ever since seen Mr Walter Pater,
in our mind's eye, decorated with a medal representing the
great *tondo*(1) of Botticelli, in everlasting memory of one
of the most incongruous and grotesque misrepresentations
ever invented by man — a criticism 'supreme', as he
would himself say, in its incomprehension of the faith and
the art of the period which he discussed. This gentleman
has done something since to wipe out youthful indiscretions;
but we allow that prejudice is strong, and that the remembrance of our Botticelli stands between us and the more
mature work, in which it is to be hoped there is a better
harvest of reflection, and less daring originality of
thought.
   We fall, however, into very thorny ways when we plunge
into the Essay on Style, in which Mr Pater's literary creed
is set forth, and which he places at the head of various
milder chapters of literary discussion or, as he calls them,
Appreciations, of sundry poets and works. To search out
the poetry in prose and the prose in poetry is, he tells
us, one of the fine operations of criticism.

> To find in the poem, amid the flowers, the allusions,
> the mixed perspectives, of 'Lycidas', for instance, the
> thought, the logical structure: — how wholesome! how
> delightful! as to identify in prose what we call the
> poetry, the imaginative power, not treating it as out
> of place and a kind of vagrant intruder, but by way
> of an estimate of its rights, that is, of its achieved
> powers, there.

This sentence is a little difficult to follow, and its
cadence is not flowing; but there is no reason why a man
should necessarily embody his theory in his own utterance.
For though Mr Pater recognises more or less the virtue
of a just selection of facts or ideas in literature, and
of that individual view which distinguishes history, for
instance, from a mere record of events, the chief point
upon which he insists in his discussion of style is the
manipulation of words, of which he speaks as a French
painter talks of the values of colour, yet in a more absolute sense. For colour has a gradation and meaning of its
own, and it is possible to produce something that will
please the eye and be pleasantly suggestive to the mind by
a study in tones and tints, a sort of simulated landscape

or drama; whereas it would be difficult so to mass and
group words dissociated from their meaning as to please
anybody or attain any serious effect. This is a distinction which it is very necessary to draw when the writer
uses terms belonging to one art to elucidate and explain
another. It is possible, for instance, to work out the
scheme of a picture so as to concentrate its effect, as if
that were the sole effect intended, in one clear tone, the
high light which gives soul and animation to the picture;
but when Mr Pater tells us that he 'fears to miss the
least promising composition' among the poems of Wordsworth,
'lest some precious morsel should be lying hidden within —
the few perfect lines, the phrase, the single word, perhaps, to which he often works up mechanically through a
poem almost the whole of which may be tame enough', — we
fail to follow his argument. To what single word could
Wordsworth, or any other poet, work up mechanically, so
as to move us to rapture at the end when the effect was
attained? Could it be Helvellyn? (a beautiful word), or
Skiddaw? (not so fine) or — what? We have all heard of
Mesopotamia, though we little expected to find an advocate
for its sweetness in such an apostle of the cultured.
    We submit that this is as nearly pure nonsense as it
is possible for any assertion given forth *ex cathedra* and
with a bland consciousness of authority, to be. Mr Pater
himself has used as many words as most men — more, we
think, in many cases than his subject demanded — and nobody would have been better qualified to give examples of
the one single word to which a great poet may be working
up through all the long range of a poem otherwise tame
enough; but he does not suggest any that would be worth
so elaborate a process.

[Anecdote, about a personal friend who attempted to write
an ode but collapsed after writing the word 'Oh', omitted.]

    We have here, however, diverged a little from Mr Pater's
canons of style, this being a simple reference to one of
its highest efforts attained. In the following page we
are permitted to see the process by which such success is
achieved.

[Quotes Style: 'Any writer worth translating' to 'a fine
fastidious scholarship throughout'.]

    We should have been disposed to say without so many
phrases that Tennyson, like all other great poets and
masters of style, seized his words where he found them,
without pausing to think whether they were monosyllabic or

metaphysic, or 'savoursome' Latin, so long as they run
well into his music; and that if he had left the phraseology of science alone he would have done better, in our
modest opinion; but the thoughts of the *Précieux*(2) are
not as ours. We are, however, sadly at a loss to know what
is the finer edge of *ascertain*, *communicate*, and *discover*,
which are very good serviceable words, and which our conscience for one is quite free of any intention to harm.
How has it been Mr Pater's 'business' (the commas are his
own) to misuse them? What has our Professor done to those
innocent parts of speech that lies so heavily on his mind?
The offended ones are too magnanimous to complain, and we
fear that our own perceptions are not sufficiently delicate
to find out this most exquisite crime. Perhaps he will let
us know another time, when he has done his penance and made
amends. Here are three other words which do not seem to
have been misused, but which Mr Pater exhorts his scholar
to employ. 'Correctly recognising the incident, the colour,
the physical elements or particles in words like *absorb*,
consider, *extract*, to take the first that occur, he will
avail himself of them as further adding to the resources
of expression'. Now here is a case in which we find ourselves in the exact position of M Jourdain,(3) who found to
his delight that he had been speaking prose all his life
without knowing it. We have availed ourselves of the words
absorb, *consider*, and *extract*, for — centuries we had well-
nigh said, without, we fear, any more regard for the incident, colour, or physical elements in them than if they
had been such detestable compounds as suck-up and take-out.
What it is to be a scholar! But such a subject as this
cannot be exhausted in a single sentence. We claim from
Mr Pater at least a pamphlet on the right use of these six
words, for the instruction of persons, experienced and in-
experienced, whose trade it is to work with words, but
whose education has been arrested before it had reached
the perfection of this eclecticism. We wish to be instructed as to the finer edge of *Ascertain*, *Communicate*, and
Discover (we give them capitals, which Mr Pater has not
taken the trouble to do), and how to acquire it: along
with fuller details of the incident and colour of *Absorb*,
Consider, and *Extract* — words of which, in the uninten-
tional contempt which is bred by familiarity, we, it is
evident, have not been half respectful enough. But we are
very willing to make up for our irreverence if our learned
instructor will only show us how, and tell us why.
    Mr Pater is, however, to the common intelligence, unen-
lightened in such recondite particulars, much more agreeable as a companion when he has a thread of something tangible to guide him, and does not dwell upon abstractions,

which, indeed, he believes to be bad for style in general,
as leading towards the classical instead of the romantic
treatment. It is rather terrible to meet with this old
classical and romantic business in the discussion of English literature. We have had, Heaven knows, enough of it
in French to bewilder anybody's brain, and a new definition is more than human nature can support, especially
where it makes nothing clear, and is not wanted in a language like ours, and amid traditions always romantic, though
the word is quite unnecessary. But it is evident, we may
say in passing, that Greek as Mr Pater is in soul, his
models of style are all French. This is, we think, a great
mistake: for nothing can be more certain — and it is a
truth far more obvious to the common understanding than
the supreme meaning in 'ascertain', 'absorb', etc. — than
that each language has an individual genius and rhythm of
its own, and that excellence in one cannot be the standard
of excellence in another. Flaubert, we do not doubt, was
a great artist, but the secret of his skill, and his eclecticism in words, could not be copied by an English writer
whose idioms are entirely different, and whose characteristic excellences ought to be, if he is true to his own
tongue, of another kind. Nothing, accordingly, can be more
false than the attempt to bring us to this standard, which
is not ours. France has an Academy, and we have none, nor
every will or can have any such arbitrator of excellence.
By the way, we cannot but ask in passing what the Academy
thinks of 'five-o'clocker' as a verb, or 'struggle-for-
lifer'? It is evidently the duty of that august body to
interfere and pronounce, once for all, as is its right,
against such debasing adaptations. And we must protest,
on our side, against a foreign model which is altogether
out of the question as affording any rule for us. Our
chief enjoyment in French style is, in fact, its unlikeness
to our own, just as friends and lovers are supposed to suit
each other better when they have no feature alike. The
concise and logical clearness, the lucidity of French narrative, is a thing to admire and emulate; but those keen
words which are ever apt to become a little shrill in the
using, and which cut, with a clean edge, the tangles of
history, are not congenial to our ways of working; and even
if we would adopt them, would grow not only shrill but hard
and toneless in our hands: while French rhetoric is even
more completely out of our habitudes, and might easily
become rant in English. Take, for instance, the French
fondness for the first person in narrative: how tawdry it
becomes in English, and what trouble a judicious translator
has to turn it into the historical tense, — a fundamental
difference which makes it at once apparent how different

are the methods of the two tongues. It is amusing, however, to find that, if Mr Pater's French standard leads
him away from the natural English censors, we are able to
meet him at every turn of his preciousness with Molière,
and to prove the unity of human nature as well as of a
national language in the fine touch of a satirical critic,
whose frank laugh over learned nonsense will never be anti-
quated while that type of folly lasts.

We were about to say, however, when we were led astray
into this digression, that Mr Pater was a much more agreeable companion when he had a more definite theme in hand.
His essay on Wordsworth is a pleasant variety upon a subject which has been driven to death, but which, were not
the statement almost too strong to be believed, we might
venture to say he had treated with something like novelty.
Novelty, indeed, is unquestionably in the statement already
quoted, that the poet of the lakes and mountains occasionally composes a long poem which is tame enough, for the
sake of a phrase or single word which may come in the middle of it. Wordsworth himself was no critic, and probably
liked the poem which Mr Pater thinks tame, and was not
aware of the word in it which flashes jewel-like upon the
consciousness of his disciple. But there are other chapters in this volume, to do him justice, in which we find
not only comprehension of, but reverence for, his subject.
Still more excellent is the article on Sir Thomas Browne,
which is a pleasant study of a man whose personality we
know too little about, and of whom we are always glad to
have something more. It would have been more excellent
still had there been further details of the life of the
excellent physician of Norwich. We can only note that
some of the criticisms of Shakespeare are also good, delicate, and discriminating, though a little too subtle, as
is Mr Pater's way.

Notes

1 Painting, carving in relief, with circular shape.
2 Blue Stockings: see Molière's 'Les Précieuses ridi-
  cules' (1659).
3 Character in Molière's 'Le Bourgeois gentilhomme' (1670).

46. LIONEL JOHNSON ON PATER

1890

Signed article entitled A Note, upon Certain Qualities in
the Writings of Mr Pater; as Illustrated in his Recent
Book, in the 'Century Guild Hobby Horse' (January 1890),
vi, 36-40. See Nos 72, 93 and 95 and Introduction, p. 30.

Lionel Pigot Johnson (1867-1902), a gifted poet and
critic, was a prominent member of the Rhymers' Club. He
published two volumes of verse, 'Poems' (1895) and 'Ireland' (1897), and one book of criticism, 'The Art of
Thomas Hardy' (1894), which established his reputation.

Johnson met Pater in 1887 in the rooms of Arthur Galton
(1852-1921), the scholar, critic and priest, when he was a
student (1886-90) at New College, Oxford. Pater showed
his esteem for his enthusiastic disciple by giving him a
presentation copy of each of his books (Wright, ii, 204).
Johnson remained a close friend of Pater in his last years
and helped C.L. Shadwell to 'sort out Pater's literary remains and advised him in the preparation of the three
posthumous volumes' (LWP, 108n). He recorded his reminiscences in The Work of Mr Pater, published in the 'Fortnightly Review' (September 1894), lxii, 352-67.

For Pater's response to Johnson's article, see Introduction, p. 10. Pater wrote to Johnson on 20 February 1890:

I have read with great pleasure your careful and scholarly paper on my work; and value it. You write with
great refinement: pleasantly, at once, and with a pervading air of thoughtful concentration (LWP, 108).

Some of those rare essays of Mr Pater, which give to a few
old numbers of our magazines a lasting value, are here
gathered by their author into a book: the fourth of his
laborious and perfected books. 'Appreciations', Mr Pater
calls it: 'Appreciations, with an Essay on Style'. In
the French tongue of our day, that word has come to mean
no more than Essays or Studies; critical estimates. But
to our English the word, I think, is new: and we may
fancy in it a meaning something more delicate and subtle;
it would seem to promise a quality of reserve, a judgment
very personal, a fine tolerance towards the reader. However this be, the book has these excellences, in full measure: each essay has a certain stateliness of progression,

it is sure of itself;   yet, its handling of things is so
gentle, that the reader finds himself confirming the
author, assenting to his appeal.   And here is a witness
to the author's triumph, an assurance of the reader's satisfaction.

The whole book deals with literary things and men of
letters; an Essay on Style, that mysterious thing! heads
it with propriety.   Mr Pater has written nothing that is
styleless, that is lawless: nothing, also, that is not
most absolutely the work of his proper genius.   And here
he is telling us what style means: how it means the production of work through an harmony of excellences;   on
one side the liberty of power, on the other the law of
restraint.   Is this, asks the artist, a fine discovery of
beauty? or is it a temptation disguised in beauty for the
moment?   Am I honouring Art, by obedience to these traditions? or dishonouring myself, in the rejection of fine
chances?   As the artist decides, so does he find his salvation, or determine his failure: if he decide well, his
work is alive with style;   he will live.   But the difficulty of decision! for it requires a very casuistry to
lay at rest questions of the artistic conscience: a knowledge of the ends of Art, an insight into the perplexed
issues, the tangled ideas, which beset the artist's mind,
and confuse his plain morality.   It is a saying of Mill:
'The course of nature is not only uniform, it is also
infinitely various'.   And just so, *forma*, the beauty of
Art, is *indivisibilis*, *multipartita*:(1) many ways lead to
the Kingdom, but they meet at last.

In perfect sympathy, then, with the great differences
of successful Art, Mr Pater has written ten essays upon
literary work: these I am not called upon to examine; nor
have I that right to do so, which only a practised ability
confers;   but I will try to say something, that may explain the effect of these essays upon an ordinary mind.

In reading Wordsworth; who has not felt an exaltation
in the mind, a sense of meditative beauty, a spiritual
calm?   Lamb, too; who, after an while in his company,
has not felt a glow of the affections, a cheerful thanks-
giving going out towards the writer?   But these are only
sentiments;   they explain nothing: it is one distinction
of the critic in Mr Pater, that he does not rest upon the
expression of sentiments;   that he makes us understand
them, at least in the sense of his understanding.   We read
Wordsworth and a score of his critics with pleasure, with
indiscreet emotion;   we read Mr Pater upon Wordsworth with
an illumination of the intellect, a light which illuminates
in Wordsworth the farthest beauty, and the last refinement.
The second thoughts, or meditations, of understanding,

222 Walter Pater: The Critical Heritage

interpret so the first thoughts, or raptures, of pleasure:
point after point, refinement upon refinement, proceeds
this great interpretation. And, since nothing of the mind
is quite simple, this search after the final truths in
Art exacts much, of all who undertake it: patience, to
endure subtilties to the uttermost; reflection, to make
sure of the way; sincerity, to withstand the seduction of
theories. Constantly observing these careful methods, Mr
Pater does not fail to 'pluck the heart' out of the 'mysteries' of imaginative work: with insistence here, and
with warning there, he brings home to us, he makes clear
to us, what it is that charms us, or surprises, in an artist's quality. So perfect a light is 'broken over' the
matters in hand, that we become intimate with the artist;
we become his internal and spiritual audience, the ini-
tiates of his mystery. Milton has defined, with truth,
the conditions of pure criticism:

> Who reads
> Incessantly, and to his reading brings not
> A spirit and judgment equal or superior,
> Uncertain and unsettled still remains,
> Deep versed in books, and shallow in himself,
> Crude or intoxicate.(1)

To 'enjoy' a book, to relish its quality, confers no right
to criticise it: not that alone. The true criticism is
not a rapture of delight, a cry of enthusiasm; but, much
more, the result of a profound and prolonged meditation.
Ours is an age of infinite talk about books: easy talk,
by men trained in the school of affectation and loose
feeling: let us be grateful to Mr Pater, who can make of
criticism a thing creative and illuminating; creative of
new perfections, whilst it illuminates the old.
 This, then, is one excellence of Mr Pater; his intellectual hold upon things, and a second is, his intellectual presentation of them. There are some writers, reviewers, critics, doing honour, they suppose, to Mr Pater, who
speak as though he did for us, in prose, what 'the idle
singer of an empty day' has done in verse: they take him
for a composer of charming phrases, a discoverer of curious
thoughts. This is to move upon the surface of things, to
deal with truths by halves. Mr Pater is, indeed, full of
such charm, he abounds in outward beauty, but to the construction of his work, to its reasoned form, they are blind.
No doubt Mr Pater does not obtrude a philosophical learning, nor parade a philosophical purpose, yet, all his
work is wholly steeped in profuse thought; so orderly,
as to be taken for granted; so won for literature, as to

lose all harshness of the schools. There is a philosophic
rigour of phraseology, a scientific precision of statement; but tempered by the saving graces of an wider comprehension, than may belong to the man of science only, or
of mere metaphysics. A knowledge of Art, of history, of
literature, a singular mastery over such things, it is on
all hands recognized that Mr Pater possesses; perhaps imperfect justice has been done to the way in which philosophic theories, and facts of science, and methods of
logic, are taken by Mr Pater into the service of literature.
Nothing is harder than to do this; than to seize upon the
'aesthetic' value, say! of 'Darwinism', or of 'Idealism',
and to get from them their essence of life, that quality
in them which is their contribution to the mind's treasury.
And here I must make one quotation from Mr Pater's Postscript:

[Quotes Postscript: 'For the literary art' to 'after the
mode of Elizabeth'.]

Of such scholarship as he praises, Mr Pater has set an
example, bringing to bear upon his work an wealth of re-
source, within the possession of few, and availing himself
of it, with a conception of propriety and of order, within
the reach of fewer still. It was a great saying of Blake,
that visionary! as we call him, 'grandeur of ideas is
founded on precision of ideas':(3) that is, time and
place, conception and execution, sweetness and strength,
must agree together; a complete moderation, an infallible
'sanity of true genius', alone discover the right procedure. An apostle has left us his account of the construction of sanctity in the soul: *Totum corpus compactum, et
connexum per omnem iuncturam subministrationis, secundum
operationem in mensuram unius cuiusque membri, augmentum
corporis facit in aedificationem sui.*(4) A soul, thus edi-
fied, is full of sweetness and of strength, is clear,
grave, and tranquil: Literature, if it be good, if it have
any virtue, is composed upon no different principles. Construction gives truth, the truth of harmony, the single-
ness of intention, the concord of ideas: all these things
are shown forth in work that has been elaborated within the
mind, before it has been furnished with final graces. It
is exhilarating, it is no less than inspiring, to read a
page of these essays, to note how each careful word, and
careful sentence, lies in its true place, gives out its
proper tone, diffuses its just influence over the neighbouring words and sentences.
Let me dwell a little upon one more excellence: upon the
touching gentleness, the winning tenderness, prevalent over

Mr Pater's work. There is a terrible facility in pathos;
the stroke of sentiment, the touch upon the nerves of sensibility, how easily are these effected! But in Mr Pater's
work we are ever remembering with Blake, that 'a tear is an
intellectual thing';(5) with Virgil, remembering the *lacrimae rerum*,(6) that tears are of the nature of things,
really in them. And in this way the pitifulness, the loving kindnesses, found throughout these writings, are a part
of their intellectual worth: the discrowned Richard;
Rossetti and Coleridge in their world of shadows; Lamb
with 'the whole woeful heart of things' open before him;
these troubles and sorrows are as moving, as were those of
'Marius', of Sebastian. Moving, because revealing; revealing, each of them a little more of that 'woeful heart',
than our minds had already known: or, at the least, more
than we had appreciated intellectually.

'On this short day of frost and sun', as that recovered
Conclusion has it, a great experience by the way of intellectual light, or of sensuous beauty, is most desirable;
singularly so, when it reaches us in the forms of Art,
those perfected forms: Let us be thankful, then, to Mr
Pater; who has now placed within our reach a fresh indulgence of that desire.

Notes

1 Form; indivisible; multipartite.
2 See p. 94n.
3 From Annotations to Sir Joshua Reynolds's 'Discourses'.
4 The body is a unity and it is interconnected in every
  joint according to the efficiency and the role of every
  single member, hence the improvement of each of these
  is the improvement of the body as a whole. See 1 Corinthians xii, 12-26.
5 'I Saw a Monk of Charlemaine', 1. 25.
6 '*Sunt lacrimae rerum et mentem mortalia tangunt*': Here
  are the tears of things; mortality touches the heart.
  'Aeneid', i, 462.

47. L.C. MOULTON, SIGNED NOTICE, BOSTON 'SUNDAY HERALD'

5 January 1890, 24

See Introduction, p. 30.

Ellen Louise Chandler Moulton (1835-1908), American poet
and writer of juvenile stories. She married (1855) a journalist and publisher from Boston; many prominent musi-
cians, writers and artists attended her Friday salons.
From 1876 she frequently spent the summer in London and
made the acquaintance of a wide number of British writers
and artists. Throughout 1886 to 1892 she contributed a
weekly letter on books to the 'Sunday Herald'.

Pater may have solicited the notice or 'Chat' (see
Introduction, p. 11). It was said in the 'Dial' (September 1887) that her 'Chats' were 'light and informal, well
adapted to the exigencies of idle moments or hurried readers' (viii, 103). Pater sent her a 'late but sincere word
of thanks' for the 'kind notice' in his letter of 25 February 1890 (see LWP, 109).

... I chanced, one day last summer, to sit next Mr W.H.
Mallock(1) at dinner, and heard him say something about
style which impressed itself on my memory.

A man who writes prose and expects an audience of cultivated readers, owes them three things. First of all
he should have some ideas of his own, something to say,
in short. Next he should say this something in good
English, with a just sense of the value of the words
he uses, but I do not think his duty ends there. He
should, in addition, study the melody of his sentences.
Not that his prose should be rhythmical, like verse;
but it should have melody — it should caress the ear.
A sentence should be so well balanced that it should
linger harmoniously, and not discordantly, upon the
memory.

These words of Mallock's recurred to me when I began to
read

Walter Pater's Latest Work,

'Appreciations', just published by Macmillan & Co. Mr
Pater fulfills all Mr Mallock's conditions. He has something to say; he says it in English undefiled, and his
sentences caress the ear and linger like music in the
memory. But, in addition to these, he has yet another
gift to the last degree individual — he has the power of
illumination. In a single phrase he flashes a new light
on the subject he is discussing, and yet what he says

seems so inevitable that we all wonder we have not thought
of it before. Thus it is, for instance, when he says that
'contemplation — impassioned contemplation — is with
Wordsworth the end in itself, the perfect end'. What can
be finer than his description of the passion and the pathos
which made Wordsworth immortal — a pathos of which we
are all aware; a passion which, perhaps, is too seldom
acknowledged? Wordsworth did not choose the scenes of
rural life to repose in their passionless calm, but rather
that the stage might be cleared of extraneous things, of
the transient agitations of the outward world, and left
for the strong exhibition of elementary emotions.
    As Mr Pater beautifully says:

[Quotes Wordsworth: 'The great, distinguishing passion
came to Michael by the sheepfold' to 'our best modern fiction has caught from him'.]

It seems to me that nobler tribute than this to the best
gifts of Wordsworth has never yet been paid.

The Paper on Charles Lamb

is altogether delightful. Mr Pater sees in Lamb's disinterested love of literature — his interest in the
things which abide, rather than in the transient circumstances of any special epoch — the secret of his perennial
hold upon our interests. Lamb cannot be old-fashioned,
since he deals with things of which the fashion does not
change.
    I like greatly, too, the paper on Coleridge, who talked
so much and did so little — of whom De Quincey said that
'he wanted better bread than could be made with wheat', and
Lamb said that 'from childhood he had hungered for eternity'. Mr Pater emphasizes the most curious fact in Coleridge's literary history — the marvellous fact that nearly
all the works by which his poetic fame will live were composed, or at least planned, in the single wonder year of
1797-1798. Coleridge did not, like most true poets, present
us with the gradual development of a poetic gift: but the
sudden blossoming, through one short year, of a gift suddenly perfect, and destined to deteriorate as suddenly as
it had blossomed. I can think of nothing like this brief
and matchless unfolding (which took place in Coleridge's
25th year) in the whole range of literary history.
    There is no critic writing today who seems to me so
helpful and so stimulating as Walter Pater. This volume
also includes, besides the papers I have mentioned, an admirable essay on Style, and seven others, devoted, respec-

tively, to Sir Thomas Browne; 'Love's Labour's Lost',
'Measure for Measure', Shakspere's English Kings, Aesthetic
Poetry, Dante Gabriel Rossetti, and a Postscript. There is
not one of them which is unworthy of its neighbors. If we
miss the subtle and marvellous creative power which gave
us 'Marius the Epicurean', or sketched for us the exquisitely beautiful 'Imaginary Portraits', we find, instead,
the sanest and subtlest appreciation of other men's works,
and the clearest insight into the sources of their power.
It is criticism with which it is almost a liberal education to be familiar.
    I especially enjoyed the paper on Style. Who, save Mr
Pater, can give you the whole character of

                A Man's Work in an Adjective;

as, for instance, where he says that prose is picturesque
with Livy and Carlyle; musical with Cicero and Newman;
mystical and intimate with Plato, and Michelet and Sir
Thomas Browne; exalted or florid it may be with Milton
and Taylor. He speaks of Pascal as belonging to the 'persuasive writers'; and of Livy and Tacitus and Michelet as
moving, full of poignant sensibility, amid the records
of the past.

    Different classes of persons, at different times, make,
    of course, very various demands upon literature. Still,
    scholars, I suppose, and not only scholars but all dis-
    interested lovers of books, will always look to it, as
    to all other fine art, for a refuge, a sort of cloistral
    refuge, from a certain vulgarity in the actual world.
    A perfect poem like 'Lycidas', a perfect fiction like
    'Esmond', the perfect handling of a theory like Newman's
    'Idea of a University', has for them something of the
    uses of a religious 'retreat'....

To these examples of what is highest, cited by Mr Pater, I
wish to add criticism like his own, in which it seems to me
one can take refuge from the base and transitory judgments,
and the clamor of the noisy hour....

Note

1 William Hurrell Mallock (1849-1923), novelist, went up
  to Balliol College, Oxford, in 1869, but became disil-
  lusioned with Oxford Liberalism, especially with the
  views of Benjamin Jowett, the Master of the College. His
  satiric defence of old and traditional beliefs against

the encroachments of liberalism, 'The New Republic' (1877), caused a considerable stir in Oxford. Pater is caricatured as 'Mr Rose' the 'arch-aesthete' who always speaks of 'self-indulgence and art' in an undertone.

48.   J.A. SYMONDS ON PATER

1890

Extracts from 'The Letters of John Addington Symonds' (1967-9), ed. Herbert M. Schueller and Robert L. Peters. See Nos 2, 3 and 21.

(a)   From a letter dated 19 January 1890 to Horatio Forbes Brown

This influenza is a very singular thing. It has left me all to bits. What I resent most is that my head is gone. I cannot write — literature I mean — and hardly a decent letter. And I cannot follow a difficult book. I tried Pater's 'Appreciations' to-day, and found myself wandering about among the precious sentences, just as though I had lost myself in a sugar-cane plantation — the worse for being sweet. (iii, 440)

(b)   From a letter dated 16 October 1890 to the Reverend Arthur Galton

Pater made his great mark in letters by a volume of carefully finished essays, penetrated through & through with the unity of his peculiar personality. (iii, 510)

49.   AGNES REPPLIER, UNSIGNED REVIEW, 'CATHOLIC WORLD'

February 1890, 1, 704-6

See No. 78 and Introduction, pp. 5 and 30.

Agnes Repplier (1858-1950), American essayist, became
a contributor to the 'Catholic World' and the 'Atlantic
Monthly' at the age of nineteen. She travelled widely in
Europe, won a number of honorary doctorates, as well as
the Laetare Medal of Notre Dame University in 1911 and the
gold medal of the Academy of Arts and Letters in 1935 and
became known as the cultural leader of Philadelphia. Henry
James met her on a lecture tour and held her in high
regard.

This review expresses the characteristic response of
the Catholic Church to Pater as the chief spokesman for
the Aesthetic Movement (see also No. 71). Compare Symons's
view, headnote to No. 58.

A book from the pen of Mr Walter Pater is certain of a
welcome from all those whose welcome is worth the having.
There is that about his style that marks him as painstaking and exacting even to the turn of a phrase — perhaps more painstaking as regards the turn of a phrase than
as regards the whole truth of a statement. Still, his
book is such as scholars delight in, even when bound to
differ with him. 'Appreciations' is not always easy reading. The sentences lack directness and point. They are
not unfrequently labored — the sentences of one groping
after fresh material and new form in which to clothe it.

The book contains suggestive essays about Wordsworth
and Coleridge and Charles Lamb. But the authors with whom
Mr Pater seems to be most in sympathy are William Morris
and Dante Gabriel Rossetti. The whole bent of his mind is
towards the school of modern aestheticism. Indeed, his
writings may well be taken as the best prosaic exponent of
that school. There is the same devotion to art for art's
sake; there is the same careful structure of sentences;
there is the same sense for the weird and the bizarre;
there also is the same anxiety to leave all beaten paths
and explore new fields of thought and construct new forms
of expression.

To our mind the most thoughtful essay in the book is
the opening one on Style. It is fresh and suggestive. It
has the advantage of being written by one who has made a
study of his subject, and who knows whereof he speaks. The
very names he mentions show the high ideal he has set up.

[Quotes Style: 'Different classes of persons' to 'the uses
of a religious "retreat"'.]

In this quotation we find Mr Pater's central idea of
literature — the point of view from which he regards it —
as well as his ideals. Literature is to him a fine art,
'like all other fine art'. As such it must possess form.
The form may be severe and unadorned, as in some of Stendhal's best work; it may be luxuriant in ornament, as in
'Les Miserables' of Victor Hugo; it may be rich in the
graces of unpretentious and unconscious beauty, as in 'The
Vicar of Wakefield'; so long as it contains the unity of
design, the proportion of parts, 'the one beauty' that is
of the essence of the subject and is 'independent, in prose
and verse alike, of all removable decoration', so long will
the work be appreciated as a piece of art. According to
Mr Pater, the great element that enters into the construction of artistic form is 'self-restraint, a skilful economy
of means'. 'The artist,' says Schiller, 'may be known
rather by what he omits.' But, as we shall see later on,
this artistic omission has various aspects, all of which
must be taken into account when criticising a work.

It is to be regretted that Mr Pater barely touches
upon the rhythm of prose. It is a fruitful theme and it
may yet lead to the construction of laws of prose rhythm
as well defined as those of poetic rhythm. It underlies
every form of approved style. It varies with a music all
its own. The rhythm of Milton's 'Areopagitica' is distinct from that of Hooker's celebrated definition of law
in the 'Ecclesiastical Polity'; these, again, are distinct from that of Macaulay's well-known passage on the
church or Newman's classic sentences on music. Then,
also, is there variety in each author. Now he writes in
a minor key, now in a major.

But a more serious oversight in Mr Pater's discussion
of style is the fact that he loses sight of the possibilities of style. He speaks as though all the best
forms of style were exhausted. Indeed, he is almost a
Humanist in his conception of the importance of form. But
we cannot make the past the exclusive measure of the
future. Every innovation of every great artist has been
a shock to his contemporaries. We have before us a remonstrance of a friend and admirer of Michelangelo's when that
great artist painted 'The Last Judgment' in the Sistine
Chapel. The artist represented every vice in all its hor-
rors as his vast brain conceived it, and the friend objected to the boldness of the conception and the freedom of
its execution. He was shocked. No doubt we shall all be
shocked on that dread day — 'that day of wrath'. A complacent painting of that subject must needs be a failure.
The remedy for Michelangelo was not to clothe his naked,
loathsome figures, but to wipe out the great masterpiece.

Again, the admirers of Mozart and Bach and Beethoven
found in the music of Wagner nothing but the discord and
the shrieks of nature. But who will say to-day that
Wagner has not given music a new and a noble form? So
also with Browning. He seems to have smashed every mould
of literary expression, and out of the fragments fashioned
unto himself a rough and rugged mould in which he throws
his magnificent soul-readings. Does not our disappointment arise from our bringing to the reading of him our
preconceived literary notions? Of course we do not find
them. His work is not that of rehearsing and re-echoing.
He has a mission all his own, and he expresses himself in
language all his own. We look, for instance, for growth
and development of character as exemplified in a series
of words and acts. Browning has nothing to do with growth
and development of character. He leaves that to the novelist. His work is to take a soul in the supreme moment —
the great crisis of its life — and show forth the making
or the marring of that soul under the touch of adversity
or prosperity. Or, in a mediaeval tale, he mirrors forth
some old-new thought as applicable to-day as when the
story was first told. Take as an example of his last volume of poems, 'Asolando',(1) over which the critics are at
this moment so much divided. Take the story of the lawyer
who has grown wealthy out of the money extorted from the
widow and the orphan, and whom the devil is waiting to
strangle as soon as he gives up saying the little prayer
that he had learned in his youth. The lawyer is on good
terms with himself and with the whole world. He gives
liberally to the church. He has the ecclesiastical digni-
taries to dine at his table. But once read, can that incident of the Father Superior wringing from his napkin the
blood that had been coined into the means by which the
lawyer could live so sumptuously ever be forgotten? And
are there no deacons, no pillars and mainstays of our
churches, on whom everybody smiles, who have coined the
money they are so liberal with out of the sweat and blood
and tears of the poor and the oppressed? Is not the evil
spirit of greed and rapine awaiting the opportunity to
strangle such men? No; there is depth in Browning; his
meaning is hard to get at, but once you enter into his
point of view and read from that outward the whole grandeur of his conception stands forth in all its rugged pro-
portions.

We may not admire the new forms; we may prefer the old
ones; but it were unwisdom to quarrel with that which
does not please us.

Note

1 Published on the day of his death, 12 December 1889.

50. OSCAR WILDE, SIGNED NOTICE, 'SPEAKER'

22 March 1890, i, 319-20

Reprinted in 'Reviews'(1908), 538-45. See No. 31 and
Introduction, pp. 30-2.
    Pater solicited the review (see Introduction, p. 10).
He wrote to Wilde on 4 January 1890:

> It seems an age since we met. I had hoped to be able
> to call this afternoon. I have been reading the
> 'Speaker': it seems very clever and excellent, and
> makes me anxious that should my recent volume be no-
> ticed there, it may not fall into unsympathetic hands.
> If I am intrusive in saying this, I am sure you will
> forgive me. (LWP, 106)

Pater wrote to Wilde on the day the notice appeared:

> I have read your pleasantly written, genial, sensible,
> criticism in the 'Speaker' with very great pleasure.
> How friendly of you to have given so much care and
> time to my book, in the midst of your own work in that
> prose of which you have become so successful a writer.
> (LWP, 109)

The review is significant for its self-revelation, especially for the emergence of the paradoxical. It also
foreshadows Wilde's essay on The Critic as Artist, which
he published in the 'Nineteenth Century' in July and September.

When I first had the privilege — and I count it a very
high one — of meeting Mr Walter Pater, he said to me,
smiling, 'Why do you always write poetry? Why do you not
write prose? Prose is so much more difficult.'
    It was during my undergraduate days at Oxford; days
of lyrical ardours and of studious sonnet-writing; days

when one loved the exquisite intricacy and musical repe-
titions of the ballade, and the villanelle with its linked
long-drawn echoes and its curious completeness; days when
one solemnly sought to discover the proper temper in which
a triolet should be written; delightful days, in which, I
am glad to say, there was far more rhyme than reason.

I may frankly confess now that at the time I did not
quite comprehend what Mr Pater really meant; and it was
not till I had carefully studied his beautiful and suggestive essays on the Renaissance that I fully realised
what a wonderful self-conscious art the art of English
prose-writing really is, or may be made to be. Carlyle's
stormy rhetoric, Ruskin's winged and passionate eloquence,
had seemed to me to spring from enthusiasm rather than from
art. I don't think I knew then that even prophets correct
their proofs. As for Jacobean prose, I thought it too
exuberant; and Queen Anne prose appeared to me terribly
bald, and irritatingly rational. But Mr Pater's essays
became to me 'the golden book of spirit and sense, the
holy writ of beauty'. They are still this to me. It is
possible, of course, that I may exaggerate about them. I
certainly hope that I do; for where there is no exaggeration there is no love, and where there is no love there is
no understanding. It is only about things that do not
interest one, that one can give a really unbiassed opinion;
and this is no doubt the reason why an unbiassed opinion is
always absolutely valueless.

But I must not allow this brief notice of Mr Pater's
new volume to degenerate into an autobiography. I remember
being told in America that whenever Margaret Fuller(1)
wrote an essay upon Emerson the printers had always to send
out to borrow some additional capital 'I's', and I feel it
right to accept this transatlantic warning.

'Appreciations', in the fine Latin sense of the word, is
the title given by Mr Pater to his book, which is an exquisite collection of exquisite essays, of delicately wrought
works of art — some of them being almost Greek in their
purity of outline and perfection of form, others mediaeval
in their strangeness of colour and passionate suggestion,
and all of them absolutely modern, in the true meaning of
the term modernity. For he to whom the present is the
only thing that is present, knows nothing of the age in
which he lives. To realise the nineteenth century, one
must realise every century that has preceded it, and that
has contributed to its making. To know anything about oneself, one must know all about others. There must be no
mood with which one cannot sympathise, no dead mode of life
that one cannot make alive. The legacies of heredity may
make us alter our views of moral responsibility, but they

cannot but intensify our sense of the value of Criticism;
for the true critic is he who bears within himself the
dreams and ideas and feelings of myriad generations, and
to whom no form of thought is alien, no emotional impulse
obscure.

Perhaps the most interesting, and certainly the least
successful, of the essays contained in the present volume
is that on Style. It is the most interesting because it
is the work of one who speaks with the high authority that
comes from the noble realisation of things nobly conceived.
It is the least successful, because the subject is too abstract. A true artist like Mr Pater, is most felicitous
when he deals with the concrete, whose very limitations
give him finer freedom, while they necessitate more intense vision. And yet what a high ideal is contained in
these few pages! How good it is for us, in these days of
popular education and facile journalism, to be reminded
of the real scholarship that is essential to the perfect
writer, who, 'being a true lover of words for their own
sake, a minute and constant observer of their physiognomy',
will avoid what is mere rhetoric, or ostentatious ornament,
or negligent misuse of terms, or ineffective surplusage,
and will be known by his tact of omission, by his skilful
economy of means, by his selection and self-restraint, and
perhaps above all by that conscious artistic structure
which is the expression of mind in style. I think I have
been wrong in saying that the subject is too abstract. In
Mr Pater's hands it becomes very real to us indeed, and he
shows us how, behind the perfection of a man's style, must
lie the passion of a man's soul.

As one passes to the rest of the volume, one finds
essays on Wordsworth and on Coleridge, on Charles Lamb and
on Sir Thomas Browne, and some of Shakespeare's plays and
on the English kings that Shakespeare fashioned, on Dante
Rossetti, and on William Morris. As that on Wordsworth
seems to be Mr Pater's last work, so that on the singer of
the 'Defence of Guenevere' is certainly his earliest, or
almost his earliest, and it is interesting to mark the
change that has taken place in his style. This change is,
perhaps, at first sight not very apparent. In 1868 we
find Mr Pater writing with the same exquisite care for
words, with the same studied music, with the same temper,
and something of the same mode of treatment. But, as he
goes on, the architecture of the style becomes richer and
more complex, the epithet more precise and intellectual.
Occasionally one may be inclined to think that there is,
here and there, a sentence which is somewhat long, and
possibly, if one may venture to say so, a little heavy and
cumbersome in movement. But if this be so, it comes from

those side-issues suddenly suggested by the idea in its progress, and really revealing the idea more perfectly; or from those felicitous after-thoughts that give a fuller completeness to the central scheme, and yet convey something of the charm of chance; or from a desire to suggest the secondary shades of meaning with all their accumulating effect, and to avoid, it may be, the violence and harshness of too definite and exclusive an opinion. For in matters of art, at any rate, thought is inevitably coloured by emotion, and so is fluid rather than fixed, and, recognising its dependence upon moods and upon the passion of fine moments, will not accept the rigidity of a scientific formula or a theological dogma. The critical pleasure, too, that we receive from tracing, through what may seem the intricacies of a sentence, the working of the constructive intelligence, must not be overlooked. As soon as we have realised the design, everything appears clear and simple. After a time, these long sentences of Mr Pater's come to have the charm of an elaborate piece of music, and the unity of such music also.

I have suggested that the essay on Wordsworth is probably the most recent bit of work contained in this volume. If one might choose between so much that is good, I should be inclined to say it is the finest also. The essay on Lamb is curiously suggestive; suggestive, indeed, of a somewhat more tragic, more sombre figure, than men have been wont to think of in connection with the author of the 'Essays of Elia'. It is an interesting aspect under which to regard Lamb, but perhaps he himself would have had some difficulty in recognising the portrait given of him. He had, undoubtedly, great sorrows, or motives for sorrow, but he could console himself at a moment's notice for the real tragedies of life by reading any one of the Elizabethan tragedies, provided it was in a folio edition. The essay on Sir Thomas Browne is delightful, and has the strange, personal, fanciful charm of the author of the 'Religio Medici'; Mr Pater often catching the colour and accent and tone of whatever artist, or work of art, he deals with. That on Coleridge, with its insistence on the necessity of the cultivation of the relative, as opposed to the absolute spirit in philosophy and in ethics, and its high appreciation of the poet's true position in our literature, is in style and substance a very blameless work. Grace of expression, and delicate subtlety of thought and phrase, characterise the essays on Shakespeare. But the essay on Wordsworth has a spiritual beauty of its own. It appeals, not to the ordinary Wordsworthian with his uncritical temper, and his gross confusion of ethical with aesthetical problems, but rather to those who desire

to separate the gold from the dross, and to reach at the
true Wordsworth through the mass of tedious and prosaic
work that bears his name, and that serves often to conceal him from us. The presence of an alien element in
Wordsworth's art, is, of course, recognised by Mr Pater,
but he touches on it merely from the psychological point
of view, pointing out how this quality of higher and lower
moods gives the effect in his poetry 'of a power not altogether his own, or under his control'; a power which
comes and goes when it wills, 'so that the old fancy which
made the poet's art an enthusiasm, a form of divine possession, seems almost true of him'. Mr Pater's earlier essays
had their *purpurei panni*,(2) so eminently suitable for
quotation, such as the famous passage on Monna Lisa, and
that other in which Botticelli's strange conception of the
Virgin is so strangely set forth. From the present volume
it is difficult to select any one passage in preference to
another as specially characteristic of Mr Pater's treatment.
This, however, is worth quoting at length. It contains a
truth eminently useful for our age:

[Quotes Wordsworth: 'That the end of life is not action
but contemplation' to 'amid awful forms and powers'.]

   Certainly the real secret of Wordsworth has never been
better expressed. After having read and re-read Mr Pater's
essay — for it requires re-reading — one returns to the
poet's work with a new sense of joy and wonder, and with
something of eager and impassioned expectation. And perhaps this might be roughly taken as the test or touchstone
of the finest criticism.
   Finally, one cannot help noticing the delicate instinct
that has gone to fashion the brief epilogue that ends this
delightful volume. The difference between the classical
and romantic spirits in art has often, and with much over-
emphasis, been discussed. But with what a light sure
touch does Mr Pater write of it! How subtle and certain
are his distinctions! If imaginative prose be really the
special art of this century, Mr Pater must rank amongst our
century's most characteristic artists. In certain things
he stands almost alone. The age has produced wonderful
prose styles, turbid with individualism, and violent with
rhetoric. But in Mr Pater, as in Cardinal Newman, we find
the union of personality with perfection. He has no rival
in his own sphere, and he has escaped disciples. And this,
not because he has not been imitated, but because in art so
fine as his there is something that, in its essence, is
inimitable.

Notes

1 American critic and social reformer (1810-50): she published a review of Emerson's 'Essays' in the New York
  'Tribune' for 7 December 1844.
2 Purple passages.

51. W.J. COURTHOPE, SIGNED REVIEW, 'NINETEENTH CENTURY'

April 1890, xxvii, 658-62

See No. 12 and Introduction, pp.30 and 32. This is Courthope's first review devoted solely to Pater. He continues
the attack on the lack of standards in Pater's criticism
which he began in 1874, but with noticeably less asperity.

This is an extremely interesting and characteristic collection of essays. For more than a century the world has been
living in revolution, and the revolution has affected the
arts as well as religion and politics. The dominant tendency in artists is now to set tradition at defiance, and
to rely solely on the force of genius. The artist casts
his bread upon the waters. After many days, if he be a
man of genius, he finds it, not perhaps in the enjoyment
of contemporary applause, but at least in the admiration
which is lavished on his memory, when it is discovered
that what he has made is really bread. From the prevailing tendency in art has naturally arisen a corresponding
tendency in criticism. Many critics now make it their object, not so much to judge the artist's work by their conception of the laws of art, as to expound to the world the
nature of the artist's motives. The method of this school
of criticism is admirably indicated in the title and illustrated by the contents of Mr Pater's book.
    It is a method with conspicuous excellences and defects.
Its merits are due mainly to the exertion of the power of
sympathy. Sympathetic criticism is the direct opposite of
that criticism of antipathy which was employed with such
deplorable results in the early part of this century,
against the poetry of the Lake school and of Shelley and
Keats. Doubtless it is a better method. The value of an
artist's performance cannot be justly estimated by the

critic, unless he endeavours to *appreciate* his intentions.
Mr Pater never fails to do this. His volume comprises
among others essays on Wordsworth, Coleridge, Charles
Lamb, Mr William Morris, and the late Mr Rossetti. All
these writers may be described as innovators in art, yet
in Mr Pater's judgment of their work there is rarely to
be found a word of depreciation. He confines himself to
discovering by delicate analysis the working of each individual mind, and the external forces by which it was influenced. In this he is admirably successful, and if, in
the style which he employs to communicate the results of
his analysis, simplicity is somewhat painfully conspicuous
by its absence, the fault — if fault it be — is due, not
to the love of rhetorical display, but to a conscientious
attempt to embody in words the most subtle complexities of
thought. Perhaps his best essays are those on Wordsworth
and Charles Lamb. With both of these writers he seems to
be in special sympathy, and his 'appreciation' of their
motives is marked by an exquisite refinement. How pregnant with suggestion of the essential character of Wordsworth's genius are the following sentences!

> The stimulus which most artists require of nature
> he can renounce. He leaves the ready-made beauty of
> the Swiss mountains that he may reflect glory on a
> mouldering leaf. He loves best to watch the floating
> thistle-down because of its hint of an unseen life in
> the air.

The appreciation of Charles Lamb is even more sympathetic, and very naturally so. Every reader of 'Marius the
Epicurean' and 'Imaginary Portraits' will detect in these
works, instinct with real genius, the same imaginative
sympathy with the spirit of old customs, the same fine perception of the life associated with places, which give so
much of their peculiar flavour to the 'Essays of Elia'.
A few sentences from this essay may serve as a sample of
the genuine excellence of Mr Pater's criticism.

> 'The praise of beggars', 'the cries of London', the
> traits of actors just grown 'old', the spots in 'town'
> where the country, its fresh green and fresh water,
> still lingered on, one after another, amidst the bustle;
> the quaint, dimmed, just played out farces he had re-
> lished so much, coming partly through them to under-
> stand the earlier English theatre as a thing once really
> alive; those fountains and sundials of old gardens, of
> which he entertains such dainty discourse; — he feels
> the poetry of these things as the poetry of things old

indeed, but surviving as an actual part of the life of
the present, and as something quite different from the
poetry of things flatly gone from us and antique, which
come back to us, if at all, as entire strangers, like
Scott's old Scotch-border personages, their oaths and
armour.

At the same time this excellence should not blind us to
the accompanying defect of Mr Pater's method. There can
in fact be no thoroughly just appreciation without a mixture of depreciation. Even the good Homer is supposed
sometimes to nod; and it is surely right that the critic
should judge an artist's work, not merely by the skill the
latter shows in executing his own intentions, but by those
ideal laws to which, if criticism is anything more than a
name, every work of art must be assumed to be subject.
Mr Pater would not deny this; but his tendency is to
assume first principles of taste which seem to explain the
practice of his favourite authors, rather than to estimate
their performances by reference to the practice of the
greatest writers. For example, he says very truly:

> An intimate consciousness of the expression of
> natural things, which weighs, listens, penetrates, where
> the earlier mind passed roughly by, is a large element
> in the complexion of modern poetry.

Later on he explains this practice on the following principle:

> That the end of life is not action but contemplation
> — being as distinct from doing — a certain disposi-
> tion of the mind: is in some shape or other the prin-
> ciple of the higher morality.... Wordsworth, and other
> poets who have been like him in ancient or modern times,
> are the experts in this art of impassioned contempla-
> tion.

Now I think it can scarcely be denied that in the work
of all the greatest poets — Homer, Virgil, the Greek
dramatists, Shakespeare, Milton, even Dante — Doing, to a
greater extent than Being, lies at the foundation of their
art. There is therefore a sanction of between two and
three thousand years in favour of the law that action, in
some form or other, must be the predominant principle in
every great poem. More than this. It can be shown that
what are acknowledged to be defects in modern poets are
due to the excessive preponderance in their work of the
contemplative element. Mr Pater accepts Wordsworth's

defence of his system of poetic diction, as if it were an
exposition of a sufficient law of art. He allows that a
very large portion of Wordsworth's poetical compositions
is artistically worthless; but he does not seem to see
that the frequent flaws in his genuinely pathetic poems
(such for instance as 'Simon Lee' and 'Resolution and Independence'), the mistaking of homely triviality for artistic simplicity, and of a garrulous prosiness for a *natural*
manner of writing in metre, arise from his exaggerated attachment to his own conceptions, and his neglect of positive rules of art.

Mr Pater's appreciation of Coleridge is more severe, and
therefore more just; yet he pronounces Coleridge (of whom
it was said, 'He talks like an angel and does — nothing')
to be 'the perfect flower of the *ennuyé* type'; and he even
finds in 'The Ancient Mariner' 'a perfectly rounded whole-
ness and unity'. Surely it would be much truer to say
plainly that this poem and 'Christabel' are the splendid
tours de force of a great but fragmentary genius; and that
Coleridge's constant struggles as a philosopher after a conception of the Absolute were, in themselves, the cause of
his infertility as a poet.

The estimate of Charles Lamb, admirable as it is, leaves
us with a certain impression of exaggeration. Lamb's art
is delightful, but it has very definite limits. Compare
him as a creator with Addison; Mrs Battle's(1) portrait
with that of Sir Roger de Coverly.(2) In each case the
art lies in the delicate portraiture of certain humorous
aspects of a character which is, in a sense, a survival.
But the figure of Sir Roger is drawn from enduring elements in the constitution of English society: it has therefore a moral significance, and is entitled in consequence
to rank higher as a creation than the conception of Mrs
Battle, which is constructed out of more purely local materials. Both characters have in them the element of contemplation; but Addison's is the work of a man familiar
with the sources of action in the English nation; Lamb's,
of an imagination enamoured with the *picturesqueness* of
family life. So again, as a critic, Lamb's judgments are
often vitiated by an excess of meditative sympathy. Many
of his criticisms are only charming excursions of capricious fancy: we can scarcely, for example, give any serious consideration to his whimsical apology for the Caroline
dramatists. Of this characteristic in his work, however, Mr
Pater, who bestows high and just praise on his critical insight, takes no account.

The fallacy involved in Mr Pater's method of judging
artistic conception makes itself felt in his remarks on
style, which are otherwise often just and opportune. In an

incidental reference to Gustave Flaubert he remarks on his
painful struggles after exact precision in language. Now
Flaubert's experience in this respect is the reverse of
Horace's — a great artist in words, if ever there was
one — who says:

> *Cui lecta potenter erit res*
> *Nec facundia deseret hunc nec lucidus ordo.* (3)

How is this? Mr Pater ascribes Flaubert's efforts
(which, from his own account, amounted to agony) to a
boundless love of art. But they are surely capable of
another explanation. Neither Shakespeare nor Scott
troubled themselves greatly to find the *one* word to express their thought, because they wrote out of full minds
on subjects of general imaginative interest. Flaubert's
aim, on the other hand, like that of so many modern artists, was to discover the imaginative secret underlying
commonplace objects, and actions, while he was obliged to
use as his instrument of expression a language built up
by men who judged of such objects and actions by the light
of common sense. Putting aside all moral considerations,
Flaubert, in an artistic sense, 'considered too curiously'.
For instance, in 'Madame Bovary' he takes eight lines to
describe, in the most refined words, the action of a woman drinking a glass of liqueur. No wonder that he was
oppressed by a feeling of artistic impotence!

To sum up: Mr Pater's criticism, in my opinion, suf-
fers from the same defect as Lamb's — excess of sympathy.
In his fine perception of the motives of his authors, and
in his delicate description of their styles, his 'Appreciations' are all that can be desired; but he seems to me
to flinch from the severe application of critical law. He
exhibits invariably the taste of a refined literary epicure. But the taste of an epicure is not always that of
a judge.

Notes

1 Subject of one of Lamb's 'Essays of Elia' (1823).
2 A character described by Addison in the 'Spectator'.
3 He whose choice has made him master of his subject
  neither fluent diction nor clear arrangement will for-
  sake him. 'Ars Poetica', 11. 40-1.

'Plato and Platonism'
February 1893

52. J.R. THURSFIELD, UNSIGNED REVIEW, 'THE TIMES'

16 February 1893, 12

James Richard Thursfield (1840-1923), journalist and naval
historian, was Pater's contemporary as a student (1859-63)
at Corpus Christi College and Fellow (1864-81) of Jesus
College, Oxford. Thursfield later became the chief leader
writer for 'The Times' (VLL, 229), in charge of the Books
of the Week section. In addition, he frequently contributed to the 'Naval Annual' and other journals.
    Pater likely prompted the review (see Introduction,
p.11). On 12 February 1893 he sent Thursfield a note calling attention to the book:

   Macmillan has just published for me a volume on 'Plato
   and Platonism'. I daresay you would come across it in
   any case, but venture to send you a few lines on the
   subject, as I think if you have time to look at it, you
   may like it, or some part of it. (LWP, 137)

Of 'Plato and Platonism', a series of lectures by Walter
Pater, Fellow of Brasenose College (Macmillan and Co), the
author tells us that the lectures 'were written for delivery to some young students of philosophy, and are now
printed with the hope of interesting a larger number of
them'. This hope well deserves to be fulfilled. Mr Pater
discourses of Plato and Platonism in the very spirit, and
with not a little of the grace, of Plato himself, and we
cannot readily recall a work dealing with Plato as a man

and a thinker which is at once more suggestive in presentation and more attractive in style. Mr Pater's method, like
Plato's own, is philosophic without being formal, and he
presents Platonism, as it really is in its essence, rather
as the consummate literary flower of Greek modes of thought,
than as its formal expression in purely philosophical categories. 'By Platonism,' as he says, 'is meant not Neo-
Platonism of any kind, but the leading principles of
Plato's doctrine, which I have tried to see in close connexion with himself as he is presented in his own writings.'
We have already noted Mr Pater's hope that his lectures as
now printed may interest a larger number of students of
philosophy than those to whom they were originally delivered, and we may add, perhaps, that they are better adopted for study in the printed page than for oral delivery in
the classroom. Mr Pater is a master of style, and his
sentences rarely fail to exhibit that finished *limae labor*
(1) which, as we know, Plato himself was wont to give his
writings. But for that very reason they demand attentive
study from a reader who desires to appreciate their full
import and significance. Such a study is amply repaid in
the result, but it is hardly compatible with the conditions of oral delivery, and, therefore, it is not impossible that those who read Mr Pater's lectures for the
first time will appreciate them more fully than those who
originally heard them delivered. At any rate, no serious
students of Plato and of his place in Greek philosophy can
fail to acknowledge that Mr Pater has presented both in a
clear, original,and singularly suggestive fashion, while
his incidental picture of the life and polity of Lacedaemon is an admirable example of his characteristic literary method, remarkable alike for its breadth and vividness of presentation, its distinction and delicacy of
touch.

Note

1 Labour of revision.

53. RICHARD LE GALLIENNE, UNSIGNED REVIEW, 'STAR'

23 February 1893, 2

From Mr Pater on Plato — Mr Oscar Wilde's 'Salome'. See

Nos 30 and 62 and Introduction, p. 34.   It is likely that
Pater solicited the review.   He wrote to Le Gallienne two
days later: 'One line of thanks.   I had already read your
interesting but too generous notice of my book' (LWP, 137).

It is curious how some authors contrive to impress their
individuality upon the externals of their books, and by
some subtle influence create a harmony between type, paper,
and binding and the spirit which they clothe.   One can
even tell our best loved books by their feel, and certain
it is that our Swinburnes, our Morrises, our Stevensons,
and perhaps, most of all, our Paters have all characteristic physiognomies familiar as the faces of dear friends.
There is no more curious witness to the power of personality, for fonts of type, one would say, are unimpression-
able things, not readily responsive to the delicate influence of the spirit.   Yet in cases where men use the
same font, there will something steal into the page, it
may be the 'leading', or in the arrangement of the paragraph, in the length of sentences, the preference for
Latin or Saxon words, that will give each of their books
a distinctive complexion.   Some writers hold that their
reader loses much by not being able to read them in manuscript.   M Mallarmé, for instance, was at one time so
careful of his 'moi' that he had his poems published in
lithograph from his original manuscript.   We are not all
so sensitive as that, but one does not need to be hyper-
sensitive to feel the Paterian aura about all Mr Pater's
books.
     The gracious union of the austere and the sensuous,
so characteristic of Mr Pater's writing;   the temperate
beauty, 'the dry beauty' beloved of Plato, and advocated
with such winning charm in the 'series of lectures' before
us ('Plato and Platonism: a Series of Lectures', Macmillan and Co), find expression too in the sweet and
stately volume itself, with its smooth night-blue binding,
its rose-leaf yellow pages, its soft and yet grave types.
So distinguished and yet so far removed from the eccentric.   To merely hold one of Mr Pater's books in the hand
and turn over its pages, is a counsel in style.   As the
Greek women during conception would look often and long
upon the statue of Apollo, so the dreamer of beautiful
books should often handle such books as these of Mr Pater.
They will refine even the sense of touch.   How little does
he know of books who deems them only to be read?

But I dally too long in the portal. And yet, how can I
presume in the short space at my disposal here to glibly
'review' so beautiful a gift as these new essays of Mr Pater?
It is true that by this time I have read them through; but,
once reading! what is it? and not the reading of the happy scholar, fellow of his college, who in cloistered peace
gives his whole heart for full untroubled hours to the book
of his love — but the snatched, worried reading of the distracted journalist who must snatch his spiritual meals now
and then as best he can. I can but, like the divining rod,
point here and there where the gold is hid, and leave you
to find it for yourself.

Mr Pater's lectures are 10 in number:- 1. Plato and the
Doctrine of Motion; 2. Plato and the Doctrine of Rest;
3. Plato and the Doctrine of Number; 4. Plato and Socrates;
5. Plato and Sophists; 6. The Genius of Plato; 7. The
Doctrine of Plato (the Theory of Ideas and Dialectic);
8. Lacedaemon; 9. The Republic; 10. Plato's Aesthetics.
Mr Pater, with nice artistic sense, has not striven, like
most other writers, to disguise the fact of their origin
as lectures, but here and there he has preserved little
hortatory phrases which remind one that he is addressing
himself to a band of youthful students of philosophy.
Doubtless he has felt that the mere knowledge of the papers having to be thus addressed to an audience would, in
however slight a degree, modify them from the essay proper, and that to attempt to disguise such modifications
would be a delicate loss in sincerity of appeal. Thus a
favorite exhortation, frequent in his other writings, is
here more frequent than ever, constantly reminding us of
the lecture-room, or rather, we would say, the Academe.
'Well!...' The reader knows the charming cadence. '...
Well! Life was like that.' There is something curiously
seductive about this very characteristic interjection,
something that puts the reader in instant rapport with the
writer. It conveys the very sound of his voice into the
sentences. I don't know any recent writer, except, perhaps, Mr Stevenson, who has this intimate accent. Another
charm of Mr Pater's attitude to his reader is his urbane
indifference in regard to the amount of his learning. He
does not affect the assumption that the reader knows everything, but when he occasionally implies his possible non-
acquaintance with certain matters he does it in a way that
seems to say that, no doubt, the reader knows many things
of which he is ignorant. Thus he doesn't even take it for
granted that his students should know Wordsworth's great
Ode. Literature is so vast, life so short, that they may
well have not come up to it yet. But when they do....

Verily, these are but the crumbs that fall from the
master's table, but they are indicative of the feast. The
chapter which charms me most of all is the first. It deals
with the Heraclitean doctrine of the eternal flux in
things —

> ... all flits away
> Light and life together

as the old Anglo-Saxon scop sang. Mr Pater never writes so
beautifully as when on this theme. You will remember the
pages upon it in 'Marius'. In this first and the two subsequent chapters Mr Pater criticises the usual conception
of Plato as an absolute pioneer of philosophy, and traces
his several obligations to Heraclitus, Parmenides, Zeno,
Pythagoras, and Socrates. And in doing so it is wonderful
what a sense of vista his imagination is able to throw for
us behind a world that one rather thinks of as but just
beginning. I cannot make a more characteristic or more
beautiful quotation than a few passages from this opening
chapter.

[Quotes ch. 1: 'Plato's achievement may well seem' to 'the
mere matter is nothing'.]

Much of Mr Pater's book is taken up with suggestive exposition of what one might call Plato's aesthetic apprehension of ideas — the power his sensuous instincts gave
him of realising for himself and his readers abstract ideas
as though they were visible appearances. For, austerely
regulated as it was, Mr Pater reminds us that Plato's nature was a richly sensuous one, the temperament of 'the
lover'. 'He is a lover, a great lover, somewhat after the
manner of Dante.' And even more suggestively does Mr Pater
show us that the apparently paradoxical banishment of the
arts from Plato's Republic was not because he condemned
them, but because he feared that the citizens must love
them too well. 'Art, as such, as Plato knows, has no purpose but itself, its own perfection. The proper art of
the Perfect City is, in fact, the art of discipline. Music'
(in the broad platonic sense), 'all the various forms of
fine art, will be but the instrument of its one overmaster-
ing social or political purpose, irresistibly conforming
its so imitative subject units into type; they will be
neither more nor less than so many variations, so to speak,
of the trumpet-call.'
Of Lacedaemon, the city that seemed to Plato nearest to
his august ideal, Mr Pater in his eighth chapter gives us
a wonderful 'imaginary portrait', one of the most beautiful
passages of his beautiful book....

54.   E.J. ELLIS, SIGNED REVIEW, 'BOOKMAN'

March 1893, iii, 186-7

See Introduction, pp. 33-5.

Edwin John Ellis (1848-1916), Irish poet and painter who was fascinated by nineteenth-century spiritualism. Ellis was a champion of William Blake when the poet-painter's reputation was being established. He wrote, in collaboration with W.B. Yeats, 'The Works of William Blake, Poetic, Symbolic, and Critical' (1893), which purported to reveal the secret system behind all Blake's writings, and 'The Real Blake' (1906).

This work is a collection of lectures 'written for delivery to some young students of philosophy, and now printed with the hope of interesting a larger number of them'. It is not a handbook of information. It is not intended as a treasure-house of facts, suitable for reference; still less is it adapted to assist any one who wishes to 'cram'. It does not even guard itself against this possible misconception by a single word. But in his 'hope of interesting' students the author is on safe ground. In this effort he certainly and pleasantly succeeds.

Yet although these lectures presuppose a moderate amount of acquaintance with their subject, such as 'young students' must needs have acquired, without perhaps any very keen enjoyment in the acquisition, there is information of a very useful and vital kind to be found all the way through. The personalities of the different platonic and pre-platonic philosophers are made to reveal themselves as if by accident. We seem to hear the voice of a personal acquaintance giving impressions that he has an authoritative right to convey. Platonism is shown as though it were a thing of yesterday — a sort of Oxford Movement — whose chief character, Plato himself, stands forth as the Newman, and as something even more than the Newman of the group of men in whom the Movement lived. The gradual building up of his system, with its origin in his own restless desire for rest, his own questioning search for certainty, is described from the standpoint of a sympathetic biographer. Much, but not too much, is made of the effect of the time, the place, and the teachers that were the surrounding framework of his mental life. The claim made for Plato from the first, at once a modest and an important claim, is that he brought to

philosophy a 'literary freshness'. By this faculty he
erected a lasting monument in the mental territory of the
race.

This also is just what Mr Pater brings to his account of
that great achievement. Yet he never allows its temptations to master him. He allures us by the vividness of
his fancy, yet does not repel or chill by any tendency to
become fanciful. What he says is firmly rooted in what he
has read, and with almost every utterance is an allusion,
or at least a hint, of chapter and verse, skilfully woven
into the tissue of the narrative, without marring by any
unseemly knots our pleasure in passing the rich tapestry
through our hands.

From a severely literary point of view the style is
loose and wandering. Sentences nearly half a page in
length are not uncommon. Verbs are divided from nominatives by *sotto-voce*(1) cross currents of unmarked parentheses, that our attention must continually hold itself
ready to ford without allowing itself to be drowned by the
way. Here and there is a fine passage of gently sonorous
and almost entrancing prose. Yet unless the reader con-
ceives the book as uttered aloud by a voice that modulates
itself intelligently, and groups by its tone the phrases
that are but carelessly arranged under the indications of
punctuation and grammar, he misses half the effect and most
of the true value. Nevertheless, the book is full of a
stimulating charm, and neither the student nor the general
reader who begins the first page will lay it down without
reading to the last, and regretting that he finds himself
at the end so soon.

Note

1 Undertone.

55.   EDMUND GOSSE, SIGNED REVIEW, 'NEW REVIEW'

April 1893, viii, 419-29

See Introduction, pp. 33 and 34.

Sir Edmund Gosse (1848-1928), poet, critic, biographer
and civil servant, rose to a prominent position in the
world of letters as an authority on Scandinavian and French

literature and as a promoter of Ibsen. He was assistant
librarian of the British Museum, translator to the Board of
Trade, lecturer (1884-90) in English at Trinity College,
Cambridge, Librarian to the House of Lords and chief reviewer (1914-25) for 'The Times'. He was knighted in 1925
and is now best remembered for his childhood recollections,
'Father and Son' (1907).

Gosse contrived to make the acquaintance of almost every
contemporary author of note. He met Pater in 1872 and their
friendship lasted for more than twenty-two years.

Pater may have solicited the 'appreciative' summary of
the book. He wrote to Gosse on 30 March 1893:

> Of course I read your very skilful paper in the 'New
> Review' with great pleasure, and thank you sincerely
> for the pains you have taken with it. Though it is all
> about my own very limited self and production, I think
> the general readers of the 'Review' will not find it in
> the way; so much of your own good work and charming
> manner of saying things have you put into it. I hope
> to give good heed to your friendly advice on some
> points, and that my *next book* will be 'really good',
> as an excellent painter told me he always felt when he
> had finished a thing. (LWP, 138)

The opportunity of appreciating Mr Pater's scholarship, or
of estimating his contributions to the science of philosophy, will, no doubt, not be neglected by those whose
claims to authority are academic or sacerdotal. There is,
of course, a sense in which the only valuable appreciation of the book he has written on 'Plato and Platonism'
would be one signed by such an expert as Dr Jowett or
Dr Henry Jackson.(1) The anise and cummin of Mr Pater's
scholarship must be numbered not here, but in the pages of
the 'Classical Review'.(2) Yet those who are interested
in pure literature as in itself a delightful form of
artistic discipline may well claim that a book composed
with a conscious regard to form should not be shut off
altogether from their consideration, because it deals with
a subject primarily associated with non-artistic branches
of intellectual labour. It is becoming a serious misfor-
tune that specialisation tends more and more in each
generation to exile from the province of pure literature
all themes which deal directly with facts, or require exact definition. Early in the eighteenth century science
began to be divorced from literature, but it is only in
our own day that philosophy has determined to follow her

example. When we consider how very differently Evelyn and
Boyle and Berkeley(3) would have been obliged to express
themselves had they lived to-day; when we realise that
even a new Huxley, or a new Tyndall,(4) publishing for the
first time in 1893, could scarcely afford the sacrifice to
style of one evidence of their erudition, we may conceive
how much we have lost, and are losing, by so rigidly
narrowing the sphere of subjects in which the manner of our
writings may be taken into consideration. Mr Pater's new
book is written with too deliberate a charm to be abandoned
to the academic controversialist.

He justifies the general reader, I think, in claiming a
place at the somewhat abstruse feast that he spreads, by
the tenour of his own prefatory words. 'The lectures of
which this volume are composed,' he says, 'were written for
delivery to some young students of philosophy, and are now
published with the hope of interesting a larger number of
them.' We may imagine ourselves seated in some lecture-
room at Brasenose, and ever and anon may seem to catch
hint of an appeal made not so much to the young and ardent
students seated round the table, as to elder, more sceptical, more world-worn auditors. For these the actual truths
delivered may seem less important than the art with which
they are imparted, the fact less valuable than the impression or the parallel. And, as we wait for the lecturer
to begin, as he arranges his notes before him, we may reflect what an important figure his has grown to be in the
literary life of our time. Almost unobserved at first in
the hurry and bustle of Oxford, attracting little or no
attention in the midst of its political and educational
revolutions, Mr Pater, who has now for nearly a quarter of
a century been saying similar things in the quiet voice of
his books, has rather suddenly been perceived by the world
to be, in a certain sense, the very oracle of Oxford. None
less than Mr Pater has striven or cried. One of our novelists has been described as always writing at the top of
his voice; Mr Pater, the same symbolist might aver, never
writes above a whisper. Yet this whisper is so poignant,
so deliberate, so delicate, that it has succeeded in piercing the Babel of our modern world, and among the intellectual forces of the moment, its faint, strenuous note can
now no longer be neglected by either friend or foe.

Among the serious English critics of the day — a body
of men to whose variety and charm and strength a good deal
less than justice is commonly done — Mr Pater stands pre-
eminent. It would probably be generally allowed, among
those whose opinion counts for something, that Mr Pater
is the first of our living critics. Certainly, since the
death of Matthew Arnold, it is difficult to see who is

quite Mr Pater's equal in the art of analysing the creations of others in a style at once brilliant, distinguished,
and consistent. He has gained this position in spite of
the modesty and the infrequency of his appeals to the public tribunal. It is just twenty years since he published
his first work, his 'Studies in the Renaissance'. For
twelve subsequent years, years in which youth is commonly
ebullient and ambition imperious, he refrained from making
the smallest attempt to increase the audience which that
solitary volume had secured him. At length, in 1885, his
admirers were rewarded by the philosophical romance called
'Marius the Epicurean'; in 1887 there succeeded the slender volume of 'Imaginary Portraits', delicate essays in
criticism by fiction; and in 1889 some wandering studies
were united in the volume called 'Appreciations'. These,
to which 'Plato and Platonism' must now be added, form the
slender library with which Mr Walter Pater, in these noisy
days of over-production, has been content to make his appeal to us; but it is sufficient. It reveals to us a
sharply individualised and precisely defined talent, not,
of course, without its defects and limitations; but, in an
age where versatility runs riot, admirable, if for nothing
else, for its distinguished cultivation of a definite personal type. So personal and so definite is the quality of
Mr Pater's work, for those whom it repels as for those
whom it attracts, that if he now wrote a book on Chinese
Pagodas, or on the Habits of the Water-rat, those people
who have already read him would devoutly read him still.
And, they would insist, his volume must not be snatched
from them on the pretence that it was either a contribution to architecture or to zoology.
    In considering one who is himself so unfailingly exer-
cised about the form of his discourse, there may be no in-
discretion in at once disposing of the question of his
style in the present volume. No one can read a page of
'Plato and Platonism' without recognising the hand that
wrote it; and yet the Pater of this volume is by no means
the Pater which we have grown accustomed to. The style is
still sustained, to speak musically, at a high, even pitch;
it is still, to speak decoratively, heavy like a brocade
with rich and concentrated ornament; but in this new book
it is far less highly coloured than ever before. The seriousness of the theme, and its antiquity, have made appropriate a certain archaic and monochromatic purity. There
never was a book of Mr Pater's, in short, with so few purple passages. The determination of the writer to detach
himself from the academic attitude, to emphasise the fact,
as it were, that he has descended from the lecturing-desk
to the chair at the fireside, is expressed by what some

readers will think a too-perpetually conversational tone.
Little deprecating parentheses, courteous appeals, as one
may say, appeals to a possibly wandering attention, inces-
sant divagations from the direct road of thought, all these
serve to introduce an element which is novel and unfamiliar.
Sometimes the result is very charming, the harmony of utterance being sustained unbroken, although the orator insists on adopting this attitude of slippers and the dres-
sing-gown. But, occasionally, I must confess, the deprecating parenthesis is too often introduced, especially for
a writer who, like Mr Pater, has almost rudimentary ideas
about punctuation. It is perhaps not an unfair way of
exemplifying what I mean, to quote a sentence, for once,
not of Mr Pater at his best, but, as I think, of Mr Pater
at his worst:

> It was something quite new, unseen before in Greece,
> inspiring a new note in literature — this attitude of
> Socrates in the condemned cell, where, fulfilling his
> own prediction, multitudes, of a wisdom and piety,
> after all, so different from his, have ever since as-
> sisted so admiringly, this anticipation of the Chris-
> tian way of dying for an opinion, when, as Plato says
> simply, he consumed the poison in the prison.

When we pass from the mere style to the general method,
we discover that Mr Pater, in his own way, is passing
through something of the same change and development of
which the death of Taine(5) has, within the last few weeks,
once more reminded us; that change, which is so inevitable
in the career of every critical artist, the gradual resignation of what is magnificent in favour of what is sound,
precise, and penetrating. But Mr Pater has one quality
which no determinist like Taine would be likely to possess
at any period of his development: a sensitive perception
of the beauty of proportion; and the manner in which he
has approached his work cannot be better suggested than by
quoting words of his own, words without some acceptance of
which, as a critical principle, the book before us is
scarcely to be accepted at all:

[Quotes ch. 1: 'The thoughts of Plato, like the language
he has to use' to 'and the mere matter is nothing'.]

Desiring, then, to make clear what constitutional tendencies in this older poetic world had exercised their
authority over Plato, and built up the materials from
which he constructed his palace of the intellect, Mr Pater
leaves us standing on the threshold of 'The Republic', and

descends within our sight, in succession, into three quar-
ries, which he designs to us as the now dead, but once active and fruitful, sources of the material out of which the
radiant structure we are about to enter was originally hewn.

[Summary of chs 1-7 omitted.]

   There is probably no chapter in this monograph which is
in itself more perfect, or presents us with a more finished
specimen of literary art than that on Lacedaemon. Desirous
of enabling us to enter for ourselves into the half romantic, half ironic Laconism of Plato, Mr Pater opens with a
long quotation from the 'Protagoras', in which we learn
what the Athenian's view was of the spirit then existing at
Lacedaemon. That this spirit had much to do with inspiring Plato's own conception of the perfect Republic may be
taken as a matter of course, but it is almost equally certain that Plato and those around him did not regard the
condition of things at Lacedaemon with unmitigated approval.
They frankly admired, but with their admiration was mingled
something of the disdain irresistibly instinctive to a
polite and pleasure-loving people in contemplating an austere and rather savage community. Pausanias tells us that
'the Lacedaemonians appear to have admired least of all
people poetry and the praise which it bestows'. The general impression in Greece seems to have been that this remote mountain nation, which disdained poetry, exiled all
strangers when it wished to talk about philosophy, and pretended to be an 'unlearned people', were enemies to all the
ornamental part of life. Their splendid prestige in the
battlefield, their reputation for skill in manifold cryptic
branches of philosophy, earned them respect rather than
sympathy. It is, interesting, no doubt, to ascertain as
far as possible what the feeling of a young Athenian personally instructed by Plato would be towards Lacedaemon.
He would have much to learn, much to unlearn, and the best
of all ways to correct the errors of fable and of prejudice
would be to undertake a journey to the mountain fastness
itself.
   This is what Mr Pater imagines. Some youthful Anachar-
sis, determined to overcome the political and material difficulties of such an expedition, sets out between the ridges
of the Eastern Arcadian mountains, and descends at length
into the broad and hollow valley of Laconia. Here let our
new Pausanias speak for himself:

[Quotes ch. 8: 'The country through which our young traveller' to 'a solemn, ancient, mountain village'.]

Not until we clearly comprehend what life was in the obscure and hieratic community of Lacedaemon, can we realise the basis of recorded experiment upon which Plato was able to build his immortal dream of 'The Republic'. The consideration of that treatise properly follows the chapter on Lacedaemon. To this, again, succeeds one on Plato's aesthetics, on his conception, that is to say, of Beauty existent in the visible world. The Platonic aesthetics are found, when we look narrowly, to be in closer relation with the ethics of their founder than we may have been ready hastily to suppose. It is valuable to have the fact brought home to us that no real disparity exists between the intellectual discipline of Plato and those beautiful arts and handicrafts which flourished around him in Athens. No vulgarities of the eye could be imagined in that perfect city of which Plato dreamed. Faultless taste must be presupposed in those who have learnt to move within the discipline of intellectual melody and symmetry. Where all is to be under the control of rhythm nothing can be awkward or discordant, and little change would have been needed to make the best decoration of Plato's living Athens worthy of his mystical city of the soul. Surely the broad and simple Dorian architecture, surely the sculpture of Phidias and the verse of Sophocles, were temperate enough, were at once impassioned enough and sober enough, to bear the dry light of Platonic criticism. The Perfect City, such as Plato conceived it, was the capital of no fabulous Utopia, no fairy town built immediately in the dim inane, but a practical, and even, in certain aspects, a homely reconstruction of the Athens of which Plato was a fortunate citizen, an Athens purified and harmonised and idealised, but essentially the Athens that he knew.

Mr Pater is not to be accused of so inartistic an intention as by a squinting comment upon passing events to pass off a monograph on ancient philosophy. Yet it is impossible to read his book and not to perceive how eminently apposite much of it is to the intellectual and political life of to-day. An ingenious person might descry the shadow of every modern malady thrown across these pages. Here, if we choose to look for them, are Panama and Egypt and Ireland, Wagner and Ibsen and Degas. Without being too fantastic in these excursions after actuality, we may admit that the secret of all freshness in aesthetic presentment, of all harmony in political progress, is to be divined in Plato. Do we not see amongst us to-day as plainly as any Athenians of old might do the eternal warfare going on between the centrifugal and inorganic tendency on the one hand, and the centripetal, or disciplined and harmonised tendency on the other?

The Sophist is with us to-day. At no previous moment of
the world's history, perhaps, was he so plausible and potent;   because never so confident of the value of his own
opportunism. The radical evil which made sophistry hateful to Plato was its practical denial of the existence of
real things. The Sophists were content to take ideas, not
as in themselves realities, but as figments, the specious
use of which might persuade the multitude to proceed to
certain more or less desirable positions. The democratic
Sophist is as active now as he was when he attempted to
persuade Phaedrus 'that it is not necessary to learn what
is really *just*, but rather what seems just to the multitude who are to give judgment. Nor, again, what is good
or beautiful, but only what seems so to them'. Those who
desire to know what truth is, who wish their lives to be
not only easy but distinguished and organic, need as much
as ever to be upon their guard against those insidious
flatterers of the native indolence of the conscience.
We must, however, pursue no further our companionship
with the latest of the Platonists. Mr Pater's book will
certainly have many readers who will keep it close to their
hands and make it one of their habitual companions. We
must leave him to those silent friends, 'enranged with
those ideas on high which Plato admired', risen into the
spheres of Spenser's Divine Beauty.

Thence gathering plumes of perfect speculation,
To imp the wings of his-flying mind,
Mounting aloft through Heavenly contemplation.(6)

Mr Pater has proved himself once more a scrupulous
craftsman in prose, and apart from all the metaphysical
and historical attractions of his book he may claim to
have achieved another success as an artist. No competent
person can read 'Plato and Platonism' without perceiving
what an exquisite thing the literature of criticism can be.

Notes

1 Benjamin Jowett (1817-93), Fellow (1838) of Balliol,
  Regius Professor of Greek (1855), and Master of Balliol
  College (1870-93), translated the 'Dialogues of Plato'.
    Henry Jackson (1838-1921), prelector in ancient
  philosophy (1875-1906) and Regius Professor of Greek
  (1906-21) at Cambridge.
2 See No. 59.
3 John Evelyn (1620-1706), diarist of the period (1641-
  (1706) of Charles I. Robert Boyle (1627-91), physicist,

chemist and natural philosopher. George Berkeley (1685-
1753), Irish philosopher, author of 'A Treatise Concerning the Principles of Human Knowledge' (1710).
4 Thomas Henry Huxley (1825-95), biologist and teacher,
best known for his defence of the theory of evolution and
for his lectures and writings popularising science. John
Tyndall (1820-93), Professor of Natural History at the
Royal Institution (1853), remembered as a populariser of
science.
5 See p. 6.
6 Hymn to Heavenly Beauty, 11. 134-6.

56. PAUL SHOREY, SIGNED REVIEW, 'DIAL'

1 April 1893, xiv, 211-14

See Introduction, p. 33-6.
   Paul Shorey (1857-1934), American classical scholar, was
Professor (1892-1933) in the Department of Greek at the
University of Chicago, acting as head from 1896 to 1927.
He published 'The Idea of Good in Plato's Republic' (1895)
and 'The Unity of Plato's Thought' (1903).
   For the views of another classical scholar, see No. 59.

It would be superfluous to dwell on the felicitous diction
and artistic unity of composition of Mr Walter Pater's exquisite little volume of lectures on 'Plato and Platonism'.
What I wish to emphasize is its value as an aid to the
serious interpretation of Plato's thought. Slight as the
performance may seem to the specialist, notable as are its
limitations and occasional lapses from accuracy in point
of erudite detail, it has the rare distinction of being
right and just throughout; it is the first true and correctly proportioned presentation of Platonism that has been
given to the general reader. Mr Pater has, in Emerson's
phrase, succeeded in 'nestling into Plato's brain', and,
if not thinking thence, at least in looking out from it
upon the Greek world of the fourth century B.C. Historic
criticism, as he justly says, is in the end the only
scientific criticism, and yet 'the trial-task of criticism
begins when we touch what is unique in the individual genius, which contrived after all by force of will to have its

own masterful way with that environment'. To this double
task of criticism Mr Pater brings sufficient scholarship,
and the broad historic culture and refined literary instinct without which the highest merely linguistic scholarship is impotent to interpret a literature like the
Greek. He has brought Plato into intelligible relation to
the life and thought of his time, has clearly apprehended
the chief elements of his complex personality, the distinctive note of his genius, and so has interpreted the
work from within, from the 'man and the environment' that
brought it forth.

Perhaps the most acceptable service of the reviewer of
such a book will be to resume in simple direct language
some of the thoughts which the 'indefectible' — to compliment Polus in his own peculiar style, — the 'indefectible' graces of the author's elaborate diction may obscure for some impatient readers. The central idea of the
book is Plato's two-fold relation to that fundamental Greek
and human antithesis of the Ionian and Dorian temperament,
the ideals of progress and conservativism, of expansion
and self-restraint. Himself the noblest type of that
graceful Athenian many-sidedness, of which Pericles made
such magnificent boast, but writing in an age when the
living force of Athens and of Greece was flaming itself
away in the fever of unrestrained individualism, watching
the society that had produced Marathon, Salamis, and the
Aeschylean drama, 'dying of the triumph of the liberal
party', Plato was led by inevitable reaction to seek salvation for Athens and mankind in the contrasted Dorian ideal
of simplification and austere self-control.

This key-note is struck in the first chapter, where, in
a brilliant exposition of the ancient Heraclitean and modern evolutionist philosophy of mutability and the flux of
form, we learn how to Plato motion 'becomes the token of
unreality in things, of falsity in our thoughts about
them', so that in his very vocabulary such innocent or pleasant words as 'manifold', 'embroidered', 'changeful', become the synonyms of what is evil. In opposing to this
world of flux his ideal world of changeless, formless,
colorless, impalpable, essence, Plato was consciously under
the influence of Parmenides and the Eleatic pantheism that
taught of one immovable being, the only true Godhead behind
the fantastic shapes of the Homeric and Hesiodic mythology,
the only reality underlying the kaleidoscopic figures of
change. And from Pythagoras he learned (besides the poetic
dream of a prenatal existence which Wordsworth has made familiar to us) to conceive the Heraclitean motion as beats
or waves of measured harmony rippling into rhythmic life and
activity the cold inert ocean of Parmenideal being. All

this is very well said (as Mr Pater says it) and is delightful reading. A more philosophic treatment would
point out that Plato, while yielding to the charm of these
earlier half-poetic lisping philosophies, consciously dom-
inates them from a higher plane of thought. He is quite
as well aware as his most literal-minded modern critic that
he is playing with symbols, and that it is somewhat fantastic to charge these catchwords of primitive generalization with all the weight of moral significance which he
discovers in them. But to make this clear, Mr Pater would
have been obliged to follow the master into some of those
metaphysical disquisitions from the pedantry of which he
shrinks with the true Oxford Platonist's pedantic affectation of abhorrence of pedantry.

Guided by this central conception of Platonism, Mr Pater
finds something new (in form, at least) to say about the
Sophists. Rising at once above the region of the tiresome
debate initiated by Grote's(1) defence of the Sophists, he
shows how 'the great Sophist was the Athenian public itself, Athens, as the willing victim of its own gifts, its
own flamboyancy'. The Sophists by their teaching rein-
forced this dangerous centrifugal tendency, this 'ruinous
fluidity', this excessive individualism, stimulating the
over stimulated and excitable Athenian temperament to burst
all bonds of convention that fettered self-expansion, not
excepting the prejudice of morality. In politics, morals,
and literature no real things existed for them; they recognized only counters and pawns to be placed and moved in
a skilfully played game.

To these teachers and the tendencies they embodied Plato
opposed the world of absolute ideas and his dream of an
ideal republic in which the judgments of the philosophic
few should be fixed by education and consecrated by religion and art as the immutable prejudices of the disciplined many. A faint adumbration of such a society Plato,
with pardonable anti-patriotic bias, seemed to discern in
that mysterious Lacedaemon lying concealed among the hollow
hills, where stern Dorian discipline, though narrow and
harsh, still continued to produce from generation to generation the noblest physical types of Hellenic manhood.

And so, with exquisite art, before proceeding to portray
for us Plato's ideal state, Mr Pater takes us to Lacedaemon
in the company of a supposed curious visitor from the Academy. A barren abstract would give the reader no conception of this beautiful chapter. It is a prose poem in
which all that fragmentary tradition has told us of Sparta
and her ways, all that the Dorian discipline symbolized
for the Athenian philosopher's idealizing imagination, is
blended in exquisite harmony with the conjectures of German

science and the permissible fancies and modern English
analogies that suggest themselves to one who has mused and
studied year after year in that richly-laden Oxford air.
Thus prepared we pass to the 'Republic', the dialogue which
the author seems to have studied most diligently — to which
the entire book indeed is in a sense an introduction. One,
perhaps the chief, aspect of Plato's many-sided masterpiece
Mr Pater has clearly apprehended and set forth — that it
is the philosopher's day dream of a city of the perfect
made strong by law, custom, and wide prejudice to resist
the great goddess Mutability, and the play of those centrifugal forces which were then destroying Greece and to which
every combination formed by man must sooner or later yield.
But Plato explicitly affirms that the main theme of the
'Republic' is ethical — the demonstration (where formal
logic fails) by psychological and social analogies, of the
everlasting truth that righteousness is better than unright-
eousness. Plato may have misconceived or misstated the
dominant thought of the 'Republic', but no treatment of
Platonism is quite satisfactory that does not assign their
due place to the ethical discussions of the 'Gorgias',
'Philebus', and the ninth book of the 'Republic'. Mr
Pater's readers, however, will not regret that he has chosen to depict a personality and a conception of human life
rather than to follow the windings of an argument. Still
seeking to interpret Platonism from within, he finds the
peculiar quality of Plato's genius to reside in the blending of diverse elements seemingly contradictory. A disciple of Socrates, the barefoot philosopher with whom the
Stoic and Cynic traditions began, Plato was himself endowed with a complex and richly sensuous nature. He
might have been a poet of the order of Catullus or Sappho,
or a rhetorical sophist with more philosophy than Gorgias
and more courage to confront the conflicts of real life
than Isocrates. The philosopher of pure 'being', he was
yet a man 'for whom the visible world existed', a 'seer
with a sensuous love of the unseen', one who came very near
to persons and who felt all things in an intense vivid personal fashion. This is the secret of his fascination for
Mr Pater, whose reasoned preference for 'Cistercian Gothic',
Gregorian church music, sober monastic greys, and awful
youthful beauty tempered by asceticism, seems to require
constant stimulus from reflection on the juxtaposed contrast of florid and flamboyant decoration, complex Wag-
nerian harmonies, the scarlet and cloth of gold of gorgeous papal functions, and youthful beauty that dedicates
itself more freely to the sun. But though the uninitiated
may be provoked to a philistine smile by the imagery in
which the writer strives to convey to us not merely his

thought but its emotional accompaniment, there is no question that this chapter on the genius of Plato is a more
serious contribution to the right understanding of Platonism than tomes of the ponderous analysis in which German
science disputes the genuineness of his most characteristic works, or endeavors to trace the evolution of his
thought by counting his particles.(2)

After thus penetrating to the heart of the man, to the
central core of his personality, Mr Pater is able to dis-
miss in one chapter the formal doctrine — the theory of
ideas and the dialectic. He attempts no exact analysis of
the logical and metaphysical problems so curiously inter-
mingled in Plato's abstruser writings. That would necessitate the use of ugly words in 'osity and 'ation and a
style of hard pedantic precision justly abhorrent to his
fastidious taste. His aim is merely to remove certain
stumbling blocks from the pathway of the young Platonist,
and to bring out the essential significance of the ideas
and the dialectic from the side of personality — as an attitude of mind, a point of view, a trick of expression. The
tone is apologetic — 'not here, O Apollo, are haunts fits
for thee' — 'of course we are not naturally formed to love
or be interested in or attracted towards the abstract as
such'. But something, he thinks, may be said by way of
'apology for general ideas, — abstruse or intangible, or
dry and seedy and wooden as we may sometimes think them'.
Something, indeed! Mr Pater must be aware that there
exist men who would define education as the acquisition and
progressive rectification of general ideas, men to whom
abstraction and generalization are naturally interesting,
men who are supremely bored both in real life and in realistic or aesthetic literature by the visible tangible world
with its insistent intrusion of concrete and irrelevant detail; men whose pulses are stirred by a subtle generalization, but who would pass unheeding by the finest intarsia
work of 'Fra Damiano of Bergamo'. Plato was not thus limited, having (as the old anecdote puts it) the eye to discern both man and humanity. But it is precisely as the
author of those 'barren logomachies' of the 'Theaetetus',
'Sophist', and 'Parmenides', from which aesthetic Oxford
shrinks with such fastidious dread, that he has attracted
some of the disciples who have done him most honor in
every age. Within its self-imposed limits, however, nothing could be clearer or more illuminating than the account here given of the ideas. They are primarily a way
of regarding and speaking of 'general terms such as "useful" or "just", of abstract notions, like "equality", of
ideals such as "Beauty", or "the Perfect City"'. These
are first conceived as things, as entities quite as real

and definite as the fleeting particulars of individual
sensation, and then, in certain select instances, and under
the influence of certain exalted moods, they are personified and gather to themselves all the associations of real
persons — and yet always as a fashion of speech, a way of
feeling, never as a rigid and systematic doctrine. These
ideas, mythologically said to have been contemplated by the
soul in the infinite voyagings of its prenatal life, are re-
coverable now only by the dialectic process — a communing
of the soul with itself, or better yet with some kindred
spirit, whereby the essential significance of the facts of
common experience is struck out as the spark of fire (it
is Plato's figure) glints from the fire-sticks of primitive
man. Only through such flexible, ever renewed, self-
checking, and sometimes self-contradicting induction can
reminiscence recover the memory of that lost vision, and
the thinker steadying himself amid the flux of sense attain
to 'perfectly representative ideas and a reasoned reflex of
experience'. Even then our truth may prove to be only relative truth, an adumbration of the postulated absolute. And
thus it happens that Plato, the philosopher of 'absolute
being', is also the true spiritual father of the long and
illustrious line of sceptics and eclectics — the New Academy, Cicero, Abelard, Montaigne, Victor Cousin, and our
English Jowett and Arnold. Such, in general, is the conception of Plato's 'doctrine', which Mr Pater sets forth
with inimitable felicity of diction and aptness of illustration. I know nothing in Platonic literature at once so
sound and so illuminating for the young student.
   The concluding chapter on the Platonic Aesthetics, while
in the main luminous and just, needs, I think, to be supplemented. For Plato the style is (of) the very man. His
own style is the expression of a rich sensuous imagination,
informed and guided by the severest logic, of the ascetic
chastening of an originally passionate nature, and his
aesthetic doctrine is based on the conviction that such
chastening is indispensable to the welfare of man, to the
salvation of the versatile and lively Greek. Man is an
imitative animal, unconsciously, inevitably imitative. His
nature is subdued to what he works and lives in. Beauty
born of a murmuring sound does really pass into the maiden's
face. Art can never be a morally indifferent thing if, as
Ruskin says after Plato, every work of art tends to reproduce in the beholder the state of mind and temper that
brought it forth.(3) It is therefore more than a mere meta-
phor to speak of an 'incorrigibly lewd style', a base and
degrading music, a vulgar and incontinent architecture.
'*Entbehren sollst du, sollst entbehren*'(4) is the law and
lesson of life. How shall we learn it if we abandon our

souls to be played upon and fretted by the alluring solici-
tations of an art without restraints and without reserves?
It is not good, says the sage old counsellor of Xerxes in
Herodotus, to teach our souls to be ever reaching out after
new things. Let us then (this is Plato's inference), let
us shut ourselves within narrowing nunnery walls of an austere hieratic art, and turn our eyes away from the brilliant Homeric epic — that lucid Ionian mirror of the var-
ious-colored world, 'all the wealth and all the woe'. It
is not good to dabble in the fount of fictive tears and
divorce the feeling from its mate the deed. We must banish
gorgeous Tragedy with her sceptred pall; hymner of auto-
cratic kings and unbridled democracies. For all her august
mien, she cares nothing to make us better, but only to
minister to the pride of eye and ear. And if we admit the
honeyed Muse into our state, 'pleasure and pain will be
the lords of our city instead of law and the rule of that
right reason shall have pronounced to be the best'. Hymns
and psalms and song services of praise must be the only
music and poetry of the city of the perfect. And yet there
is no hard puritanic insensibility in Plato's banishment of
Homer and his train. He is only too susceptible to the fas-
cinations of the honeyed Muse, as the fond and frequent
citations scattered over his pages prove. 'We are very conscious of her charms — and thou too, dear friend, art thou
not thyself beguiled by her and chiefly when thou dost contemplate her through Homer?' But great is the prize for
which wé are striving, and what shall it profit a man if
he gain the whole world of poetry and art and lose his own
soul?

> But all those pleasant bowers and palace brave
>   Guyon broken down with rigour pitiless,
> Ne aught their goodly workmanship might save
>   Them from the tempest of his wrathfulness.(5)

Mr Pater seems to close his eyes to this culmination in
Plato of the eternal tragedy of the conflict in imperfect
human nature between the artist's apprehension of the beautiful and the thinker's conception of the salutary and the
true. He finds consolation in the sterner charm of 'Saint
Ouen of the aisles and arches' or Notre Dame de Bourges.
But Plato cherished few if any such illusions as to the
superior loveliness of the 'dry beauty', and had the *anima
naturaliter pagana*(6) that lurks in every one of us, cries
out: Ah no, —

> Not as thine, not as thine was our mother, a blossom
>   of flowering seas.

We may dream of a time when these discords shall be resolved in a higher harmony. But to-day in the noonday of
science they are felt no less poignantly by sensitive natures than then in the dawn of speculative philosophy. As
the wayward Nietzsche (himself an intelligence at war with
a temperament) profoundly says in his half-mystical language: 'Art is like wine. Better it is for man to need
neither, but to keep to cold water, and change the water
into wine by the inward fire, by the indwelling sweetness
of the soul.'(7)

Notes

1 George Grote (1794-1871), historian and author of the
  ten-volume 'History of Greece' (1846-56).
2 See the concluding paragraph of No. 59.
3 See Part III of the third volume of 'Modern Painters':
  Of the Real Nature of Greatness of Style.
4 'You must go without, go without.' 'Faust', I, 1. 1549.
5 'The Faerie Queene', II, xii, lxxxiii.
6 The soul is by nature pagan.
7 See 'Human, all too Human' (1909), ii, 109.

57. R.H. HUTTON, UNSIGNED REVIEW, 'SPECTATOR'

1 April 1893, lxx, 422-3

See Introduction, pp. 33-5.
    Richard Holt Hutton (1826-97), editor, theologian, aca-
demician and prolific man of letters. With Walter Bagehot
(1826-77), he edited (1855-62) the 'National Review'; and
with Meredith Townsend (1831-1911), he edited (1861-97) and
was proprietor of the 'Spectator'. He took charge of the
literary section of the 'Spectator', and won wide respect
for his sound criticism.

Mr Pater has written a very fine and delicate study of
Plato and Platonism, the study of a scholar and an artist
even more than the study of a metaphysician. The motto he
takes from Plato describes the leading idea of his book,
asserting, as it does, that philosophy is essentially the

principle of harmony in human life. As a matter of fact,
the thinkers whose names have been the leading names in
philosophy, have hardly ever, except in Plato's own case,
illustratéd the full force of this assumption. Plato himself was a 'mighty harmonist'; so, perhaps, if we may accept the tradition about him, was Pythagoras; nor have
there been wanting some more modern names in philosophy
with which we associate, in some degree, the conceptions
which Plato regarded as interpreting the higher order and
beauty of the universe, — Bacon, for instance, Descartes,
Malebranche, Berkeley, Coleridge. But, for the most part,
we must go to the poets, and not to the philosophers, to
find representatives of the sort of teaching which Plato
understood under the word μουσική,(1) — the teaching that
chiefly fascinates Mr Pater in Plato's writings. The most
notable names in philosophy, from Parmenides onwards, including, for instance, Aristotle and his Arabic commentators, Occam, Hobbes, Hartley, even Butler, Leibnitz, Wolff,
Condillac, Helvétius, Hume, Kant, Bentham, Hegel, Mill,
Herbert Spencer, suggest to us nothing so little as the
Platonic conception of philosophy as the highest kind of
harmony; nor would Mr Pater, we suspect, have undertaken
to give a course of lectures on any philosopher of the
ordinary type. His love for Plato is due greatly to what
he justly terms Plato's 'sensuous love of the un-seen'.
Nevertheless, what he says of Parmenides as one of the most
potent influences moulding Plato's thought, is well and
admirably said. Mr Pater delineates truly and skilfully
Plato's recoil from the doctrine of perpetual change and
flux, — the doctrine of Heraclitus, — which undermined
the whole principle of constancy and fidelity in human
life, and which made of the mind of man a mere moral and
spiritual chameleon. It was recoil from this philosophy
for ephemeral rather than immortal beings, which led to
that aspiration after fixity and constancy which fascinated Plato with the petrified immutability of the One
Absolute Being as Parmenides taught it. This it was that
appealed to Plato's thirst for lofty and inflexible principles of conduct. He saw that the doctrine of perpetual
flux was really a doctrine which made life a mere phantom,
— a rapid succession of transitory sensations, without
any permanent meaning or end. If perpetual change is the
only law of our being, we are mere dancing atoms, — nay,
not so much as atoms, flickerings of capricious change,
which can have no more responsibility for what we are, or
are not, than the shadows which fly and shrink and lengthen
as the sun moves over the leaves of a forest. It was the
passionate eagerness for something fixed, for something of
permanent significance in human life, which made Plato

drink-in the teaching of Parmenides as a grateful refuge
from the mockery of a philosophy of perpetual flux, and
therefore of perpetual illusion.

And in his chapter on Plato's doctrine of ideas, Mr
Pater shows with great skill how the one eternal, indivisible, and immutable Being of Parmenides, has for Plato

> been diffused, divided, resolved, refracted, differen-
> tiated, into the eternal Ideas, a multiple, numerous,
> stellar world, so to call it, — abstract light into
> stars: Justice, Temperance as it is, Bravery as it is.
> Permanence, independency, indefectible identity with
> itself, — all those qualities which Parmenides sup-
> posed in the one and indivisible reality, — belong
> to every one of those ideas, severally. It was like a
> recrudescence of polytheism in that abstract world; a
> return of the many gods of Homer, veiled now as abstract
> notions, Love, Fear, Confidence, and the like; and as
> such, the modern anthropologist, our student of the
> natural history of man, would rank the Platonic theory
> as but a form of what he calls 'animism' (pp. 152-3).

We hesitate at the words 'animism' and 'polytheism'. Mr
Pater goes on to explain what he calls this 'animism',
this spiritual 'polytheism', as if only the existence of
intrinsic life, of a kind of personality in the Platonic
ideas, could account for the reverent passion which they
inspire in Plato, — the enthusiasm with which, when really
beheld by the soul, they are supposed to fill it, — so that
even a temporary vision of them is sufficient to renew the
fountains of moral strength and religious hope. But is
this a correct reading of Plato's drift? Did he not really
mean that there are intellectual and moral conditions of
life which are, in some sense, prior to life of any kind,
divine or human, independent of it, and by the observance,
or non-observance, of which conditions, the moral and intellectual character of all life, divine or human, is
really determined? To modern thinkers, no doubt, it seems
as if there were a contradiction in terms in talking of
an idea as existing outside a living mind; but it looks
to us very much as if Plato's ideas of Justice, Temperance,
Beauty, and the like, were conceived by him as independent
of any mind, though the great purpose and object of them
is to animate, subdue, and control minds. As far as we
can judge, Plato craved an ideal standard which was independent even of the divine personality itself, and one
therefore which could not be identified, as Berkeley
subsequently identified it, with that personality. He
wanted the ideas of Justice, Beauty, Temperance, and the

rest, to be as independent of God as of man. He foresaw,
we imagine, the danger of a theology which places the *will*
of God above these great moral and spiritual ideas, and
places character therefore at the mercy of an omnipotent
caprice. And surely the history both of Mahommedanism and
of Calvinism has shown us that in shrinking from any philosophy which makes the moral attributes of God dependent
on his absolute will, he had some reason on his side.

The only point, then, on which we venture to differ
from Mr Pater, is in the inference he supposes Plato to
have drawn from the passionate love with which these eternal ideas possess minds worthy to gaze upon them in their
purity, that they were in any sense living persons, —
that his view was a kind of abstract Polytheism. On the
contrary, we believe that he looked upon these ideas as in
some way much *more* than living persons, though *not* living
persons, as partaking in some respects of that Greek conception of Destiny which regarded Destiny as beyond the
control of the gods. These ideas determined all that was
really worthy of enthusiastic love in living beings, God
or man, but they were not themselves conceived as personal.
The very passage which Mr Pater quotes from the 'Phaedrus'
to show why it is that men have a clearer idea of Beauty
than they have of Justice, and the rest of the eternal
ideas, — namely, that Beauty alone of these eternal ideas
has left in this lower world any adequate copies of itself,
copies 'out of all proportion in their truthfulness and
adequacy to any copy left here with us, of Justice, for
instance', seems to us to prove this.

> As regards Beauty, as I said, it both shone out, in its
> true being, among those other eternal forms; and when
> we came down hither we apprehended it through the clear-
> est of all our bodily senses, gleaming with utmost
> brightness. For sight comes to us keenest of all our
> bodily senses, though Wisdom is not seen by it. Mar-
> vellous loves, in truth, would that [namely, Wisdom] have
> afforded, had it presented any manifest image of itself,
> such as that of Beauty, had it reached our bodily vision,
> — that, and all those other amiable forms. But now
> Beauty alone has had this fortune; so that it is the
> clearest, the most certain, of all things, and the most
> lovable.

In other words, Beauty is clearest to us and most lovable
because it can be discerned by the bodily sense as well
as by the spiritual sense, while the other divine qualities
are discerned by the spiritual sense alone. Yet there is
nothing so *personal* in Beauty as there is in Wisdom and

Courage and Temperance. We discern beauty in a sunset,
in a landscape, in a flower, whereas we cannot discern
wisdom or courage or temperance without some personality
real, or at all events imagined, in whom wisdom and courage and temperance shall be illustrated. Yet Plato chooses
Beauty — least personal of all these ideas — as the one
divine idea of which we possess the clearest vision on
earth. We cannot but think that he regarded these eternal
ideas, not as living, but as above life, as presenting
superpersonal standards by which persons, whether divine or
human, if they are to be worthy to gaze upon them, shall
guide themselves. He had the greatest fear of subordinat-
ing the eternal standards of conduct to the will even of
divine omnipotence, and his device was to represent that
there are eternal conditions, or, as we should say, 'laws',
of personal life which can only be apprehended by persons,
but which are independent of, and raised above, the persons who apprehend them. His doctrine of men's partial
reminiscence of a prenatal vision, and of the eternal
verities of which in a former existence men have had a
fleeting glimpse, is Plato's equivalent for Kant's doctrine of a *priori* truths and conceptions, and we doubt if
to Plato these dominating moral conditions affecting the
higher personalities were a bit more of the nature of the
distinct personalities than a *priori* categories were to
Kant.

Mr Pater does full justice to the asceticism which
Plato so constantly inculcates in spite of his 'sensuous
love of the un-seen'. But we wonder that he does not lay
more stress than he does on the doctrine approaching very
nearly to the Christian doctrine of retributive as distinguished from merely corrective punishment, which is so
vividly represented in the 'Gorgias', where, in our opinion, Plato comes very near to a doctrine, not merely of
retribution, but of penance. If Mr Pater does injustice
of any kind to Plato, — and we would not say that he does,
— it is in rather underrating the depth and intensity of
his moral convictions. On the other hand, we do not think
that he insists sufficiently on the very low estimate Plato
must have formed of the claims of the domestic affections
upon human nature, before he could have given us his ideal
of the domestic life of his model republic. His whole conception of human life was too artificial. As Mr Pater
puts it, he wished every man to make himself 'a work of
art', and, of course, to a certain extent he was quite
right; but there is always a great danger that, in making
yourself 'a work of art', you may make yourself stiff,
artificial, *unnatural*, perhaps even distorted; and such,
no doubt, would have been the vice of the citizens of his
model republic.

There is the greatest possible charm in the whole book,
though we think that Mr Pater sympathises a little more
with Plato as an unsatisfied searcher after truth than he
does with Plato as a spiritual moralist of the highest
rank. Here is one of the finest passages, in which he
sums up Plato's services as a thinker:

[Quotes ch. 7: 'Since Zeno's paradoxes' to 'nor a system
of propositions, but forms a temper'.]

And, he observes very happily a little further on:
'Κινδυνεύει, "it may chance to be", is, we may notice, a
favourite catch-word of his. The philosopher of Being,
or, of the verb "to be", is, after all, afraid of saying
"It is"'. But this applies much more to questions of
metaphysics than to questions of ethics, in which last
Plato's judgments are as explicit and affirmative as any
human judgments could be.
    One of the best characteristics of Mr Pater's book is
that he translates, as we may say, Plato's theory, with
the greatest freedom and vivacity, into its true modern
equivalents. We have seldom read, for instance, a more
telling passage than that in which he explains (pp. 142-
46) how much fresh light and meaning the abstract and
generalised 'idea' throws on the individual and concrete
example, how the scientific knowledge of species and genus
adds even to the imaginative, as well as to the intellectual, apprehension of every individual specimen of a class.
Plato's 'sensuous love of the un-seen' helped him greatly
in the sensuous realisation even of the seen.

Note

1 Music.

58. ARTHUR SYMONS ON PATER'S STYLE

1893

Extract from a signed article entitled The Decadent Move-
ment in Literature, in 'Harper's New Monthly Magazine'
(November 1893), lxxxvii, 858-67. See Nos 35 and 94 and
Introduction, p. 35.

According to Symons, 'The latest movement in European
literature' is best defined by the epithet 'Decadent'
rather than by such terms as 'Symbolism' or 'Impressionism'.
The works of the brothers Goncourt, Verlaine, Mallarmé,
Maeterlink and Huysmans possess the qualities of the Greek
and Latin decadence: 'an intense self-consciousness, a
restless curiosity in research, an over-subtlizing refinement upon refinement, a spiritual and moral perversity'.

... The prose of Mr Walter Pater, the verse of Mr W.E.
Henley(1) — to take two prominent examples — are attempts
to do with the English language something of what Goncourt
and Verlaine have done with the French. Mr Pater's prose
is the most beautiful English prose which is now being
written; and, unlike the prose of Goncourt, it has done
no violence to language, it has sought after no vivid effects, it has found a large part of mastery in reticence,
in knowing what to omit. But how far away from the classic ideals of style is this style in which words have their
color, their music, their perfume, in which there is 'some
strangeness in the proportion' of every beauty! The
'Studies in the Renaissance' have made of criticism a new
art — have raised criticism almost to the act of creation.
And 'Marius the Epicurean', in its study of 'sensations
and ideas' (the conjunction was Goncourt's before it was
Mr Pater's), and the 'Imaginary Portraits', in their evo-
cations of the Middle Ages, the age of Watteau — have
they not that morbid subtlety of analysis, the morbid curiosity of form, that we have found in the works of the
French Decadents? A fastidiousness equal to that of Flaubert has limited Mr Pater's work to six volumes, but in
these six volumes there is not a page that is not perfectly
finished, with a conscious art of perfection. In its
minute elaboration it can be compared only with goldsmith's
work — so fine, so delicate is the handling of so delicate,
so precious a material....

Note

1 Symons refers to Henley's (1849-1903) 'Book of Verses'
  (1888) and 'The Song of the Sword' (1892). He claims that
  'The poetry of Impressionism can go no further, in one
  direction, than that series of rhymes and rhythms named
  "In Hospital".'

59. LEWIS CAMPBELL, SIGNED REVIEW, 'CLASSICAL REVIEW'

1893, vii, 263-6

See Introduction, pp. 33-5.
    Lewis Campbell (1830-1908), Scottish classical scholar
and editor of Sophocles and Plato, was Professor of Greek
and Gifford Lecturer at St Andrews (1863-94). He completed
Benjamin Jowett's translation of 'The Republic' (1894) and
wrote 'The Life of Benjamin Jowett' (1897) in collaboration
with Evelyn Abbott.
    Campbell knew Pater for many years and furnished Wright
with recollections for his 'Life'. He remarked: 'Pater's
conversation always seemed to me more interesting than his
books. Such easy flow of perfect expression, often paradoxical, but always suggestive. His personal excellence,
his kindness and devotion to home duties were well-known
to all his friends' (Wright, ii, 212).

'*Nil tetigit quod non ornavit*'(1) is the commonplace which
rises to the lips on taking up this last and largest of Mr
Pater's 'Appreciations'. 'Last year he gave us Raphael(2)
in a comely guise and now he presents Plato to us, no doubt
as suitably apparelled.' But as we read onward we are
charmed and interested in a more serious manner than heretofore. The book is in fact a brilliant critical essay of
the kind which, in Mr Pater's view, is, ever since Montaigne
employed it, the best vehicle for modern philosophic
thought. Readers of 'Marius the Epicurean', who remember
the subtle exposition there of Cyrenaicism will be prepared
for similar *tours de force*. Yet it is not without a feeling of pleased and exhilarating surprise that they will
alight on such pages of the present volume as that in which
the character and mind of Zeno the Eleatic are delineated
(p. 23), or those which explain perhaps more luminously than
has been done hitherto the value which Plato set on Dialectic (pp. 161-4). The following statement, one of cardinal
import, deserves to be quoted at length, both for the felicity of its expression, and for its undeniable truth:

[Quotes ch. 7: 'Platonism is not a formal theory' to 'which
reduce "the Many to the One"'.]

    The author's characterization of the 'historic method'
may also be repeated here:

Dogmatic and eclectic criticism alike have in our own
century, under the influence of Hegel and his predominant theory of the ever-changing 'Time Spirit' or *Zeit-
geist*, given way to a third method of criticism, the
historic method, which bids us replace the doctrine, or
the system, we are busy with, or such an ancient monument of philosophic thought as 'The Republic', as far
as possible in the group of conditions, intellectual,
social, material, amid which it was actually produced.

It is in some ways fortunate for Mr Pater's readers
that he has not thought it necessary to confine himself
within the cogent limits which the method so prescribed
might seem to impose. He has made a strong and earnest
effort on his own account thus to understand and realize
Plato. But in setting forth his conception he has freely
availed himself of the wealth of illustration readily afforded by his own full and fertile mind. His readers are
insensibly drawn within a magic circle of quintessential
flame that has been fed with all the choicest products of
art and literature. Not one century alone is present here.
Much rather, all the centuries, the bloom of every civilization, flowers culled from every soil, are intertwined to
form the delicately broidered framework. Talk of ποικιλία!
(3) Why here are Isaiah and the children of Sion, Louis
the IXth, Fra Damiano of Bergamo, the Gregorian Chant, St
Ouen and Notre Dame de Bourges (confessedly a 'far cry'
from Athens), Montaigne and Thackeray, Dante and Berkeley,
Wordsworth and Henry Vaughan — not to mention Marcus
Aurelius, Spinoza, Descartes and Bacon (whose business in
such affairs is more obvious) — contributing their several
tones to the production of this symphony in prose! These
cross-lights, as from 'storied windows richly dight' on
forms of alabaster, shed a manifold radiance on the firm
outlines of the solid central work, which is also permeated by a remote Hegelian influence and by the writer's
personal idiosyncrasy, in which refined aesthetic sensitiveness is blended with a quiet intensity of religious
feeling. Something of this mode of sentiment appears in
the comparison of Ionian pessimism to the moodiness of
adolescence, 'when it is forced suddenly to bethink itself
and for a moment feels already old, feels the temperature
of the world about it sensibly colder':- also in the frequent adaptation of Scriptural expressions. A pleasing
result of the writer's power of religious sympathy is his
just and penetrating view of the religious vein in Socrates.
The Essayist has many privileges, which Mr Pater's
genius turns to good account. He may isolate and draw out
tendencies, he may accentuate contrasts, he may seize on

salient features, he may press analogies; he need not
shrink from iteration, nor from glaring discrepancies
(which it is the reader's business to harmonize); he
may steep his work in the atmosphere of a pervading sentiment, without incurring blame for 'subjectivity'. He may
use words in new or foreign senses ('assistant' p. 85,
'amiable', p. 158, 'παραλειπόμενα'(4) p. 257), and may indulge, after Hegel's fashion (p. 88), in fanciful etymolo-
gies:- even an occasional pun (like that on *carrière
ouverte*(5) p. 96) may be permitted him. He need not profess to have overtaken a voluminous and wearisome 'literature'. He is not tied, as the mere interpreter is, to the
avoidance of minute errors, which take little from the essential value of his work. He can concentrate attention
on the form, without being haunted by distracting anxieties
on account of material exactitude.

The *matter* of the book before us has, much of it, been
common property for about forty years, commencing from the
time when the historic method was first seriously applied
to criticism. But it is not the less a solid gain to possess this bright and genial exposition of truths which we
have long potently believed. For, however he may try to
veil his gift, Mr Pater is essentially a poet. And if
Goethe and Hermann(6) offered to discourse on Homer, who
would not be tempted to exclaim 'Dear Gottfried, we will
gladly listen to you εἰσαῦθις,(7) — on some other day'?
The siren voice of Mr Pater will be heard, where that of
the unkempt Heraclitean 'Sibyl' could not penetrate. That
is why such sentences as these are of peculiar value:

Think, for a moment, of the difference, as regards
mental attitude, between the naturalist who deals with
things through ideas, and the layman (so to call him)
in picking up a shell on the sea-shore; what it is
that the subsumption of the individual into the species,
its subsequent alliance to and co-ordination with other
species really does for the furnishing of the mind of
the former. The layman, though we need not suppose
him inattentive, or unapt to retain impressions, is in
fact still but a child; and the shell, its colours and
convolution, no more than a dainty, very easily des-
tructible toy to him. Let him become a schoolboy about
it, so to speak. The toy he puts aside; his mind is
drilled perforce, to learn *about* it; and thereby is
exercised, he may think, with everything except just
the thing itself, as he cares for it; with other shells,
with some general laws of life, and for a while it
might seem that, turning away his eyes from the 'vanity'
of the particular, he has been made to sacrifice the

concrete, the real and living product of nature, to a
mere dry and abstract product of the mind. But when he
comes out of school, and on the sea-shore again finds
a fellow to his toy, perhaps a finer specimen of it,
he may see what the service of that converse with the
general has really been towards the concrete, towards
what he sees, — in regard to the particular thing he
actually sees.... What broad-cast light he enjoys! —
that scholar, confronted with the sea-shell, for instance,
or with some enigma of heredity in himself or another, with
some condition of a particular soul, in circumstances which
may never precisely so occur again.... He not only sees,
but understands (thereby only seeing the more) and will
therefore, also remember.... So much by way of apology
(!) for general ideas (pp. 142-4).

The last words are characteristically significant. Mr
Pater is really charmed with Plato; but there are other
and rival charms which he will not forego. Some of the
discrepancies to which I before alluded may be thus ac-
counted for. He admires Marcus Aurelius (p. 242), yet he
is struck with a 'mortal coldness' (p. 40) in thinking of
him. 'Monotheism' has his good word upon occasion; yet he
finds it 'repellent'. At one moment Form is everything and
Matter nothing (p. 4), though by and by precipitancy of
Form without Matter is shown to be a mark of Sophistry
(p. 101). In writing on metaphysical subjects he appears
like some strong-winged butterfly which now mounts into the
pure azure, now flits about the tree-tops, but anon is
sure to be found hovering amongst the fragrant garden-
flowers. The words of Descartes come back to us as we read:

*Nec aliter quam captivus, qui forte imaginaria libertate
fruebatur in somniis, quum postea suspicari incipit se
dormire, timet excitari, blandisque illusionibus lentè
connivet; sic sponte labor in veteres opiniones.*(8)

What most fascinates him in Plato is precisely the coexis-
tence in him of the supreme visual faculty with the severity
of abstract reasoning:

It is in the blending of diverse elements in the mental
constitution of Plato that the peculiar Platonic quality
resides. Platonism is in one sense an emphatic witness
to the unseen, the transcendental, the non-experienced,
the beauty, for instance, which is not for the bodily
eye. Yet the author of this philosophy of the unseen
was, — Who can doubt it who has read but a page of him!
this, in fact, is what has led and kept to his pages many

who have no turn for the sort of questions Plato actually discusses:- The author of this philosophy of the un-
seen was one, for whom, as was said of a very different
French writer, 'the *visible* world really existed'. Austere as he seems, and on well-considered principle
really is, his temperance or austerity, aesthetically
so winning, is attained only by the chastisement, the
control of a variously interested, a richly sensuous
nature (p. 114).

Plato's writings form an exceedingly complex whole, and
it is not surprising that each new writer on the subject,
approaching it at a different angle, should accentuate a
different aspect, diverging perhaps in each case somewhat
from the 'entire point'. To Mr Grote's(9) apprehension,
the 'Protagoras' was of all the dialogues intellectually
the most mature. Mr Pater appears to dwell with most complacency on the 'Phaedrus', 'Symposium' and 'Charmides'.
And I venture to think that, of the eternal triad, Beauty,
Goodness, Truth, the first obtains more importance with him
than in the long run with Plato, — that of the terms composing his motto (φιλοσοφία, μουσική)(10) he lays undue emphasis on the second. In saying that Beauty alone has a
visible antitype, Plato did not mean to subordinate Wisdom
to Beauty. It is true that under Plato's influence Mr
Pater declares himself as the upholder of a 'dry beauty',
— of severe simplicity in art and life. But is the con-
notation of 'καλὸν'(11)when applied to conduct any longer
coextensive with that of 'beautiful'? Or is not the Puritanism of the 'Republic' (especially in Book x) even more
thoroughgoing than our author imagines, and is it quite
fair to infer from isolated positions in Book i that Art
is to be for Art's sake alone, and not rather for the sake
of Life? — Meanwhile the book before us is in every sense
of the words an unmistakable τόκος ἐν καλῷ.(12)
Plato's attitude towards mysticism is another point
where Mr Pater's view appears hardly adequate. Not re-
gress, but progress seems to me the distinguishing note of
Platonism. There is an important difference (well displayed in Professor Caird's(13) fine chapter on God as the
End of Knowledge) between Spinoza's *Omnis determinatio est
negatio*'(14) and Plato's *Omnis negatio est determinatio*'.
(15) The 'Phaedo' indeed counsels withdrawal from the
world, the meditation of death. But this is not the lesson of the 'Symposium', nor the spirit of the prayers at
marriage festivals in the 'Republic', nor the motto of the
great victory of primaeval Athens over Atlantis.
The incidental chapter on Lacedaemon has been universally admired. It is a prose poem, in which all that is

most valuable of K.O. Müller's(16) great work has been
condensed, so as to bring out the significance of Plato's
reaction towards Laconism. But (1) was the actual dividing line between Ionian and Dorian so wide and deep as
Pericles and Mr Pater would have us think, or had the
Dorian consciously that sense of the beauty of austerity
which Mr Pater attributes to him? (2) Granting that Pytha-
goreanism found a congenial habitat in Dorian cities, is
there any ground for supposing that Laconian culture 'held'
in any way directly of Pythagoras? (3) Why are the Perioeci
passed over almost silently? May not they as well as the
Helots have contributed to relieve the monotony of Spartan
discipline:- for instance by fine work in iron:- of which
the 'street of the smiths' in Tripolitza reminds the traveller of to day?

I have already hinted, -- I trust in no pedantic sense,
— that there are occasional oversights ('παραλειπόμενα')
(17) which in another edition one would be glad to see
removed. On p. 82 'Cebes' (*bis*) should have been 'Phaedo'.
On p. 84 Socrates is credited with the argument of Simmias,
and the words ἄνευ ἀποδείξεως κ.τλ,(18) in which Simmias
acknowledges the weakness of his own position, are taken
for the expression of Socrates' own 'immovable personal
conviction'. 'The fling round the bat' (whatever that picturesque phrase may mean) is no equivalent for τῆς βολῆς
πέρι (or περὶ) τῆς νυκτερίδος,(19) nor does παρ' ἄλληλα
σκοποῦντες(20) signify 'using our eyes in common' (p. 162).
Plato's school was not 'in the quiet precincts of the *Aca-
dêmus* (p. 134), nor is ἀκολουθεῖν τὸν λόγον(21) a Greek
construction. Let me hasten to set against these trivial
flaws some expression of more than common beauty:- 'the
principle of outline' (p. 98); 'youth ... willing to undergo much for the mere promise of some good thing it can
scarcely even imagine' (p. 89); 'Time ... is itself a kind
of artist, trimming pleasantly for us what survives of the
rude world of the past' (p. 250); 'the diamond, we are
told, if it be a fine one, may gain in value by what is
cut away' (p. 257).

The translations of illustrative passages are extremely
close and have a strong flavour of the original. For the
purpose of guiding students to a perception of the Greek,
they are admirably conceived. It is a matter of which I
write with diffidence, but I venture to doubt whether to
the 'English reader' they are likely to convey the feeling
of spontaneity, — of conversational ease and freedom, as
of a wind blowing where it listeth, which is an inseparable
attribute of Plato's style: — whether their very ingenuity
does not give them a certain air of quaintness and remoteness. See for example p. 95 'that private education ...

likes them'; p. 38 'Have you anything ... being unmixedly'.
The most successful of these versions, perhaps, is that of
'Protagoras' 343, prefixed to Lecture VIII.

The subject of 'Plato and Platonism' is not yet exhausted. Mr Pater has brought his delicate spectroscope to
bear upon that 'bright particular star', has registered
its prismatic colouring, and ascertained the elementary
constitution of this distant world. But if we would come
nearer, should we not know more? And there is one means
of coming nearer which has hardly yet been realized, still
less applied. Plato's industry extended over half a century. Could the problem raised by Schleiermacher(22) be
even partly solved, and the order in which the dialogues
were written approximately ascertained, our conception of
the evolution of this master mind might be in some ways
modified; his points of contact with earlier and contemporary thought and the manner of his reaction from them
might appear more evidently. The assumption, which scholars in an increasing number are beginning to accept as
proved, — that the dialectical dialogues as well as the
'Timaeus' are intermediate between the 'Republic' and the
'Laws', — seems destined to play no inconsiderable part
in future Platonic studies. For example, whatever may be
ultimately thought of Mr Henry Jackson's(23) theories, it
will some day be reckoned to his credit that he made this
assumption the starting point of his laborious investigation.

Notes

1 'He did not touch anything which was not ornamental.'
2 'Fortnightly Review' (October 1892), n.s. lii, 458-69;
  reprinted in 'Miscellaneous Studies' (1895).
3 Variable things.
4 Negligences.
5 'Open quarry': see PP, 108.
6 Gottfried Hermann (1772-1848), the German classical
  philologist.
7 Again.
8 'Like a prisoner who in his dreams enjoys freedom, then
  when after he begins to suspect that he is asleep, he
  is afraid of waking up, and slowly closes his eyes to
  the pleasant illusions, so willing I slip into old ideas.'
9 See p. 263n.
10 Philosophy, music (culture).
11 Beautiful.
12 Offspring in beauty.
13 Edward Caird (1835-1908), the Scottish philosopher and

277 Walter Pater: The Critical Heritage

theologian who succeeded Jowett as the Master of Balliol
(1893-1907).
14 'Every proposition is a negation.'
15 'Every negation is a proposition.'
16 Karl Ottfried Müller (1797-1840), German archaeologist
and author of 'The Dorian Race' (1824) and the 'History
of Greek Literature' (1841).
17 'Things omitted'.
18 Without logical proof.
19 Concerning hitting the bat: see PP, 45.
20 Studying both things together.
21 Follow the argument (employing the genitive case instead
of dative).
22 Friedrich Ernst Schleiermacher (1768-1834), Professor of
Theology and translator of Plato's works (1804-28).
23 See p. 255n.

Obituary Notices and Tributes

60. OBITUARY NOTICE IN 'THE TIMES'

31 July 1894, 10

_____

   In Mr Walter Pater, of Brasenose College, Oxford, who
died rather suddenly in that city yesterday, English letters have lost a writer of considerable originality and
refinement. Mr Pater was born in London in 1839, and was
sent to school at the King's School, Canterbury. He matriculated at Queen's College, Oxford, and took a second
class in the school of _Literae Humaniores_ in Michaelmas
term, 1862. Three years later he was elected to a fellowship at Brasenose, where he filled different offices,
being dean and lecturer at the time of his death.
   Although Mr Pater wrote an essay on Coleridge as early
as 1866, his first considerable work did not appear until
1873, when he published 'Studies in the History of the
Renaissance'. The subject was well adapted to the gifts
and the style of the author, and a second edition was
called for in 1877. It is characteristic of Mr Pater's
mind, and, perhaps, of the position he held as an unmar-
ried resident Fellow of his College, that he never allowed
himself to be tempted into over-hasty production. Tastes
may and do differ as to the excellence of the peculiar
style he cultivated. To some judgments it seems more opu-
lent and luscious than is altogether consistent with absolute purity of manner, while others find in the linked
sweetness of his carefully constructed periods a soothing
harmony they miss in writers more austere. Nobody, however, with any knowledge of literary form can fail to discern in Mr Pater's work a finish and delicacy which come
only of careful and assiduous labour. Mr Pater had a

conscience for style. He cared not only for what he said but for how he said it. Perhaps, indeed, he concerned himself more about the form than about the substance of his books, and undoubtedly it was the manner rather than the matter of his writings which appealed most powerfully to not a few of his admirers. It was, however, to the breadth of his own general cultivation that the special attractiveness of Mr Pater's style was due. He was not only widely read in the history of the periods and movements with which ordinary English scholars are very imperfectly acquainted, but he was a keen and thoughtful student of painting, sculpture, and music and of the growth and development of all these arts in antiquity and in modern times. It is the references and allusions, now direct and again half veiled, to the literature and the arts he loved which impart to his own writings much of their peculiar flavour, and no educated reader can open them without feeling half-forgotten memories and associations stirred within him.

In the interval of 12 years between the publication of 'The Renaissance' and that of 'Marius the Epicurean', which came out in 1885, Mr Pater wrote essays on such congenial topics as The School of Giorgione, The Beginnings of Greek Sculpture, and The Marbles of Aegina, The Myth of Demeter and Dionysus. Partly to this period and partly to that which has elapsed since 1885 belong the articles on 'Measure for Measure' and on 'Love's Labour's Lost', that on Charles Lamb, and the essay on A Prince of Court Painters and Sebastian van Storck. In 1887 appeared 'Imaginary Portraits' and in 1889 'Appreciations'. Only last year Mr Pater published his lectures on 'Plato and Platonism'.

As a teacher Mr Pater has exercised considerable influence on modern Oxford. The picturesqueness and, to a certain extent, the mannerism of his writings possessed much fascination for youthful minds of a particular caste. That that influence was always wholesome we do not pretend to say, but in a University which is only too prone to divide its mental activities between the work required for success in the schools and controversies of a polemical kind in theology and politics, it was something to have a scholar who steadfastly taught the beauty and excellence of literature adorned by art and of art enlightened by literature for their own sakes alone.

Mr Pater suffered from an attack of rheumatism in June, which was followed by pleurisy. He was believed to be in a fair way of recovery when the end came. As he was leaving his room yesterday he fainted and died immediately afterwards.

61. 'MICHAEL FIELD', POETIC TRIBUTE

1894

___

From Original Verse. Walter Pater (July 30, 1894), in the
'Academy' (11 August 1894), xlvi, 102.

Katharine Harris Bradley (1846-1914) and her niece
Edith Emma Cooper (1862-1913) jointly wrote eight volumes
of lyric poetry and numerous verse tragedies under the
pseudonym 'Michael Field'. After the appearance of
'Callirrhoe' (1884) their work continued to receive very
high praise from the reviewers.

They greatly admired Pater's writings and probably met
him on 22 July 1889 (see LWP, 98n). For their view of
Pater's concessions to the critics, see Introduction, pp. 9-10.

___

The freshness of the light, its secrecy,
Spices, or honey from sweet-smelling bower,
The harmony of time, love's trembling hour
Struck on thee with a new felicity.
Standing, a child, by a red hawthorn-tree,
Its perishing, small petals' flame had power
To fill with masses of soft, ruddy flower
A certain roadside in thy memory:
And haply when the tragic clouds of night
Were slowly wrapping round thee, in the cold
Of which men always die, a sense renewed
Of the things sweet to touch and breath and sight,
That thou didst touch and breathe and see of old
Stole on these with the warmth of gratitude.

62. RICHARD LE GALLIENNE, OBITUARY NOTICE

August 1894

___

Reprinted from 'Retrospective Reviews: A Literary Log' (New
York, 1896), ii, 136-41. See Nos 30 and 53.

___

Probably the entire sale of Mr Walter Pater's books from the beginning has not yet equalled the first 'subscription list' of some indecently boomed and wire-pulled novels. The man in the street knows nothing of the 'Studies in the Renaissance', 'Marius the Epicurean', or the 'Imaginary Portraits', yet in subtle indirect fashion these books will influence his children's children. After all, circulation is not everything, and Mr Pater is perhaps even likely to leave a greater mark on his time than, say — well, we won't mention names. Mr Pater, like Mr Meredith, is one of those writer's writers who reach what we call the general public at second or perhaps tenth hand. He is one of those literary springs, 'occult, withdrawn', at which the best of our younger writers have secretly drunk. He is like the unseen hand in Bunyan pouring unacknowledged oil upon the flames of their various talents. When he has exerted no more particular influence upon them, he has, at least, been responsible for their approaching their work in a more serious artistic spirit than might have occurred to them, without the example of his own fastidious practice. Few writers have had such a passion for perfection. One naturally thinks of Flaubert, and of all he suffered for 'the unique word'; and it would be interesting if some intimate would tell us if Mr Pater travailed in such agony — in Flaubert's case literally mortal — for his beautiful prose.

It is natural to think of Mr Pater first as a writer of prose rather than as a teacher or a critic, though he was both in an eminent degree. Some found his teaching enervating and his criticism thin, but really such criticisms are little more relevant against him than they would be against Charles Lamb or Izaak Walton. It matters nothing to us that Lamb brings us no profound philosophy of life, or that Walton was behind even his own times as a practical fisherman. So with Mr Pater: though to some his matter has been of considerable spiritual and intellectual significance, the abiding appeal of his writings is in their beauty of form, and that glamour of personal temperament which pervades them. Which is but to say that Mr Pater is to be regarded first and foremost as an artist, essentially a creative writer, choosing, for the most part, to work ostensibly through the medium of criticism.

When, for example, he writes of Leonardo da Vinci, no doubt he has admirable illuminative things to say about that master from the merely critical point of view; yet surely it is not in his general view of Leonardo that his essay finds its chief *raison d'être*, but in that famous passage in which he sets free his imagination to read in 'La Gioconda' wonderful mystic meanings, such as probably

no eyes save his own ever saw there; to dream his own
dream of that fair woman whose beauty was 'a beauty
wrought out from within upon the flesh, the deposit, little
cell by cell, of strange thoughts and fantastic reveries
and exquisite passions', and to whom long cycles of rich
and moving experience had been 'but as the sound of lyres
and flutes'. Mr Pater was pre-eminently of those critics
whose attitude a distinguished French critic has charmingly
hit off in the well-known sentence: *'Messieurs, je vais
parler de moi à propos de Shakespeare, à propos de Racine,
ou de Pascal, ou de Goethe. C'est une assez belle occasion.'*(1)

The interest of Mr Pater's writing is entirely subjective; whatever his themes, they but interest us for the
time as seen through, so to say, the stained-glass window
of his own rich and very idiosyncratic temperament.

'But his faults!' cries some alarmed critic of that
truly British race which approaches an artist on the principle of displaying the defects, and leaving the reader to
judge for himself upon the residual merits. Mr Pater was
not a 'simple' writer. Indeed — dreadful thought! — was
he not a 'euphuist'? Was he not mannered and very sugary?
Was he, indeed, quite 'manly'? I cannot resist asking by
what literary council has it been decided, as an absolute
law, that writing must be always simple, unmannered, unadorned, or, indeed, so-called 'manly'? Doubtless the
greatest writing possesses these characteristics; but it
takes all sorts to make a world, and to judge all literature by the greatest, and be satisfied with nothing less,
would be to lose us some of the most delightful books that
have ever been written. Because we have had a Bunyan,
shall there be no De Quincey? Because we have had a Tennyson, shall there be no Edmund Gosse? There is none of Mr
Pater's various lessons that the modern critic more needs
to learn than that of giving fair play to all schools of
art, appreciating each from its own aim and point of view.
In this comprehensiveness of appreciation, Mr Pater was the
only critic we had who approached Matthew Arnold, though
one would not think of contending that merely as a critic
he was anything like the equal of Arnold. He was less of
the centre, and more the representative of a somewhat exotic temperament. Moreover, as a literary critic, he represented the exact opposite school from that of Arnold.
Arnold was all for the 'moral idea' in literature; Pater
was, broadly speaking, for the *l'art pour l'art* conception
of it. He held that the first appeal of literature, of all
art, was to the sense of beauty; and in his famous essay
on The School of Giorgione, he contended, with much ingenuity and power, that music, in its very indefiniteness, was

the true archetype of all the arts. 'All art constantly
aspires towards the condition of music.' 'The ideal types
of poetry,' he writes in a famous passage, 'are those in
which' the distinction between matter and form

> is reduced to a *minimum*; so that lyrical poetry, pre-
> cisely because in it we are least able to detach the
> matter from the form, without a deduction of something
> from that matter itself, is, at least artistically, the
> highest and most complete form of poetry. And the very
> perfection of such poetry often seems to depend, in part,
> on a certain suppression or vagueness of mere subject,
> so that the meaning reaches us through ways not dis-
> tinctly traceable by the understanding, as in some of
> the most imaginative compositions of William Blake, and
> often in Shakespeare's songs, as pre-eminently in that
> song of Mariana's page in 'Measure for Measure', in
> which the kindling force and poetry of the whole play
> seems to pass for a moment into an actual strain of
> music.

If one is unable to accept this conception of art entirely as it stands, yet we may profitably associate it
with other maybe broader conceptions, as one of those part-
truths which contribute to that whole truth which ever remains incomplete.

In his own writings, sensuously beautiful as they are,
Mr Pater is far from living up to this aesthetic standard.
His writings abound in high spiritual counsel and subtle
psychological observations. As a study of the development
of a soul on its 'journey from this world to the next', a
soul of rare spiritual purity and refinement, 'Marius the
Epicurean' stands alone. Never were the *nuances* of such
a temperament so faithfully registered; and if the book
has its dangers for weak minds (as Mr Pater himself
feared), minds which might confound its lofty, almost
austere gospel of pleasure, of giving 'the highest quality
to our moments as they pass', with the degrading so-called
Epicureanism which profanes the name of a great philosopher, there must be many in whose lives it has been a
bracing and purifying influence. For, despite Mr Pater's
detractors, it is, in the best sense of the word, a manly
(were one writing in the seventeenth century, one might
even say godly) book. 'Not pleasure, but fulness, completeness of life generally', is a sentence which most
fairly sums up its philosophy; and for sheer beauty, glamour, fragrance — that mysterious fragrance as of incense
which clings about every word Mr Pater wrote — where in
English literature is there a book like it?

In Mr Pater's death we have lost a writer who is destined to rank as a classic along with Sir Thomas Browne
and Charles Lamb, and a temperament which upon a certain
type of mind will exert an enduring influence.

Note

1 See Anatole France, 'La Vie littéraire' (Paris, 1889),
  series I, iii-iv. 'Gentlemen, I shall talk about myself
  with regard to Shakespeare, to Racine, or Pascal, or
  Goethe. It is rather a good opportunity.'

63. F.W. BUSSELL, SERMON ON PATER

1894

A sermon (Luke xi 52) preached in Brasenose Chapel on
Sunday, 14 October 1894, and printed as Walter Pater, in
the 'Oxford Magazine' (17 October 1894), xiii, 7-8.
  The Reverend Frederick William Bussell (1862-1944),
clergyman and scholar, was Fellow, Chaplain, Tutor and
Vice-Principal (1896-1913) of Brasenose College.
  Bussell was Pater's closest companion in the later
years (Wright, ii, 198). In the sermon he takes great
pains to correct the misconceptions caused by Pater's
writings and stresses his basically 'religious' nature.

We have lately lost a pattern of the student life, an example of the mind which feels its own responsibilities,
which holds and will use the key of knowledge; severely
critical of itself and its own performances; genially
tolerant of others; keenly appreciating their merit; a
modest and an indulgent censor; a sympathetic adviser.
At an age when some men begin to turn into themselves and
lose sympathy with younger ones, and the rapid generations
of undergraduate life, he maintained (nay, latterly he in-
creased) an unflagging interest in the doings of the College, in the essays of the men, in those unique lectures,
prepared with such care, and delivered with such modesty.
It was not his way to compel the idle; he recognized (as
politicians do or must do) that the newly enfranchised must

be left to the responsibility of choice; he preferred to
be sought by those who were willing to take that trouble.
I do not think that any one who did so, can help looking
back to that first making his acquaintance as an important
moment in his university career; or that any one will forget the kind way in which he tried to discover the signs of
merit first, before he ventured to disapprove. He was a
model of forbearance; and I well remember on one occasion
his indignation with himself, and self-reproach, because
he had allowed his tongue to speak with unfamiliar severity of some one absent, and who, I believe, deserved it.

Naturally inclined to a certain rigour in discipline,
he was full of excuse for individual cases; and regretted,
and thought over stern measures more than most members of
a governing body can afford to do. The pains he took about
his frequent hospitality was a sign of the conscientious
thoroughness with which he performed the most trivial
actions of life. And this explains the slowness of his
composition; and the classical smallness of the bulk of
his writings.

To a certain extent, but to a certain extent only, these
may be taken as an index to his character, as unveiling the
true man. But to those who knew him as he lived among us
here, they seemed a sort of disguise. There was the same
tenderness, the same tranquillizing repose about his conversation that we find in his writings; the same careful-
ness in trifles, and exactness of expression. But his
written works betray little trace of that child-like simplicity, that naive joyousness, that never-wearying pleasure in animals and their ways, — that grave yet half-
amused seriousness, also child-like, in which he met the
events of the daily routine. His habits were precise and
austere, in some respects simple to the last degree: as
unlike the current and erroneous impression (which certain
passages of his books may leave) as it is possible to conceive: almost the sole luxury he allowed himself was a
bowl of rose-leaves, preserved by an old lady in the
country from a special receipt, and sent every year as a
present to him, and as a reminder of her friendship. He
did not accumulate around him an increasing number of necessary props of life, as so many men of a sedentary life are
unhappily tempted to do. He never smoked; rarely took
tonic or medicine of any kind; and has left an example
which it would be well if every student could follow;
spending his morning in writing or lecturing, some part of
the afternoon in correcting the composition of noon, and
in the evening, closing his books entirely; — regarding
it as folly to attempt to make up for idleness in the day
by unseasonable labour at a time when reading men are best
in bed.

In consequence of this ascetic and simple life, he was
never depressed; he was absolutely and always the same.
There was only one point in which he wished the sterner
regimen could be revived; namely, that Sunday morning
chapel should be made compulsory. Always regular there
himself, he felt real pain at a scanty attendance, and used
to trouble himself a good deal when some of his pupils
abandoned the idea of taking Holy Orders after coming up
with that career in prospect. The entire interest of his
later years was religious; not as some would put it, ecclesiastical, though he was keenly sensible of the influence
of stately ritual, and to the last was planning schemes of
a decoration of our East end, a hope of beautifying which
was very near his heart. In the Chapel service he took
great delight; sometimes regretting that the ardour of
singing which you showed in the Psalms, seemed to abate
when you came to the Magnificat, to him above others, the
Song of Songs. Another alteration he would have liked was
the introduction of music into our monthly mid-day celebration, from which he was never absent when resident in
College.

Many of you have doubtless read in one notice, how to
a young student(1) once he confessed that now he read
little else but the Bible, the Prayer Book, and the Bre-
viary. It is quite true that his interests, as years
passed over him, centred more and more on the liturgy and
fabrics of the Catholic church; on the truths of the creed
from a High Church standard; on the education of the young
in the faith of their fathers. He once said he 'had often
wished to become a clergyman'. He was never happier than
when discussing with child-like simplicity and submission
some of the cardinal mysteries of the Faith; and I well
recall how he would reprove any symptom of a Rationalizing
spirit.

This picture of the student of deep religious feeling,
of transparent naturalness, of ready humour, of unfailing
courtesy, of simple life, of austere and uniform diet (except when he entertained; then, nothing was too good for
his guests) — this is a very different picture from that
which some men have formed of him, judging from stray passages here and there in his writings. But this is the way
he would wish to be represented in his own College to those
who remember him, and before those, to whom, alas! he
must be but a name. Much more I could write about him, but
could not speak it, and so will end.

I am glad of the opportunity of adding a few more words;
words I could not have uttered on that occasion. For many
will be disappointed at the meagreness of the reminiscence,

or the coldness of the language. But they will, I feel
sure, pardon me for the restraint I put upon my pen, knowing that tongue and voice would have failed me had I attempted to publish my real feelings. In such a place too,
purely personal memories of an almost constant companion
would have been inopportune, unless they had conveyed some
lesson. And surely it was not wrong to confine myself
to just those secrets of his inner life, about which there
are abroad, perhaps, some false impressions, even among
those who fancied they knew him best. The genuineness of
his piety, the simplicity, cheerfulness, and unselfishness
of his daily life, his extraordinary and unusual care for
the feelings (or the comforts) of others, — these are the
things that I remember best about him; these are too the
points on which but few are qualified to speak. Others
will write with a finer appreciation of the unique style
and beauty of his literary works; which, apart from their
intrinsic art in thought or arrangement, had a strange
soothing and elevating effect even upon those who could but
imperfectly understand the language or the allusions.

  But it was my peculiar privilege (the loss of which I
have scarcely yet realized) to meet him, daily and hourly,
rather as a man than as a writer; and so to listen to his
ordinary talk, not upon art (I should have been but an
inapt scholar and listener), but upon religion, chapel-
services, sermons, undergraduates, books, essays, cats,
entertainments, and the attractions of nature, which we
noticed on our frequent walks into the country, of which
he was passionately fond. It was the happiest blending
of seriousness and mirth, of deep feeling and a sort of
child-like glee in the varying surfaces of things. His
whole life seemed to me to be the gradual consecration of
an exquisite sense of beauty to the highest ends; an almost literally exact advance through the stages of admiration in the 'Symposium', till at last he reached the sure
haven, the One Source of all that is fair and good. Not
without significance, Pascal was the last character he
undertook to portray (as only he could!) in a public lecture.

  It is not here or now that I should write about his domestic affections, the break in which is almost the only
really sad thing about his sudden departure hence. We do
not say as of old ἀρχή ἄνδρα δείξεὶ;(2) but I think we
look to home-life as to an unerring testimony to a man's
true character. Nor again can I say much about my own
private loss, which I have only just begun to feel, and
shall feel more and more keenly, daily and hourly.

  It seems strange to us, in these days of rapid disillu-
sionment with in-College life, that a man of his fastidious
tastes should have contentedly borne for eight-and-twenty

years this luxurious discomfort, this continuous residence
in a society often exuberant and boisterous in spirits.
But it never seemed for a moment to occur to him as possible to carry out the ideal or the practical side of
College life, without living within constant call of his
pupils. All these (who took the trouble to avail themselves of this wonderful chance) will remember his easy
accessibility (for spite of the many interruptions he
suffered, I never once saw his oak shut), his ready sympathy and pretended leisure, for it was the extreme of his
politeness to always appear to the visitor as having nothing just then to do; and his invariable change of seat
from fire to window, that the caller might have the benefit of the only easy chair. We miss such a man in a hundred little ways; at every turn some remembrance of his
kindness or his mirth rises up unbidden; his daily habits
(we can say that of few nowadays!) were woven inextricably
into the texture of the public life.

His death took place on the very day for which he had
planned a visit to an old farmhouse of mine in Devonshire;
with infinite forethought and care mapped out for the pleasure of his sisters, and by me expected with keen antici-
pation of walks and drives together. I well recall the
zest with which he entered into the projected excursion,
the minuteness of every detail considered, and the too-
generous payment to my tenant which he stipulated to be
allowed to make. I have left the original remarks exactly
as they were delivered, and add these few and digressive
words, partly to justify my choice of memories here, partly
to show how greatly in a College is felt the rare death of
a resident without whom it seems impossible to conceive
the Society or the daily routine. I have purposely omitted
all reference to merits known to a very wide circle, and
thought of him (as he would wish to be remembered) as an
affectionate friend, a loyal and interested College-teacher,
a devout Christian.

Notes

1 Walter Pater. By an Undergraduate, 'Pall Mall Gazette',
  2 August 1894, 3.
2 He beginning will show the man.

64.   HUGO VON HOFMANNSTHAL ON PATER

1894

Article entitled Walter Pater, in 'Die Welt' (17 November
1894), vii, 6-7, and reprinted in 'Gesammelte Werke'
(Frankfurt-am-Main, 1950), i, 235-40. See Introduction,
p. 7.

   Hugo von Hofmannsthal (1874-1929), Austrian poet, dramatist and critic, is perhaps best known to English
readers as librettist for Richard Strauss's operas, especially 'Elektra' (1903) and 'Der Rosenkavalier' (1911).
He was the leading force in the decadent culture which
characterised the last days of imperial Austria, and a
frequent contributor to Stefan George's (1868-1933)
'Blätter für die Kunst' and T.S. Eliot's 'Criterion'
(1922-39).

A first book, which appeared in the seventies, carries the
title 'The Renaissance: ten Studies'. Pico della Mirandola,
the school of Giorgione, Leonardo and Sandro Botticelli,
the poetry of Michelangelo and of other such outstanding
and distant phenomena of a great departed world are presented to us in a way which reaches their essence and
gives them life as certainly as a stab to the heart brings
death. The nature of the artist's relationship to life
has never been so well understood and presented not even
by Goethe who, in his studies and conversations on the
subject, forced the functions of the artist into an abstract ideality; Goethe's greatest difficulty was in
entering a world of lesser artists, those who were nevertheless born to be artists and yet separated from 'ordinary human beings and their lives'. Pater is the very rare
man who is born to understand the artist, a critic from
necessity and from the will of nature. He is in love with
the artist, as the artist is in love with life. In his
hands the divining rod quivers over places where treasures
of the earth no longer lie sleeping, but have already been
uncovered. To grasp the secret processes of the artist's
soul, processes which can only be compared to those of the
realm of love and which strive to express themselves in
symbolic ideas beyond the conceptual realm, ideas which
in their turn and with an obscure urge take their symbolic
expression from outer reality — to grasp these processes
represents the closest approach to the notion of 'the

artist'. One then senses soul in every one of his smallest
impulses, as one senses tree in the youngest branches, one
understands his moods, his baser nature, the paths of his
infatuation, the kind of landscape and the kind of women
that he liked to paint, the smile that he gives to the
faces of young men and the epithets with which he describes
himself; his vanities become golden flashes which light up
his soul before us, and the silly, insignificant and sterile anecdotes in Vasari(1) flow with life, as the udders of
disenchanted cow flow with good milk.

   In this, Pater's first book, one sees an excellent attempt at grasping the particular qualities of an artist
and the whole of his personality. Any line of verse, a
small ornament, a way of painting eyelids and lips — this
all makes a strong impression on us and engenders in us
for a moment that feeling of happiness, with its mixture
of longing and satisfaction, which is evoked by aesthetic
perfection. Every such type of perfection that we find
along our path is a fragment from a harmonious and foreign
world, a fragment which has lost its ways like the meteor-
ite which has somehow fallen on the paths of our earth.
What is attempted is the momentary evocation of this foreign world out of the lone fragment through a strong intensification of the imagination. Whoever is capable of this
evocation, and of that strong intensification and concentration of the reproductive imagination, is sure to be a
great critic. He will be at the same time both just and
compliant, since he will be measuring each work of art
against an ideal, but a subjective ideal created from the
personality of the artist, and he will feel the beauty of
everything that is so conceived and born of integrity.

   A second book by Pater, which appeared in the eighties,
is called 'Imaginary Portraits'. It attempts to portray
invented aesthetes as whole beings, no longer, as in the
studies on the Renaissance, to create personalities as a
whole (whatever they in fact were) from already existing
revelations of such people, that is, from works of art.

   A fictitious Watteau (whose background nevertheless
bares traces of the real Watteau), a fictitious organ-
builder with a peculiar christian-pagan character, a
bacchic musician in a gothic town of the French Middle
Ages, a fictitious Dutch painter and disciple of Spinozism, a fictitious dilettante German prince from the seventeenth century. In these imaginary portraits something is
brought to completion with which we all often occupy ourselves on a lesser scale and in an almost unhealthy manner;
and that is, to guess from the artworks of a past age the
inner life of those figures as clearly as if one could
sense their physical presence. In one way or another we

are all in love with a past that has been perceived and
stylised through the medium of the arts. It is, so to
speak, our way of falling in love with an ideal, or at
least an idealised life. This is Aestheticism, a great and
famous word in England and generally an overnourished and
over-grown element of our culture, and perilous like opium.
Nevertheless the basic function of the artist is similar
to this, and it is permissible that he inspire himself with
the past, so that he may illuminate the present: however
criticism is itself a subordinated function of the whole.
Such a fascinating and charmingly beautiful book as these
'Imaginary Portraits' clearly displays the kind of exis-
tential problems on which critical representation is
dependent. Artistic people, people who live by and for
the imagination, whose basis for life lies in individual
instances of beauty, the kind of people who do the same
with their own life as a representational artist does with
the life of 'ordinary human beings', namely artists or
dilettantes, closely related to the artist — these people
can be grasped as a whole and portrayed in a suggestive
manner by the critic. Everything else is beyond his power.
The concept of the artistic human being is brilliantly
elaborated by Pater and with 'Imaginary Portraits' it
creates a quite unique book.

The third book, 'Marius the Epicurean', shows the inadequacy of the aesthetic world-view, when one attempts to
build a whole way of life upon it. The book is extremely
clever, but its effect is sterile, without greatness and
without true humanity. If one measures it against Ecker-
mann(2) or against any other of Goethe's literary bequests,
it proves to be one-sided, almost immoral, despite the fact
that Goethe was an exclusively aesthetic nature. That
which jars in Pater's book is clearly the consciously one-
sided and systematic aspect. It is the story of a young
Roman of Hadrian's time, who has established his life on
the basis of a very fine and complicated Epicureanism. But
then life is much more colossal, much greater and more inexpressible, and this book makes a meagre impression, at
the same remove from reality as marginalia to a dead text.
Thus it is that the inadequacy of aestheticism (here Epicureanism) is demonstrated by that which in minor matters
represents its magic; namely in the choice of epoch. At
a certain semi-mature age full of longing and refinement
everyone's fantasy has at some time become firmly and
voluptuously attached to Rome at its decline, attached to
that gracious epoch where the great strong words of early
Latin become magnificent and sonorous titles, where the
naked figures of earlier poetry rise up dreamlike from the
blue sea, with naive hands and childlike brows before their

later-born countrymen, and where a people with peculiar
sphinx-eyes and narrow quivering fingers wander about,
rummaging in the treasures they have inherited, in the
carved stones, the pots of chrysoprase, the wax death-
masks, the brilliantly sculptured old verse and the individual gems of the half-forgotten language. To us they
appeared so like ourselves, living their lives away, not
completely true and yet very witty and very beautiful,
with a morbid, Narcissus-like beauty, fond of everything
allegorical and subject to a somewhat affected scepticism;
womanlike and boylike and senile and vibrating with deep
traces of beauty, with every kind of beauty, the beauty
of gently swelling vases and the beauty of jagged rocks,
the beauty of Antinous, the beauty of dying, of lying dead,
of flowers, of the goddess Isis, the beauty of the great
courtesans, the beauty of the sinking sun, of the christian martyrs, the beauty of Psyche, that weeping, wandering, naively-perverse and small Psyche from the 'Golden
Ass', every kind of beauty apart from the one, great and
inexpressible beauty of existence; this is not revealed to
weak generations.

Notes

1 See p. 73n.
2 Johann Peter Eckermann (1792-1854), German prose writer
  and secretary to Goethe from 1823 to 1832. He is remembered for his 'Gespräche mit Goethe in den letzten Jahren
  seines Lebens, 1823-32' (1836), which was translated into
  English as 'Conversations with Goethe' (1839).

65. HENRY JAMES ON PATER

1894

Extract from his letter dated 13 December 1894 to Edmund
Gosse, in 'Letters of Henry James' (1920), ed. Percy
Lubbock, i, 227-8. See Introduction, p. 38.
  Henry James (1843-1916), the celebrated American novelist, short-story writer and man of letters. From 1876
he settled in London and quickly became well known in
literary society.

James may have met Pater in 1877 through a mutual
acquaintance, Julia Constance Fletcher (1858-1938), the
American novelist who dedicated her 'Mirage' (1877) to
Pater. In the mid-eighties they frequently met at the
literary parties given by the Robinsons. Pater read 'The
Europeans' (1878) 'with immense enjoyment of its delicate
beauty' (LWP, 33).

I return with much appreciation the vivid pages on Pater.
(1) They fill up substantially the void of one's ignorance
of his personal history, and they are of a manner graceful
and luminous; though I should perhaps have relished a
little more insistence on — a little more of an inside
view of — the nature of his mind itself. Much as they
tell, however, how curiously negative and faintly-grey he,
after all telling, remains! I think he has had — will
have had — the most exquisite literary fortune: i.e. to
have taken it out all, wholly, exclusively, with the pen
(the style, the genius,) and absolutely not at all with
the person. He is the mask without the face, and there
isn't in his total superficies a tiny point of vantage for
the newspaper to flap his wings on. You have been lively
about him — but about whom *wouldn't* you be lively? I
think you'd be lively about *me*! — Well, faint, pale, em-
barrassed, exquisite Pater! He reminds me, in the dis-
turbed midnight of our actual literature, of one of those
lucent matchboxes which you place, on going to bed, near
the candle, to show you, in the darkness, where you can
strike a light: he shines in the uneasy gloom — vaguely,
and has a phosphorescence, not a flame. But I quite agree
with you that he is not of the little day — but of the
longer time....

Note

1 James refers to Gosse's article, Walter Pater: A Portrait,
  'Contemporary Review' (December 1894), lxvi, 795-810.

66.   'VERNON LEE' ON PATER

1895

Extract entitled Valedictory, from 'Renaissance Fancies
and Studies: Being a Sequel to Euphorion' (1895), 255-60.

Violet Paget (1856-1935), the essayist and art critic
who wrote under the pseudonym 'Vernon Lee', was the half-
sister of the poet and novelist Eugene Jacob Lee-Hamilton
(1845-1907). She was born in Normandy, but from 1871 lived
in Italy. From a very early age she devoted herself to
aesthetics and at twenty-four she published 'Studies in the
Eighteenth Century in Italy' (1880), a book which won her
a considerable *succès d'estime* at the time.

In the summer of 1881 she set out to extend her literary
connections and while in London she stayed with her friend,
Mary Robinson. She met Pater, one of her literary idols,
on 18 July 1881 at an Oxford dinner party given by the
Wards (see headnote to No. 23). On 21 July 1881 she wrote
to her mother:

> The Paters are all very friendly. He is plain & heavy
> & dull, but agreeable; the sisters are younger than he
> & very pleasant. What strikes me is how wholly unlike
> Pater is to the Mr Rose of Mallock; so much so that, in
> some of Mr Rose's sentiments & speeches, I could imagine
> him meant for Symonds rather than for Pater. They have
> a very pretty house, with a great many pretty things in
> it, aesthetic but by no means affected & cheap, like
> for instance the Gosses. (VLL, 80)

She frequently stayed with the Paters during the summer
months from 1881 to 1893 and was an outspoken admirer of his
writings. She dedicated 'Euphorion' (1884) 'To Walter
Pater, in appreciation of that which, in expounding the
beautiful things of the past, he has added to the beautiful things of the present.' Pater thought highly of her as
a writer and in the third edition (1888) of 'The Renaissance' he referred to 'Euphorion' as 'a work abounding in
knowledge and insight on the subjects of which it treats'
(R, 16n).

Like F.W. Bussell (No. 63), 'Vernon Lee' interprets
Pater's spiritual development as an evolution from narrow
aestheticism into a wider morality based on self-discipline.

... The spiritual evolution of the late Walter Pater —
with whose name I am proud to conclude my second, as with
it I began my first book on Renaissance matters — had
been significantly similar to that of his own Marius. He
began as an aesthete, and ended as a moralist. By faithful and self-restraining cultivation of the sense of harmony, he appears to have risen from the perception of
visible beauty to the knowledge of beauty of the spiritual
kind, both being expressions of the same perfect fitting-
ness to an ever more intense and various and congruous life.
   Such an evolution, which is, in the highest meaning, an
aesthetic phenomenon in itself, required a wonderful spiritual endowment and unflinchingly discriminating habit. For
Walter Pater started by being above all a writer, and an
aesthete in the very narrow sense of twenty years ago: an
aesthete of the school of Mr Swinburne's 'Essays', and of
the type still common on the Continent. The cultivation
of sensations, vivid sensations, no matter whether healthful
or unhealthful, which that school commended, was, after all,
but a theoretic and probably unconscious disguise for the
cultivation of something to be said in a new way, which is
the danger of all persons who regard literature as an end,
and not as a means, feeling in order that they may write,
instead of writing because they feel. And of this Mr
Pater's first and famous book was a very clear proof. Exquisite in technical quality, in rare perception and subtle
suggestion, it left, like all similar books, a sense of
caducity and barrenness, due to the intuition of all sane
persons that only an active synthesis of preferences and
repulsions, what we imply in the terms *character* and *moral*,
can have real importance in life, affinity with life — be,
in short, vital; and that the yielding to, nay, the seeking for, variety and poignancy of experience, must result
in a crumbling away of all such possible unity and efficiency of living. But even as we find in the earliest
works of a painter, despite the predominance of his master's style, indications already of what will expand into
a totally different personality, so even in his earliest
book, examined retrospectively, it is easy to find the
characteristic germs of what will develop, extrude all
foreign admixture, knit together congruous qualities, and
give us presently the highly personal synthesis of 'Marius'
and the 'Studies on Plato'.
   These characteristic germs may be defined, I think, as
the recurrence of impressions and images connected with
physical sanity and daintiness; of aspiration after or-
derliness, congruity, and one might almost say *hierarchy*;
moreover, a certain exclusiveness, which is not the contempt
of the craftsman for the *bourgeois*, but the aversion of the

priest for the profane uninitiated. Some day, perhaps, a
more scientific study of aesthetic phenomena will explain
the connection which we all feel between physical sanity
and purity and the moral qualities called by the same
names; but even nowadays it might have been prophesied
that the man who harped upon the clearness and livingness
of water, upon the delicate bracingness of air, who experienced so passionate a preference for the whole gamut, the
whole palette, of spring, of temperate climates and of
youth and childhood; a person who felt existence in the
terms of its delicate vigour and its restorative austerity,
was bound to become, like Plato, a teacher of self-discipline and self-harmony. Indeed, who can tell whether the
teachings of Mr Pater's maturity — the insistence on scrupulously disciplined activity, on cleanness and clearness
of thought and feeling, on the harmony attainable only
through moderation, the intensity attainable only through
effort — who can tell whether this abstract part of his
doctrine would affect, as it does, all kindred spirits if
the mood had not been prepared by some of those descriptions of visible scenes — the spring morning above the
Catacombs, the Valley of Sparta, the paternal house of
Marius, and that temple of Aesculapius with its shining
rhythmical waters — which attune our whole being, like the
music of the Lady in 'Comus', to modes of *sober certainty
of waking bliss*?

This inborn affinity for refined wholesomeness made Mr
Pater the natural exponent of the highest aesthetic doctrine — the search for harmony throughout all orders of
existence. It gave the nucleus of what was his soul's
synthesis, his system (as Emerson puts it) of rejection
and acceptance. Supreme craftsman as he was, it protected
him from the craftsman's delusion — rife under the inappropriate name of 'art for art's sake' in these uninstinc-
tive, over-dextrous days — that subtle treatment can dig-
nify all subjects equally, and that expression, irrespec-
tive of the foregoing *impression* in the artist and the subsequent *impression* in the audience, is the aim of art.
Standing as he did, as all the greatest artists and thinkers (and he was both) do, in a definite, inevitable relation
to the universe — the equation between himself and it — he
was utterly unable to turn his powers of perception and
expression to idle and irresponsible exercises; and his
conception of art, being the outcome of his whole personal
mode of existence, was inevitably one of art, not for art's
sake, but of art for the sake of life — art as one of the
harmonious functions of existence.

Harmonious, and in a sense harmonising. For, as I have
said, he rose from the conception of physical health and

congruity to the conception of health and congruity in
matters of the spirit; the very thirst for healthiness,
which means congruity, and congruity which implies health,
forming the vital and ever-expanding connection between
the two orders of phenomena. Two orders, did I say? Surely
to the intuition of this artist and thinker, the fundamental unity — the unity between man's relations with external
nature, with his own thoughts and with others' feelings —
stood revealed as the secret of the highest aesthetics.

This which we guess at as the completion of Walter
Pater's message, alas! must remain for ever a matter of
surmise. The completion, the rounding of his doctrine, can
take place only in the grateful appreciation of his readers.
We have been left with unfinished systems, fragmentary,
sometimes enigmatic, utterances. Let us meditate their
wisdom and vibrate with their beauty; and, in the words of
the prayer of Socrates to the Nymphs and to Pan, ask for
beauty in the inward soul, and congruity between the inner
and the outer man; and reflect in such manner the gifts of
great art and of great thought in our soul's depths. For
art and thought arise from life; and to life, as principle
of harmony, they must return.

Many years ago, in the fulness of youth and ambition,
I was allowed, by him whom I already reverenced as master,
to write the name of Walter Pater on the flyleaf of a book
which embodied my beliefs and hopes as a writer. And now,
seeing books from the point of view of the reader, I can
find no fitter ending to this present volume than to express what all we readers have gained, and lost, alas! in
this great master.

67. THEODORE DE WYZEWA ON PATER

1895

From Two Deaths: Pater and Froude, in 'La Revue des Deux
Mondes' (January 1895), lxiv, 219-23, and reprinted in
'Foreign Writers': First Series (Paris, 1896), 164-82.
See No. 89 and Introduction, p. 6.

Theodore de Wyzewa (1862-1917), Russian-born French
poet and critic, was closely associated with the early
days of the Symbolist Movement. From 1889 he contributed
articles on music, literature and painting to the 'Revue
des Deux Mondes. De Wyzewa first discussed Pater in a

review entitled The Renaissance of the Historical Novel in
England (January 1889, lx, 184-201).

Following the extract de Wyzewa compared J.A. Froude,
who 'was the most open of people, revealing to every new-
comer the most intimate aspects of his soul', with Pater,
'who all his life kept himself to himself'. A writer in
the 'Saturday Review' (1 August 1896) claimed that this
study of Pater was 'beyond doubt the first adequate review
of that extraordinary individuality which has yet appeared
on the continent of Europe' (lxxxii, 107).

Within the space of a few weeks, England has lost two of
its best writers, Walter Pater and James Anthony Froude.
The first-named was a critic, the latter an historian; but
both were above all artists. In criticism and history they
simply found a pretext for the free development of their
poetic fantasy. And so their works appear to us today to
be related: both of them remarkable above all for their
precious qualities of imagination and style.

Walter Pater, the Oxford fellow, the dilettante who
always lived and worked away from the crowd, has been
honoured after his death as the equal of the most famous
men of letters. We have been told of his life with every
detail mentioned of his habits and manners. Even controversies have been discussed on this subject: the dates of
some of his essays have been discussed as if they were
great historical events. And his fellow critics, his
friends, and his pupils have been of one opinion in extolling the nobility, the elegance and the exquisite harmony
of his work.

From now on, his fame is assured. For long only appreciated by scholars, here he is now almost a popular figure:
no more need we fear he will escape future historians of
literature. Walter Pater now has his place alongside
Thomas de Quincey and Mr Ruskin, among the most perfect
poets of English prose. So I have less fears of returning
to him, to indicate, after such reliable testimonies, the
principal features of his life and character.

I would, however, mention only one of the studies devoted to him, the one published by Mr Gosse in the 'Contemporary Review'.* This is the only one that appears to
me to have given a living portrait of Pater, the only one
where I have yet found a true appreciation of his talent.
Mr Edmund Gosse is moreover one of those who knew him
best; and more than anyone he had the good fortune to
speak with him, being himself both critic and poet.

He tells us first of all that, though of Flemish origin,
like his namesake the painter J.B. Pater,(1) the author of
'Marius the Epicurean' had in all probability no family
link with him. His family, in any case, had emigrated to
England at the time of William of Orange. But in emigrat-
ing the family appears to have retained a number of their
national customs and traditions: thus the habit was retained in the Pater family of the sons becoming Catholic,
while the daughters were brought up in the Anglican religion.

The father of the critic, the doctor Richard Glode
Pater, was the first to break with this tradition. He
renounced Catholicism, and took no other faith in its
place; so that the children were born and brought up outside the Church. And though, from his youth, Pater had
shown a lively interest in the ecclesiastical life, it is
only in his last years that he feels growing in him the
curiosity for religious problems. He was, as if in compensation, deeply moved by them.

When I met him for the first time [says Mr Gosse] he was
a pagan, following only the guide of his own conscience.
But from year to year I saw him move more and more
closely towards the firm support of a faith. His way
of speech, his way of life became more and more theological; and I am sure that had he lived a few more years
he would have taken orders and gone to live in a country
parish.(2)

He was born at Shadwell, on the Thames, on the 4th
August, 1839. At King's School, Canterbury, where he was
first a pupil, his masters were struck above all by the
slowness of his wit. And, indeed, he retained throughout
his life this peculiar slowness, which without doubt came
from his race. He needed a lot of time to study and also
to understand. But what he had studied and understood,
from then became indelibly fixed in his mind; after an
interval of twenty years, a piece of country that he had
loved remained fixed clearly in his memory. Unfortunately
his schoolteachers did not appreciate that, and there is
little doubt that throughout his days as a schoolboy,
Pater remained in their eyes a mediocre pupil. It was
the same story again at Oxford, where he later went as an
exhibitioner. With great difficulty and after four years
residence, he obtained a second-class degree. Neither he
himself, nor those around him would then have guessed that
he was soon to be one of the outstanding figures in Oxford.

That, however, is what he was: for his name is always
linked with that of Oxford. Not that he ever appeared a

brilliant teacher; his natural timidity was such as almost
to prevent him teaching at all. But it is at Oxford, that
he spent, we might say, the whole of his life; and from
year to year his influence made itself increasingly felt
there. He was to the old university town rather what Fra
Angelico must have been to his monastery in Florence. Visi-
tors were shown the windows of the room where he worked;
the purity of his life was praised, as was his indifference to the turmoil that went on outside; he was extolled
for living there in silence and repose, totally occupied
in the service of the holy cause of art. And how many fine
and solid young men who dedicated themselves, simply on
the strength of a chance encounter, to the vain pursuit of
a deceptive ideal!

It was in 1864 that Pater, having finally obtained his
degree, was named a fellow of Brasenose College, one of the
most important in the University of Oxford. And it was
only two years later, in 1866, at the age of twenty-seven,
that he wrote his first Essay. He took as his subject the
famous poet and metaphysician, Coleridge. But, strikingly,
he chose to concern himself only with Coleridge the metaphysician; there was not a line in the essay that recalls
Coleridge the major writer. It appears, further, that
literary and artistic questions held no interest at that
time for Pater. Metaphysics and logic absorbed him completely. His Essay on Coleridge is nothing more than a
clinically correct college thesis, the work of a conscientious student of philosophy. There is no trace, either
in the style or in the imagery, of the delicate poet of
the later works. The feeling for poetry and the taste for
art came to him through the intermediary of Goethe, whom
he had, a little later, the chance to study. His naturally
religious soul learned from the master to search in *beauty*
the absolute that it craved. And when, in 1867, the young
philosopher published in the 'Westminster Review' his essay
on Winckelmann, all the men of letters were aware of a new
genius that he appeared among them.

Thus Mr John Morley, who the same year took over the
'Fortnightly Review', hurried to engage Pater among his
regular contributors. And indeed, Pater contributed regularly to the 'Fortnightly Review' — regularly, but in his
own way, that is to say with the slowness of his usual
work, for it took him a year or near enough, to write an
article of twenty pages.

In 1873 he collected the Essays in one volume with the
title 'Essays On The History of The Renaissance'. It is
the most famous of his works, and it is perhaps superior,
in fact, through the simplicity of its subject and the
novelty of its ideas, to the work which follows it, 'Marius

the Epicurean'. But it seems probable that this philosophical novel had for Pater the interest of an autobiography; and one truly feels that his whole heart was expressed in these so sweet and pure sentences, that are like
a gentle song that one hears in a dream. These sentences,
in every case, demanded twelve years of work: for it was
not until 1885 that 'Marius' appeared. In the meantime,
Pater had journeyed on the continent, visiting Germany,
Italy, but above all France, which he loved as much as his
own country. Every summer he would explore some corner of
one of our regions, tiring himself so much with his explora-
tions that he would become ill. In a letter written in 1877
from Azay-le-Rideau to Mr Gosse, he writes: 'I always find
tremendous pleasure in extending my knowledge of these
small French towns, and I always come back more tired than
when I went, but with my spirit pleasantly full of memories
of stained-glass windows, tapestries and fresh wild
flowers.'(3)

But Oxford remained the centre of his life. In his last
years, he gave a series of lectures on 'Plato and Platonism';
and he even had, for a time, to lead his college in his
capacity as Dean. But all public offices terrified him; all
he wanted was peace. Several short Essays, a novel which
was never published as a volume, four or five philosophical tales: that together with his lectures on Plato and his
two great works make up all the literary luggage he left behind him. Right until the end, however, he worked, wearing
himself out, torturing himself in the search for sentences,
in a way true perhaps of no other writer.

It took so much out of him to get down a single sentence
[writes Mr Gosse] that without his extraordinary courage
he would certainly have given up literature. I remember
the pain that it took to write the first chapter of
'Marius': real pain, for the exhaustion made him ill,
bringing on a fever, persistent insomnia, and a feeling of unbelievable depression. Later, it is true, work
became a little easier for him. He told me a year ago,
that if he were able to live a few years longer, he
hoped that he would really learn to enjoy writing.(4)

Alas, that happiness was not to be granted him. Suffering
from rheumatism, he drove himself to finish an essay on
Pascal. He caught a draught from an open window, and pleurisy was diagnosed. He would still have recovered with a
little care; but his article obsessed him: he went back
to his work, shivering with fever, tried vainly to finish
a sentence, got up again, and dropped dead on his stair-
case. He was 54.

He had [wrote Gosse] a great natural gentility, and most equable temperament. I know of only one subject that was capable of annoying him; it was the memory of an act of vandalism that had once occurred at Oxford and for which he had been a little responsible. Brasenose College possessed a bronze group 'Cain and Abel', which was a genuine work by Jean de Bologne. One fine day, this group of statues began to give offence, and the college authorities sold it for its weight in bronze, without Pater lifting a finger to prevent this desecration. And in the last years of his life, a sure means of annoying him would be to ask 'whether there hadn't once been at Brasenose a group by Jean of Bologne?'(5)

No matter how wrapped up in his dreaming, he would draw himself up, and reply in a sharp tone: 'It was a work without any interest at all, I beg you to believe me!'

I cannot resist the temptation to mention here the following anecdote:

One day, in an examination, Pater had to read the English Essays of the candidates. When the examiners met to agree on the marks, it was observed that Pater had not given marks to any one. 'The truth is,' he declared, 'None of these papers impressed me!' It was, however, necessary to class them, and one of Pater's colleagues began to read out to him the names of the different candidates. But at each name he shook his head. 'No,' he would murmur, 'I don't remember!' Finally his colleague mentioned the name of a candidate named Sanctuary: immediately Pater's face was seen to light up:- 'Yes,' he said, 'I remember that one; his name delighted me!' (6)

But I have already spent too much time with this gentle dreamer who, more than any one, always loved to hide himself from the world. He was a man of another age. He admitted to his friends that he was completely ignorant of the work of most of his contemporaries, of Mr R.L. Stevenson for example, or of Mr Rudyard Kipling. I do not believe he ever expressed a political opinion. Mr Gladstone was, no doubt, as far as he was concerned, merely an average annotator of Homer, and a theologian who was more brilliant than he was serious.

Notes

* Mr Gosse has since published it in his 'Critical Kit-Kats' (1896).

1 Jean-Baptiste Pater (1695-1736), pupil and imitator of
  Watteau.
2 'Critical Kit-Kats', 260.
3 Ibid., 257. See LWP, 25-6.
4 'Critical Kit-Kats, 262.
5 Ibid., 268.
6 Ibid., 269.

68.   GEORGE SAINTSBURY: PATER AS PROSE ARCHITECT

1896

Extract from Saintsbury's 'History of Nineteenth Century
Literature' (1896), 398-401. See Introduction, p. 38.
   George Saintsbury (1845-1933), distinguished literary
critic, historian of English and French literature, Professor of Rhetoric at Edinburgh University (1895-1915)
and prolific writer of reviews.
   Saintsbury met Pater when he was an undergraduate (1863-
8) at Merton College, Oxford. He has recorded his impressions of Pater in Walter Pater, 'Bookman' (August 1906),
xxx, 165-70. For his earlier examination of Pater's style,
see his article on Modern English Prose in the 'Fortnightly
Review' (February 1876), xxv, 243-59.

... Mr Arnold, it has been said, abstained almost entirely
from dealing with art. Mr Ruskin, who has abstained from
dealing with nothing, did not abstain from criticism of
literature, but his utterances in it have been more than
usually *obiter dicta*.(1) Yet we must take the two together
if we are to understand the most powerful influence and the
most flourishing school of criticism, literary and other,
which has existed for the last thirty years. This school
may be said to halt in a way between purely literary and
generally aesthetic handling, and when it can to mix the
two. Most of its scholars — men obviously under the influence both of Arnold and of Ruskin, either in submission
or in revolt, are alive, and we reason not of them. But,
as it happens, the two most famous, one of whom was a
prose writer, pure and simple, the other a copious artist
in prose and verse, have died recently and call for judgment. These were Walter Horatio Pater and John Addington
Symonds.

The first-named was born in 1839, and went to Oxford,
where he was elected to a fellowship at Brasenose. He
spent the whole of the rest of his life either at that
college or in London, practising no profession, compet-
ing for no preferment, and for many years at least producing literature itself with extreme sparingness. It was
in 1873 that Mr Pater first collected a volume of 'Studies
in the History of the Renaissance', which attracted the
keenest attention both as to its manner and as to its matter. The point of view, which was that of an exceedingly
refined and carefully guarded Hedonism, was in a way and
at least in its formulation novel. Mr Pater did not
meddle with any question of religion; he did not (though
there were some who scented immorality in his attitude) offend directly any ethical prejudice or principle. But he
laid it down explicitly in some places, implicitly throughout, that the object of life should be to extract to the
utmost the pleasure of living in the more refined way, and
expressly and especially the pleasure to be derived from
education and art. The indebtedness of this both to the
Arnoldian and Ruskinian creeds, its advance (in the main a
legitimate advance) on the former, and its heretical devia-
tion from the development of the latter, require no comment.
But this propaganda, if so violent a word may be used, of
Mr Pater's placid creed, called to aide a most remarkable
style — a style of the new kind, lavish of adjective and
the *mot de lumière*,(2) but not exceedingly florid, and aiming especially at such an arrangement of the clause, the
sentence, and the paragraph, such a concerted harmony of
cadence and symphony, as had not been deliberately tried
before in prose. The effects which it produced on different tastes were themselves sufficiently different. Some
found the purport too distasteful to give a dispassionate
attention to the presentment; others disliked the manner
itself as formal, effeminate, and 'precious'. But there
were others who, while recognising the danger of excess
in this direction, thought and think that a distinct and
remarkable experiment had been made in English prose, and
that the best examples of it deserved a place with the best
examples of the ornater styles at any previous time and in
any other kind.
     Mr Pater was not tempted by such a popularity as his
book received to hasten publication; indeed it was understood that after beginning to print a second collection of
Essays,(3) he became dissatisfied with them, and caused
the type to be broken up. But the advance of so-called
Æstheticism was too strong an invitation, and prepared for
him too large and eager an audience, so that the last decade of his life saw several books, 'Marius the Epicurean',

'Imaginary Portraits', 'Appreciations', while others
appeared posthumously. Of these the first named is unquestionably the best and most important. Although Greek had
been the indispensable — almost the cardinal — principle
in Mr Pater's own literary development, he had been so
strongly affected by modern thought and taste, that he
could hardly recover a dispassionate view of the older
classics. 'Imaginary Portraits', an attempt at constructive rather than critical art, required qualities which he
did not possess, and even made him temporarily forget his
impeccable style: 'Appreciations', good in itself, was
inferior to the first book. But 'Marius the Epicurean'
far excelled all these. It, too, took the form of fiction,
but the story went for so little in it that deficiencies
therein were not felt. The book was in effect a reconstruction, partly imaginative, but still more critical, of
a period with which Mr Pater was probably more in sympathy
that with any other, even the Renaissance itself, to wit
the extremely interesting and strangely modern period when
classicism and modernity, Christianity and Paganism,
touched and blended in the second century after Christ
after the fashion revealed to us in the works of Apuleius
most of all, of Lucian to some extent, and of a few others.
Mr Pater indeed actually introduced the philosopher-novel-
ist of Madaura in the book, though he was not the hero; and
his own peculiar style proved itself admirably suited to
the period and subject, whether in description and conversation, or in such translation or paraphrase as that of the
famous and exquisite Pervigilium Veneris.
     For this style, however, in perfection we must still go
back to the 'Studies of the Renaissance', which is what
Mr Arnold liked to call a *point de repère*.(4) The style,
less exuberant, less far-reaching and versatile, and, if
any one pleases to say so, less healthy than Mr Ruskin's,
is much more chastened, finished, and exquisite. It never
at its best neglects the difference between the rhythm of
prose and the metre of verse; if it is sometimes, and
indeed usually, wanting in simplicity, it is never overloaded or gaudy. The words are picked; but they are seldom or never, as has been the case with others, not only
picked but wrenched, not only adjusted to a somewhat unusual society and use, but deliberately forced into uses
and societies wholly different from those to which readers
are accustomed. Above all, no one, it must be repeated,
has ever surpassed, and scarcely any one has ever equalled
Mr Pater in deliberate and successful architecture of the
prose-paragraph — in what may, for the sake of a necessary
difference, be called to scriptorial in opposition to the
oratorical manner. He may fall short of the poetic grandeur

of Sir Thomas Browne, of the phantasmagoric charm of De
Quincey at his rare best, of the gorgeous panoramas of Mr
Ruskin. But his happiest paragraphs are like *flamboyant*
chantries, not imposing, not quite supreme in quality, but
in their own kind showing wonderful perfection of crafts-
manship....

Notes

1 Incidental remarks.
2 Word of enlightenment.
3 See Introduction, pp.13-14.
4 Landmark.

69. P: PATER'S REPUTATION RECONSIDERED, 'ACADEMY'

1 January 1898, liii, 13-14

See Introduction, pp. 8 and 38. The reviewer ('P')
extols Pater as a great writer with a vivid imagination.

In and about the year 1870 a great change became apparent
in the spirit of English literature. The group of vigorous writers who had made letters subservient to morality,
and who believed in 'the man and his message', had begun
to break up. Carlyle, who had wielded a long sway over
every kind of intellect — the imaginative, the historic,
even the scientific — was feeling the effects of years,
and though, even in decay a rugged giant, his power was
no longer what it had been. All along the line the movement was being carried on with feebler hands. Whatever
was weak or imperfect in art with a purpose became glar-
ingly apparent in the work of those secondary writers to
whom the elders handed on the torch. Brilliant young men
no longer found it natural to adhere to Lord Tennyson's
theory of literature; and very soon it became apparent
that the centre of influence was shifting, and that for a
time at least an opposite doctrine was to prevail. The
rebellion — if one may be permitted to apply that word
to a perfectly natural and, within limits, wholesome movement — was not carried out by any single leader. It

sprang up simultaneously in a number of minds, not, indeed,
of the very highest rank, but of fine and genuine capacity.
In verse its clearest exponent was William Morris, who, in
lines as bold as they were sweet and tuneful, announced
that a bard had come who assumed to be neither prophet nor
messenger. 'Dreamer of dreams' sang the latter-day poet:

> Dreamer of dreams born out of my due time
> Why should I strive to set the crooked straight?
> Let it suffice me that my murmuring rhyme
> Beats with light wing against the ivory gate.(1)

But though he so beautifully found words for the creed, it
was another who was to be the dominant influence. 'Atalanta in Calydon' had appeared before the 'Earthly Paradise', and for twenty years to come its author was to be
the most sedulously imitated of poets; and the imitators
taking their cue from him and Morris ostentatiously ignored
'the message'. I am not concerned to discuss whether they
were right or wrong; indeed, I do not believe there is any
abstract right or wrong in the matter. Art will bear no
heavier moral than is carried by life itself, and if the
poet be true to life it is impossible for him to be false
to its morals. The justification of a theory lies wholly
in its fruit, and it may here be pointed out that the consciousness of a great aim in life itself, the belief that
'eyes do regard you from eternity's stillness', the feeling
that there is and must be some great and solemn object in
existence has a bracing and ennobling effect upon letters.
The wave of a great moral movement gave us 'Paradise Lost';
its reaction only the drama of the Restoration. A somewhat
similar wave produced 'In Memoriam', 'The French Revolution', and 'Adam Bede'; its reaction was flowered into no
achievement of the highest class, and is ending in something like paralysis.

Be that as it may — and I throw it out only as a suggested explanation — the late Mr Pater, just about the
time when 'Atalanta' and 'The Earthly Paradise' appeared,
began to wield in prose an influence equal to that which
Mr Swinburne wielded in verse. It ran in channels, however, that were partially concealed. He was preeminently
a writer's writer, and his power is not, as Carlyle's was,
open, conspicuous, and commanding; it has been most deeply felt by the choice minds of his age, and has been fil-
tered through them to the wider public. There is scarcely
an aspect in which he does not differ from the great moralist. Not even Goethe could make Carlyle understand what
Kunst was — 'Carlyle knows nothing of art', said Tennyson
— he used letters purely as the vehicle through which he

delivered his exhortations to the age. To Pater literature was something very different. It was 'a refuge, a
sort of cloistral refuge, from a certain vulgarity in the
actual world'. He was the first great Englishman to preach
the gospel of art for art's sake. He judged life not by
its effect on the race or the future, but by the sensations it experienced by 'the pleasure of the ideal present,
the mystic *now*'.

The creed looks foolish enough as presented by those
who may be called derivatives from Pater; his own mind was
too clear and strong to be content with its weaker aspect.
All roads lead to Rome, and it is strange to note that the
most diverse intellects, provided they be honest and capable, arrive finally at very nearly the same conclusions.
He worked out his thoughts into a creed as large and austere as that of Carlyle himself. 'Not pleasure, but fulness of life and insight as conducting to that pleasure —
energy, choice, and variety of experience, including noble
pain and sorrow' — so does he make his Marius think. Pain
and sorrow are noble only when they are nobly born, and
with this explanation the creed embodies all that makes
for submission and conciliation, for adjustment to conditions.

Nor has any moralist laid down a sterner and more un-
compromising law than this:

Truth: there can be no merit, no craft at all without
that. And, further, all beauty is, in the long run,
only fineness of truth, or what we call expression,
the finer accommodation of speech to the vision within.

Mr Pater does not himself appear to have been of a combative or aggressive disposition; but some of the more
ardent spirits, who caught up the cry of art for art's
sake without troubling about its deeper meaning, at once
began to use it as a battering-ram on the great reputa-
tions of their time. Lord Tennyson's biographer tells us
that he saw in this a beginning of decay. His words are
worth quoting. After giving the poet's *impromptu* made in
1869, after reading an attack on the 'Idylls', 'Art for
art's sake! Hail, truest lord of hell!' he goes on:

These lines in a measure expressed his strong and sorrow-
ful conviction that the English were beginning to forget
what was, in Voltaire's words, the glory of English literature — 'No nation has treated in poetry moral ideas
with more energy and depth than the English nation.'(2)

That was thirty years ago, and the young warriors who
then rushed eagerly to the fray are grizzled veterans now,
and it is their turn to be haled before the judgment-seat
and asked, not What theory did you hold? but What work
have you done? To some extent they have leavened English
letters, and the young poet and the young novelist have
been turned aside from 'the purpose', but the condemnation
of the movement from a purely literary and artistic point
of view is that it has failed to produce any book of the
first importance. Let us see why this has been so in Mr
Pater's case.

In one sense Mr Pater was a brilliantly successful
writer. He has done many things so well that one cannot
imagine how they could have been done better. But he did
not know where his own strength lay. His patient hunt for
what he called 'the exact word' was in his case, as in
that of Flaubert, doomed to futility. For a writer never
can convey any but a simple thought fully and lucidly from
his own mind to that of another. The meaning he attaches
to words is coloured not only by his learning and knowledge, but by his previous meditation and experience. And
his phrases fall on minds, each of which has a separate
and different body of experience, which contracts or ex-
pands, modifies or distorts, their significance. One
need not go further for examples than to certain shibbo-
leths of his school. The very word art, so vilely hacked
and vulgarised during the past quarter of a century, is
applied by nearly every writer to his or her own work. Sir
Walter Scott very justly called himself an artist, so did
George Eliot, so do a score of fourth-rate scribblers. In
each case it conveys a meaning coloured by personality;
it cannot be absolutely defined; it cannot, therefore, be
employed with such exactitude as to convey a meaning fully
and lucidly from one mind to another. Distinction, again,
is a term which has the same ambiguity. It is constantly
employed by critics to indicate a quality of phrase; with
Pater it describes an attitude of mind. The writer is
truly distinguished who looks at life independently with
his own eyes; it is but a bastard distinction that springs
from preciosity of phrase. Fuller and larger illustration
of the impossibility of conveying thought exactly from one
mind to another may be found in the history of any creed.
The Gospel of Christ is set forth in clear and simple words,
yet if we consider the number of creeds and sects, the divisions, arguments, and even battles to which its interpretation has given rise, how obvious must it be that the word
had one meaning in the mind of him who uttered them; another in the case of those who heard. Nay, take Mr Pater's
own teaching and compare it with that of his derivatives,

and it will be seen how distorted it has become in passing
from the master to his scholars. That he knew this himself is evident from his fear that the well-known 'conclusion' of his 'Renaissance' studies should be misapprehended,
as it undoubtedly has been.

But the great weakness of Mr Pater and his school lies
in a too great exaltation of art. He did not, indeed, as
some of his followers have done, go the length of asserting that art transcended life, but art was his chiefest
interest. His books are all those of a bookman. In no
case that I know of did he take his materials direct from
nature. His creative works, 'Marius' and 'Gaston de Latour',
are but attempts to show the development of a personality in
times to which he was a stranger, and they could be recon-
structed only through records and chronicles. The work is
done marvellously well, but within limits that fix narrow
boundaries to his sympathies. An imagination that had been
fed not only by books, but by the living stream of life,
could not have been satisfied with such a picture. It
would have been satisfied with such a picture. It would
have demanded not only the flower of the time in a refined
Marius or a Gaston, but would have used a hundred vigorous
forms from the wild, rugged surroundings to complete the
picture, and to throw those exquisite portraitures into contrast. He does, indeed, talk of life for life's sake, but
it does not work out in his conceptions. There is a passage in 'Marius' typical of so much that it deserves quotation — it describes the hero's feelings after the death of
his friend Flavian (the italics are mine):

> The sun shone out on the people going to work for a long
> hot day, and Marius was standing by the dead, watching
> *with the deliberate purpose* of fixing in his memory
> every detail, that *he might have that picture in reserve*,
> should any day of forgetfulness ever hereafter come to
> him with the temptation to feel completely happy again.

In other words, he was not living wholly in 'the mystic
now', but saving up his grief for future use. The man who
lives his life fully, and drinks the cup, be it of joy or
sorrow, to the lees, mourns or rejoices without any 'deliberate purpose'. Indeed, the moment emotion begins to be
fondled and thought about it loses its direct natural character. One sees this more clearly by considering what a
real single-hearted zest for life a great artist such as
Scott had. To him, novel-writing was not even a very noble
or grand way of earning a livelihood, and no one can imagine him treasuring his sensations, calculating his grief,
measuring his joy, either as indicating the richness of life

or to serve as stuff out of which to weave art. Far less
can it be supposed that Henry Fielding, when going out to
dine in his coach attended by his yellow-liveried servant,
had a deliberate intention to lay by experience out of
which to fabricate Squire Western. Not a bit of it. He
and Shakespeare, and all the rest of the great artists,
lived their lives without any *arrière pensée*(3) about art,
and all unconsciously gathered the experience from which
their creations were ultimately fashioned. To be conscious
of artistic intentions is enough of itself to take some of
the fine flavour from life. In Pater, too, it led to over-
bookishness and super-refinement and preciosity, so that
his books, and still more those of his followers, tend to
lose touch with the actual.

But it is the limitations of his own nature and temperament that lie at the root of the matter. The greatness of
a writer largely depends on the extent of his sympathies.
He is the interpreter of human nature, and the wider and
deeper his interests the more certain is he to command attention. A great sunny nature like that of Scott wins upon
us, because it can project itself into a thousand personalities and speak through as many different masks. King,
priest, and beggar — he projects himself by turns into
each. But there are other writers so rigid and self-
centred, so incapable of changing voice or appearance,
that they seem to speak with set features and in a mono-
tone. They tap, as it were, only one vein of interest,
and the reader who is not held by that is not held at all.

Now, Mr Pater, supreme as he is in the exercise of a
fine gift (of which more anon), is one of those strictly
limited writers. Moreover, he was of a sterling honesty
that scorned to make pretence of what he had not. Others
we know who try to rope in all sorts of readers by imitat-
ing the qualities they do not possess. They can produce
a sham humour, a sham pathos, a sham passion, that will
pass without question in the market-place. It is a mark of
greatness in Mr Pater that he never condescends to this.
He goes on sternly compressed within his narrow channel,
and never dreams of throwing out a tentacle to those not
fully in sympathy with him. He has no humour, and not even
in writing of Charles Lamb does he make a pretence of it.
With nine-tenths of the pursuits of mankind he is out of
touch, and appears to be quite content that it should be so.
Cold and austere in his own temperament, he makes no attempt to appeal to the warmth and playfulness of human nature. The great surging passions of life never beat in
view of the windows of his cloistral refuge. Indeed, it is
somewhat of a paradox that in his two novels the apostle of
art for art's sake is more of a teacher and sermoniser than

an artist. There is far more of the gust of human life in
many a novel with a purpose than in these works. So
strangely does performance often contradict intention.

But in spite of all these drawbacks he is certainly a
great writer, one of the first of his day. Neither his
doctrine nor his actual work is likely at any time to
appeal to the general public, but they are invaluable to
the student and scholar. I do not refer to the matter —
it would carry us far beyond the bounds of this paper to
touch even superficially on that — but to the style by
which he would presumably choose to be judged. The greatest quality manifest in it is that of vivid imagination.
Of what may be called pictorial English it is doubtful if
any finer exists in the language. There are whole pages
of 'Gaston de Latour' where each sentence is like a piece
of exquisite carving from purest marble, and every word is
that of a man who has conjured up the clearest image of
what took place in his fancy. Of his Cupid and Psyche
one can only say, as Tennyson said of FitzGerald's 'Omar',
that it is a 'version done divinely well'. And even in
his less important essays there are bits which could have
been composed by none but a man of strong imagination.
What could be finer than this from the paper on Charles
Lamb?

Reading, commenting on Shakespeare, he is like a man
who walks alone under a grand stormy sky, and among
unwonted tricks of light, when powerful spirits seem
to be abroad upon the air; and the grim humour of
Hogarth, as he analyses it, rises into a kind of spec-
tral grotesque.

If the historical novelists would only study Pater's pictorial manner how much more difficult, but how much more
delightful, would their work become! The plague of it is
that they cannot reproduce the 'quality' of Pater, while
there is nothing easier than to catch at the hothouse mannerisms and preciosities that are his flaws. Nor will they
amend their ways while critics bestow the epithet 'distinguished' on those who murder his style.

Notes

1 Fourth stanza of 'Earthly Paradise' (1868-70).
2 Hallam Tennyson, 'Alfred Lord Tennyson: A Memoir' (1897),
  ii, 92.
3 Ulterior motive.

70. ROGER FRY ON PATER

1891, 1898

Extracts from the 'Letters of Roger Fry' (1972), ed. with
an Introduction by Denys Sutton.
   Roger Fry (1866-1934), art critic and painter, established his reputation as an authority on Italian art with
the publication of 'Giovanni Bellini' (1899). He was a
member of the Bloomsbury Group, director (1905-10) of the
Metropolitan Museum of Art in New York, a pioneer in intro-
ducing the work of Cezanne and Slade Professor of Fine Art
at Cambridge (1933-4).

(a)   From a letter dated May 1891 to Basil Williams

Last night we stayed up till the small hours discussing
the preposterous paradox started by Symonds in real good
faith, namely that Botticelli was either a fool with a
knack of drawing who didn't understand the least what he
was about or else a puritan satirist who tried to bring the
sensuosity of the Renaissance into contempt by his pot-
bellied Venuses, etc., etc. I tried to convince him, but
in vain; he is wrong and ought to know it — the worst of
it was that defending Botticelli is not at all what I am
naturally keen on now, but such a theory demanded criticism which, alas, I was not very well able to give.
Symonds ended by saying 'Of course we are all very thankful to Botticelli for having inspired those pages of Walter Pater,' and then he added with what I think was hardly
good taste in one who is so obviously a rival, 'That is the
worst thing I've yet said about Botticelli.' (i, 146)

(b)   From a letter dated 1 March 1898 to R.C. Trevelyan

I've just been reading Pater's 'Miscellanies'. It is a
pity he makes so many mistakes about pictures; but the
strange, and for a Morelli-ite(1) disappointing, thing is
that the net result is so very just. What is wanted now in
the way of criticism is someone who will make appreciations
as finely and imaginatively conceived and take them into
greater detail as well. Perhaps Berenson(2) will get to
this if he gets over his theories. (i, 171-2)

Notes

1 Giovanni Morelli (1816-91), an Italian art critic, concentrated mainly on the problem of attribution, which he
  claimed to have reduced to scientific principles, namely
  that an artist's treatment of insignificant details
  (such as the hands or ears) was tantamount to a signa-
  ture.
2 See p. 5.   Fry refers to Berenson's theory of tactile
  values.

71. REVEREND A.D. MALLEY: A STUDY OF PATER, 'CATHOLIC
WORLD'

February 1900, lxx, 602-9

_____

See Introduction, p. 5.
   The Rev. Augustine D. Malley (d. 30 October 1921), a
priest in the archdiocese of Boston, was a graduate of
Boston College and St John's Seminary, Brighton, Massachu-
setts.
   Malley sums up the response of the Catholic Church in
America to Pater as the chief exponent of 'decadence' in
England (see also No. 49).

_____

Although judicious critics are slow to admit that any one
author can be taken as a mirror of his times, yet the late
Walter Pater may be selected as the best representative of
that growing school of English littérateurs who have devoted themselves to subtle appreciations of sensations
arising from contact with the beautiful and to the expression of them in exquisite language. For Pater, as well
as for his model in style, Flaubert (model at least in
regard to conscientiousness), out of the many possible
words for one idea there is but one word that fits exactly,
which word must be sought with most painstaking care, and
when found this serves as a mysterious connective between
the minds of the author and reader, starting in the latter
what Pater calls 'brain waves', cognate ideas and sensations
which in loose and slipshod selection of words would otherwise lie dormant. The French writers have always devoted
this care to their exquisite prose. 'A word is a human

being, a soul,' said Hugo; or rather, when the right word
comes glowing from one soul into another it is charged
with life and partakes of the personality of the writer
or speaker, truly clothed with that mind-stuff Clifford(1)
dreamed of in his atomistic philosophy.

THE ART OF SELECTING WORDS

A delicate selection of words is, then, the whole art
of Pater. He looked out on this world rather lazily; it
was to him a multicolored spectacle of pleasure with varied interests and passions. Within himself he beheld another world, sensations evoked, which were fleeting, tangled,
complex. A word seizes, clarifies, describes these transient feelings, and therefore a word was sought with all
the care a jeweller bestows in the selection of rarest gems.
As a consequence his style has sweetness, harmony, color;
not the concentrated robustness of Flaubert, for the temperament of the master was widely divergent from that of the
pupil, but the calm, reflected sensations of an aristocrat
of art, subtly aesthetic, clothing his thought in phrases
of chastened pontifical dignity.
Such exquisiteness renders Pater fastidious, academic,
impatient of the wish; he would have a cult, not general
admiration. There was something higher than popularity
which he strove for — his own approval. As a necessary
consequence of such a self-centred standard of judgment,
he is often relative and elusive. But his sensations are
of the keenest importance to himself; the 'jewel flame
of life' must be kept burning at the greatest intensity.
The whole world, physical, spiritual, affords material; it
is to seek the most delicate, to know the more complex, to
become perfect by gazing on beautiful forms. Beauty can be
seen in all things, from the natural sensuous enjoyment of
ancient Greek life to the Christian ascetic in his cell,
striving to subdue the flesh, yearning to lead on earth the
life of the angels. As a psychologist he would analyze
simply for the sake of analysis; not to pass judgment, for
that, according to him, is the province of the moralist.
This devotion to beauty wherever found won for Pater the
title of 'hedonist', a term he hated to find in descriptions
of himself, as it led the people, he said, to believe him
something bad or uncanny. But he truly had won the title.
His philosophy of life would do away with all hard-and-fast
rules of morality, making pleasure or beauty the sole criterion of action. He was indeed, as he prided himself, a
modern Greek. Not an ancient one, for between himself and
Aristippus there is a whole world. How can one be a

follower of the school of Cyrene, even if he would? It is
impossible for such men to eliminate from their personality
nearly nineteen centuries of Christian training. Our religion has so revolutionized man's thoughts in regard to life
and death, and relations with another world have so convinced him in regard to sin and judgment, and the life to
come is so intimately interwoven in the very warp and woof
of modern society, and its customs, laws, and language
itself penetrate the mind through so many hidden and unobserved avenues, that it is utterly impossible for the modern hedonist to enter with unremorseful buoyancy into the
unreflecting sensuousness of the Greek. The whole modern
world lies under the shadow of the Cross; men cannot escape it, nor close their eyes to it. Hence, when this is
attempted, the inevitable note of sorrow is heard. As
Catholics we must often have wondered at the prevailing
sadness that tinges, or rather permeates, all literature
not our own. We do not very well understand it; our own
lives have sorrows enough, but we are so buoyed up by the
great old faith that the expressions of sadness, gloom,
mystery, unrest, which we come across in the newspaper,
read in the novel or poem, awaken in us only a vague sympathy, but more wonderment. We can never fully realize the
state of the souls of those who are in darkness but hesitate to come towards the light, or the terrible and grim
misery of the others who deliberately turn their back on
the light and walk towards the valley and the shadow.
     So also with the other questions which were once uncer-
tain: Whence came we? Where are we going? How do we
enter into relationship with God? Revelation has answered,
though reason itself can answer somewhat, so that it is
impossible to doubt now in the same frame of mind as they
did in the days of Pyrrho or Lucian. A modern Epicurean
and sceptic differs from the ancient in kind, not degree;
he has had Moses and the prophets.

                    HEDONISM TRACEABLE TO KANT

     This modern hedonism of Pater, however, seems to owe its
origin, not so much to a deliberate wish to throw aside
Christianity and its restraints, but rather to the influence of German subjectivism propagated by the doctrines of
Kant. According to him, the judgment has been deceived
by the information conveyed through the medium of the senses.
They reported to him that substances existed outside himself, that he could rely on their permanency and trust implicitly to the truths deduced from them; but when he examined closely, when he strove to verify these observations,

he was convinced that outside realities resolved themselves into mere sensations, and these were found at last
to be only modifications of the sentient personality. How,
then, could he ever be sure that anything did exist outside himself, since he knew it only by a modification of
himself, and never as it was in itself? Thus what was
hitherto permanent begins to crumble into instability,
truth becomes relative and subjective, things lose their
individuality, or are resolved into manifestations of some
one force which is supreme. The only things, then, that
we can be certain of are sensations; let sensations, then,
be as exquisite as possible, concludes the hedonist.

Kant's doctrine of Beauty found in the 'Critique of
Judgment', namely, that 'the judgment of taste is not a
judgment coming from scientific rules, and therefore does
not pertain to logic, but it is aesthetic, that is, the
determining principle is purely subjective',(2) has been
adopted by many or by most of the literary men in Paris and
London, and therefore spreads the influence of scepticism
and hedonism in polite circles. Flaubert, who is perused
day and night by those who would attain force and grace of
style, makes one of his characters exclaim dramatically,
yet summing up succinctly the whole system:

> The necessity of thy reason, does it not create the law
> of things? Do not things become known to thee only
> through the intermediary of thy mind? Like a concave
> mirror, she defaces objects, and all means are lacking
> to thee for obtaining truth. Form is perhaps naught
> else but an error of thy senses, substance but a vain
> dream of thy thought, and beyond thyself there is —
> Nothing!(3)

It is to Germany, and not to Greece, we owe modern scepticism; Pater, like so many others, adopted these views,
concerning himself simply with sensations arising from contact with the beautiful, and hence only a superficial
agreement can be found in him with the old philosophers of
the Garden.

HIS GREAT STUDY OF LIFE

This mixture of Christian training, modern psychology,
ancient love of beauty, are welded together in his great
study of life, 'Marius the Epicurean'. The work is really
a masterpiece, the only example of its kind in English. It
has the same effect upon one as a piece of pure Greek art;
yet with an after-feeling of sombreness which comes from a

lost Christian hope. Yet Greece too had something of this
gloom;   there are her epitaphs that cry to us across the
ages, with their great burden of woe: 'O thou who readest
this rejoice, rejoice in life! After this there are no
more smiles, nor joys, nor bright laughter!'(4)   'Friend,
hearken unto my counsel;   prepare the cup for wine, crown
thy head with the rose;   behold, all else comes to naught.
Thou must sink into horrible night, eternal exile, a sub-
terranean sleep!'(5)   Greece had not yet been instructed;
modern hedonism has the greater sin.

In 'Marius' Pater expressed his ideal of the human being:
a youth, high-born, chaste, priestly, cultured;   a flush of
the world about him through his subdued Epicureanism.   An
unfinished life, with the subtle charm of leaving the reader's intellect unsatisfied, provoked towards more serious
speculation.   And the style of the work suits accurately
this conception: it is chaste, polished, austere;   yet
again, in places, delicately flushed.   The advice which
Marius' monitor gives him when he asks for a rule of life
is Pater's advice to the world:

> If thou wouldst have all about thee like the colors of
> some fresh picture, be temperate in thy religious mo-
> tions, in love, in wine, in all things, and be of a
> peaceful heart with thy fellows. Keep the eye clear by
> a sort of exquisite personal alacrity and cleanliness,
> extending even to the dwelling place;   discriminate
> ever more and more fastidiously, select form and color
> in things from what is less select;   meditate much on
> beautiful visible objects — on objects, more especially
> those connected with the period of youth — on children
> at play in the morning, the trees in early spring, on
> young animals, on the fashions and amusements of young
> men;   to keep ever near if it were but a single choice
> flower, a graceful animal, a sea-shell, as a token and
> representative of the whole kingdom of such things; to
> avoid jealousy in thy way through the world, every-
> thing repugnant to sight;   and, should any circumstance
> tempt thee to a general converse in the range of such
> objects, to disentangle thyself from that circumstance
> at any cost of place, money, or opportunity!

This advice is, of course, beautiful;   but it is the advice
of decadence — too refined to be vigorous or healthy.   It
enervates;   it is the soft Companion with his baths and
his perfumes.   Nevertheless it must be confessed Pater's
mind is strong and masculine;   he never trips daintily over
a problem, but strives to sound the bottom.   His tastes,
though, are thoroughly feminine, delicate, keenly sensitive

to the rarest opalescent shade in either thought or object.
He would catch even the filmiest, most evanescent feeling
and give it its proper expression; a labor, of which the
engraver blowing off invisible grains of dust from the
finished gem is the ideal.

ONCE A CATHOLIC

A mind of this kind cannot be judged by the same standards we would apply to Macaulay; it sets its own standards, and must be appreciated in its own settings.
Pater's family was once Catholic; he himself was baptized
in the church, but fell away through dilettantism. It is
interesting to note the Catholic purity which permeates all
his pictures and which he reads into old paganism:

[Quotes ch. i of 'Marius': 'Early on that day' to *Favete
linguis*'.]

This yearning in his blood, as it were, for the faith
of his fathers finds full vent in his wonderful description
of the Mass as it was celebrated in the second century:

[Quotes ch. xxiii of 'Marius': 'For the silence' to *redem-
isti mundum*'.]

HIS RELIGIOUS INSTINCTS NEVER EDUCATED

Yet notwithstanding this devotional tendency in many of
Pater's works, a tendency which we cannot help feeling is
somewhat akin to the Catholic, a legacy from his forefathers,
yet it is only superficial, for he holds himself aloof from
the really great religious problems. 'The fire so bright,
the love so sweet, the unction spiritual', are no longer his.
Modern culture has taken from him the true beauty of childhood faith, nor has it left upon him the scars of much questioning and searching after God, whom to seek is to find —
scars which are manly and honorable; but rather, it has
left him the vacancy of worldliness, moral triviality, and
the sad, wistful lassitude of the baffled seeker after pleasure. Compare the death-scenes of the wayward, brilliant
pagan, Flavius, and the half-converted Christian, Marius:

[Quotes ch. vii of 'Marius': 'But at length delirium' to
'and hear you weeping'.]

Flavius had enjoyed life as the pagans did; Marius, his friend, had restrained himself, living a life half in accordance with the maxims of the Stoics, and then again following the Epicureans, — yet good, to all seeming, '*anima naturaliter Christiana*',(6) declared Pater. His death, nevertheless, was neither better nor worse:

[Quotes ch. xxviii of 'Marius': 'It was after all a space of deep sleep' to 'a kind of sacrament with plenary grace'.]

Modern hedonism is at the bottom hopeless also; the old Greek inscriptions could still be carved over its graves. Yet, if we mistake not the signs, this theory of life is being rapidly adopted by the cultured classes here in America. A prevailing conviction of God's presence to us, of his gracious intents and purposes working in and through our best thoughts and endeavors, is by no means characteristic of the times. Rather there is the growing acquiescence that he is unknowable, and that man's desire for communication with the spiritual world can never be hardly more than

The desire of the moth for the star,
Of the night for the morrow.

To define God is to put limits to him, they say, and the moral order is not absolute for all times and all places. But the man who first wishes for a thesis proving the existence and nature of the Deity before he condescends to worship, and the man who desires to have the moral order proven absolute before he will restrain himself, have both committed spiritual suicide, and will never obtain the overwhelming answer. These facts are a Divine consciousness within us, they are 'the light which illumineth all men coming into this world'. Struggle to do away with them, and you commit the unpardonable sin against the light; the punishment thereof is darkness, intellectual and moral. Hedonism will ever have the aspect of the sad Ophelia crowned with her wild flowers, 'fennel, rue, and columbine', wandering in pathetic solitudes — babbling.

Notes

1 William Kingdon Clifford (1845-79), Professor of Applied Mathematics at University College, London, wrote philosophical treatises in which he conceived consciousness as built up of simple elements of 'mind stuff'.
2 See Division II, Section 57, of Immanuel Kant's (1724-

1804) 'Critique of Judgment' (1793).
3 A slightly corrupt quotation from ch. vi of 'The Temptation of St Anthony' (1874). The speaker is the devil.
4 See Isaiah lxvi, 14-15.
5 See Jeremiah xlix, 20.
6 'the soul is naturally Christian': Tertullian, 'Apolo-
   geticus, xvii, 29-30.

72. LIONEL JOHNSON: TWO POEMS

1894, 1902

See Nos 46, 93 and 95. The first poem, dated 1894, was
collected in Johnson's 1895 volume and in Ian Fletcher's
edition of 'The Complete Poems of Lionel Johnson' (1953),
67. Ian Small has identified Pater as its subject. The
second poem first appeared in the 'Academy' (11 October
1902), lxiii, 398, and was reprinted in 'Poetical Works:
With an Introduction by Ezra Pound' (1915) and 'The Complete Poems of Lionel Johnson'. Ian Fletcher has kindly
provided the following text, which is based on a collation of the York Public Library MS and the poem in the
'Academy'.

A FRIEND

His are the whitenesses of soul
That Virgil had: he walks the earth
A classic saint, in self-control,
And comeliness, and quiet mirth.

His presence wins me to repose:
When he is with me I forget
All heaviness: and when he goes,
The comfort of the sun is set.

But in the lonely hours I learn,
How I can serve and thank him best:
God! trouble him: that he may turn
Through sorrow to the only rest.

WALTER PATER

Gracious God rest him! he who toiled so well
    Secrets of grace to tell
Graciously; as the awed rejoicing priest
    Officiates at the feast,
Knowing, how deep within the liturgies
    Lie hid the mysteries.
Half of a passionately pensive soul
    He showed us, not the whole:
Who loved him best, they best, they only, knew
    The deeps, they might not view;
That, which was private between God and him;
    To others, justly dim.
Calm Oxford autumns and preluding springs!
    To me your memory brings
Delight upon delight, but chiefest one:
    The thought of Oxford's son,
Who gave me of his welcome and his praise,
    When white were still my days;
Ere death had left life darkling, nor had sent
    Lament upon lament;
Ere sorrow told me, how I loved my lost,
    And bade me base love's cost.
Scholarship's constant saint, he kept her light
    In him divinely white:
With cloistral jealousness of ardour strove
    To guard her sacred grove,
Inviolate by worldly(1) feet, nor paced
    In desecrating haste.
Oh, sweet grave smiling of that wisdom, brought
    From arduous ways of thought;
Oh, golden patience of that travailing soul,
    So hungered for the goal,
And vowed to keep, through subtly vigilant pain,
    From pastime on the plain,
Enamoured of the difficult mountain air
    Up beauty's Hill of Prayer!
Stern is the faith of art, right stern, and he
    Loved her severity:
Momentous things he prized, gradual and fair,
    Births of a passionate air:
Some austere setting of an ancient sun,
    Its midday glories done,
Over a silent melancholy sea
    In sad serenity:
Some delicate dawning of a new desire,
    Distilling fragrant fire

On hearts of men prophetically fain
    To feel earth young again:
Some strange rich passage of the dreaming earth,
    Fulfilled with warmth and worth.
Ended, his service: yet, albeit farewell
    Tolls the faint vesper bell,
Patient beneath his Oxford trees and towers
    He still is gently ours:
Hierarch of the spirit, pure and strong,
    Worthy Uranian(2) song.
Gracious God keep him: and God grant to me
    By miracle to see
That unforgettably most gracious friend,
    In the never ending end.

Notes

1 'worldly' in the editions by Pound and Fletcher; 'un-
  worldly' in the 'Academy'; and 'unworthy' in the manuscript.
2 Karl Heinrich Ulrichs (1825-95) coined the term 'Urning'
  (from Uranos of the 'Symposium') to denote the homosexual.

73. G.B. SHAW ON PATER

1903

Extract from a letter dated 15 September 1903 to Max Beerbohm, from 'Bernard Shaw: Collected Letters, 1898-1910
(1972), ed. Dan H. Laurence, 373-4.
    George Bernard Shaw (1856-1950), the celebrated dramatist
and social reformer, was a vigorous and versatile journalist
from 1885 to 1898. He was music critic for the 'Star', art
critic for the 'World', drama critic for the 'Saturday Review' and literary critic for the 'Pall Mall Gazette' respectively. Richard Le Gallienne noted in 'The Romantic
'Nineties' (1926) that Shaw, H.W. Massingham, William
Archer and A.B. Walkley represented the 'New Journalism',
which was marked by 'an agressive, menacing individualism'.

... the reason Bunyan reached such a pitch of mastery in
literary art (and knew it) whilst poor Pater could never
get beyond a nerveless amateur affectation which had not
even the common workaday quality of vulgar journalism (and,
alas! didn't know it, though he died of his own futility),
was that it was life or death with the tinker to make
people understand his message and see his vision, whilst
Pater had neither message nor vision & only wanted to cultivate style, with the result that of the two attempts I
have made to read him the first broke down at the tenth
sentence & the second at the first. Pater took a genteel
walk up Parnassus: Bunyan fled from the wrath to come:
that explains the difference in their pace & in the length
they covered....

Posthumous Publications

'Greek Studies'
January 1895

74. UNSIGNED REVIEW, 'SATURDAY REVIEW'

9 February 1895, lxxix, 191

It is disputed whether the virtue of Mr Walter Pater's
work resides chiefly in the depth and seriousness of his
studies or in the distinction of his literary style. Assuredly both contributed to the total result; but perhaps
what most impresses the reader of this volume is that Mr
Pater added something of the poet to the critic, and by
patience and subtlety of the imagination, and with the support of an adequate scholarship, could recover or recreate
a myth. The first essay, A Study of Dionysus, reads like
a fantasia suggested by the life of the vine and the
'spirit of sense' in the grape; but the fantasia is in
truth the tracing out, by a learned sympathy, of strange or
beautiful sequences of feeling and fancy in the Greek mind.
Such criticism approaches as near to creative work as is
permitted to work that is critical. Mr Pater would probably have shuddered had any one named him a 'prose-poet',
for he recognized the delicate severance of literary kinds,
and believed that the finest effects were to be attained
by the observation of limits; but he possessed some of the
poet's unifying power, which discovers the single life
running through manifold diversities, and he possessed
some of the poet's delight in a chastened richness of details. He presses gently, yet without feebleness or a wandering touch, towards the dark root of the primitive myth,
and then he endeavours to follow its development from stem
to branch, and from branch to leaf and flower and coiling
tendril. Such work is a reconstruction of genius, demanding
a fine artistic instinct and certain ventures of imaginative

faith.   In the picture finally presented there must, as Mr
Pater perceived, be some artificiality;   'things near and
far, matter of varying degrees of certainty, fact and surmise, being reflected and concentrated, for its production,
as if on the surface of a mirror'.   Artificiality there is,
but it is an artificiality endeavouring to follow the track
of Nature.

Mr Pater took an opportunity in his essay on Demeter
and Persephone to criticize that view of Greek religion,
partly sanctioned by the authority of Goethe, which assigns
no place in it to 'the worship of sorrow'.   He noticed a
romantic spirit in Greek art and poetry, the sense of a
beauty born through pain and difficulty, and he pointed to
the legend of Persephone as in itself sufficient to show
the function of a reverent sorrowfulness in the religion
of a wistful, anxious people.   This is one of those qualifications of a common view which it is just to observe,
but which do not really disturb the received and central
truth.   The Greeks knew sadness, as all men must know it,
but in the main *Heiterkeit*, cheerfulness, is characteristic of their feeling and of their work.   What we should
rather correct in the popular theory is the supposition
that Christianity is a 'worship of sorrow'.   More than any
other religion Christianity — it matters not as regards
this historical fact whether Christianity be false or not
— is the religion of joy attaining victory over sorrow.
Mercy rejoices over judgment, salvation rejoices over sin,
grace rejoices over trial, the ascended Christ rejoices
over the cross, life rejoices over death — 'O death, where
is thy sting?   O grave, where is thy victory?'(1)   And the
conception of Christian art as an art which worships sorrow
obliterates in an instant the central meaning of every
great work produced by the artists of Christendom.   The
representation of the martyr's agonies is not a glorification of physical pain, but of a faith which is the evidence
of things not seen, and a hope that does not fail.   The
central figure of Christianity 'for the joy that was set
before Him endured the cross'.   His birth is heralded by
carols of angels;   His absence for a season is solaced by
the presence of the Paraclete.   The sadness of Christian
art can be understood aright only by perceiving that it is
the shadow thrown by a deep and solemn light.

Very admirable is Mr Pater's warning against a too intellectual or abstract view of Greek sculpture.   Students
of antiquity, he justly remarked, have

for the most part interpreted the creations of Greek
sculpture, rather as elements in a sequence of abstract
ideas, as embodiments, in a sort of petrified language,

of pure thoughts, and as interesting mainly in connexion
with the development of Greek intellect, than as elements of a sequence in the material order, as results
of a designed and skilful dealing of accomplished
fingers with precious forms of matter for the delight
of the eyes.

Mr Pater loved to dwell rather upon the purely sensuous
aspects of Greek art, the side of Greek art which expresses
the Ionian influence, and he in some degree suspected what
he calls the Dorian influence, recognizing its homage to
sanity and reason, but dreading its coldness and its tendency to extreme simplification. He could almost be
pleased to think of the Venus of Melos as the most majes-
tic of *bibelots*. Here again Mr Pater expressed an important lesser truth, and it will be the fault of his readers
if they replace by it the major truth, which has rightly
been recognized as central. Spirit and sense — both of
necessity play their part in all artistic work, but the
spirit is not necessarily cold and abstract. It may well
be like the descending figure in Blake's design of the
reunion of the soul and body — instinct with rapture, fire,
and passionate longing.
    Mr Pater's style, as all rightly qualified readers have
felt, is excellent in its kind. But it would be unfortunate if its kind were supposed the highest, or if it became
a model. Each word is studiously chosen, each clause is
nicely poised, but the total effect is not quite admirable.
There are none of those large fluctuations of feeling, none
of those irrepressible thoughts which break through language and escape, that characterize the greatest writers.
By a steady system of levelling up, each sentence being
equally charged with meaning and emotion, the rise and fall
of passion and idea are lessened if not lost. We admire
the fine manipulation of language, and are conscious that
we admire it.   And at length we grow a little weary even
of our own admiration.

Note

1 1 Corinthians xv, 55.

75. F.G. KENYON, UNSIGNED REVIEW, 'ATHENAEUM'

23 February 1895, 244-5

See Introduction, p. 37.
    Frederick George Kenyon (1863-1952), classical scholar,
was chief librarian of the British Museum from 1909 to 1930.
He was responsible for a number of classical and biblical
texts and he edited 'The Centenary Edition of Robert Browning '(1912).

Collected magazine articles though the contents of this
volume are, they yet possess a unity of conception which is
generally wanting to such collections. Their subject is a
single one — the Greek genius, as exemplified alike in the
beliefs, the literature, and the art of the Greek people.
Grouped round this central idea, they gain greatly by
being united in a single volume. There was something incongruous in finding, amid the usual miscellaneous assem-
blage of ephemeral articles in a monthly magazine, a delicate study of a Greek myth, in the refined and thoughtful
style which was characteristic of all Pater's work. Readers
are apt to skim a magazine article; and to skim an essay
of Pater's is to miss all its charm and most of its thought.
Now that these studies are gathered from their heterogen-
eous surroundings, it is possible to read them more deliberately, and to enjoy them more thoroughly. Whether they
would have appeared in precisely this form had Pater lived,
we cannot tell; probably not, since the essays on Greek
sculpture, with which the volume ends, were to have been
continued, and would have formed a separate work by themselves; and we may reasonably suppose that he would not
have left an ungrammatical sentence at the close of the
second essay (p. 78, 'a fragment ... were ... adopted ...
and have figured', &c). Nevertheless they form, as they
now stand, a harmonious and satisfying work, worthy to
take its place with the other charming volumes which represent the life-work of this conscientious artist and thinker.
    There are nine essays in all, and of these five are con-
cerned with mythology and four with sculpture. The two
subjects may seem to fall rather far apart; but in the
hands of Mr Pater they are in perfect harmony. In neither
is he the researcher, the historian; in both he is the
interpreter of the forms in which the Greek genius expressed itself. Pater's life was one continuous study of

beauty, whether in mediaeval art or Greek literature or
religious thought; and if his interpretations of a myth
or a sculpture sometimes seem far-fetched, it must be remembered that study brings insight, and that Pater's
chastened sobriety of thought is very far removed from the
undisciplined enthusiasm which so often runs riot in the
fields of mythology and folk-lore. Fanciful he may sometimes be, but never rhetorical; rather, he sees further
into the truths which underlie the ancient myths than
they can who have not undergone the same prolonged training in insight and refinement. The first essay, that on
Dionysus, is a singularly delicate study of the nature-
conceptions embodied in the legends of this deity, in whom
Mr Pater sees 'the spiritual form of fire and dew'. Dionysus is the person 'in whom, somehow, all those impressions of the vine and its fruit, as the highest type of
the life of the green sap, had become incorporate; — all
the scents and colours of its flower and fruit, and something of its curling foliage; the chances of its growth;
the enthusiasm, the easy flow of more choice expression,
as its juices mount within one'; in some such image as
this 'you have the idea of Dionysus, as he appears, entirely fashioned at last by central Greek poetry and art, and
is consecrated in the Οἰνοφόρια and the ’Ανθεστήρια, the
great festivals of the Winepress and the Flowers'. Around
this central idea are grouped studies of the various forms
in which Dionysus figures in Greek legend and literature,
culminating in the separate essay on the treatment of the
subject by Euripides in the 'Bacchae'. We have called them
'studies', as the title-page of the book so describes them;
but the word is somewhat too heavy for these delicate meditations, musings which flow gracefully from one detail to
another, taking various aspects of the subject into successive consideration, and finally leaving behind a general impression of beauty, the less precise perhaps because of the charm of the language, which diverts the
reader's attention from the sequence of the thought.

  Two essays, or rather lectures, follow on the myths of
Demeter and Persephone. The treatment is the same, the
style rather less attractive. Perhaps the chill of the
lecture hall was unfavourable to the delicate grace of
Pater's finer style. However this may be, the next study,
that entitled Hippolytus Veiled, is open to no such charge.
Lighter in touch than many of Pater's writings, it has all
his most delightful charm of thought and description, and,
to us at least, is unquestionably the gem of the volume.
It is but the story — familiar enough in its general outlines — of Hippolytus, the son of Theseus and the Amazon
queen Antiope, whom Phaedra loved too well; but Pater's

poetic imagination has had free play in filling up the
details, until the picture of the simple life of the lad,
in a retired corner of Attica, becomes a perfect idyll of
a pure and healthy boyhood, trained by the finest influences of nature. Here, as a specimen, is the description
of the home in which King Theseus placed the babe and his
mother:

[Quotes Hippolytus Veiled: 'The white, paved waggon-
track' to 'the white fleeces heaped warmly round him'.]

The essays on Greek sculpture treat only of the beginnings of the subject, from the earliest relics of Mycenaean
art to the age of Myron amd Polycleitus, leaving off, unfortunately, before reaching the masterpieces of Pheidias,
the Parthenon and the Olympian Zeus. The materials for a
treatment of these early periods are scanty, just as our
knowledge of the origins of Greek myths is often scanty;
but, with the one as with the other, Pater delighted to
follow out every indication and make the most of every
trace of beauty. His treatment of both is similar, always
seeking, behind the legend or the statue, the thought embodied in it, and keenly alive to every beauty of conception as well as of execution. All that is beautiful in
Greek art or literature had its attraction for him, and
he was quick to see beauty and poetry where others see only
quaintness and archaism — a quality shown particularly in
his appreciation of primitive Greek sculpture and metal
work. His general attitude towards sculpture is well expressed in one of the earlier essays:

These two tendencies [copiousness of imagination and
precision of realization] met and struggled and were
harmonised in the supreme imagination, of Pheidias, in
sculpture — of Æschylus, in the drama. Hence a series
of wondrous personalities, of which the Greek imagination became the dwelling-place; beautiful, perfectly
understood human outlines, embodying a strange, delightful, lingering sense of clouds and water and sun. Such
a world, the world of really imaginative Greek sculpture, we still see, reflected in many a humble vase or
battered coin, in Bacchante, and Centaur, and Amazon;
evolved out of that 'vasty deep'; with most command,
in the consummate fragments of the Parthenon; not, indeed, so that he who runs may read, the gifts of Greek
sculpture being always delicate, and asking much of the
receiver; but yet visible, and a pledge to us of creative power, as, to the worshipper, of the presence,
which, without that material pledge, had but vaguely
haunted the fields and groves.

In the course of his brief preface Mr Shadwell takes
occasion to protest against the conception of Pater as
merely a master of style. The truth is that, in some respects, he was not a master of style at all. The charm of
Pater's writing lies, not in the elaborate structure of
sentences, but in the exquisite choice of words. His
sentences are often amorphous, a succession of participial
clauses with a baffling accumulation of pronouns, and often
ending with an unexpected abruptness. But the words and
phrases themselves are full of a quiet beauty and a perfect
fitness of language to thought. That is really the secret
of the matter. The style follows the thought. It is simply the careful, artistic choice of the most refined language in which to express beautiful thoughts; never a deliberate aiming at literary effects. It is the style of
Plato rather than of Demosthenes, reminding one at times
of the language of Mr Ruskin without his rhetoric; a
refinement of mind expressed in a refinement of words.
Pater sympathized to the fullest extent with both sides
of the Greek genius — its sensuous delight in every kind
of beauty, and its artistic self-restraint in expression,
which he characterized as the Dorian element in the race;
and both qualities combine to produce his literary style.
The charm of that style, expressing the charm of a retir-
ing, but keenly appreciative personality, will always give
delight to those who value beauty and grace in language.
His audience during his life was never a very large one;
but an audience, fit if few, he is likely to retain so long
as English literature is read and good workmanship is held
in honour.

76. ANDREW LANG, SIGNED REVIEW, 'ILLUSTRATED LONDON NEWS'

9 March 1895, 299

See Introduction, pp. 4 and 37.
    Andrew Lang (1844-1912), the Scottish scholar, settled
in London in 1875 as a journalist. He quickly established
a reputation as a prolific writer in a wide variety of
literary forms, publishing novels, poetry, translations of
Homer, research in Scottish and French history, anthropolo-
gical studies of primitive religions and numerous collections of fairy tales.
    Although Pater referred to Lang as his 'friend' in a
letter dated 27 November 1872, little is known of their

relationship (see LWP, 11n). Lang received a presentation
copy of 'The Renaissance' and in a footnote to the third
edition (1888) of the book Pater acknowledged a translation
of 'Aucassin and Nicolette' 'from the ingenious and versatile pen of Mr Andrew Lang' (R, 16n).

I am conscious of not being the right critic of Mr Pater's
'Greek Studies' (Macmillan), for the critic should be more
sympathetic. In a review of Mr Symonds's 'Life', Mr
Symonds is said to have compared Mr Pater's style to a
civet cat.(1) I am not familiar with that sort of cat,
but, clearly, no compliment was intended. On myself, in
this posthumous work, Mr Pater's manner has a very different effect. I seem to be in a gallery almost hieratic in
its stately repose, rather chill, full of good things, but
not very interesting, somehow. The words 'fine', 'dainty',
'delicate', 'strange', 'subtle', eternally repeated, become as dull as modern copies of Greek decorative designs.
They are good words, but staled by constant use. One has
the feeling that they could be stuck on anywhere, and that
it would be agreeable to take some of them away. One compares a vocabulary like Mr Stevenson's, with its constant
surprises, usually delightful, and only surprising by their
unexpected aptness.

So much for style; on my head be it! As to matter,
having given a good deal of time to Greek mythology, religion, and early art, I may have become pedantic. I want
facts and authorities, though, to be sure, I know most of
the authorities. Again, I really do not think that the
Greeks (or any other people) were like Mr Pater's Greeks.
What he squeezes out of their religion and art, they did
not — at least, did not consciously — pour into these
vessels. The book is full of pretty and even poetic ideas
which the relics of Greece suggested to Mr Pater. The
inner sense of Dionysus, as the spirit of the vine, in
flower and fall, the inner sense of Demeter, are finely
expressed; but only a very rare Greek here and there
would have thought about them as Mr Pater thinks. Then,
being a kind of 'specialist' (*mea culpa*),(2) I cannot but
see how much he omits, and how important it is.

There is no smell of roast pork about his *Mystae*, yet,
from Aristophanes, we know that it was there. He omits
the figurines of pigs in the precinct of the Cnidian
Demeter; he does not tell us the odd fact that each
initiated person took a swim in the sea with his pig at
Eleusis. We get a prettified picture of Greek faith and
custom from Mr Pater. The comparative method he abjures.

The Goddess of Theocritus at the Harvest Home is our Kirna-
baby, is familiar to ancient Peruvians; and this makes
Greeks and other peoples much akin. The peculiarity of
Greece is only beauty, the inexplicable, unparalleled genius for plastic and poetic art. OEno and the other girls
who turn out wine and corn and oil are in all the fairy
tales of the world. Greece merely made them classical.
Every farm had its chapel of Demeter, a tool-house; but
in the Cnidian tool-house was the statue of the Greek
Mater Dolorosa, now in our Museum. To me it is a highly
interesting and curious fact that the Pawnees have the
Attic rite of the Bouphonia, in essentials. They also
have their Eleusinian mysteries. Father de Smet(3) chronicles the accompanying and explanatory sacred story of
Manabozho and Chibiabos. Taking a young brother in place
of a daughter, this is exactly the Eleusinian tale of
Demeter and Persephone. Instead of dressing in the dark-
est blue, like Demeter, Manabozho blackens his face. He
laments, like Demeter, for six years. The Muses do not
sing and dance before him, but the Manitous do. He is
consoled, the Mysteries are established. Chibiabos, like
Persephone, is brought back from the dead. He, like her,
now presides over the Land of Souls.
     Is this the result of transmission, or of coincident
fancy? Such questions get the better of me, when I am
brought to contemplate mythology. For Mr Pater (if he
was acquainted with the facts) such questions appear to
have no interest. Again, speaking of Mycenaean art, he
seems to deny an Egyptian influence (p. 224): 'The theory
which derived Greek art, with many other Greek things,
from Egypt, now hardly finds supporters.' The theory was
sadly overworked. But there, in the Mycenaean graves, are
the daggers, of which the spirit is Achaean (or early
Greek), while the technique is of the Age of Aah Hotep, a
process of inserting divers-coloured golds into bronze;
and, in at least one case, the landscape is Egyptian, with
a view of papyrus reeds. To these facts I do not observe
that Mr Pater makes any allusion. Now, all this may be
brutally pedantic on my part, but in archeology and mythology one does like facts. The real, and impossible, problem is to discover how and why Greece, working on the
same savage fancies as the rest of the world, 'turned all
to favour and to prettiness'. In that 'favour' Mr Pater
is perfectly at home, and in the similar 'favour' of the
French and Italian Renaissance. From the works of France
and Italy, in the Middle Ages and in the fifteenth century,
he draws many pleasant and beautiful illustrations. Art,
in fact, is his province, not this kind of science. His
knowledge of art is manifold, and is informed by an exqui-

site sense and taste.   But his intellect lived in an air
infinitely refined, and peopled by the grave and beautiful Spartans of his essay on Lacedaemon.   The ruffianly
element in these Spartans he winks at, so that he gives us
a life as ideal as that lived in the 'Hypnerotomachia' of
Poliphile.(4)   It is magnificent, but it is not history.
It is as one-sided as Mr Barlow's Spartan existence in
'Sandford and Merton'.(5)   These coarse remarks would not
have been penned had Mr Pater been here to read them.
They amount to no more than this — that he was an idealist,
no less, or rather more, than Plato.   He does not show us
(nobody does!) workaday Greece, that medley of barbarism and
beauty, so lovely, happy, wise, lustful, dirty, and cruel.
Could we live a day in Athens, we should be delighted and
horrified, and at night, the insects!   Think of the narrow,
muddy street, with the wild swine charging down it, tramp-
ling on the wayfarers!   Such facts do not enter into Mr
Pater's view of Hellas.   Conceive a morning call in Greece,
as in that dialogue of Herondas, which horrifies M Jules
Lemaître.   Not in Greece are we, with Mr Pater, but in a
Hellas of dreams, going delicately, as one of their own
poets says, in delicate air.   His work needs human beings,
human interest, of which we have a little in his essay, or
romance, The Veiled Hippolytus.   But, taking the dream as
a dream, no one has seen and told it more excellently than
the accomplished writer, and, as Mr Shadwell truly says,
the laborious and conscientious scholar, whose most valuable work here, probably, is in the later essays on the
more accomplished Greek sculptors.   Nothing is more common
or more stupid in criticism than to blame an author for not
being something else than he is, and for not doing what he
never intended to do.   Mr Pater did not set out to write
comparative mythology, or, perhaps, to paint Greece and the
Greeks as they were.   And so, here I am blaming his work
for the absence of elements which it was not meant to include.   But that comes of my having taken up Greece, as
Epictetus says, 'by another handle', and such are the ways
even of the least special specialist.

Notes

1 See Symonds's letter to Henry Sidgwick (No. 21b); this
  expression was quoted in Horatio F. Brown's life of
  Symonds, which was published in 1895.
2 My fault.
3 Pierre Jean de Smet (1801-73), Belgian Jesuit, wrote
  three books on his mission work among the American
  Indians.

4 'Hypnerotomachia Poliphili' (1499).
5 Mr Barlow is a character in 'The History of Sandford and
  Merton' (1783-9), a moral tale for children written by
  Thomas Day (1748-89).

77. W.M. RAMSAY, SIGNED REVIEW, 'BOOKMAN'

April 1895, viii, 18

See Introduction, pp. 36 and 37.
   William Mitchell Ramsay (1851-1939), Scottish historian
and archaeologist, was an authority on the geography of
Asia Minor and early Christian history. The most notable
of his books is perhaps 'The Church in the Roman Empire'
(1893).

The most important and permanently interesting essays in
this book are those which express Mr Pater's ideas about
the nature and origin of Greek mythology and its relation
to Greek religion. In The Myth of Demeter and Persephone
he has stated his views most clearly; and it might have
been, perhaps, a more lucid arrangement if the editor had
placed that 'study' first in the volume; moreover, the
arrangement would then have been the chronological order
of publication. In many respects, however, the Study of
Dionysos is the most striking part of the book, and this
fact, presumably, weighed with the editor when he placed
Dionysos before Demeter. According to Mr Pater, each
characteristic Greek legend passed through three stages of
development — the instinctive, the poetical, and the
ethical.(1) In the first stage the Greek mind, contemplating the nature that surrounded it, 'divined a number
of living agencies, corresponding to those ascertained
forces, of which our colder modern science tells the number and the names'. In the second stage, the plastic,
creative imagination gave definiteness and fixed character
to those living agencies, and formed them into a group of
human or divine persons, who were connected with one another by ties of relationship and lived a common life, 'the
incidents and emotions of which soon wove themselves into
a pathetic story'. Then, in the third stage, the reflec-
tive and ordering imagination, pondering on this tale and

its persons and incidents, found in it the expression of
moral and religious ideas about the nature of human life
and the relation between man and God.

It is not easy to understand why Mr Pater gives to the
first instinctive stage the alternative epithet 'mystical'.
That seems to imply an inadequate and even erroneous conception of mysticism and of the Greek Mysteries. It is
the third stage that is the mystic stage, for mysticism
co-ordinates and gives an intelligible religious explanation of the poetical forms of primitive thought; and the
Mysteries saw in Persephone 'the goddess of death, yet
with a promise of life to come', and set that lesson on
the Eleusinian stage in the most impressive surroundings
before the eyes of the initiated.

On p. 100 are some exquisitely expressed sentences on
the growth of the religious myth,

> which grew up gradually, and at many distant places, in
> many minds independent of each other, but dealing in
> a common temper with certain elements and aspects of
> the natural world, as one here and another there seemed
> to catch in that incident or detail which flashed more
> incisively than others on the inward eye, some influ-
> ence, or feature, or characteristic of the great mother
> — the goddess of the fertility of the earth in its
> wilderness.

But in almost every page of the essay on Demeter and
Persephone occurs something that invites quotation and
repays attention, something that expresses in delicate
and carefully weighed terms a luminous and impressive —
though perhaps one-sided — view, as Mr Pater traces the
development of the idea of the 'great mother' in the mind
of her worshippers. She is the complete embodiment of
their science and of their religion; in her their civi-
lisation is crystallised in a definite presentation. In
an earlier stage she is the expression of their theory and
their practice in agriculture, when agriculture was a
young art. But, as Mr Pater says in his Study of Dionysos,
p. 2, 'the thought of' Demeter and her 'circle was a
complete religion, a sacred representation or interpretation of the whole human experience, modified by the special limitations' and circumstances of her worshippers.
Demeter, therefore, is the founder of civilised order, the
guardian of married life; and society is held together by
the bonds of her religion.

The picture presented to us by Mr Pater of the myths of
Dionysos and of Demeter is not, in the historical point of
view, complete. It has to be supplemented from other

methods of study; and especially we must call in Mr Lang
(2) and Mr Fraser(3) to help us to understand the primitive and barbaric elements that cling to and clog the religious thought of the Greeks. It was not possible for that
thought to separate itself wholly from the actual ritual
and ceremonial of religion, with its survival of early acts
and things, quaint or interesting or grotesque or disgust-
ing as they were by turns. But within their proper limitations Mr Pater's studies of religious myth are suggestive
and charming throughout; and stand in striking contrast
with the deadness and barrenness of that method which
finds its most prominent exponent at the present day in
Dr Roscher,(4) the method which sees in each divine being
the envisagement of some single fact or phenomenon of
nature — which looks on Hermes, for example, as 'the wind-
god', and deduces all the religion and mythology of Hermes
from that initial idea.

The studies in Greek Art do not seem to the present
reviewer to reach such a high standard as those on religion.
In them too much is evolved from the inner consciousness,
and too little comes from direct interpretation of the
actual works of art. There is also a distinct absence of
knowledge; Mr Pater is too much dependent on Overbeck,(5)
the least sympathetic and least suggestive of German writers on Greek art. It was a doubtful service to the auth-
or's memory to reprint essays resting upon a stage of knowledge that was perhaps adequate at the time, but is certainly inadequate now. Of course, it need hardly be said
that there are many striking paragraphs and fine thoughts
in these, as well as in the religious essays.

Notes

1 See GS, 91.
2 See No. 76.
3 Sir James Frazer (1854-1941), Scottish scholar and an-
  thropologist, is best known for 'The Golden Bough' (1890-
  1915).
4 Wilhelm Heinrich Roscher (1845-1923), German classical
  philologist and scholar, wrote chiefly of Greek and Roman
  mythology.
5 Johannes Adolf Overbeck (1826-95), German archaeologist
  and art historian.

78. AGNES REPPLIER, SIGNED REVIEW, 'COSMOPOLITAN'

May 1895, xix, 116-17

See No. 49. A paraphrase of Pater's treatment of Dionysus
has been omitted.

Readers who have loved Mr Pater's work sincerely and unob-
trusively, who have found in him a stimulus to culture, and
a wholesome corrective for the slipshod cleverness of the
day, will receive this last volume of essays with mingled
pleasure and pain. Alas! for the unavailing regrets that
haunt and disturb us at every page. This is the final gift
of one who gave but sparingly, yet whose rare good fortune
it was to increase the conscious joy of living. Echoes
of that finely tempered and restrained content which succeeded the rapturous license of youth, and which reached
its highest spiritual development in 'Marius the Epicurean',
relieve and lighten the more somber pages of his later studies. If he turns now and again to the 'worship of sorrow',
even among the happy Greeks; if he dwells unsparingly upon
the vengeful grief of Demeter, or the mysterious suffering
of Dionysus (a subject which, in 'Imaginary Portraits', has
awakened his subtlest powers of imagination), his true
charm and helpfulness lie still in his recognition of
beauty as a factor in life, and in his delicate philosophy
of 'happy moments', by which we snatch, even amid sordid
and fretful cares, some portion of serenity and delight.
    No writer of modern times has surpassed Mr Pater in sym-
pathetic appreciation of classic literature and art. He
strives, indeed, as others have striven before him, at a
too exhaustive interpretation of ancient myths. Iris bringing to Demeter the message of Zeus is, for him, the rainbow
signifying to the earth the good-will of the rainy skies.
He is capable of finding the Homeric Hecate, 'sitting as
ever in her cave, half veiled with a silver veil, thinking
delicate thoughts', to be no other than the chaste and
fleet-footed Artemis; and he fails to make these connections quite clear to the ordinary mind. But who save the
author of 'Greek Studies' could so interpret and reveal the
Demeter of the wheat-fields, the homely goddess, blithe
and debonair, who visits the pastures in the springtime,
when the young lambs are bleating, and the autumn barns
well stocked with yellow corn; who watches the farmers
threshing their grain, and stands by the women baking bread

in the ovens. Who but Mr Pater could describe with such
charming grace the infant Pans with their hairy little
shanks, and the peevish trouble of babyhood in their puck-
ered faces, and their 'small goat-legs and tiny hoofs
folded over together, precisely after the manner of a
little child'.

The conception of Dionysus in this volume is singularly
beautiful and pathetic. The youngest of all the gods, his
worship carries us back to the vineyards of the Greek hillsides, 'and is a monument of the ways and thoughts of
people whose days go by beside the wine-press, and under
the green and purple shadows, and whose material happiness
depends on the crop of grapes'. He is the beneficent god
whose fiery birth was heralded with joy, and whose tender
babyhood was the object of Jove's solicitous care. Mr
Pater's description of the child Dionysus reads like a
translation into letters of the frieze which decorates that
worn and beautiful old vase found at Formia, and now preserved in the museum of Naples....

79. W. WORRALL, UNSIGNED REVIEW, 'SPECTATOR'

20 June 1896, lxxvi, 876-6

Probably by Walter Worrall (b. 1862), who attended the
Liverpool Institute and became a classical scholar (1880-
4) at Worcester College, Oxford. Worrall edited 'The
Essayes or counsels, civill or morall of Francis Bacon'
(1900) and 'Milton: Sonnets' (1910).

Compare this laudatory appraisal of Pater's 'aesthetic'
criticism with Lang's demand for the 'comparative' method
(No. 76).

This posthumous volume is devoted to ancient Greece. The
essays here collected (to quote the editor's preface) 'fall
into two distinct groups, one dealing with the subjects of
Greek mythology and Greek poetry, the other with the history of Greek sculpture and Greek architecture. But these
two groups are not wholly distinct; they mutually illustrate one another, and serve to enforce Mr Pater's conception of the essential unity, in all its many-sidedness, of
the Greek character'. To the student of aesthetics, bent

upon interpreting the idea of Beauty and its various expression in art, no other people and no other period perhaps offer so much completed material. Mr Pater's name
is, for many readers, associated more especially with that
mediaeval art and thought which he expounded, with original
and illuminating insight, in his earliest volume, 'The
Renaissance'. But the central ideas which guided him in
those studies were won quite as much from the ancient world
as from the mediaeval. We may venture even to say that
the artistic achievement of the Middle Ages — perfect often
in its many forms, and yet veiled and clouded with the shadows of mysticism and symbolism — gives up its secrets
most readily to the critic who has imbued his mind with
the principles of the simpler and purer art of the Greeks.

The second set of essays in this book 'are all that remain of a series which, if Mr Pater had lived, would, probably, have grown into a still more important work'. Each
paper is, however, complete in itself; and the author's
real bent was scarcely towards the composition of a continuous and complete history of any art. What he has here
actually done is to present (following the historical order) a series of fine 'appreciations' of the chief phases
in the evolution of Greek sculpture. He does not compete
with the 'standard' histories, though he has evidently read
them carefully, and uses their results to assist him in his
own direct study of the existing remains. The following
passage, from the paper on The Marbles of Ægina, exempli-
fies his method of delicate, picturesque, and vivifying
criticism, which, while interpreting the ideal significance of a work of art, never loses sight of technical
considerations of form and material:

[Quotes 'And although the actual material of these figures
is marble' to 'the Chaucer of Greek sculpture'.]

But it is in the first set of essays that the writer's
peculiar faculty for imaginative criticism finds the most
striking expression. The Study of Dionysus and The Myth
of Demeter and Persephone are a brilliant effort to re-
vivify and recreate for the modern reader those old fundamental stories of religion which, in their essence always
mysterious, were yet in a sense so real, and meant so much,
to the Greek mind. Every one has felt the difficulty
of comprehending these intangible shadow-pictures (as they
now seem) of the Greek religion; every one, that is to
say, who has turned his attention to Greek art and literature, which are pervaded with allusion to them. Mr Pater,
taking two of the most profound of these myths for his
theme, has excellently exemplified one way of interpreting

their meaning. It is not the strait way of modern 'comparative' science; he has not sought assistance from the
'variants' of savage beliefs; Dionysus is not assimilated
to a totem in his hands, nor is Demeter explained as a
comparative type. His method is simply to study the myths
themselves in their authentic sources, — the extant literature and art — remains; 'as regards this story of
Demeter and Persephone, what we actually possess is some
actual fragments of poetry, some actual fragments of sculpture'. It is half way or more towards grasping the significance of a myth when its leading incidents, and the aspect of its leading figures, are so skilfully described as
in this elaborate account of the 'dread goddesses', drawn
from Homer and all later poets, and from monuments such as
the famous statues of Cnidos. But the author also attempts
to unfold, in each case, the inner and spiritual meaning of
the story, — to show that these conceptions of Greek religion, 'because they arose naturally out of the spirit of
man, and embodied, in adequate symbols, his deepest
thoughts concerning the conditions of his physical and
spiritual life, maintained their hold through many changes,
and are still not without a solemnising power even for the
modern mind'. He has not neglected the suggestions of
modern theorists where they are legitimate and valuable;
he finds Dionysus to be 'the spiritual form of fire and
dew', while Demeter and Persephone symbolise 'the earth,
in the fixed order of its annual changes, but also in all
the accident and detail of the growth and decay of its
children'. But he employs such explanation imaginatively,
not with the cold handling of modern science. He does not
merely refer the myth to its origin in some aspect or
phenomenon of Nature, but explains by the virtue of his
own creative insight and sympathy what was essentially a
spiritual and poetic process in the Greek mind. An example or two will illustrate the successful charm of his
treatment. First, of Demeter, as she appears in the
Homeric Hymn, 'the *mater dolorosa* of the ancient world,
with a certain latent reference, all through, to the mystical person of the earth':

[Quotes Demeter and Persephone: 'Her robe of dark blue' to
'hidden in the wrappings of the dead'.]

And again of Dionysus, the vine-god, in these passages of
exquisite fancy and exquisite expression:

[Quotes A Study of Dionysus: 'He is' to 'final victory
through suffering'.]

The essay on The Bacchanals of Euripides, while it
serves to give further illustration of the writer's conception of Dionysus, also does much to elucidate this
beautiful but difficult work of the sophist-poet. The
remaining essay, Hippolytus Veiled: a Study from Euripides, though admirably written in parts, is over-fanciful
and unduly romantic in its point of view; it is not so
much a study of Euripides' play as a set of variations
on the same theme, from which the dramatist's name were
best omitted. This Aphrodite, in particular, who 'was
just then the best-served deity in Athens', and who,
having 'looked with delight' upon the young Hippolytus,
'was by no means indifferent to his indifference', — this
is surely not the mysterious goddess of Euripides, but a
quite modern Aphrodite of the boulevards.

These essays show Walter Pater at his best as a writer.
He was first and last an aesthetic critic of a high order.
And his characteristic and peculiar merit is that he can
deal subtly with things that are in their nature subtle
and elusive; that he can interpret the mystical, or the
suggestive, or the symbolical without losing himself or
his reader in the merely vague. He has written with sincerity and feeling and felicity on topics which many a
critic wisely shuns, — on the spiritual and inner meaning
of a concrete work of art, the half-lights of an ancient
myth, the shifting daedal aspects of Nature; on things
which it is hard to see and feel truly, harder still to
convey one's vision of them to others. This was always
his chosen function as a writer: and for his instrument
he elaborated a style which has been variously praised or
blamed in different quarters, but cannot fairly be denied
the merits of originality and fitness. At its worst, it
is lax, involved, fatiguing; or over-ornamental, luscious,
with a tendency to *préciosité*.(1) Self-conscious it is
invariably. But, on the other hand, it is often flexible,
graceful, incisive, and picturesque; a style altogether
his own, unlike anything else in English prose, and invaluable for the work he set himself to do. It is true
that his sentences and constructions are often strangely
loose and incoherent, adverbs and participles dislocated,
and nominatives left hanging. But along with this looseness he has succeeded in shunning the formula, the stereotyped phrase, the unyielding mould in which so many writers
straiten and deform their thought; his epithets, however
loosely inserted, are in a high degree expressive and
beautiful, — 'the best words', in fact, if not always
'in the best order', though there is often a charm in the
dislocation itself. It was a style consciously contrived

to express ideas and impressions which were novel and not
easy to express in regular prose; it was to a large extent an artistic experiment in language, and at its best
it has achieved a singular success.

Note

1 Preciosity.

'Miscellaneous Studies'
October 1895

80. UNSIGNED NOTICE, 'THE TIMES'

25 October 1895, 14

See Introduction, p. 23.

These scattered essays, gathered from the pages of magazines, are the last gleanings of the late Mr Pater's
singular genius. The volume, says Mr Shadwell, who has
collected and edited them, has no such unifying principle
as the 'Greek Studies', published early this year. Some
of the papers would naturally find their place alongside
those collected in 'Imaginary Portraits', or in 'Appreciations', or in the 'Studies in the Renaissance'. This
miscellaneous character, however, is, in some respects,
an attraction to the appreciative reader. It serves to
show the writer in his various moods, all individual, all
inspired by serenity and detachment of temper, by rare
delicacy of insight and perception, and by fastidious
distinction of thought and expression. Mr Pater's work
is not of the kind which takes the multitude. It embodies
an exotic element which appeals only to the few, and, perhaps, it sometimes attempts to do in prose what can only
be done quite fitly in verse of a very high order. But
in spite of its laborious refinement, which sometimes
almost wears the air of affectation, it is the natural
expression of a personality of rare delicacy and distinction, of a genius which in reality was creative rather
than critical, synthetic rather than analytic. By those
to whom these qualities appeal through affinities of

temper and taste, this volume of 'Miscellaneous Studies'
will justly be regarded as a treasure, and certainly none
can read it without recognising in it literary genius of
a high order and a remarkably gifted mind.

81.   AGNES MACDONELL, SIGNED REVIEW, 'BOOKMAN'

November 1895, ix, 58

See No. 88 and Introduction, p. 37.
   Agnes Harrison MacDonell (d. 1925) was a gifted novelist and wife of Sir John MacDonell (1845-1921), the famous
jurist and writer.   She wrote 'For the King's Dues' (1874)
and 'Quaker Cousins' (1879).

In this new volume Mr Shadwell has collected essays dif-
fering in quality as well as in subject; but they are all
welcome.   There is less perfection than in the 'Studies in
the Renaissance', the 'Appreciations', or the 'Greek Studies'; but the book has this peculiar interest, that it
sounds Mr Pater's whole gamut.   The mind that conceived
'Marius' is distinctly visible, as are likewise the methods of the 'Imaginary Portraits'.   The things written of
with love and enthusiasm in the 'Renaissance' book, and
the 'Appreciations', have supplementary homage done them
here.   From the editor's preface, which contains a chronological list of the published writings, we see how large a
part of his life is represented by the present essays.
Diaphanéité dates from 1864, The Child in the House from
1878, while the architectural chapter on Amiens and Vézelay,
and the study of Pascal, were published in the year of his
death.
   The Diaphanéité, 'the only specimen known to be preserved of those early essays of Mr Pater's by which his
literary gifts were first made known to the small circle
of his Oxford friends', has, says Mr Shadwell, been added
with hesitation.   But the hesitation was surely unjusti-
fied.   It is structurally weak, a fault Mr Pater never
mended, but it has passages that fill us with wondering
admiration.   Was his mind ever crude, that he could produce this at twenty-four? for it is not merely pretty
wording we find, but a calm, mature philosophy.   It is a

rare type of character he is describing, and after which he is aspiring, the type to which the ideal man of à Kempis would have approached on the spiritual side. Here the pure character is seen using his qualities with fewer ascetic limitations. The mental habit of such is described 'as wistfulness of mind'.

> Its ethical result is an intellectual guilelessness, or integrity, that instinctively prefers what is direct and clear, lest one's own confusion and instransparency should hinder the transmission from without of light that is not inward. He who is ever looking for the breaking of a light he knows not whence about him, notes with a strange heedfulness the faintest paleness in the sky. That truthfulness of temper, that receptivity, which professors often strive in vain to form, is engendered here less by wisdom than by innocence. Such a character ... has something of the clear ring, the eternal outline of the antique.

The imaginative pieces, The Child in the House, Emerald Uthwart, and Apollo in Picardy, may possibly make the widest appeal. But while owning their grace, their refinement, they seem to me to show Mr Pater on his weakest side. I can conceive of several other persons writing that favourite, The Child in the House, and this is not praise when employed to so individual a writer; it hovers now and again on the merely pretty; there is a great deal of the same kind of thing, just less good, in fiction today. Apollo in Picardy is not faultless in plan, but there is more of the stuff in it that Mr Pater could weld, and you find in it some of the finest patches he ever wrote. The walk to the Grange is unforgettable.

> Prior Saint Jean, then, and the boy started before daybreak for the long journey; onwards, till darkness, a soft twilight, rather, was around them again. How unlike a winter night it seemed, the further they went through the endless, lonely, turf-grown tracts, and along the edge of a valley; at length — vallis monachorum, monks vale — then aback by its sudden steepness and depth, as of an immense oval cup sunken in the grassy upland, over which a golden moon now shone broadly. Ah! there it was at last, the white Grange, the white gable of the chapel apart amid a few scattered white gravestones, the white flocks crouched about on the hoarfrost, like the white clouds, packed somewhat heavily on the horizon, and nacrés(1) as the clouds of June, with their own light and heat in them, in their hollows, you might fancy.

It is in his criticism that his highest imaginative
qualities are revealed, where he is lightest, brightest,
and also most profound. For his philosophy strives to
express itself not in metaphysical guise; he never longed
after 'a visible loveliness about ideas'. The convincing
force of an appeal to poetry is half of his critical
method. And so in this representative collection you not
only find more robustness, more intellectual vigour in the
masterly essays on Mérimée or Pascal, and on French architecture, than when he played delicately with fiction, but
a greater stimulus to the imagination as well. For all
his fastidious exclusiveness, it is not the severe scholar
that speaks in his critical work. His first interest is
always in the man that made the books he is writing of.
This is pathetically noticeable in dealing with the 'impossible, unfamiliar, impeccable' Mérimée, who reflected
no feature of himself in his writing, save in the letters
he never meant for publication. His critic probes to find
the man beneath; finds him, indeed, quite different from
his creations, yet finds something also which explains how
his creations must be as they are, since made by pure *mind*,
unhelped by soul, by a man with a harsh ideal, 'as if, in
theological language, he were incapable of grace'. It
is, too, the man Raphael, the man Pascal, he is interested
in; but he examines their medium of expression with great
and unostentatious learning; for there are no short cuts
to his desire. Mr Pater, at least, is not impersonal. His
loves and ideals are written plainly here; his delight in
clearness and order, his wholesome love of beauty, his
shrinking from disease in art, or religion, or thought,
his reverence even for the things that clothe his spirit
no longer (like Raphael's, the 'scholar who never forgot
a lesson'), his gentle conscientiousness.

Strange, Raphael has given him a staff of transparent
crystal. [It is of the Baptist of the Ansidei Madonna
in the National Gallery he is speaking.] Keep, then
to that picture as the embodied formula of Raphael's
genius. Amid all he has here already achieved, full,
we may think, of the quiet assurance of what is to
come, his attitude is still that of a scholar; he
seems still to be saying, before all things, from
first to last, 'I am utterly purposed that I will not
offend.'

Note

1 Nacreous.

82.   C. MILMAN, UNSIGNED REVIEW, 'SPECTATOR'

28 December 1895, lxxv, 937-8

See Introduction, p. 37.
  Listed in R.H. Hutton's record book as 'Miss Constance
Milman' of 61, Cadogan Square, Miss Milman may have been
one of the daughters of the Rev. Henry Hart Milman (1791-
1868), author of verse dramas and church histories.

These 'Studies' have been gathered from various sources,
and sufficiently deserve their title of 'miscellaneous'.
It is perhaps a happy accident that this posthumous collection of Mr Pater's essays should contain varied specimens of his writings that might well have been included
in one or other of the books that have already made his
name well known to lovers of literature; but there is a
certain sadness in looking through the volume and coming
upon an 'Imaginary Portrait', or an 'Appreciation', or a
'Renaissance Study', much as there is sadness in looking
over a man's smaller possessions after his death, brought
together in a heap, orderly enough, but in their incongruous association losing the exact fitness of familiar usage.
The 'study' of Pascal, written for delivery as a lecture
at Oxford in July, 1894, is interesting, not only for Mr
Pater's treatment of the subject, but as containing his
last utterance on a theme on which he has often dilated.
After noting that Pascal's irony in the 'Provincial Letters' may remind us of the 'Apology' of Socrates, but that
his style reminds us of the 'Apologia' of Newman, he goes
on to say:

[Quotes Pascal: 'The essence of all good style' to '*la
manière qu'il voulait*'.]

It is this reverence for those who can say what they wish
in the precise way they wish to say it, this excessive
admiration for 'style', for the 'search after the phrase',
and the necessity of an accurate balancing of the value of
each word that is at once Mr Pater's chosen message to his
generation, and the reason why his circle of admirers is
necessarily somewhat limited. His admiration for those
masters of prose who can choose their words, and fit them
into the exact niches they are to occupy, amounted to a
passion. Readers of 'Appreciations' will remember the

description of Flaubert searching for the 'one phrase',
and Mr Pater's argument that literature is one of the fine
arts:

[Quotes Style: 'The one word for the one thing' to 'the
possibility of which constitutes it a fine art'.]

In Mr Pater's own writings this nice adjustment and balance
of words, this pause, as it were, to listen and 'search
for the phrase', makes itself almost unduly felt. The
style is overloaded and becomes mannerism, and the sentences seem built up and laboured with involved parentheses until there is a distinct sensation to the reader of
perpetual strain and even breathlessness in the effort to
follow such subtleties of expression. Still, the writings
of Mr Pater have a peculiar flavour and charm of their own,
and all students of literature must revere so careful a
steward of the English language, one who set before him a
high standard of felicitous phrase and choice expression,
and scorned to produce work that to his fastidious taste
was in any way imperfect.
    The 'Study' of Mérimée is interesting both for its cri-
tical remarks and as revealing Pater's sympathy with the
French author, whom he likens to a 'veritable son of the
old Pagan Renaissance'. It seems almost as if, in discussing Mérimée's works of fiction, with their 'clarity'
and 'antique force of outline', that Mr Pater becomes imbued with the characteristics of his subject, and for a
time drops his own somewhat artificial manner; as, for
instance, in the following remarks:

> Mérimée, a literary artist, was not a man who used two
> words where one would do better, and he shines espe-
> cially in those brief compositions which, like a minute
> intaglio, reveal at a glance his wonderful faculty
> of design and proportion in the treatment of his work,
> in which there is not a touch but counts. That is an
> art of which there are few examples in English; our
> somewhat diffuse, or slipshod, literary language hardly
> lending itself to the concentration of thought and ex-
> pression, which are of the essence of such writing. It
> is otherwise in French, and if you wish to know what
> art of that kind can come to, read Mérimée's little
> romances; best of all, perhaps, 'La Venus d'Ille',
> and 'Arsène Guillot'.

Though Pater admired the strict impersonality of Mérimée's
writings, he confesses that he is glad that Flaubert
failed entirely to efface *himself* in his works, and we

welcome with interest the slight personal touches in the
present essays, as we should always welcome them in writers
whose individuality impresses us with the fact that 'the
style is the man'.   In the imaginary portrait called The
Child in the House, we suspect that the retrospect is in
the main a fragment of the author's own 'shadowy recollections', of the gradual unfolding to a highly sensitive
nature of the closely allied mysteries of beauty and pain,
the recognition of sorrow, and the awakening of sympathy.
The 'imaginary child' yields himself easily to religious
impressions, but he seems to be content with outer symbols, all that 'belonged to the comely orders of the sanctuary', the vestments and fonts of clear water are types
of purity and simplicity to him, but there his attitude
towards religion seems to end.   There is a longing for an
ideal, mystical companionship, but how far such a longing
would suffice as a weapon in the great warfare of life we
are not told, and the fragment ends abruptly.   In the description of Emerald Uthwart's school-days we have an acknowledged reminiscence of Mr Pater's own boyhood, as he was
himself a scholar of the King's School at Canterbury, which
he speaks of with almost passionate affection:

> As Uthwart passes through the old ecclesiastical city,
> upon which any more modern touches, modern door or win-
> dow, seem a thing out of place through negligence, the
> diluted sunlight itself seems driven along with a spar-
> ing trace of gilded vane or red tile in it, under the
> wholesome active wind from the East coast.   The long,
> finely weathered, leaden roof, and the great square
> tower, gravely magnificent, emphatic from the first
> view of it over the grey down above the hop-gardens,
> the gently-watered meadows, dwarf now everything beside;
> have the bigness of Nature's work, seated up there so
> steadily amid the winds, as rain and fog and heat pass
> by.   More and more persistently, as he proceeds, in the
> 'Green Court' at last, they occupy the outlook.   He is
> shown the narrow cubicle in which he is to sleep; and
> there it still is, with nothing else, in the window-
> pane, as he lies; — 'our tower', the 'Angel Steeple',
> noblest of its kind.

It was with the same enthusiasm that Dickens embalmed his
boyish recollections of Canterbury in 'David Copperfield',
and recalled the venerable towers, the ancient houses, and
the serene air that breathed over them.
    In the 'Study' of Raphael, there is a characteristic
passing note that he is a master of style, and that the
Madonna del Gran Duca, the 'loveliest of his Madonnas,

perhaps of all Madonnas', contains a 'consummate example
of what is meant by *style*'; while he recommends the lover
of Renaissance art to study again and again the treasure
we have in London, the 'Blenheim' Madonna, as 'the embodied
formula of Raphael's genius'. The notes on North Italian
art, on Moretto and Romanino, on Borgognone and Ferrari,
equally with the fine description of Notre Dame d'Amiens,
and the Romanesque Abbey of Vézelay, are good examples of
Mr Pater's keen perception of beauty, and of his skill as
a 'word-mosaic artificer'. Apollo in Picardy is an illustration of the insight Mr Pater seemed to have into the
old, half-forgotten pagan world. It is a mediaeval survival of the shepherd-god, of which a brief hint had already been given in the mention of Raphael's 'Apollo and
Marsyas', which Mr Pater says contains a 'touch of truth,
of Heine's fancied Apollo "in exile", who, Christianity
now triumphing, has served as a hired shepherd, or hidden
himself under the cowl in a cloister'. There is a mingling
of pagan rites, of golden lyres and syren music, of mystic
flowers and dazzling lights, with the austerity of a mediaeval monastery, that is wholly characteristic of Mr Pater's
half-sensuous, half-ascetic theories of religion. We seem
to catch sight of a grotesque monkish devil peering out
from the foliage and fruit of some sculptured Romanesque
capital; there is a hint even that the figure of 'Apollyon', as the mysterious shepherd is called, with a strayed
sheep on his shoulders, reminds the good monks of the great
carving over the chapel-door in their own monastery. The
strange, irresponsible being, at once healer and destroyer,
and his playmate Hyacinth, server to the Prior Saint Jean,
are woven into the web of monasticism, while all that the
strange illumination of learning brings to the Prior is a
thwarted purpose and an intellect devastated with intellectual lightning. We have left to the last the study
called Diaphanéité, which Mr Shadwell says in his preface
is the only specimen extant of 'those early essays of Mr
Pater, by which his literary gifts were first made known
to the small circle of his Oxford friends'. There are
slight traces of his more mature writings in this early
fragment, which attempts to construct a 'basement' or
ideal type of absolute simplicity and purity. We doubt
whether Mr Pater has succeeded in conveying by the medium
of his pen a figure possessing what he often calls the
'eternal outline of the antique', though, no doubt, it
was presented clearly enough to his own mind. We learn
more of what it is not, than of what it is. It is a
character of negations, achieving the perfect life, but by
some grace innate, rather than by victory over a lower
nature; filled with wistfulness of mind rather than hope

of attainment; full of repose, yet discontented with
society as it is; possessing not so much a mind of taste
as the 'intellectual manner of perfect culture assumed by
a happy instinct'. Such a nature must of necessity be expressed by a form of outward beauty; it will be full of
discontent with the world, and of sympathy with revolution-
ists, but it is revolution harmonised and softened down,
'with an engaging naturalness, without the sound of axe
and hammer'. Crude and fanciful as this essay is, it still
contains the germ of that nature that is fully pictured in
'Marius the Epicurean'. There is the 'mind of taste
lighted up by some spiritual ray within', the earnest seeker after beauty, the wistful desirer of perfection without
hope of present attainment; and it is this wistful desire
for perfection that is the keynote of all Mr Pater's writings.

83. UNSIGNED REVIEW, 'OUTLOOK'

25 January 1896, liii, 160

The review is illustrated by a reproduction of the frontis-
piece to 'Greek Studies'. See No. 81, which also identifies
Pater's capacity to evoke an artist's 'personality' as the
chief attraction of his criticism.

This last volume, now posthumously published, of Mr Pater's
essays is made up almost entirely of the work of the last
few years of his life. It contains also a curious study,
printed as 'the only specimen known to be preserved of
those early essays ... by which his literary gifts were
first made known to the small circle of his Oxford friends',
and the exquisite Child in the House, which, though published seventeen years ago, has only of late come to general notice. But the other essays come within the last
five years, and as a whole the book gives a good idea of
the later developments of Mr Pater's work and thought.
    Like Matthew Arnold and Ruskin, Mr Pater was always in-
terested in art, not for itself alone, but in its relation
to life. He wanted always to know, not merely what it was,
in what forms it was manifest, but what kind of element it
made in the great complex of circumstance that envelops

each one of us. Indeed, in his real interest in actual
life he went far beyond the two other great critics of our
time, having in fact such a feeling for concrete humanity
that he was himself not merely a critic, but a creative
artist as well, and hence came 'Marius the Epicurean' and
the 'Imaginary Portraits', of which, by the way, three are
contained in this volume, as fine as any of the others.
Matthew Arnold regarded literature as a sort of guide to
conduct, but always in a largely intellectual way. Ruskin
looked at all art as didactic, and at almost all works of
art as symbolizing universal ideas. But Pater always
sought for the actual people who had produced any artistic
thing; he always strove to see the artist behind and in
his work.

The particular direction which this effort took was
toward an emphasizing of the representative character of
style. Where Ruskin presents at length the allegoric significance of the quatrefoils in the façade of Amiens,(1)
Mr Pater is interested in the cathedral as being one of
'the grand and beautiful *people's* churches of the thirteenth century', so that he chooses as a companion study
(both essays are here republished) the monastic church of
Vézelay. The way in which the style represented the artist,
the personal note in style, that was Mr Pater's great interest, even as in the lecture on Mérimée here, where
'Mérimée's superb self-effacement, his impersonality' is
the personal trait. In his earlier work other principles
seemed more important to Mr Pater, but as he grew older
this one seems to have become more dominant.

This idea, however, even when urgently insisted upon,
is not in itself strikingly original; in Mr Pater's mind
it seems to have been connected with another: not the representative quality of style only, but the moral quality
of it, the formative power of good style, the transmuta-
tion, in a way, not here of conduct into expression, but of
expression back again into conduct. The formative power of
style — he never stated exactly his conception of it. In
his earlier days he pressed his conviction that the function of art was to give the highest quality to the passing
moment; pressed it in a manner so focused and surcharged
that it is not easily forgotten. But the later conception,
that style may be a force in life, an influence on character, this idea never came to perfectly definite expression
in Mr Pater's work. It is by stray hints here and there
that one becomes conscious of it — by stray hints and by
its reflection on his own writing. In the last chapter of
'Plato and Platonism' is there something approaching a
clear statement, but in this volume only dim allusions.
Still, this vaguer, less definite conception of the influ-

ence of art in life seems largely to have taken the place
of the earlier theory which has offended so many who only
half understood it.

If, however, this last volume gives us no new light upon
the problem opened in the last lecture on Plato, it does
show us clearly enough another development of the representative power of style, and that in the style of Mr Pater
himself. His earlier way of writing — the Conclusion to
'The Renaissance' is the best example, although the passage on La Gioconda seems to be most quoted — his earlier
style has here given place to a mode of expression very
different. We have an example of the early work in the Oxford essay in this volume, which forms a quaint contrast
with the writing of later years — a sort of journeyman's
masterpiece, it seems. Interesting also is this lecture
on Mérimée, which in the beginning is as diamond-like as
if he had written it twenty years ago, perhaps consciously
so with a view to its subject. But in a few pages we have
the later style, the suggestion, the colloquial tone, which
marks all his later writings. Instead of the clear, direct
statements, we have all the armory of suggestion, the conjecture, the approximation, the remark to the reader, the
exclamation. And, instead of the brilliancy and grace of
literary tradition, we have countless indications of an
effort to come nearer to real speech. So his style becomes less and less of a formal court costume, and more
and more the every-day working-dress of an intense and cultivated intellect. To some degree also is it the mirror —
and here let us recall that idea that style has a formative
power, a molding quality — the mirror, not so much of Mr
Pater's actual temper, probably, as of the temper which we
may think one of his ideals. Sensitive it is, subtle
enough, and yet masculine and persistently truthful, putting persuasion in the place of crying and striving, attaining its end by reasonable influence instead of by authority,
looking on all sides of the matter, dissatisfied with cut-
and-dried conventionalities, scholarly but not pedantic, and
therefore clear-sighted and keen, judging possibilities and
probabilities rather than setting the thing down *ex cathedra*,
and very human all the time, speaking to the reader as a
friend to a friend. And all these characteristics, which
might be of a man rather than of a way of writing, may have
been to some extent qualities of the temper which Mr Pater
conceived of as best for one who would see clearly all the
shows of this world, what they were, and through them all —
whatever such a one might see.

Note

1 See ch. iv of 'The Bible of Amiens' (1880-5). Ruskin's
  editors maintain that his insistence upon the purity of
  its Gothic character 'served as the starting-point, for
  Mr Pater's essay on the Cathedral' ('Works', XXXIII, lx).

84. UNSIGNED REVIEW, 'NATION'

9 April 1896, lxii, 291-3

See Introduction, pp. 36-7.

These final gleanings of Mr Pater's work lack, in some
instances, the latest touch of his hand; but in none except the essay on Pascal can they be called incomplete.
All that they want is unity; they are so many codicils to
his studies in art or in literature. The most precious
and significant are in the nature of autobiography. Mr
Pater's readers will find them all characteristic and
worthy of preservation; his admirers will consider one,
at least, unique and indispensable.
    The chapters on Raphael, on Romanino and Moretto of
Brescia, on the Cathedral of Vézelay and Notre Dame
d'Amiens, are the continuation, by a skilled and matured
hand, of those eloquent essays on Botticelli and Luca
della Robbia and Leonardo da Vinci which appeared more
than twenty years ago. It is not for a mere layman to
criticise these, but simply to express the opinion that
fortunate indeed is the student who shall make his first
acquaintance with these less-known painters, and with
these cathedrals, under the guidance of such a cicerone.
Mr Pater here writes in the plain and direct manner of one
who has much to tell and has complete mastery of his subject, one who has eyes to see what many cannot see by themselves, and who has all the historical equipment, the acquaintance with the life and thought of a period, without
which even the artist's eye cannot see straight and intelligently. A far safer and less whimsical guide than Mr
Ruskin, a guide more poetically sensitive than Mr Hamerton,
(1) we always feel that he is most inspiring, most felici-
tously occupied, when his theme is art. We are not now

speaking as a connoisseur, but as a learner who has found
in him his Virgilio, in some sort — his gracious and illuminating conductor in strange regions to whose atmosphere
he was not born. To the literary critic, at any rate, it
is quite clear that Mr Pater moves most easily and most
winningly, with fewer temptations and snares for his footsteps, when, as we have said, his theme is Art. When he
is not treating of Art directly, he strays into it inevitably. His 'Marius' is a series of brilliant and imaginative pictures; his philosophy is the philosophy of an
artistic spirit, of the Platonic lover of beauty.

The fundamental endowment of his nature is most strikingly revealed in the sketch entitled The Child in the
House, here first published in the collected works. It
was called originally, when it appeared in 'Macmillan's
Magazine', 'an imaginary portrait'; but it is undoubtedly
a portrait of Mr Pater's own childhood. It has a singular
interest and value because it sums up all the peculiarities
of his style and manner, as well as of his temperament. It
is a picture of an extremely sensitive artistic temperament, taken with all the shades, the nuances, of some peculiarly delicate process. This hyperaesthesia, which verges
upon disease, which one sees distinctly reaching disease
in many pages of Maupassant's 'La Vie Errante'(2) remained
with Mr Pater simply an exquisite organ, a superfine sense
with which he took in the world so vividly that his impressions became far more real to him than any thoughts or
processes of reason. He began 'to assign', as he himself
says, 'very little to the abstract thought, and much to
its visible vehicle or occasion. He came more and more to
be unable to care for or to think of soul but as in an actual body, or of any world but that wherein are water and
trees, and men and women look so or so, and press actual
hands.' One can understand from this how Marius proceeded
in his conversion. He accepted, in the house of Cecilia,
an ocular demonstration of the Christian religion. He
saw there a family living lives of sweetness and charity,
peace and contentment; he saw this life moving in an atmosphere of decorum and ritual that appealed to his taste
and his sense of fitness; he looked upon the beauty of
holiness, and he surrendered at discretion. It is not an
intellectual process at all. There is no inquiry for cre-
dentials, no inquiry as to whether this belief be true or
false. The intellect has no part in his choice any more
than it has in the decision whether a woman is beautiful.
We look and we make up our mind without hesitation. From
the same natural bent proceeds his fondness for the ritual
and symbolism of religion; his 'love for the comely order
of the sanctuary, the secrets of its white linen and holy

vessels and fonts of pure water, its hieratic purity and
simplicity, became the type of something he desired always
to have about him in actual life'. It is this same feeling that gives us the wonderfully sympathetic and vivid
picture of the rites of Aesculapius, and of the Christian
worship and ceremonial at the house of Cecilia — a scene
which shows us what sort of familiar appeal may have won
the minds of the early Christians at a time when their
religion, 'hardly less than the religion of ancient Greeks,
translated so much of its spiritual verity into things
that may be seen'. As a final touch we have the confession that this passion for the visible emblems and conso-
lations of religion was fed in the child's soul by his
early fear of death, 'a fear of death intensified by the
desire of beauty'.

The essay on Pascal is a further revelation of our
author's temperament and of his necessary point of view.
It would have received some additions if he had lived, but
its general outline and drift would not have been altered.
He describes the 'Pensées' as evincing a malady of genius,
a typical malady of soul, which, he observes, anticipates
certain modern conditions of thought — the ailing help-
lessness of Obermann,(3) for example. Pascal's malady, he
goes on to say, 'reassures sympathetically, by a sense of
good company, that large class of persons who are *malades*
in the same way'. '*La maladie est l'état naturel des
Chrétiens*',(4) he quotes with a sort of acceptance, and
adds, 'We are all ailing more or less with this disease,'
not perceiving the irony of his own admission nor the profound irony of Pascal's attitude in such an utterance. For
the 'Pensées' present chiefly the spectacle of a powerful
and penetrating intellect which has stultified itself by
the acceptance of certain irrational dogmas, and which
bears the consequence in an agonized endeavour to make this
attitude square with the rational scheme of things. To
achieve this impossibility, he wrests and twists his own
powerful logic, he vilifies man, he vilifies the Deity
whom he professes not to know. To his credit be it said
that his yoke is too heavy for him to bear, and it causes
him unutterable misery. With lesser spirits the penalty of
such a surrender is a growing indifference to truth, a decay of conscience that ends in dishonesty; no sight is
more pitiable to the student of human nature than the certainty with which this degeneracy affects certain classes
of men, even the best of men. But, for Pascal, sincerity
and power of intellect were a supreme endowment. He could
not quench it without groaning and travail of spirit; he
had made *il gran rifiuto*,(5) the abdication of his own
reason, and so he necessarily belonged to the class he so

pathetically describes as the band of those 'qui cherchent
en gémissant'.(6) It is the tragedy of a Samson who has
put out his own eyes. Yet it is a Samson who has not
wholly succeeded in blinding himself; the light still
glimmers, and the light gives pain, the mortal pain of a
great intelligence at war with itself, an intelligence
made to apprehend life and the world, not (like Mr Pater's
Marius) chiefly by the senses, but with the inward eye. To
his serious apprehension, the aesthetic charms, the ritual
of the Catholic Church were, indeed, as Mr Pater himself
admits, often weary and unprofitable, 'an extra trial of
faith'. The vision of things must come to him not by
their beauty, but by their reality, by their truth. And
hence, with this fundamental sincerity, there is a horror
of compromise, a tendency to paradoxes and contradictions,
a readiness 'to push all things to extremes'. He is ready
to push even his scepticism to an extreme.

Mr Pater notes the influence of Montaigne on some of
the 'Thoughts', the sceptical influence of Montaigne, as he
calls it. It is quite true that in those later years of
illness described by his sister with a naïve fidelity of
diagnosis, Pascal has lost the self-poise, the wit of the
'Lettres Provinciales'; he has parted company with the
large and sane spirit, the transcendent good sense, of
Montaigne, which looked so far and so serenely beyond the
mists and prejudices and conventions of his time. But Mr
Pater fails to see that Pascal is never so thorough-going,
so absolute a sceptic as when, in the 'Thoughts', he denies altogether the validity of his own reason in favor of
a mystical scheme inspired by an ecclesiastical authority.
'Nous ne connaissons ni l'existence ni la nature de Dieu.'
(7) 'Il n'y a rien de si conforme à la raison que ce dé-
saveu de la raison.'(8) Such phrases go far beyond the
Pyrrhonism of Montaigne. We can hardly conceive them as
uttered before that last period of shock and hallucina-
tions and ascetic pietism which his sister so vividly por-
trays. They anticipate, it is true, the language of some
theologians of the present century; yet they are the ne
plus ultra(9) of agnosticism, for they affirm not merely
that we do not know, but that we cannot know, the realities
of the Universe.

Apollo in Picardy is the realization of a conception
which had haunted Mr Pater's mind for many years, the earliest hint of it appearing in the series of papers on the
Renaissance. It is a delicate fantasy played about a
theme which Heine suggests. The ex-deity Apollo, a wander-
er to northern climes, brings to the chill seasons of
Picardy an alien supernatural brightness, and plays strange
pranks with the monastic brethren among whom he is a

sojourner. Masquerading as Brother Apollyon, he still re-
tains his lyre, and helps by its magic notes to raise the
rhythmical and classic lines of some monastic edifice; he
still keeps his bow, and his ancient dominion over the
creatures of the forest; and, by the spell of his weird
and baneful beauty, he ensnares, as of old, young Brother
Hyacinth to wrestle and play quoits with him. It is a
fateful game played on some late autumn evening, when the
scene dissolves before the earliest blast of winter, and
the vagabond god at last flees with the whirling leaves,
tricksy and conscienceless, leaving the stain and suspicion
of murder on the innocent mad Prior St Jean. The antics of
the exiles deity, wavering between monk and wizard and
daemon, and retaining in his fallen estate the relics and
reminiscences of his ancient dignities, are traced with the
fine and dexterous strokes of learning and imagination
which painted the Amazon in the Hippolytus Veiled. It is
a pretty bit of moonshine, lighting up the fretwork of some
old ruin — a fancy which few writers would have dared to
entrust to the matter of fact vehicle of prose.

But Mr Pater likes to demonstrate that prose is not
necessarily prosaic, that it is an intrument of many stops,
from which a varied music may be drawn. The proof of this
is easy enough, if you know how — *solvitur ambulando*;(10)
and Mr Pater does offer us a rather convincing solution.
Yet we like his work best when he is not pursuing these
wire drawn fancies and clothing them in a web of elaborate
and ingenious spinning. We like him best when he is so
charged with his subject that he has no time left to
think of embroidery. Nothing that he has since done moves
with a flow so free and impassioned as those early essays
on the Renaissance. Nothing, for example, quite equals
his description of Leonardo's 'La Gioconda', as a spontaneous flight of sustained imagination and eloquence.
There is many a paragraph in his later works that moves
with curious artifice, on the wings of Icarus. But the
flight makes us uneasy. There is something in the movement, tortuous, baffling, ineffectual; it affects us like
some of the nocturnes of Chopin. These periods are intended
to imitate with cunning carelessness the freedoms of conversation, its digressions and parentheses; but the art is too
evident, it reminds us of Mr Pater's favourite *askesis*.(11)
There is indeed too much *askesis* for the reader; and readers, with proper justice, object to any athletics of the
understanding which are not demanded by the intrinsic
weight and difficulty of the theme. Mr Pater speaks somewhere of the 'long victorious period'; some of his periods
are long and not victorious — not victorious as Plato's
longest periods, or like Mr Ruskin's, both of which bear

the reader without fatigue triumphantly on the wings of a
passionate and powerful eloquence. Therefore it is that
we most admire Mr Pater when he lets himself go, when he
forgets his artifice and yields to the current of thought
and emotion of the moment. He did this oftenest, as was
natural, in the ardor and abandon of youth.

But the word *abandon* can never be rightly used of any
period of Mr Pater's work. It was always under the control of an artistic conscience that tended to austerity.
For, mingled with this pathetic precocity of The Child in
the House, that susceptible spirit nurtured on delicate and
dainty sights and sounds, it is a singular trait to discover an admiration for the Spartan training of youth,
whether in English schools or in Lacedaemon. The foundation for this admiration is, we suppose, the feeling for
restraint and measure in art, for an *askesis* which may
emerge in asceticism; and the theory that masculine
beauty is developed by such training. This feeling is
embodied in the imaginary portrait of Emerald Uthwart,
which is the counterpart of the sketch of the Laconian
'noble slavery', one of the most brilliant chapters on the
Platonic system and ideas. Uthwart is a young Englishman
with the ideal temperament of a soldier, the tastes of a
scholar, and the susceptibilities of Mr Pater's own childhood. He leaves Oxford after the training of an English
school, and serves in a brief campaign in Flanders, where
he receives an honorable wound. He is finally dismissed in
disgrace because of some irregular exploit, which, though
punished by a court-martial of martinets, won, after later
investigation, the applause of his countrymen and the reversal of the military decision. The reversal comes too
late, and he dies of the double wound at his heart. Uthwart is the embodiment of that *askesis* which Mr Pater so
much admires, of the monastic discipline and obedience, the
vigorous rule in play and study, of a Rugby or a Winchester,
'a sort of hardness natural to English youths', crowned by
the subtler influences of Oxford, 'the memory of which made
almost everything he saw after it seem vulgar'. This last
sentence evidently comes from Mr Pater's heart. No one
can blame him for loving that one ideal shrine in the world
of σχολή, of scholarly leisure and quiet, where wisdom may
be worshipped and pursued in ideal temples, amid habita-
tions which Plato himself might have found no less fitting
than his own Academy.

Notes

1 Philip Gilbert Hamerton (1834-94), artist and essayist,

was the founder (1869) and editor (1869-94) of the art periodical the 'Portfolio'.

2 Guy de Maupassant (1850-93), French short-story writer and novelist, published 'La Vie Errante' in 1890.

3 'Obermann' (1804) is an analytical, introspective novel written in the form of letters by Etienne Pivert de Senancour (1770-1846).

4 'Sickness is the natural state of Christians.'

5 The great refusal: see 'Inferno', iii, 160.

6 'Who seek while groaning.'

7 'We know neither the existence nor the nature of God.'

8 'There is nothing more consistent with reason than this disavowal of reason.'

9 The highest point attainable.

10 It is solved walking.

11 'Military hardness': ME, i, 169.

'Gaston de Latour'
October 1896

85. G.S. STREET, SIGNED REVIEW, 'PALL MALL GAZETTE'

12 October 1896, lxiii, 4

See Introduction, pp.37-8.

George Slythe Street (1867-1936), novelist, drama critic
for the 'Pall Mall Gazette' and His Majesty's Examiner of
Plays, was associated with the counter-Decadent movement.
His parody of the aesthetic type, 'The Autobiography of a
Boy' (1894), received considerable acclaim.

It is too general a habit to write of Mr Pater as the
master of a style, and that alone. No doubt in a period
when English prose is especially lacking in rhythm and
colour, on the one hand, and in simple force, on the other,
his prose is eminent at once, since it is melodious and
finely-coloured, minutely as well as broadly effective,
beautiful always in its deliberate sureness. But it is
well to remember that the master of words was also a master
of thought. His own philosophy and his peculiar appreciation of ancient philosophies — with which his appreciation
of later modes of thought is invariably implicated — may
or may not be consonant with that commonly wearisome abstraction, the spirit of the age. Most probably, indeed,
not a tithe of those who have been impressed in a measure
by his style have been influenced by his ideas, the finished epicureanism — of one whom assuredly Epicurus would
not have 'scourged from his garden' — combined so fitting-
ly with an implicit doctrine of catholic understanding and
sympathy. But to estimate a writer by his immediate influ-

ence on his contemporaries is to reach strange results,
and it is not hazardous to say that when the artistic and
intellectual influences of the century are old enough to
be estimated, the place of Mr Pater's will be found exalted, as it is even now unique: it will be found that he
excited a desire not only of beauty in expression, but of
instructed sanity in thought.

In 'Gaston de Latour' at least the thought is more remarkable than the expression. Yet this latter is fine as
ever; a little more reserved and contained than in 'Marius', as though (did not dates forbid) Mr Pater had seen
dangers in the imitation of his richness, but wonderfully
and variously appropriate. For the most part it is serene
and even, having to deal with such themes as a sixteenth-
century manor in central France and its surrounding
country, as the early life of Gaston, as the poetry of
Pierre de Ronsard and the poet himself, as the talk and
habits of Montaigne. But it rises in the last chapter (an
exposition of Giordano Bruno's(1) philosophy and a portrait
of the wonderful Italian) to a sustained flow of sympathetic enthusiasm — subtle enthusiasm, of course, but enthusiasm. To quote examples of either of these manners would
be to quote pages: Mr Pater's gems are worked into an
ordered whole, not set conspicuously here and there. But
it is noticeable that he does not disdain altogether the
ruder forms of eloquence: witness this, of the time before
St Bartholomew: 'Charles and his two brothers, keeping
the gates of a mimic paradise in the court of the Louvre,
while the fountains ran wine — were they already thinking
of a time when they would keep those gates, with iron purpose, while the gutters ran blood?' A quite ordinary form
of eloquence, but how well it is managed! And we note
elsewhere a touch, not uniquely characteristic either, but
conveyed with amazing effect. Gaston had been sojourning
with Montaigne, and listening to his philosophy of the
relativity of everything, true and false, good and bad, and
of that genial 'egotism' which is after all a wisdom dangerous to youth. Mr Pater barely notices the danger in
the chapter; he is concerned with the wisdom and the attractiveness; and he ends it: 'These were the questions
Gaston had in mind, as, at length, he thanked his host one
morning with real regret and took his last look around
that meditative place, the manuscripts, the books, the
emblems — the house of Circe on the wall.'

It is the thought, however, which is the more interesting feature of 'Gaston de Latour'. Mr Charles L. Shadwell,
who has prepared the book for the press, gives us its history succinctly; it was probably begun not long after
'Marius' was finished; the first five chapters appeared

in 'Macmillan's Magazine' in 1889; the seventh (and last)
was published separately as an essay on Bruno; the other
chapter was left unfinished among Mr Pater's manuscripts.
It will be seen that the book, in so far as it concerns
the personal history of Gaston, is fragmentary. One regrets
the fact, but not overmuch. For it is in abstract subtlety,
not in subtlety of personal divination, that Mr Pater's
genius lay. One might say without great licence that he
was the abstract counterpart of Mr Meredith: his subtlety
in appreciation of the scope and applications of a principle or a system is matched by and is quite distinct in
mental habit from the novelist's subtlety in following a
personal train of thoughts and impressions. 'Marius' was
a full character, though always in connection with larger
matters; 'Gaston de Latour' is but a shadow. It does not
signify; the generalizations concerning the philosophies
with which he is brought into contact, the appreciations
of the age in which he lived — these are the things that
matter. Mr Pater, turning from his own age, loved to
focus on another, as Matthew Arnold, disliking his own age,
was impelled to run a-tilt at it. In this case he has
chosen an age as interesting intellectually and far more
picturesque than the age of Marcus Aurelius. He has gone
to the France of Charles IX and his successor, with its
barbarous instincts running free under an artificially
elaborate refinement, largely of Italy, with Ronsard singing its joys, and Montaigne — may one say without deep
meaning? — excusing its morals. What he has made of it
is here to see. But certain lines of treatment may be
indicated. Pierre de Ronsard gives him the theme of poetry
in relation to youth, of living poetry in relation to dead
poetry. Montaigne is curiously analyzed, in his life and
in his teaching. The influence of outward religion and of
moral oppositions on a religiously minded youth is touched
in very gently and fully. Lastly, Bruno gives him occasion for the wonderfully eloquent chapter referred to above.
These are the subjects; to follow them at all with detail
would be to submit a vastly inferior paraphrase. One may
disagree at times, may think a quality over-stated, or an
inconsistency ignored, or an over-wide significance suggested: but always one admires. At times — very often,
in truth — there is over all the subtlety and discrimination, a certain dimness of manner, a 'twilight', as Mr Pater
says of Gaston: 'Physical twilight we most of us love in
its season. To him that perpetual twilight' — he speaks
of the church of Chartres — 'came in close identity with
its moral or intellectual counterpart, as the welcome re-
quisite for that part of the soul which loves twilight,
and is, in truth, never quite at rest out of it, through

some congenital uneasiness or distress, perhaps, in its
processes of vision'. It is not, of course, literally
true of himself; yet one could not but think, as one read
the passage, of its author. A certain pleasant twilight
there is over his philosophy; but it is only a twilight:
it needs but eyes to penetrate. Mr Shadwell announces that
no more of Mr Pater's manuscript can be published. This,
then, is the last of his books, to the sorrow of all men
who care for letters.

Note

1 See p. 376n.

86. T.B. SAUNDERS, UNSIGNED REVIEW, 'ATHENAEUM'

17 October 1896, 518-19

See Introduction, pp. 36 and 38.
    Thomas Bailey Saunders (1860-1928), man of letters,
translator of Schopenhauer and frequent contributor to
the 'Athenaeum' and the 'Dictionary of National Biography'.
    Thomas Wright notes that the review was written by a
friend of Pater (Wright, ii, 104).

At the close of last year, in reviewing(1) the volume of
'Miscellaneous Studies' in which Mr Shadwell had collected
and republished a number of Pater's fugitive essays, expression was given in these columns to the hope that he
would go on to republish the fragments of a romance which
began to appear in 1889 under the title of 'Gaston de
Latour'. Yielding to this and many other wishes to the
same effect, both public and private, those who have the
charge of Pater's unpublished writings have authorized the
appearance of the present volume: a step for which, it is
almost unnecessary to assure them, the greatest gratitude
will be felt by all who had the privilege of being his
personal friends, and indeed by all who possess any taste
or judgment for what is good in contemporary literature.
It is, unhappily, the last of Pater's works that will see
the light; nothing more, it is stated, remains of his

writings in a shape sufficiently finished for publication,
nor is it unapparent that his executors have entertained
some positive doubts as to the propriety of issuing even
this volume. Only a part of it had been given to the
world; and that part — with which, as Mr Shadwell suggests, and as the present writer can from his own knowledge affirm, Pater was dissatisfied — had been deliberately abandoned, or rather, perhaps, put aside for future
reconsideration. If his executors had felt free to consult
none but their own desires, it is plain that their inclina-
tion would have been to leave the fragments as they were,
out of a pious regard to the writer's known dislike to
republishing any work that had not been carefully revised;
and they protest that it is not their wish that anything
that he wrote should appear in a form less complete than he
himself would have approved. With this saving caution they
place the book in the reader's hands.

'Gaston de Latour' was originally planned on the model
of 'Marius the Epicurean', the most complete and perfect
of all Pater's writings, and, according to Mr Shadwell, the
expression of his deepest thought. It may be of interest
to mention that of that work he observed to a friend at
Oxford, in an intimate conversation soon after it appeared,
that it was written 'to show the necessity of religion'.(2)
There is reason to believe that a similar motive was present, consciously or unconsciously, in the conception of
the scheme which was to have been carried out in 'Gaston
de Latour'. 'Marius' had illustrated the contact of the
best results of Greek philosophy with the new doctrines of
Christianity. 'Gaston' was to show how the later Revival
of Letters, in the form and with the issues which the movement assumed in a thinker like Montaigne, might be subdued
and overcome by the spirit of the same faith. This is in
perfect accord with the tendency of Pater's intellectual
development in the last years of his life; nay, it is the
outward reflection and visible result of that tendency.
If 'Gaston de Latour' had been completed, it is possible
that 'Marius the Epicurean' could not be held to represent
the profoundest lessons which the author had been taught;
and that it remains a fragment is an additional reason for
regretting his untimely death.

Still, it is a fine fragment, or, rather, a collection
of fine fragments; and there is a peculiar, almost unique
pleasure in handling some of the separate parts and pieces
out of which the work was to be put together. It begins
with the description of Gaston's ancestral home in the
pleasant level of La Beauce, and of 'the great, quiet
spaces' of the country about it; of his dedication to the
life of the Church in the chapel of the manor; of the old

weather-beaten cathedral at Chartres, of its bishop, and
the free and fashionable life of young probationers for
the priesthood. Then Ronsard is introduced — Pierre de
Ronsard, prior, although a layman, of Croix-val; and in
a college professedly religious Gaston comes under the
sway of thought and influence which are frankly pagan.
Ronsard's Odes are a revelation to the novice of his own
fundamental desires, and he discovers that that which
had shown him his own nature was not the product of any
one individual, but the general bent or fashion of the
time. He finds he has strayed from the choice and consecration of his boyhood. Ronsard perceives him to be a
youth by no means conventional, and, anxious for his intellectual furtherance, gives him a letter of recommendation
to Monsieur Michel de Montaigne.

Gaston sets forth on his journey to the country of
'peach blossom and wine', and in due course presents himself at La Rochelle to the writer of the 'Essays'. Montaigne is thirty-six. He has returned from his travels,
disgusted with the business of the world, and is settled
quietly in the high tower among his books, absorbed in the
'continual observation of new and unknown things'. It is
a beautiful picture that Pater gives of him, and the long
chapter entitled Suspended Judgment shows a profound grasp
of the meaning and true significance of his doctrines. It
is an excellent example of Pater's exquisite power of
seizing the essential thought of a philosophy, and rendering it again in picturesque phrase and discriminating epithet. The effect of the method is enhanced — nay, the
method itself is almost dramatized — by the device which
makes of Gaston an imaginary listener to the philosopher's
talk, and in places the direct object of it.

It is a delicate art which prepares the way for Montaigne by an acquaintance with Ronsard and the influence
which that pagan poet represented, so that at La Rochelle
Gaston can feel himself at home in the company of one 'for
whom exceptions had taken the place of law'. He remains
nine months, rides and walks with him, sees the essays in
the making, and finds in them later, when they are published, 'many a delightful actual conversation re-set',
having the key to their capricious turns. Nor is a suggestion of criticism absent from this picture, though perhaps *criticism* is a harsher word than is applicable to
the very faint indication that is given of the attempt at
the end of the chapter to find a consistent motive for
Montaigne's sceptical activity. It is contained in a reflection of Gaston's, when, many years later, he heard of
Montaigne's 'seemingly pious end': after all, he thought,
his philosophy of ignorance had not, and was not likely to

have, despised such intimations in favour of a venerable
religion as might be entertained in the experience of the
wise or the simple. To deny would be, in defiance of the
essayist's own observation, 'to *limit* the mind by negation'.
This, however, was not the aspect of his philosophy most
attractive to Gaston when he left him.

The scene is shifted to Paris, the Paris of the massacre
of St Bartholomew. Gaston is discovered in the company of
'a yellow-haired woman, light of soul, whose husband he had
become by dubious and irregular Huguenot rites'. Charles
IX and Coligni, Henry of Navarre and Margaret of Valois,
flit across the stage, and the massacre is suggested rather
than described. Gaston is summoned home just before it,
and his young wife is left to perish, half suspecting that
she has been intentionally deserted — a suspicion which
to Gaston becomes a feeling of abiding remorse. He returns to Paris at the time that Giordano Bruno is lecturing at the Sorbonne, and an opportunity is thus made for
subjecting Gaston to the influence of Pantheism, in the
shape in which it was expounded by the Dominican philosopher, and the doctrine he preached that the world was informed by a Divine Spirit. At the point at which Gaston
is brought to a consideration of the theory of 'the co-
incidence, the indifference, of opposites', and just as
he begins to question it, the fragment ends.

What Pater would have made of a romance of which these
are some of the ingredients can be guessed from the plan
and development of 'Marius the Epicurean'. To attempt any
comparison with that work, except in respect of the leading idea of both, would be a vain proceeding. Something,
indeed, may fitly be said of the style of 'Gaston de
Latour', even though it lacked revision. A reviewer(3)
has already hazarded the opinion that the sense of style
is less present here than in Pater's other books, and that
thus he gains in distinction what he loses in elaboration.
But what a curious canon it is which supposes that the
sense of style is less present when its efforts are less
observed, or that distinction is a sign of little elaboration. The reverse is the truth. If Pater's style is
easier and less elaborate in this volume — and of parts
of it the remark may justly be made — than in any other
of his writings, it is because the art of it is more concealed, and therefore more perfect. He was a most conscientious writer — no one, indeed, was more so. He said himself that the essence of all good style was expressiveness,
the facility of saying what a man wants to say. The effort
was sometimes made too obviously, and where aims are high
the failure is all the more manifest. But up to the end of
his career his style was as progressive as his thought. He

was always improving, and had he lived to the full maturity of his powers, there is evidence in this work that his
style would have been largely freed from its more obvious
defects, and have left very little to be desired.

Notes

1 T.B. Saunders, unsigned leading review of MS in the
  'Athenaeum', 7 December 1895, 783.
2 See Wright, ii, 87; LWP, 52, and Introduction, p. 14.
3 Perhaps No. 85.

87. UNSIGNED REVIEW, 'SATURDAY REVIEW'

17 October 1896, lxxxii, 421

See Introduction, p. 37. The reviewer shrewdly comments
on the mixture of fact and fiction in Pater's criticism.

With this romance the series of Walter Pater's published
writings closes. In his lifetime he issued six volumes,
and Mr Shadwell has added three more of the same size and
character. The material, then, for producing a final
estimate of this remarkable writer is now before the world
in a convenient form. But such a final estimate criticism
will be long in forming, for the subject is intricate, difficult, and various. One thing, at least, seems certain.
If Pater is not immediately raised to the hierarchy of the
literary saints, if his position as a great writer is not
immediately acknowledged, he is sure of that constant discussion and reverberation which are the very food of cele-
brity. Whether he is 'great' or not is really an idle
question, which it may be left to posterity to settle; it
is obvious that he is captivating. If any one gives attention to the formal part of writing among his contemporaries, he is sure to be preoccupied with Pater. He may be
attracted or repulsed, he may approve or dislike, but he
cannot overlook this exquisite, elaborate, personal manner,
so persistent, so concentrated, so penetrating.
   Of these seven chapters of a philosophical romance, six
are here reprinted from the pages of a magazine, where they

appeared seven or eight years ago. With the extreme labour
of composition habitual to him, Pater took up this scheme
for a story of life under the Valois after putting down
'Marius the Epicurean'. It grew very slowly beneath his
hand, and although some portions of other chapters have
been found among his manuscripts, they do not indicate
clearly what the ultimate conduct of the story would have
been. Mr Shadwell has decided not to print these fragments,
and we believe that he is right, for they had not received
the final revision, without which the work of that minia-
turist who was Walter Pater lacks its most prominent characteristic. One short chapter, hitherto unpublished,
called Shadows of Events,(1) will be eagerly turned to by
students of his writings. It introduces us to more positive incident than all the rest of the book, for here
Gaston marries a Huguenot girl in Paris, and leaves her
with her brothers on the very eve of the Massacre of St
Bartholomew, having been hastily summoned down to Chartres
to the deathbed of his grandfather. While he is gone the
relatives of his wife are murdered, and she, half demented
and near the time of her delivery, escapes wildly and
vaguely into the country, where she dies. Gaston seeks her
a long time in vain, and at last discovers her tomb. It
seems as though Pater grew conscious of a want of progression and continuity in the book, and by these means proposed to make it readable. He was, however, no dangerous
rival of Mr Stanley Weyman(2) or Mr Conan Doyle.

It is not for the story that any one will read 'Gaston
de Latour', but as a chain of remarkably ingenious and
subtle essays on a phase of the Renaissance in France. The
chapters of this romance are really studies of the Cathedral of Chartres, of Ronsard, of Montaigne, of the Valois,
of Giordano Bruno. Pater had a great delight in settling
on one phase or facet of a character, and evolving the
rest of the character from it. A familiar example is the
essay on Joachim du Bellay, in the 'Studies on the Renaissance', where one short lyric is actually made the *nodus*
round which a whole web of ingenious and various criticism
is woven. The same mode is preserved in 'Gaston de Latour'.
The author, desiring to produce a picture in his own peculiar style of the characteristics of Montaigne, fixes at
last on the single aspect of that writer's genius for qualification, the undulating elasticity of Montaigne. On this
theme Pater embroiders fact and fancy, an anecdote here, a
picture there, until we hold, not all the man, perhaps, but
certainly a remarkable insight into 'his keen, constant,
changeful consideration of men and things'. A main advantage of this method was that it enabled Pater to get rid
of the mass of more or less unessential detail which

trammelled his somewhat slow and toilsome step in moving
through literary history. Most critics endeavour to obtain a wide, general view, and then fill up the detail;
Pater liked to concentrate his thought on a single fact or
condition, and then cautiously, almost furtively, to expand his vision and annex surrounding forms.

'Gaston de Latour', then, consists of a very thin and
sinuous thread of story about the adventures of a young,
devout gentleman of La Beauce, a clerk in orders, half a
soldier, half a priest, and all a poet, who was a witness
of the frantic deeds done by Charles IX and his successor,
who visited Ronsard, and lived nine months with Montaigne,
and who finally died (we know not how) in 1594. On this
bare scheme are embroidered, not merely those critical and
philosophical reflections which were to be expected, but
also little vignettes of a freshness and delicacy quite
extraordinary. We do not think that in any other work of
Walter Pater's the pictorial quality of his fancy is seen
to so much advantage as in 'Gaston de Latour'. The book
is full of delicious little pictures, each finished like
some illumination of Giulio Clovio,(3) and always with
fruit or bird or leaf to enliven the setting of it. The
impression of Chartres Cathedral, as the traveller of
today may see it, sailing like a great ship in the corn-sea
of La Beauce; the charming arrival of the noisy boy-king,
unannounced, in the courtyeard of Daux-manoirs; the sensation of Gaston in reaching the coast as he descends the
Loire to its mouth, 'imperceptibly along tall hedgerows of
acacia, till on a sudden, with a novel freshness in the
air, through a low archway of laden fruit-trees it was
visible — sand, sea, and sky, in three quiet spaces, line
upon line' — all these are exquisite, and there are a
score as good. We are tempted to quote the scene in which
the young pilgrims of poetry, in their gallant enthusiasm,
come at last upon the prime object of their worship,
Ronsard, in his retirement in the Vendomais:

[Quotes ch. iii: 'Gaston came riding with his companions'
to 'the vanity of great men aware and pleasantly tickled'.]

The first six chapters of 'Gaston de Latour' hold together with a tolerable adhesion. The seventh, called The
Lower Pantheism, is less obviously connected with the main
thread of the story. It is a study of Giordano Bruno's
gift to the singular generation into which he was born, an
appreciation of the lucidity and breadth of intellect of
that mundane mystic. Gaston comes to hear him, the runaway
Dominican monk, lecture to the gay world of Paris in his
comely Dominican habit. And so we part, quite abruptly,

from the visionary companion of so many years of Walter
Pater's imaginative life, glad to have this flotsam drawn
to shore and saved for us, but inconsolable to think of
what has gone down for ever into the uncommunicating deep.

Notes

1 Ch. vi.
2 Stanley John Weyman (1855-1928), novelist, wrote a series
  of cloak-and-dagger romances with a French historical
  background, as well as period novels with an English
  setting.
3 This painter and illuminator was born in Croatia but
  spent most of his life (1498-1578) in Italy. In his
  illuminations he made frequent use of motifs from the
  work of Michelangelo and Raphael.

88.   AGNES MACDONELL, SIGNED REVIEW, 'BOOKMAN'

November 1896, xi, 41-2

See No. 81 and Introduction, p. 37. Compare Theodore de
Wyzewa's views on Pater's method of portraiture (No. 67).

If for a moment we look at 'Gaston de Latour' in the light
of a historical romance — and in a sense it is such —
Mr Pater's methods of portraiture and scene-painting will
flash on us by contrast with those pursued by almost every
other writer in the same field. Like the others, he takes
pains to make the distant age real to us; but they have
ever the air of stoutly determining they will bring it
actually to our door. By pageants, antique costumes,
strange oaths, archaic forms of speech, echoes of the
noise or the brutality that may strongly suggest an earlier, rougher time, by various means, and with very various skill, they shape pictures that aim at supplanting our
own familiar surroundings while we read. Mr Pater is not
careless of scenic details: but he has the air of mis-
believing that far away time can ever come back to us in
its familiar daily aspects, of being struck by the distance
between the physical conditions of our life and of theirs.

At all events, willingly or not, his men of the past look
at us through a mist; we discover their features bit by
bit, and here and there a telling circumstance; the rest
of the space is blank and nebulous, for he will not invent.
This is not the robust and the captivating way, perhaps.
Just because we do not care a jot for accuracy we clamour
for the fullest detail. But truth is not always lusty and
loud-tongued, and art and truth are with Mr Pater. A different age is even more a reality to us by his vague, misty
hints than by strange oaths shouted in our ear. To the un-
changing part of man, the heart and soul, rushes his desire
to completely interpret, and if, bodily, his men of long
ago, even the best of them, are but feeble shadows, he has
shown us with careful accuracy the ways and fashion of
their thought.

Yet his method in 'Gaston de Latour' is not merely to
describe states of mind. In fact, each stage of this unfinished romance is marked by a scene, or an incident,
clothed in effective circumstance. Only he does not trans-
port us to the scene — save now and again to a landscape,
and then marvellously — and make us, as it were, bodily
witnesses of the incident, but insists rather that we are
looking back through a glass that time has blurred. Through
this glass then we see Gaston in the home of his fathers
being made a clerk, Gaston at Chartres, in the episcopal
household, Gaston on his first sally into the modern world,
visiting Ronsard in the priory of Croix-val, going at Ronsard's recommendation to see Montaigne, and sojourning in
his sunny house; a hint of him among the Huguenot
troubles — he had married a Huguenot wife, and lost her;
then later, at Paris, listening to Giordano Bruno lecturing on 'De Umbris Idearum'.(1) The story, all we have of
it, can be measured off in such a way; and wherever externals are presented they are presented exquisitely and
with force. How time and place, the wide La Beauce country
during the Religious Wars, are suggested in the description
of the boy Gaston lying

awake in the absolute, moon-lit stillness, his outward
ear attentive for the wandering footsteps which,
through that wide, lightly accentuated country, often
came and went about the house, with wierd suggestions
of a dim passage to and fro, and of an infinite distance. He would rise as the footsteps halted perhaps
below his window, to answer the questions of the tra-
vellers, pilgrims, or labourers who had missed their
way from farm to farm, or halting soldier seeking
guidance.

And see this picture of the rustic peace that no wars and commotion can altogether disturb —

> If you were not sure whether the gleaming of the sun in the vast distance flashed from swords or sickles ... still those peasants used their scythes, in due season, for reaping their leagues of cornland, and slept with faces as tranquil as ever towards the sky, for their noon-day rest. In effect, since peace is always in some measure dependent on one's own seeking, disturbing forces do but fray their way along somewhat narrow paths over the great spaces of the quiet realm of nature.

Mr Shadwell, who has prepared the book for press, says 'the interest' of the romance 'would have centred round the spiritual development of a refined and cultivated mind, capable of keen enjoyment in the pleasures of the senses and of the intellect, but destined to find its complete satisfaction in that which transcends both'. 'That which transcends both' is not in the foreground when we are forced to leave Gaston in the midst of his intellectual hunger and restlessness. Strange that the theory of education and the history of educational systems should, of all theories and all histories, be the most sterile, the most deadening, yet that the education, the development of any soul, shrewdly, gently watched, should be the most fascinating thing in the world. Mr Pater chose the soul of all souls he could perfectly keep pace with, and the inner life of this shadowy Gaston, about whose 'romance' we shall ever wonder without satisfaction, is a reality. He is of no particular time; he is of every shifting, restless age, a nature very reverent and very sensitive, so that he is peculiarly open to the religious influences that breathe about his youth, and no less to the new thoughts and impulses in the air that are real to him before he has heard any exposition or condemnation of them, or even their names, a nature hospitable to the past and stretching out to the coming days, one that will long be at war with itself, and yet have great capacities as well as desires for reconcilement. Mr Pater was feeling his way very surely to his hero's development, if not to the final presentment of his story, when the work was broken off, and Death forbade its resumption. But I cannot regard it as a mere fragment. Gaston's spirit moves along a path clearly marked out. There is no reason for the writer's most fastidious friends to regret that the incomplete MS has been given to the world. The style, for beauty and interest, he never surpassed, save perhaps in his Greek

Studies. It is his own style at its best, which had every
quality save vivacity.

And, at all events, we have three finished portraits
here, of Ronsard, Montaigne and Bruno. It was the Ronsard
of middle age and failing health the young man saw, his
court days over, as also his creative days. Gaston looked
at the first book of the never finished 'Françiade' in
'jerky, feverish, gouty manuscript', watched the face 'all
nerve, distressed nerve', of the man who had brought youth
to French poetry, in an unyouthful age — 'a haggard generation, whose eagerly-sought refinements had been after all
little more than a theatrical make-believe — an age of
wild people, of insane impulse, of homicidal mania. The
sweet-souled songster had no more than others attained
real calm in it.' It was, we gather, about 1569 when
Gaston visited Ronsard and made his pilgrimage to Montaigne.
The 'Essays' were then only in the making, but the matter
of them existed and was sociably uttered to the guest in
the 'conversation begun that morning, and lasting for nine
months', a time long enough to shake all the foundations
of Gaston's mental house, to let distracting lights in at
all the crevices. Nine months with such a talker, one who
used every human instrument as a stimulus to his thought!

> To Gaston there was a kind of fascination, an actually
> aesthetic beauty, in the spectacle of that keen-edged
> intelligence, dividing evidence so finely, like some
> exquisite steel instrument with impeccable sufficiency,
> always leaving the last word loyally to the central in-
> tellectual faculty, in an entire disinterestedness.

> But could one really care for truth, who never even
> seemed to find it. Did he fear, perhaps, the practical
> responsibility of getting to the very bottom of certain
> questions? That the actual discourse of so keen a
> thinker appeared often inconsistent or inconsecutive,
> might be a hint perhaps that there was some deeper
> ground of thought in reserve; as if he were really
> moving, securely, over ground you did not see.

These fragments are hints of the interest of this masterly
essay on Montaigne in the chapter called Suspended Judgment.

As Bruno came to Paris in 1579, it is an older, but a
still searching, growing Gaston that listened to him dis-
coursing on Lully's system, with his own original interpretations. 'The truly illuminated mind, discerning spiri-
tually, might do what it would.... Of all the trees of
the garden thou mayest freely eat! If ye take up any
deadly thing, it shall not hurt you! And I think that I,
too, have the spirit of God!' These doctrines were not to

be applied beyond their 'proper speculative limits';   but
the last we see of Gaston is as he watches and listens
and wonders on the practical outcome of this liberating
philosophy on the world as it is.

Note

1 Giordano Bruno (1548-1600), Italian philosopher, was
  forced to leave (c. 1576) the Dominican order because
  of his unorthodox views. He travelled widely (as far
  as Oxford), lecturing, teaching and writing. In 1592
  he was arrested by the Inquisition, and he was burned
  at the stake on 17 February 1600. His mnemotechnic work,
  'De Umbris Idearum', was published in Paris in 1582.

89.   THEODORE DE WYZEWA: PATER'S CONFESSION

1896

From Pater's Posthumous Novel: 'Gaston de Latour', in 'La
Revue des Deux Mondes' (November 1896), lxvi, 458-68, and
reprinted in 'Foreign Writers: Second Series' (Paris,
1897), 248-68. See No. 67.
    De Wyzewa believes that 'Gaston' could have been Pater's
most important work.

Here is another posthumous novel, unfinished at that. Along
with R.L. Stevenson's 'Weir of Hermiston', these seven
chapters of 'Gaston de Latour' must be the main literary
event of the year. It also seems that the wind of death
is currently blowing on English Letters. Poets, novelists,
historians, philosophers, all the masters are going in one
fell swoop, leaving behind nobody who could even pretend
to replace them: Tyndall and Huxley, Freeman and Froude,
Browning and Tennyson, Stevenson and Pater, and the admirable William Morris, whose 'Defence of Guinevere' must
remain the most perfect 'Pre-Raphaelite' masterpiece;   it
is at once archaic and new, as simple as a fairy tale under
the striking richness of its rhythms and images. Mr Ruskin
and Mr Swinburne are now the only survivors of the glor-
ious line of great English writers. Moreover, Mr Ruskin

is now a very old man, and Mr Swinburne seems extremely
tired. When they go in their turn, a literature which
was formerly so alive will be totally empty; unless Mr
Rudyard Kipling finally decides to fortify the hopes of
those who used to see in him a new Dickens, or Mr Alfred
Austin(1) uses his position as Poet Laureate and comes up
finally with a good poem.

At least the English know how to treasure religiously
the memory of their dead. Tennyson today is better known,
more admired and loved, than ever before. Dickens continues to enjoy more readers than Kipling. And with the
posthumous piece by R.L. Stevenson, the main literary
event of the year must be 'Gaston de Latour', a posthumous
piece by Walter Pater.

I have spoken frequently of Walter Pater, so I have no
need to say again what a fine writer he was and for what
fine studies he directed, even sacrificed, his life. He
is without equal in his own country for that special form
of literary honesty which refuses to translate its thoughts
in any but the most perfect sentences. Or rather, no one
else has carried to such a high degree, or so completely,
the taste and search for perfection; for the fact is, the
choice of his thoughts cost him as much pain as the shaping
of his sentences, and the best things only interested him if,
in addition, they were perfectly beautiful. But the strangest thing is that these artistic instincts were with him
not at all unconscious, and that, though he was born a
poet, his overriding concerns were with philosophical and
moral problems. He even ended up despising art as the most
futile of all pastimes, and he studied Plato, and dreamed
of writing a Defence of Christianity,(2) without realising
that even there what really attracted him were their symbolic harmony and aesthetic perfection.

For all that, he was a marvellous poet: and it is even
possible that his sentences were at their most musical and
pure in tone in those writings that he intended most especially for our edification in his lectures on Platonism,
in his philosophical novel 'Marius the Epicurean', and in
these truncated chapters from 'Gaston de Latour', where
he has tried to take up and refine the moral conclusions
reached in 'Marius'.

It was, in fact, on his own admission, 'to prove the
necessity for a religious faith',(3) that he had formerly
written that story of a young Roman dilettante, moving in
turn from one system to another, admiring Christianity
without deciding to embrace it, and striving for faith in
the very act of martyrdom. But he had met along the way
so many fine people and elegant doctrines that he quickly
lost sight of the purpose of his narrative: and his

'Marius' had seemed to us more like the confession of a
sceptic too erudite, too troubled, and too completely absorbed in formal beauty, to give itself over completely to
the religion of the 'poor in heart'. We, and the public
with us, mistook the real meaning of that unusual 'Apology': in our naïveté we saw in it a forerunner of the
fantasies of Renan,(4) or of the ingenious 'Serenus' of
Jules Lemaître.(5) And, to put us right, the following year
Pater conceived the idea of a new book where the same doctrine would be laid out in clearer terms. For 'Gaston de
Latour', unlike 'Weir of Hermiston', does not mark the
last moments of its author's life. Of its seven chapters,
six date from 1889 in 'Macmillan's Magazine' and the 'Fortnightly Review'. They were to form the first part of a
large novel, but Pater, spontaneously and independently,
one fine day stopped its publication. And although he did
not stop working on it during the years that followed, as
the many notes found among his papers testify, he seems
never to have seriously taken up the task of finishing it.
One discouraging factor, without doubt, made him give up
his fine project. Had he realised that his contemporaries
were decidedly too difficult to convince, and that, under
this new form, as under the old one, his true thoughts always ran the risk of escaping them? Or, more likely, was
it the work itself that he had judged too difficult to
write? His confidants, if he had any, have told us nothing. Thus, we have to fall back on hypotheses as to the
motives which prevented him from finishing a book, which
was to have revealed his innermost feelings.

The plan of the book nevertheless can be seen clearly
enough from these first chapters, which have just been
presented to us by a colleague of Pater, Mr Charles Shadwell, fellow of Oriel College, Oxford. It is, with few
exceptions, the same plan as that in 'Marius the Epicurean'. Once again Pater wished to tell the story of a
young man, intelligent and idle, who, having done the tour
of all the artistic, philosophical, and moral doctrines of
his age, finally finds peace in a complete acceptance of
Christian dogma. But in order to make the lesson clearer
and to put over the example of his hero, he thought of
making him no longer a Roman of the time of Marcus Aurelius, but a French gentleman of the Renaissance, a student
of Ronsard, Montaigne, and Giordano Bruno. It is through
the teaching of these masters that Gaston de Latour was to
climb step by step towards a higher truth. Alas! the work
breaks off just at the moment when he is about to start
climbing; and from what we gather of him in this fragment,
never to be finished, the novel's hero is still just a
young dilettante, further away than Marius the Epicurean
from any certainty or any belief.

But how pleasant and touching he is, with his scepticism! And how careful Pater has been to describe the for-
mation of that young soul, among so many diverse and conflicting influences! For the delicacy of its psychological analysis, for the elegance of its imagery, and for the
music of its style, 'Gaston de Latour' is indisputably the
most beautiful of his books. And it is certainly the one
most likely to interest a French reader, since it has a
Frenchman for its hero, and French society during the
Renaissance as its background. Why is it, though, that
this most perfect of prose styles is also the least trans-
latable of all! That it is so is no doubt due to its perfection. An indefinable thread links the ideas with the
verbal forms with which they are clothed: translated, the
purest parts of their charm would be destroyed. So it is
extremely difficult to quote the odd passage, here and
there, which can give an idea of the novel's plot or at
the very least to suggest its high literary and philosophical standing.

[Summary of plot omitted.]

It is nevertheless certain — and this rapid analysis will
certainly suffice in making this apparent — that 'Gaston
de Latour' was a fine effort on Pater's part. From the
way in which he had first dreamed of treating it, from the
way in which he treated it in the first five chapters, his
'Gaston de Latour', had he finished it, would have been
the most beautiful of philosophical novels. All aspects
of the great moral problems would have been dealt with in
their place, presented in a living, concrete form, with
the supplementary attraction of an artfully woven narrative. And even when we have to admit that it is the difficulty of the task which prevented Pater from following
it to the end, the event seems perfectly natural.

The enterprise was, in fact, too difficult. It needed,
above all, a constant attention in reconciling the philosophical element with the novel-element, and to think, as
it were, only through the skull of Gaston de Latour. It
needed a deep knowledge of the life and customs of the
French Renaissance, a knowledge at once external and internal, and an ability in not falsifying the colour of the
narrative. And these were merely secondary difficulties.
The main obstacle was in the subject itself, in the
necessity Pater found this time in facing it head on, and
in pursuing it resolutely to its final conclusion.

For if Christianity had been for the Roman Marius simply
a doctrine of resignation and love, a voluntary giving-up
of worldly pleasures, Gaston de Latour, fifteen hundred

years later, was necessarily held to a more exact faith.
He had to choose between the Christianity of Calvin and
that of Saint Ignatius; and, since at the end of the novel
he would have been converted to Protestantism or would have
come back to the beliefs we have witnessed in the first
pages, the direction and scope of the book would have been
altered. A Catholic author would have had no difficulty,
a Protestant author little more. But Pater, unfortunately,
was neither Protestant nor Catholic: divided throughout
his life between his artistic instincts and his English
habits, seduced by the poetic beauty of Catholicism without being able to resign himself to the rigidity of its
dogma.

And one feels that the work he had set himself was too
important to him for him to hazard a conclusion. In the
history of Gaston de Latour his own history was embedded,
the history of his own dreams, of his own deceptions, and
of the long detours that his thoughts followed. The opening chapters of the narrative have such an engaging feeling
about them, the smallest details are so fine and drawn with
such love, that at every moment, by changing the time and
the place, we can guess a strong element of perfect memory. 'Gaston de Latour' is Walter Pater's confession, in
so far as his secret soul could allow itself to admit to
self-confession. And perhaps he waited, before resuming
and finishing his novel, until he had a definite idea of
the best shape? Of his religious faith, the need of which
he wanted to prove?

Notes

1 Alfred Austin (1835-1913), poet laureate (1896) and
  joint editor with W.J. Courthope (see No. 12) of the
  'National Review' (1883-95).
2 By 1892 Pater was considering a tripartite work on religion: 'Hebrew and Hellene', 'The Genius of Christ' and
  'The Poetry of Anglicanism'. See Mountstuart Grant Duff,
  'Notes from a Diary: 1892-95' (1904), i, 134.
3 See p. 14.
4 See p. 138n.
5 François Élie Jules Lemaître (1853-1914), French playwright, short-story writer, and critic. Pater reviewed
  'Sérénus' (1883) in 'Macmillan's Magazine' (November 1887),
  lvii, 71-80.

90. UNSIGNED NOTICE, 'CATHOLIC WORLD'

December 1896, lxiv, 407-8

See Introduction, pp. 5 and 36. The writer regrets the publication of 'Gaston de Latour'.

The works of Walter Pater are not so widely known in this country as they should be. He was gifted with a rare sense of the beautiful in nature and art, and his fine taste is reflected in a literary style which many consider incapable of improvement, in English diction. He may be regarded as the literary hierophant of that aesthetic school in England which found its highest inspiration in Hellenism and the pantheism of nature, yet oscillated between the Greek expression of beauty and the exquisite poetry and color of mediaeval architecture, art, and song. This dubious condition leaves its traces deeply in the last of his works, a fragment of a novel entitled 'Gaston de Latour'. The early chapters of the work appeared in two English magazines, but the author appears to have been dissatisfied with the composition itself, as he left it derelict and unfinished. We think it would have been well if his own wishes had been respected, for some of the chapters in this reproduction can certainly add nothing to his literary reputation. Mr Pater wrote a book(1) on literary style, which is justly regarded as a safe guide. In 'Gaston de Latour' he often makes painful departure from his own canons and gives us sentences which are labyrinthine both in thought and prosidy, and strongly suggestive of a mind beyond its depth, or finding some difficulty in fitting itself to language.

We may conjecture that the motive of the story was an apology for the eccentricities of Giordano Bruno, and the influence of his contradictory pseudo-philosophy upon the mind and action of the title character. Of story there is but little in the work. Each chapter is a long essay, not an epic composition. But some of these essays are amazingly beautiful in their subtility of thought and iridescent portrayal of substantial personages and things. The picture of Notre Dame de Chartres, for instance, to which one chapter is devoted, is full of touches which are like a superb note on a violin, conjuring up whole worlds of beauty and delight. There are sketches also of the poet-priest, Ronsard, and the odd, gay philosopher, Montaigne, which are as mentally satisfying as a painting by Van Eyck.

The voluptuous, fanatical royalty of the France of the
Four Henrys period is lit up by the weird gleams of a
fancy which often acts like the colored lights of a thea-
tre, converting the commonplace and shocking into the glit-
tering and intoxicating. Fine essays all, but not very
serviceable to the seeker after truth in the French wars
of the Reformation.

Note

1 I.e. 'Appreciations'.

91.   UNSIGNED REVIEW, 'CRITIC'

5 December 1896, n.s. xxvi, 359

See Introduction, p. 37.

To our regrets for both the great masters of English who
were taken from us with so little an interval between the
two blows, alike not only in their careful and finished
style, but to some extent in their personal charm for
those who never knew them — Pater and Stevenson, — there
has been a certain solace in the reverent gleaning of the
last ears of corn before the harvest should be ended, in
the trying to cheat oneself (as one read these posthumous
fragments with the old delight) into the belief that death
had not cut us off from minds which had such inspiring
powers. But there is a sadness about the reading of 'Gaston de Latour', since Mr Shadwell definitely announces that
nothing more remains of Mr Pater's writings in a shape sufficiently finished for publication, and that it is not the
wish of those entrusted with his papers that any work of
his should appear in a form less complete than he himself
would have approved. One cannot but respect this feeling,
with whatever regret one may think of the value of even
unfinished notes from such a hand, and be all the more
grateful for the substantial portion given to us here of
what bid fair to be a worthy companion to 'Marius' in
scope and execution, as well as to a curious extent in the
motif of its story. Of the seven chapters now published,

five appeared consecutively during 1889 in 'Macmillan's
Magazine', another (though afterwards largely revised) as
an independent article under the title of Giordano Bruno
in the 'Fortnightly', while the remaining one is printed
from the hitherto unpublished manuscript as a connecting
link which may help to indicate the direction the story
would have taken.

[Summary of plot omitted.]

   Yet the book ends (and we are more than ever sorry when
we have read so far) with the resurgence of questioning.
So, indeed, it might have ended had its author rounded it
out to completion. Mr Shadwell says that 'we can only
guess how Mr Pater would have developed the story', that
'it seems not improbable that he was himself dissatisfied
with the framework which he had begun and deliberately
abandoned it'. After all, perhaps we should have got no
nearer to the heart of things; perhaps the abrupt close
is as fitting as any that could have been devised to a
book of which we cannot but be thankful to have so much.
It is a book to be read three times — once for its deep
and searching thought, once for the poignant beauty of
the pictures which pass before us, and once again for the
music of the style, which is Pater's. There is no need
to say more on that head, if Mr Max Beerbohm(1) is bored
by it, and 'from that laden air, the so cadaverous murmur
of that sanctuary, would hook it at the beck of any jade'.
Unfortunately there are many 'jades' who write books nowadays; there were, alas! not many Paters.

Note

1 In Be it Cosiness, first published in 'Pageant' (1 December 1895), and reprinted as Diminuendo in 'The Works of
  Max Beerbohm' (1896). Max Beerbohm (1872-1956), critic,
  essayist, and caricaturist, expressed his anger that
  Pater 'should treat English as a dead language' (p. 129).

92. UNSIGNED REVIEW, 'OUTLOOK'

27 March 1897, lv, 853

There is a pathetic interest attaching to the last book of

a great writer when it is cut in two by death and we have
but the half of it. What might it not have been? But
'Gaston de Latour' was written by Walter Pater long since,
and abandoned before it had been carried half way. In the
years following the 'Imaginary Portraits' Pater published
the first five chapters in 'Macmillan's Magazine'. In
the next year he wrote an article on Giordano Bruno, which
seems to have been a carrying further of the same idea.
The book, as now published, gives also the half-elaborated
notes of an intermediate chapter. 'Gaston de Latour', then,
although the last of Pater's works to appear in book form,
is not another 'Denis Duval' or 'Edwin Drood' or 'Doctor
Grimshaw'. It was not cut short; it was abandoned. The
reason is not far to seek: we think it lies partly in
Pater's lack of constructive imagination, partly in the
fact that at the time of writing he had hardly secreted
material enough for the task. 'Marius the Epicurean' re-
tains our interest from beginning to end, not by its constructive power, but by the inherent interest of the problems in question, by the development of character, and by
the charm of its background. 'Gaston de Latour' was conceived as a Renaissance Marius. Living in a world poised
between a great past and a great future, as the age of
Marcus Aurelius was poised between Paganism and Christianity, living in a world where men were weighing the
value of the old and speculating as to the value of the
new, Gaston de Latour was youth to whom the problem of
constructing a theory of life came precisely as it came to
Marius. But it is obvious that Pater had never thought
out the character as he had thought out Marius. Gaston is
not so clearly defined, even, as the more slightly indicated Sebastian van Storck or Duke Carl. In the first
chapters, if we compare him with Marius, he is shadowy;
afterwards he is barely mentioned. We do not think that
Pater ever had a definite conception of just what should
be the development of the character, the opinion, in the
work he had undertaken, nor do we think it curious that
such should have been the case. 'Marius the Epicurean'
was carefully thought out, but that book was almost the
sole product of five years. Three years after 'Marius',
Pater began to publish 'Gaston de Latour', and in those
years he had also published the 'Imaginary Portraits'.

It is true that a certain order in development may be
perceived, or, more accurately speaking, guessed. Gaston
passes his earlier days in a kind of regulation of divine
order which had unconsciously become the fitting garment
for unthinking childhood. Even during his life in the
cathedral town of Chartres, however, though it harmonizes

with a certain sacerdotalism of his character, he begins to
feel the spirited energy of his companions, and finally
experiences the fresh modernity, the romanticism, of
Ronsard. From Montaigne the skeptic, then, he learns the
infinite flexibility of the human spirit, and afterwards
by Giordano Bruno he is initiated into an idealism by which
that spirit may almost be said to form a universe for itself, in so far as it is able to apprehend its relation to
the spirit which is in the life of all things. Such, perhaps, was the transition as Pater had it in mind, but it
is indicated only by a hint here or there, rarely by anything so direct as the introspection of the young Roman.

Such a vagueness of development may be an annoyance to
the reader who suspects it and cannot make it more definite.
Get rid of this drawback, if it be one, and the book is
delightful and contains some work in Pater's best vein. Get
rid of the idea that it is a single whole, and you can more
fully enjoy the parts. The scene is alluring in itself —
the beautiful France of the days of Charles the Ninth,
more attractive to most of us than the Italy of Marcus
Aurelius. The beautiful places, the Château of Deux-man-
oirs, the cathedral of Chartres, the fascinating personalities, Ronsard and Montaigne, the appreciation of the
strangely shifting, unaccountable, fiercely passionate time
coming to a flash in the bloody outburst of St Bartholomew's
day — such matters as these are material much to our mind,
and such material as was well suited to the soft casuistries
and the subtle refinements of Walter Pater. He has written
nothing much better than the first three chapters of 'Gaston
de Latour'.

An infinitely curious book, take it all in all; a book
of great delightfulness and of some disappointment; a book
very representative of the man who wrote it, more representative in some ways than anything else of his that we
have. It is the last thing of Walter Pater's that will be
published, and makes a singularly appropriate final volume
to his complete works.

'Essays from "The Guardian"' Privately printed, October 1896

93. LIONEL JOHNSON: A NOTE ON PATER, 'ACADEMY'

16 January 1897, li, 78-9

Reprinted as Mr Pater's Humour in 'Post Liminium' (1911),
ed. Thomas Whittemore, 11-14. See Nos 46, 72 and 95.
  Johnson again champions Pater as a scholar who 'wrote
with quiet mirth', rather than strict solemnity. For a
discussion of Pater as a humorist, see Nos 63, 69 and 95.

A little ingathering from the 'Guardian' of nine reviews
by Mr Pater, though privately made and published, appeals
to an audience not greatly fewer in number than the honest
lovers of that still obscure great man. They are not his
honest, or at the least his fortunate, lovers who praise
but his grave beauty, passionate scholarship, elect restraint, and who read his measured sentences with only a
devout, a careful 'recollection'. Such solemnity, brought
by some to an owlish perfection, is most needless and inappropriate: it is not the right way to read an humorist.
Mr Pater ceaselessly, as it were, pontificating; stiff and
stately in his jewelled vestments; moving with serious
and slow exactitude through the ritual of his style: that
is a Mr Pater of the uneasy reader, to which his rich
humanity seems but a laborious humanism. That reader cannot catch the wise laughter rippling so pleasantly beneath
the studied phrases: he is blind to the quiet smile, sometimes innocently *malin*,(1) which lies as a charm upon the
ordered utterance. Humour, that is gentle in its strength,
humour rooted in philosophy, humour gravely glad and

gleaming, has not the popular chances of humour militant
and pranksome, a thing that jerks surprisingly on wires. A
great saint is, of necessity, a great humorist, since, like
his Maker, he 'knows whereof we are made': so too are the
princes of poetry and philosophy, and thus we are sad at
thinking that Milton and Mill were both without one part
of their birthright. 'Has God a sense of humour? Can He
laugh?' asked a correspondent of Kingsley. 'Yes!' came the
answer: 'because God has all perfections in perfection'.
Celestial humour, joyous and radiant and undoubting, is an
obvious attribute of Omnipotent Omniscience, both in Itself,
and as It contemplates free will in man; so, if we go to
authority, have Shakespeare and Heine told us. And in
proportion to a man's reach and range of vision is his
share in the divine humour, his appreciation of 'Things in
Themselves', to quote Kant, of 'Things as They Are', to
quote Mr Kipling. A heroic sense of sorrow, the very pro-
fundity of melancholy, are not incongruous with the very
clarity of humour: only the narrow and the sour look as-
kance at the sound of the wise laughter. And there are
some to whom from early boyhood Mr Pater, then the author
of one book, gave an exhilaration, which it were priggish
to call intellectual merely, but which rippled into laughter the growing intellect.

Let us have done with the fabled Mr Pater of a strict
and strait solemnity, that travesty false and foolish!
Flesh and blood, life multiform and variegated, things
charged and eloquent with humane emotion, a world starred
with points of interest and concern — among that moved
the loving and patient genius of the man. Moved, obeying
laws of art: so absolute and imperative was the obedience,
that it seemed to many the one great thing of note; each
single word deliberately chosen! Never a harmless laxity!
always a passion of precision! And it was inferred thence
that Mr Pater was a votarist of style for its own exacting
sake, not by reason of the reverent value that he set upon
his matter, upon the humanities that were his reverent
theme. Yet he was instinct with veritable *fun*, and wrote
with quiet mirth, as he elaborated his sense of life's
meanings and contents. Never a sentimentalist, he is never
found pluming himself upon his pathos or his humour: the
notes are never forced. But his descriptions of things
gone, old philosophy or old furniture, are steeped in a
peaceful irony: his tales of young ambitions now in ashes,
of ardent ideals laid in dust, have touches of Horace and
of à Kempis, of Pascal and of Montaigne. Loving-kindness,
which cares for the vast world's dead, for the live world's
'little ones', for what moves or has moved the affections
of men — he possessed that loving-kindness in its pleni-

tude. Maudlin tears were far from his eyes, facile laughter from his lips: his 'humours' were philosophic and
natural, like those of Mr Patmore and Mr Meredith. But
they are direct creators: he an indirect. So, many have
read him with the loins girt, the brows knit, because he
is a scholar, a critic, a humanist, an academic: when they
fall upon a positive and patent jest, it disturbs them:
this is levity, Mr Pater forgets himself! They have been
deaf and blind to the winning insinuations of a delicious
pleasantry upon every page: they would be horrified with
much amazement, to learn that some readers, in some moods,
waver long between the election of Lamb or of Mr Pater for
a winter night's companion. But *truth* involves *delight*:
it is so universally. And both Lamb and Mr Pater were
solicitous for the expression of truth, not in its naked-
ness, but in its felicity: so that many of their perfect
sentences communicate a thrill of consentient joy. To
masters of the whimsical or the fantastic, our startled
admiration may cry *Wonderful!* To masters of the truth
in its beauty, we give a simple *Yes!* of personal thanks,
with a glow at the heart and eyes. '*Sudden Glory*', says
Hobbes, 'is the passion which maketh those *Grimaces* called
Laughter'. Hobbes meant that somewhat severely, and for a
reproach: but it is an exquisite account of the nobler
laughters, those of perceptive joy. To find the intrinsic
value of Webster the tragedian, or of Marcus Aurelius the
tragic, perfectly estimated and set down, raises a 'sudden
glory' in the reader, a joy which laughs at the perfect
capture of *a* truth, the perfect triumph of *the* truth: and
the reader knows that the writer of the royal sentences
had his 'sudden glory' also, the joy of having created
what is 'very good'. Most of us view art and all intellectual products with far too awed a seriousness: we cannot take them radiantly, we shrink from gaiety in high
places, we check the incipient smiles. Humour in the 'hieratic' Mr Pater! It seems a sacrilegious thought. But the
humour is there — there in profluent abundance — as it is
in Plato and in Berkeley.
    This little book of reprinted reviews is rich in charm.
Courtesy of protest and qualification, generosity of praise
and appreciation, a note both personal and classical: we
find them here. And here, in work of no necessary elaboration, we still find that charm of leisureliness and punc-
tilious ease which is so lovable a mark of Mr Pater's writing. For he is ever reminding us of the rich talker who
cannot but talk perfect grammar in pleasing rhythm, yet
without a wearisome effect of pose or strain. Such a talker will be still more happily correct in his correspondence:
his public writing will be flawless. So here, as in the

review of some Wordsworthian books, we have an early
version of Mr Pater's essay upon Wordsworth: it is excellently educative to note the differences.   But, indeed,
distinction could not fail to wait upon his lightest word
and work: distinction, which means an exquisite nicety
of carriage, at once natural and cultivated, equal to all
occasions and never doffed.   For he respected the universe,
and neither optimists nor pessimists do that.   He felt himself to be moving among mystery and beauty, things exceeding great.   He spent his life in realising how his fellow-
men of the past and of his day behaved themselves under
those conditions, what potencies and possibilities were
theirs: he was clear of flippancy and of pedantry.   Confronted with the world's 'magnalities', or with its ephemeral littlenesses, his heart burned within him, and his
fine spirit was finely touched.   Of great men only can
that be often said, and of good men, whose greatness is
to be good and unknown.

Note

1 Evil (-minded).

94.   ARTHUR SYMONS, UNSIGNED REVIEW, 'ATHENAEUM'

12 June 1897, 769-70

See Nos 35 and 42 and Introduction, p. 36.

The journalism of a distinguished writer, when, as in the
case of Walter Pater, it has been scanty, and seems to
have been done from careful personal choice, may be permitted to have more than the interest for us of an idle
curiosity.   It is certain that the reader will find in it
some indication of tastes, some perhaps freer passing of
judgments, some valuable side-lights upon the finished
work of which it was never intended to be more than a marginal note.   And, while he should not look specially for
passages of beautiful writing, it is probable that he will
find them;   at all events, in individual sentences, perhaps a little entangled with the too insistent subject-

matter of the review. The charming little book which has recently been printed contains only a portion of Pater's literary journalism, but it contains not the least interesting portion in the nine reviews which he contributed to the 'Guardian' between 1886 and 1890. The titles and dates are as follows: English Literature (17 February 1886); Amiel's 'Journal Intime' (17 March 1886); Browning (9 November 1887), 'Robert Elsmere' (28 March 1888), Their Majesties' Servants (27 June 1888); Wordsworth (27 February 1889), Ferninand Fabre: an Idyll of the Cevennes (12 June 1889); The *Contes* of M Augustin Filon: Tales of a Hundred Years Since (16 July 1890); Mr Gosse's Poems (29 October 1890). To this list it may be interesting to add a few uncollected, and in some cases unsigned, reviews of Pater, probably unknown to many students of his work: 'The Complete Poetical Works of William Wordsworth', edited by J. Morley ('Athenaeum', 26 January 1889); 'Correspondence de Gustave Flaubert' (Deuxième Série: 'Athenaeum', 3 August 1889); J.A. Symonds's 'Renaissance in Italy: The Age of the Despots' ('Academy', 31 July 1875); M Jules Lemaître's 'Sérénus', and other Tales ('Macmillan's Magazine', November 1887, unsigned); 'The Life and Letters of Flaubert' ('Pall Mall Gazette', 25 August 1888); Fabre's 'Toussaint Galabru' ('Nineteenth Century', April 1889); Lilly's 'Century of Revolution' ('Nineteenth Century', December 1889); A Poet with Something to Say: Mr Arthur Symons's 'Days and Nights' ('Pall Mall Gazette', 23 March 1889, unsigned); It is Thyself ('Pall Mall Gazette', 15 April 1889, unsigned); 'Dorian Gray' ('Bookman', November 1891); Mr George Moore as an Art Critic ('Daily Chronicle', 10 June 1893). To these others could no doubt be added, but, we think, not many. To one who wrote as slowly and carefully as Pater the writing of a review was really not worth the labour it cost, and it was only occasionally that he gave way to what, in his case, was in the nature of a temptation.

Five out of the nine reviews in the volume before us may be taken, in their different ways, as models of what reviewing should be, of what the best kind of review can be. These are the Engligh Literature, Browning, Amiel's 'Journal Intime', 'Robert Elsmere', and Mr Gosse's Poems. The article on Wordsworth will be for the most part familiar to readers of the 'Appreciations'. The essay on Wordsworth, perhaps the most intimately critical of any of Pater's criticisms, appeared for the first time in the 'Fortnightly Review' many years ago. Part of it was used, word for word, in the 'Guardian' and in the 'Athenaeum' review, so that Pater may certainly be said to have signified his own sense of the value of what he had to say in

this notable passage of the Wordsworth essay by using it
three times over before its appearance in the book. The
review of M Filon's 'Contes' is occupied almost entirely
with telling the story — not a particularly interesting
one — of a single tale in it, and it makes one wonder at
the sometimes uncritical indulgence of a great critic's
leisure moments. The review of M Fabre has one charming
and delicately felt sentence, brought in by way of illustration:

> The reader travelling in Italy, or Belgium perhaps,
> has doubtless visited one or more of those spacious
> sacristies, introduced to which for the inspection of
> some more than usually *recherché* work of art, one is
> presently dominated by their reverend quiet: simple
> people coming and going there, devout, or at least on
> devout business, with half-pitched voices, not without
> touches of kindly humour, in what seems to express
> like a picture the most genial side, midway between
> the altar and the home, of the ecclesiastical life.

The remaining review — that on Dr Doran's 'Annals of the
English Stage' — is a quaint, gossiping little paper, admirably done, certainly, and amusing to read because it is
written by Pater, and ending with its ingenious moral, so
delicately just:

> Contact with the stage, almost throughout its his-
> tory, presents itself as a kind of touchstone, to bring
> out the *bizarrerie*, the theatrical tricks and contrasts,
> of the actual world.

'He was meant,' says Pater, speaking of Amiel,

> if people ever are meant for special lines of acti-
> vity, for the best sort of criticism, the imaginative
> criticism; that criticism which is itself a kind of
> construction, or creation, as it penetrates, through
> the given literary or artistic product, into the men-
> tal and inner constitution of the producer, shaping his
> work.

How admirably this defines, in its definition of what to
Pater was the ideal criticism, his own realization of that
ideal! And in this very essay, perhaps the best in the
book, there is a passage which may be quoted as an instance
of just this kind of imaginative insight into 'the mental
and inner constitution' of a writer not easy to seize
through all his disguises:

Yet, in truth, there are but two men in Amiel — two
sufficiently opposed personalities, which the attentive
reader may define for himself; compare with, and try
by each other — as we think, correct also by each other.
There is the man, in him and in these pages, who would
be 'the man of disillusion', only that he has never
really been 'the man of desires'; and who seems, therefore, to have a double weariness about him. He is akin,
of course, to Obermann, to René, even to Werther, and,
on our first introduction to him, we might think that
we had to do only with one more of the vague 'renun-
ciants', who in real life followed these creatures of
fiction, and who, however delicate, interesting as a
study, and as it were picturesque on the stage of life,
are themselves, after all, essentially passive, uncreat-
ive, and therefore necessarily not of first-rate importance in literature. Taken for what it is worth, the
expression of this mood — the culture of *ennui* for its
own sake — is certainly carried to its ideal of negation by Amiel. But the completer, the positive, soul,
which will merely take that mood into its service (its
proper service, as we hold, is in counter-action to the
vulgarity of purely positive natures), is also certainly
in evidence in Amiel's 'Thoughts' — that other, and far
stronger person, in the long dialogue; the man, in
short, possessed of gifts, not for the renunciation,
but for the reception and use, of all that is puissant,
goodly, and effective in life, and for the varied and
adequate literary reproduction of it; who, under favourable circumstances, or even without them, will become
critic, or poet, and in either case a creative force;
and if he be religious (as Amiel was deeply religious)
will make the most of 'evidence', and almost certainly
find a Church.

In this essay, and, at greater length, in the review of
'Robert Elsmere', we find a more definite statement on the
subject of religion than Pater cared usually to give.
'Robert Elsmere', to quote the most separable passage from
the latter,

was a type of a larger number of minds which cannot be
sure that the sacred story is true. It is philosophical, doubtless, and a duty to the intellect to recognize
our doubts, to locate them, perhaps to give them practical effect. It may be also a moral duty to do this. But
then there is also a large class of minds which cannot
be sure it is false — minds of very various degrees of
conscientiousness and intellectual power, up to the

highest. They will think those who are quite sure it
is false unphilosophical through lack of doubt. For
their part, they make allowance in their scheme of life
for a great possibility, and with some of them that
bare concession of possibility (the subject of it being
what it is) becomes the most important fact in the world.
The recognition of it straightway opens wide the door to
hope and love; and such persons are, as we fancy they
always will be, the nucleus of a Church.

This scrupulous moderation, this entirely scholarly
subtlety in judgment, is the most distinguishable characteristic of these reviews. The delicate weighing of justice: we find that in the consideration of Amiel, where
not the most generous or plausible of prejudices in favour
of an interesting defect is permitted to disturb the exact
balance of the scales; we find it in the careful, forbear-
ing review of 'Robert Elsmere', a model of the good manners
of literary criticism, with its keen, at times droll, side-
lights: 'And their goodness,when they are good' (he is
speaking of the men in that novel), 'is — well! a little
conventional; the kind of goodness that men themselves
discount rather largely in their estimates of each other.'
We find it in the delicate, kindly criticism of the article
on Mr Gosse's poems, saying so prettily, and with such
charm of lightness in the touch, all that needs saying,
all that can be said, on its subject. We find it in the
review of Mr Arthur Symons's 'Introduction to the Study
of Browning', where the art of quotation is carried to
perfection, passage after passage from the book being
pieced together, from every corner of it, with an admirable effect of *ensemble*, the reviewer's far more valuable
comments being introduced but sparingly. 'Imaginatively,
indeed,' he says of Browning in one place, 'he has been a
multitude of persons; only (as Shakespeare's only untried
style was the simple one) almost never simple ones.' And
again:

In the preface to the later edition of 'Sordello',
Mr Browning himself told us that to him little else
seems worth study except the development of a soul, the
incidents, the story, of that. And, in fact, the intellectual public generally agrees with him. It is because
he has ministered with such marvellous vigour, and
variety, and fine skill to this interest, that he is
the most modern, to modern people the most important,
of poets.

The essay on English Literature, which opens the volume,
is not less admirable in its adjustment of four books of
prose selections into the scope of a single and perfectly
continuous essay. It contains, too, some valuable criticism of the course and capacities of English prose. Speaking of Elizabethan poetry, it adds:

> That powerful poetry was twin-brother to a prose, of
> more varied, but certainly of wilder and more irregular
> power than the admirable, the typical, prose of Dryden.
> In Dryden, and his followers through the eighteenth
> century, we see the reaction against the exuberance and
> irregularity of that prose, no longer justified by
> power, but cognizable rather as bad taste. But such
> reaction was effective only because an age had come —
> the age of a negative, or agnostic philosophy — in
> which men's minds must needs be limited to the super-
> ficialities of things, with a kind of narrowness amount-
> ing to a positive gift.

'A kind of narrowness amounting to a positive gift'! How
perfectly that describes so much of the correct writing
on which unimaginative writers in all ages are so confident in priding themselves! And could anything be more
suggestive, coming from Pater more significant, or, rightly
taken, more valuable in its counsel, than this summing up
of the question of style in prose?

> Well, the good quality of an age, the defect of
> which lies in the direction of intellectual anarchy
> and confusion, may well be eclecticism: in style, as
> in other things, it is well always to aim at the com-
> bination of as many excellences as possible — opposite
> excellences, it may be — those other *beauties* of prose.
> A busy age will hardly educate its writers in correct-
> ness. Let its writers make time to write English more
> as a learned language; and completing that correction
> of style which had only gone a certain way in the last
> century, raise the general level of language towards
> their own.

It was in the finest sense, certainly — in the sense
in which he means it in this passage — that Pater himself
wrote English as if it were a learned language. It did not
seem to him that one should treat a living language, because it is living, and one's own, with less respect than
a dead language which had once been living to the people
of another nation.

The *Édition de Luxe*
1901

95. LIONEL JOHNSON: FOR A LITTLE CLAN, 'ACADEMY'

13 October 1900, lix, 314-15

Reprinted as Mr Pater and His Public in 'Post Liminium'
(1911), ed. Thomas Whittemore, 14-19. See Nos 46, 72 and
93.

Shortly after Mr Pater's sudden death it was the present
writer's bitter-sweet privilege to examine much of his
unpublished and unfinished MS.: fragments of rich treasure were there, unfulfilled promises to us of fresh delight in the perfected achievements of his lovingly laborious art. It had been less sad to have seen nothing; to
have been untantalised, unprovoked, by the revelation of
what might have been but for that swift intervention of
death. Fifty-five years of life, some thirty of literary
labour: it affords room for production in goodly quantity
when, as in this case, there are also leisure, felicitous
circumstances, scant hindrance from the pressure of the
world. Yet Mr Pater published but five works. Since his
death there have been published three volumes — or, if we
take note of a privately printed little volume, four. Only
one of his works is of any considerable length, designed
upon an elaborate scale. 'Gaston de Latour', which would
have been, in that and other respects, a companion of
'Marius the Epicurean', is a fragment. To the reckoners
by quantity this does not seem a notable tale of work
achieved, designs accomplished. True; but to the worker
himself, in the first place, and secondarily to all who

knew him, it represented as great an amount of intellectual
and emotional toil and pains as those thirty years could
contain. The fruits of them are presently offered to us
in an especial form of honour, in an *édition de luxe*.

Certainly, if jealous vigilance on behalf of artistic
purity, and the utmost strenuousness of aesthetic self-
examination, ever had their consequences in work worthy of
distinguished honour, Mr Pater's work is the consequence
of those disciplinary virtues. The edition will present
its possessors with nothing of 'happy negligence', easy
inaccuracy, blemishes of haste, or indifference or ignorance or sloth. The athlete, whether of Greek games or
of philosophic study, or of religious passion, or of artistic devotion, was ever an image dear to Mr Pater; asceticism, in its literal and widest sense, the pruning away
of superfluities, the just development or training of essentials, the duty of absolute discipline, appealed to him
as a thing of price in this very various world. He wrote
with certain literary virtues, in what theology calls the
'heroic degree' of virtue, and was obedient to 'counsels
of perfection': the right word for the right thought,
the exact presentation of the exact conception, matter and
manner 'kissing each other' in complete accord, and truth
throughout prevailing. With what austere patience, what
endurance of delay, he wrought for that, content with
nothing less, even physically hurt and vexed by less! To
disentangle good from evil in the conduct of life, to be a
master of honest casuistry in the matter of moral right and
wrong, tasks the holiest of men hardly; and Mr Pater, beyond most writers of his time, felt the hardness of the
kindred task in art. Clearness of vision, integrity of
thought, he held difficult of attainment, exacting ideals.
We find him always striving to disintegrate, to set free,
in dealing with an age or a temperament or a work of art,
that soul of value which makes it what it is, makes it
important, considerable, vital. Others might think themselves 'born free' of the kingdom of art; with 'a great
sum', at a great expense of the spirit, distrustful of
light first impressions, Mr Pater acquired his freedom;
and so, little modern writing is so remarkable for its air
of finality; his reader may dissent, but can never doubt
that Mr Pater has expressed what, for himself at least, is
the last truth, or a part of the last truth, about Wordsworth or Botticelli or Lamb or Plato; never doubt that
every sentence, in its every phrase and word, represents
a profound quest after exactitude, and had its discarded
predecessors. Had he, as the saying goes, had 'nothing to
say', such intensity of workmanship would have perforce
been ranked beside the foolish and vain kinds of Alexandri-

aniam, Ciceronianism, Euphuism. Having had much to say,
his zealous resolve to say it in a form of ultimate precision did but mean that to his mind anything short of
entire correspondence between the things to be said and
the mode of saying them was an injury and an insult to
those things. To any readers, should any still exist, who
conceive of Mr Pater as primarily an artificer in words,
let us commend the consideration of this fact: that where-
ever a sentence or a paragraph fails in part to please, it
is never through an affectation in language, some excess
of curiousness and strangeness in the use of words, but
always through a too great compression of meaning, assem-
blage of ideas. We do not claim perfection for Mr Pater;
but when we seem to take less than our customary delight
in some page of his writings, it is because the man with
much to say has been too much for the man who says it.
Wealth of thoughts, not of words, is to blame for any
falling away from lucid grace in Mr Pater; and such falling away is very exceptional and rare. Perfect correspondence between conception and expression was ever his aim,
and miraculously well he was wont to find it: it was what
he prized above all artistic excellences of a wayward and
casual character. Writing anonymously, we do our modesty
no violence by quoting some words of generous praise in a
letter from Mr Pater to ourselves; deserved or not, they
express his instinctive relish of 'congruity' between matter and form. 'By the way,' he wrote, 'I was much pleased
with a poem of yours I read in the — . A certain firmness
and definition in the sentiment there expressed, congruous
with the thoughtful finish of the manner, mark it very
distinctly.'(1)
     FitzGerald, writing to an American friend,(2) confesses
more than once that he cannot appreciate Hawthorne, cannot
take to him comfortably, though he feels that Hawthorne
is a writer of distinction. These repugnances, or, in
milder phrase, ineffectual attempts at admiration and enjoyment, are matters of temperament. We can drill and
school ourselves into respect for a writer, seldom into
genuine pleasure in his writings. Mr Pater brought to bear
upon his large scholarship and various culture a personality of exceeding distinction, an individuality most marked.
His works have plenty of pathos, plenty of humour, an abundance of human sympathies; he can dwell upon 'little'
common things with no less pleasure than upon the Roman
Catholic Church or the genius of Michael Angelo. It is
wholly a misconception to conceive of him as confined to
the chambers and precincts of a palace of art, shudderingly
averse from the spectacle or the intrusion of the 'vulgar'
world. Yet, if his inevitable mode of presenting life and

thought distress you, if his style, which is himself, dis-
please you, you will with difficulty see the rich appreciation of life in his books, his faculty of intimacy with the
ways of life and feeling among many various vanished generations of men. We speak of writers who make an 'universal
appeal'. The phrase is very questionable, even when applied to Homer, Shakespeare, the Bible, to Rabelais or
Cervantes. And assuredly it is no reproach to any writer
that he is not, probably will never be, widely popular.
Messrs Macmillan's *édition de luxe* of Mr Pater is to con-
sist of less than a thousand copies; that number, for certain, does not profess to represent the number of those who
honestly delight in him, of those to whom his genius is a
friend and full of charm. But, if it did, were that anything against him? To court obscurity by wilfulness is
not the same thing as to accept it upon the dictates of
conscience, by obeying the *daimon* within you and 'hearken-
ing what the inner spirit sings'. Mr Pater kept the laws
of his literary conscience as the monk keeps the rules of
his order; their rigour was often burdensome, but relaxation would have been treason. They limited his productive-
ness and the number of his readers, but they were imperative; self-dedicated to his art, he accepted its limitations. If he died 'leaving great' prose 'unto a little
clan' of appreciators, 'a little clan' sure of increase and
of successors, *satis est*,(3) for him as for them. 'It is
not to be thought of' that Marius and Sebastian van Storck,
and Duké Carl and Denys of Auxerre and Emerald Uthwart,
should fade from sight with all their plenitude of bright
wistful youth; that the portraits of Ronsard and Montaigne,
Marcus Aurelius and the Christians of Rome, should lose
their poignancy and fascination. None will surpass in nobility of interpretation those lectures upon Plato and
Platonism given at Oxford: few will with greater subtlety
of skill pluck out the heart of the secret than he who
explored and expounded the secret of Coleridge, Sir Thomas
Browne, Winckelmann, Giorgione. Courtliness, suavity, an
elegant severity, an excellent persuasiveness, are qualities
making for life in literature; they are preservatives
against decay, a 'savoursome' salt. And Mr Pater could be,
in a peculiar and characteristic way, almost homely also,
with little confidences and asides to his reader. Many
pages, to some honoured with his friendship, recall the
gravely measured voice, in which there was often an undertone of quiet humour, gentle irony, delightful and bland.
Learned as he was, he wore his learning lightly. It is
possible to read 'Marius' over and over again, and at each
reading to discover some fresh proof of those toils and
studies whence sprang the book, but which were carefully

bidden to conceal themselves. If there be weight in all
his writings, there is no touch of pedantry; that was as
far from him as slovenliness and flippancy. He will live,
by virtue of much else, but in great measure by virtue of
the lovableness, the winning personality, of his gracious
writings. There is a sedulous avoidance of 'I' in them,
yet they have some spiritual affinity with Montaigne and
Lamb. They will live, 'if precious be the soul of man to
man'. Their *édition de luxe* will prove no sumptuous cas-
ket enshrining fine gold waxen dim, scentless spices, and
treasure turned to dust.

Notes

1 See Pater's letter of May 1893 to Johnson (LWP, 139).
2 Letter of 23 January 1876 to C.E. Norton (see No. 27).
3 It is enough.

'Essays from "The Guardian" '
September 1901

96. RICHARD GARNETT, SIGNED NOTICE, 'BOOKMAN'

April 1902, xxii, 29

See Introduction, p. 36.
   Richard Garnett (1835-1906), poet, literary historian,
critic and biographer, was on the staff of the British
Museum for nearly fifty years, eventually becoming Keeper
of Printed Books (1890-9). He published 'Relics of Shelley'
(1862), 'The Twilight of the Gods' (1888), biographies of
Milton, Carlyle, Emerson and Coleridge and a 'History of
Italian Literature' (1897).

We cannot, with some, regret the re-publication of these
essays. If they were in any respect derogatory to the
character of the writer, their preservation should certainly be deprecated. But it is clear that Pater's own
intimates do not so regard them, since a few years ago they
welcomed their issue from a private press, and accepted
copies for themselves. The essays might, of course, have
expressed opinions which it would have been judicious to
have confined to a limited circle, but their original appearance in the staid and orthodox 'Guardian' is a sufficient proof that they cannot be freighted with combus-
tibles. Their comparative slightness, which might have
been a good reason for withholding them in the case of a
writer of less artifice and elaboration, rather makes for
their publication in Pater's case, as a proof that he was
not always in full dress, and could, in case of need, ac-
commodate himself to the requirements of a weekly newspaper.

400

There seems, then, no reason against publication except
that this may impair the value of the privately printed
copies, which would have prohibited many other reprints of
greater importance.

We cannot regard the appearance of the present reprint
as a literary event of great moment. There is little novelty of view in any of the essays; but most of them deal
with subjects allowing of considerable diversity of opinion, and it is interesting to learn which side of a question enlisted Pater's support. His mind and Amiel's, for
instance, had enough in common to render it an appreciable
aid to the study of the latter to know what Pater thought
of him. Both in this essay and in the review of 'Robert
Elsmere' the instinctive preference of picturesqueness to
verity is always noticeable. Opinions and habits of mind
are advocated without reference to their absolute veracity,
which is admitted to be uncertain, but to their beauty, or
their comfortableness, or their associations. This is but
the hedonism of Mr Pater's early writings in clerical garb:
Cucullus non facit monachum.(1) The review of Mr Gosse's
poems is distinguished by its grace; and if the essay on
Wordsworth, partly reprinted in the author's 'Appreciations', adds little to what others have said, it is at
all events a beautiful piece of writing. On the whole, the
volume leaves the impression that Pater, while not less of
an intellectual epicure than we had deemed him, was less
fastidious, and better adapted for the ordinary work of the
world.

Note

1 Wearing a hood does not make one a monk.

The Library Edition
1910

97. JOHN BUCHAN, UNSIGNED REVIEW, 'SPECTATOR'

25 June 1910, cix, 1075-6

See Introduction, pp. 35 and 39.

John Buchan, First Baron Tweedsmuir (1875-1940), the
well-known Scottish novelist, was also a biographer, historian, publisher, lawyer and diplomat. From 1935 to
1940 he was Governor General of Canada. Despite his busy
public life, Buchan wrote more than fifty books, among
them his best-selling novels 'The Thirty-Nine Steps' (1915)
and 'Greenmantle' (1916).

It is more than fifteen years since Walter Pater died, and
his more famous books have been before the world for a
quarter of a century. If it is still too soon to determine his exact place in English letters, there can be no
doubt that that place is a permanent and a high one. He
is already a classic, ranking not among the greater kings
of literature, but among the sovereigns of small and exclusive territories, like De Quincey and Peacock and
Landor. The popular school with which he seemed to have
affinities has long since disappeared. The aestheticism
which flourished in the early 'eighties' is as *démodé*(1)
as the Della-Cruscans. The world has gone after other
gods, and in judging Walter Pater we are not hampered by
the illegitimate developments with which a school is always apt to credit a master. We can take him wholly on
his merits as a sincere scholar and thinker, who had much
to say to his generation, and who strove to say it, not in

the easy phrases of popular rhetoric, but in a style of a
rigorous and classic perfection. It is one of the ironies
of literary history that work so laborious, so laden with
thought, so morally serious and sincere, should have been
adopted as the gospel of a school of facile impressionists.
Mr Rose in 'The New Republic'(2) is a good caricature of
certain Paterians, but he has no sort of resemblance to
their master. Pater was never foolish, never flippant,
never petty. In all his work there is the evidence of a
strong and penetrating intellect. So far from deifying
sensations, it was the intellectual element in them, the
discipline of their evaluation, which interested him. He
combined, indeed, two qualities which are generally dissociated, — an intense love of the concrete, and a passion
for some principle which would link natural beauty to the
life of the human soul.

The starting-point of his intellectual development was
probably a revolt from easy metaphysics. He got his Fellowship at Oxford on his work in philosophy, and he was
well read in the classics of speculation; but he never seems
to have had any of the passion for unification which we
associate with the philosopher. Among the many imaginary
portraits which he has drawn, only one — that of Sebastian
van Storck — is a metaphysician, and he is the most tra-
gically fated of Pater's types, and obviously the least
sympathetic to its author. In the 'seventies' the revolt
against the narrow ratiocination of Mill and Mansel(3) was
driving the better minds to Hegel and German metaphysics.
Pater was sensitive to this influence, as he was to all
others, but something in him reacted against it. Like
Nietzsche in a later day, he protested against a unification which made life a featureless plain. He became the
apostle of the concrete, the individual. He insisted upon
a value in the sensation which the thinkers who merely
regarded it as the raw material of a concept would not
grant it. It is necessary to be very clear as to this attitude. He did not revive any crude version of the old
Cyrenaicism; he laid down no metaphysical theory; he
merely insisted upon a greater reverence, a fuller analysis,
a more dignified destiny, for the content of sensation, the
phenomena of our everyday life. He wished to rationalise
it, but without depleting it, an aim which he shared with
Hegel, and, indeed, with all metaphysicians worthy of the
name. But for Pater the interest was always less rectitude
of thought than rectitude of conduct. He was a humanist,
and therefore a moralist. Nowadays we are inclined — not
without justice perhaps — to put the moralist outside
philosophy proper. His point of view is embarrassing in
the quest for truth. Most modern heresies take their

origin in his plea that man wants a rule of conduct
rather than the reason of things. So, leaving the narrow
and thorny path of metaphysics, Pater sought for a principle which would, as they say in the schools, 'maximise'
life. With his intense love of beauty in art and Nature,
his temperament responding like a sensitised plate to the
nuances of atmosphere and memory, he strove to give men a
key to the rich datum of life. But he never lost sight of
his own metaphysics. The beauty of Nature and art was im-
pregnated with spirit. Every detail of a picture, every
line of a statue, every delicacy of a spring morning was
alive with a vast and spiritual significance. The truly
spiritual were they whose souls were like a transparency,
in which the wonders of the sensuous world could be reflected through a fine medium. Hence he created the 'diaphanous' type — for, like Plato, he always thought in types
— the soul which is aloof from the bustle of action,
which does not create or construct, but which reflects
and transmits the subtleties of beauty which would otherwise be lost to men.

The true ritualist is wholly passive, and the earlier
Pater was an austere ritualist. He was like some community
of mystics, waiting with hushed breath on the blowing of
the Spirit. Marius, the greatest of his creations, is a
harp played on by every wind. Few more searching and
beautiful histories of the progress of a soul have been
written than the study of this Falkland(4) of the Roman
Empire. He dies on the eve of finding salvation in the
Church; but, remember, he does not find it. He is too
diaphanous; creeds and emotions are too adequately appreciated by him to remain; they flit through his soul and
find no resistance. But as the years went on Pater's mind
turned to something harder and less passive. Instead of
the unconscious discrimination between good and evil of a
delicately poised soul, he groped after active principles
of selection. There is always a discipline in ritualism,
but it is a prison discipline; one endures because one
has no other choice. But the *ascêsis* which Plato taught,
and Pater began to emphasise, is the discipline of free
men. The soul is master of itself, and will shape the
world to its will. Sensations, the sensuous world, are
still vital things, but the mind is not subject to them;
it uses and adapts them. In his last work, 'Plato and
Platonism', it is permissible, we think, to see a real
change of attitude. The chapter on Lacedaemon would not
have been written by the writer of the postscript to 'The
Renaissance'. The discipline of the ritualist was changing
to the discipline of the thinker. He has not lost his grip
upon the infinite and various beauty of the world; but he

is ready to subdue it consciously to spirit, to select and
recreate and remodel. The soul is no longer a mirror, but
a fire.

Some such spiritual development we may with justice,
using the books as our evidence, attribute to Walter Pater.
He has left no autobiography and no materials for a biography, so we are driven to read the history of his soul
in his writings. And when all is said, what a performance
these ten volumes constitute! Where else in English letters are we to find so much subtlety of thought and feeling embodied in so adequate a medium? It may be that later
generations will care little for our old controversies of
the spirit. Some new master may supersede all our conun-
drums with some profounder organon. But by the happy law
of things style cannot be superseded, and Pater will be
read for the unique blandishments of his style. In this
matter he has been vastly overpraised, and vastly under-
rated, and in both cases on the wrong grounds. His is
not a model of English prose. It is far too cumbrous, too
recondite, too unworkable. The exact meaning is hammered
out laboriously; it does not spring up fresh and unexpected like a spring flower. There is always the air of heavy
thought and effort about the sentences. It is not, therefore, a true working weapon, like Milton's tremendous
periods, or Burke's golden flow of eloquence, or Ruskin's
transmuted poetry. Still less is it a model, like Huxley's
or Newman's prose, which the humble man may strive after
because it is English in its simplest and most central
form. Pater wrote great sentences, sometimes great paragraphs, but he rarely wrote a great page. The vital force
ran low in his style. For one thing, in the successful
search for the right word he forgot sometimes to look for
the right cadence, and there are many passages where there
is not a word wrong, but yet the sentence does not please.
Nevertheless, languid, overstrained, and overstudied as he
often is, there are many moments when he attains the purest
melody. From the too famous postscript to 'The Renaissance'
and the description of Mona Lisa, through a dozen passages
in 'Marius' and the 'Imaginary Portraits', to the grave
dignity of some of the 'Greek Studies' and of 'Plato and
Platonism', he has left us a treasury of prose which will
endure. No man perhaps can come so near giving our rugged
prose language the exquisite and intangible effect of music.
He is a *petite chapelle*(5) in style, like Lamb, and Borrow,
(6) and Stevenson, but it is a *chapelle* whose walls are
well founded and whose worshippers will not decrease.

Notes

1 Old-fashioned.
2 See p. 227n.
3 Henry Longueville Mansel (1820-71), Professor of Ecclesiastical History at Oxford (1866-8) and Dean of St Paul's
  (1868-71), published an exposition of Hamiltonian philosophy, 'Metaphysics', in 1860.
4 Possibly Lucius Cary Falkland (1610-43), a famous Royal-
  ist whose sympathies wavered between Parliament and a
  King whom he distrusted. He is said to have died for
  'a cause that was not his own'.
5 Small chapel: figuratively, a clique or literary set.
6 George Borrow (1803-81), author and linguist, compiled a
  lexicon of Romany (1874).

98.   J. BAILEY, UNSIGNED REVIEW, 'TIMES LITERARY SUPPLEMENT'

1 September 1910, 305-6

Reprinted in 'Poets and Poetry' (1911), 187-94.   See Introduction, p. 39.
    John Cann Bailey (1864-1931), critic and essayist, was
a regular contributor to the 'TLS'.   He promoted the study
of English literature as Chairman (1912-15) and President
(1925-6) of the English Association.   He is remembered for
'The Poems of William Cowper' (1905), 'Dr Johnson and his
Circle' (1913) and 'Milton' (1915).

We live in an age in which, till recently at any rate, the
battle has been more than commonly believed to be to the
strong.   Materialism, *real-politik*,(1) business methods,
survival of the fittest — these are the things that apparently rose on the ruins of the optimistic idealizing
Liberalism of the mid-nineteenth century.   Mommsen replaced
Niebuhr(2) and Arnold, Mr Kipling became a kind of national
Laureate to a people who possess Wordsworth and Shelley,
the young 'intellectuals' who formerly sat at the feet of
John Stuart Mill took to sitting at those of Nietzsche.
The tendency has been reflected even in style.   The pulpit
thunders of Ruskin leave no more room for doubt than a
Papal decree.   Delicacy, fine shades of thought, the

hesitations and distinctions that belong to the perception
that life is an elusive, many-sided business, requiring
very tactful handling, are necessarily excluded from these
sweeping pontifical utterances. It is the same again with
Carlyle. If pity is often a note of his work, tolerance
never is. His method of bringing his opponent round to
his own position is always to knock him down and drag the
dead body to the required spot, never to feel his way tentatively to the place where the opponent stands so as to
let him see that there is a path leading from the one to the
other, and to tempt him to follow back alont it. 'Ye know
not what spirit ye are of.'(3) The very men who most hated
and scorned the age of 'bagmen', and its high priest, Macaulay, were still full of one of its worst characteristics,
its positive and blustering self-assurance. Not Macaulay
himself is fuller than they of that conviction, which properly belongs only to the uneducated, that things are
quite plain, and statements about them are to be made cate-
gorically without doubts, cautions, or reservations. The
very tongues that most loudly rebuked democracy and materialism did so with the confident violence of a street orator.
   These were the voices that all could hear, that could
not have been heard by all unless they had had in them
something with which all felt some sort of kinship. But
meanwhile there was another side of the life of the time,
a critical, questioning, balancing side, turning over all
these loud assertions and testing them by the dry light
of a reason which insists on weighing all things, of a
sympathy which is ready to believe that opposite opinions
have each some reconciling element of truth in them. Of
this other side no man was more representative than Walter
Pater. Minds like his can never achieve a popular success.
They have neither the merits nor the defects that make for
that; neither the revealing lightning-flash of genius nor
the darkness which generally precedes and follows it; neither, it would be more exact to say, the piercing vision
which not only sees a thing, but makes it alive, gives it
motion, force, name, personality, all the gifts that can
only be given by creative power; nor, on the other hand,
that blindness which is the companion of the vision, the
blindness of genius averting the eye from all but that
which it is its especial and immediate business to see.
They try to look at the world from all possible sides, to
prove all things; and, if they end in Montaigne's *Que
scais-je*?(4) it is not necessarily in Montaigne's spirit
of amused indifference, as of a person playing a game,
whose object is not to win it but to pass the afternoon
away pleasantly, but often rather, and certainly in Pater's

own case, in the spirit, as he says, of the Platonic
Socrates, with whom the right sort of doubt was 'nothing
less than a religious duty or service'.

This was just the part that Pater played, in his own
field, all his life. That he played it in the end with
success, the only kind of success such a man was likely
to care about, securing the attention of people who felt
that he helped them to understand life and to live, is
proved by this new edition of his works. It is not, one
may be sure, brought out for the ordinary member of the
circulating libraries. Neither the men who want to get
through a day at the seaside, nor the ladies who have
nothing to do when they have finished feeding the parrot,
are likely to read Pater. When he is read at all it is
by people who make a practice of considering their ways,
and not their own only, but the ways of the human spirit,
the way of thought, the way of art, the way of religion.
Many such people find that the things Pater had to say on
these questions are among the most fruitful, the most suggestive, and even, just because of their cautious economy
of assertion, the most convincing that have been said in
our own generation or in the last. They therefore read
him, and read him again, and that is the same thing as
saying that they wish to buy his books and keep them. And
hence, no doubt, the new edition of an author who could
never be exactly popular.

The old notion that Pater was an epicurean and a hedonist may be supposed now to be finally dismissed, though
there were some strange indications of its persistence in
Mr Algernon Cecil's 'Six Oxford Thinkers'.(5) The reading
of a very few chapters of any of his later works would be
sufficient to disprove it; 'χαλεπὰ τὰ καλὰ'(6) is their
note; and their atmosphere much nearer that of the cloister than that of any of the abodes of the Epicureans,
whether palace or pigsty. The truth is that the key to
the understanding of the author of 'The Renaissance', of
'Marius', and of all that lies between them is always to
be looked for in the same place, in the philosopher who
was so much more than a philosopher, in Plato. Pater is
only a fragment of Plato, of course. No one could be further than he, for instance, from Plato's incomparable
lightness of style. For that gracious ease, as of a river
flowing delightedly in the sunshine, Pater substitutes a
style which is often of involved and halting obscurity,
turning and returning upon itself in endless coils of
hesitation. It is true that he writes with a felicity and
precision of phrase which makes it always an intellectual
delight to read him, and, more than that, that his language
seems at its best to have a kind of emotional kinship with

its subject; but high merits as these are, they cannot
prevent our seeing that he is altogether without some of
the most necessary virtues of a writer of prose, has no
swiftness, little beauty of motion, far too little clarity
of construction. 'The "Apology" ... we may naturally take
for a sincere version of the actual words of Socrates;
closer to them, we may think, than the Greek record of
spoken words, however important, the speeches in Thucydides, for instance, by the admission of Thucydides himself, was want to be.' How structureless, how top-heavy
it is, all that long sentence crushing the last four unim-
portant little words with its weight, and they adding nothing to the sense, scarcely seeming to have any business
there at all. There are too many of such sentences in
Pater; and they, if there were no greater things to do
it, would show that the servant is, in a good many ways,
not as his master. But still the essential Pater is the
Platonist.
    What, after all, is a Platonist? Let Pater himself
give the answer. He remarks that there are two opposite
Platonic traditions in the history of philosophy, the one
resting in an intuitive assurance of the highest acts of
knowledge, enjoying a 'vision' of the truth, the other
balancing and measuring and questioning, but ending in an
'Academic' suspension of judgment. Aristotle, who embraces
all actions of the mind, is on the whole the father of the
first tradition, which develops through the Neo-Platonists
to medieval mystics and modern poets, in a line which
stretches from Plotinus to Wordsworth. The other tradition,
coming straight from Plato's own Academy, finds it representatives in such names as those of Lucian and Montaigne.
The first represents the Parmenidean side of Plato, the
firm faith in an absolute and ultimate truth, the doctrine
of the Ideas; the second, the inconclusive wanderings of
the human mind as it moves this way and that through the
long course of the Platonic 'Dialogues'. Now, the point is
that Pater represents both traditions. He has the temper
of mind characteristic of the 'Dialogues', that which has
an appearance of never forcing the argument but letting it
go its own way, lying in wait for the truth to descend by
some act of grace upon the discussion, hurrying nothing,
anticipating nothing. But he has also, and more and more
as he grew older, the instinctive and unshakeable assurance
of the ultimate truths which underlie the argument and make
it real. Beauty, truth, goodness — nothing ever shook his
faith in the supreme reality of these. They are his ideas,
his patterns laid up in the heavens, and all the tentative
wanderings of his mind, all its hesitations, only hung on
the difficulty of finding them amid the confusion of their

earthly counterparts and shadows. He spent his life in
writing essays, and he says somewhere that the essay, 'a
little trench or hole which they dig to search for ore',
as an old dictionary defines it, is the proper literary
form of an age like ours, in which truth is realizable
chiefly as 'the elusive effect of a personal experience'.
His notion of it is that of a kind of dialogue with oneself; a formulated and public part of that 'continuous
company we keep with ourselves through life'; and, with
such subjects as he chose for his continuous self-ques-
tioning, he might well have justified himself for so spending his days and years by those words of Plato's Glaucon:-
'Well, for the wise, at any rate, the proper time to give
to such discussions is the whole of life.' The whole of
life, because the complete solution, the answer that does
not itself ask another question, is never reached; but
also — and this is the other side of the Platonic tradition — the whole of life, because there is never a doubt
that a true and final solution exists. And even for a
higher reason still; for the reason that he, too, no
doubt felt, as his own Marius felt that summer morning at
Tibur, that the long dialogue was not, after all, with himself alone, but shared all the while with another companion;
an unfailing invisible companion,(7) at his side all the
way through; one that might, for him as for the dying
Marius, lay a friendly hand upon his shoulder amid the
obscurities of the world, and make some explanation of
them at the last.

There is another thing. It was no small part of Plato's
philosophic achievement to have fashioned a meeting-place
for 'the one' and 'the many', the grey, motionless shadows
of the Parmenidean unity and the restless, many-sided, many-
coloured flux of Heraclitus. A man of thought and a man of
religion, he must needs bring his world together under one
central Idea: a lover of art, a liver of life, he cannot
be content with an abstraction; his Idea must take visible
shape, must play a hundred visible parts in a complex world.
This last side of himself, however much he may appear sometimes to pass upon it a philosophic condemnation, was, one
cannot but feel, very real in Plato. Certainly it was very
real in Pater, nor did he ever desire to deny or conceal it.
The note of his first and in some respects his most remarkable book may be given in a single sentence of its preface
— 'Our education becomes complete in proportion as our
susceptibility to these impressions' (i.e., the impressions
of pleasure to be derived from nature, art, and human life)
'increases in depth and variety'. And the business of the
essays which it contains is to draw out, by a kind of Soc-
ratic midwifery, the special birth of meaning, the special

intellectual pleasure which lies hidden in each of the
subjects with which it deals. But also, like Plato, and
even in this book, the most detached, the most purely
aesthetic of his works, he desires a unity in his diversity. Part of the attraction which throws him into the
study of that age of the Renaissance is that it is one of
the rare epochs in which the many interests of the intellectual world — 'art and poetry, philosophy and the religious life, and that other life of refined pleasure and
action in the open places of the world', all 'combine in
one complete type of general culture'. And all through
his work there runs that increasing note of reconciliation.
Human life, he more and more says, is a whole: all that
the human mind can embrace must somehow and somewhere find
its unity. Plato may banish poets and speak unkindly of
art, but all through the world's history he has been
honoured and loved by poets and artists at least as much
as by philosophers and saints. And Pater may begin by an
appearance of pure aestheticism, of Hellenic aloofness from
moral preoccupations, but that pressing need of unity will
draw him on till it comes to be his especial business to
interpret art in terms of thought and still more of religion, to clothe philosophy and religion in a human garb of
colour and feeling and varied life. What is his Marius but
an attempt to trace 'the one in the many' of the human
spirit, the likeness between the thoughts of a young Roman
of the second century and a young Englishman of the nineteenth, the links that unite all religious, the natural,
almost imperceptible, progress which in those days of
Marcus Aurelius a devout mind might make from Paganism to
Christianity? For Pater's unity is not one of lifeless
immobility, but that of a process, or rather of a growing
organism; so that in the field of literature he will once,
by a curious freak, dare to say that the chief use of
studying the old masters is the help they give in interpreting the new. But, whatever we may think of that, his
controlling desire of unity is everywhere evident. He is
interested in Goethe as illustrating the union of the subjectivity and adventure of the romantic spirit with the
rationality of Hellenism; he delights, in his 'Greek
Studies', especially Demeter and Persephone, in finding
traces of things commonly denied to Greece, the Christian
'worship of sorrow' and the romantic power of extracting
beauty out of things strange and painful; and all through
'Plato and Platonism' he is for ever using Hebrew and
Christian language, applying 'sitivit anima mea in Deum,
in Deum vivum'(8) to Socrates, closing his account of the
violently attained unity of the Platonic Republic with
'that they all may be one', often bringing in such words

as 'sacramental' and 'penitential', yet not forcing any
parallel, but letting the mere fitness of the alien words
bear its silent witness to the human kinship of Jew and
Greek, to the ordered, harmonious, not unnatural progress
of the world.

This is, at any rate, one aspect of Pater, and perhaps
not the least interesting. In a time of loud voices and
much eloquent striving and crying, art scorning morals and
morals denouncing art, the Church anathematizing the criticism of culture, culture dreading the obscurantism of the
Church, Pater felt his way along, through hesitations and
scruples, to a unity for which no serious effort of the
human spirit could be an object either of scorn or of
dread or of denunciation. He was the high priest of the
artistic world of his day; but he was also a Puritan, an
ascetic of the asceticism which, as he liked to relate,
was practised in Sparta and took its place in the ideal of
the Hellenic world through the immortal pages of Plato.

Notes

1 A political term signifying a mixture of Bismarckian
  and Machiavellian pragmatism.
2 Theodor Mommsen (1817-1903), German classical scholar,
  historian and author of the celebrated 'History of Rome'
  (1854-6). Barthold Georg Niebuhr (1776-1831), historian,
  statesman and philologist.
3 Luke ix, 55.
4 'Who knows?' PP, 176.
5 Published in 1909.
6 'Things which are noble are difficult.'
7 Ch. xix of 'Marius'.
8 'My soul thirsts for God, the living God': Psalms xlii, 2.

99. LAURENCE BINYON: A POSTSCRIPT TO 'THE RENAISSANCE',
'SATURDAY REVIEW'

15 October 1910, cx, 481

Robert Laurence Binyon (1869-1943), poet, art historian,
critic and translator. He was a member of staff (1893-
1933) of the British Museum; from 1913 he was Keeper of
paintings and drawings. His study of 'Painting in the Far

East' (1908) was the first European treatise on the subject.
Binyon achieved a reputation as a poet untouched by *fin de
siècle* ideas, strongly in the tradition of Wordsworth and
Arnold.

In the preceding paragraphs Binyon discusses Finberg's
(see p. 415n) assertion that 'the contemporary criticism
of art is bankrupt.

... Current criticism of art, I should say, to speak of
the general fashion, not the exception, derives from
Pater's essay on the school of Giorgione, helped out by
the memory of some of Whistler's witty sayings. Now
Pater's essay is an excellent starting-point for one who
wishes to appreciate the arts, just as Whistler's epigrams often hit the nail on the head with remarkable precision; but at second or third hand the ideas suggested
by these originals are apt to become blunted, vague and
flaccid. To Pater we owe the use in criticism of art of
the word 'literary', since so unthinkingly repeated; to
Pater indirectly and to Whistler directly we owe the notion of employing musical terms for pictorial qualities;
and what was once a useful corrective, full of right suggestion, has been hackneyed into staleness. Since original
doctrines always tend to become perverted and obscured in
use, let us return for a moment to Pater and see what he
really said.

'All art constantly aspires towards the condition of
music.'(1) Whether this is true or not I am too ignorant
of music to decide; but when Pater says that the ideal
condition of art is for the matter to be inseparable from
the form, I understand and agree. As interpreted by other
people, however, it seems to me that this saying has been
made to express the theory that perfection lies not in
the perfect melting of matter into form but in the emptying
of matter from form. Not fusion but attenuation has been
proclaimed the principle, as if the ideal achievement of
art were an arabesque devoid of ulterior meaning. Pater
does not say this. What he is emphasising is the extreme
importance of the sensuous element in all the arts; on
the fact, which we have only to consult experience to
verify, that by appeal to something in us which lies deeper than everyday consciousness, or than language can arti-
culate, sounds, forms and colours, ordered by creative
genius, move and affect us more powerfully than abstract
ideas, however exalted, expressed and explainable by pure
intelligence; nay more, that ideas only inspire and impress us when embodied in rhythmical form of one kind or

another. But far from drawing the conclusion made by
Pater himself that the lyric, for instance, is 'the highest and most complete form of poetry' and the painting
which corresponds to the lyric the highest and most complete form of pictorial art, I maintain that the richer,
the more complex and more significant the material fused
in the form, the greater and more splendid the work of art,
the higher and completer the triumph of the artist. I will
not admit that any lyric is more perfect in its fusion of
the elements it contains than the 'Agamemnon' or 'King
Lear', or any painting of an impression than the 'Bacchus
and Ariadne'.(2) More than this: the best works in a
slight kind have been produced, for the most part, not by
those who limited themselves to such forms but by those
who brought to these the rich experience gained upon more
complex themes. Perhaps the most memorable landscapes
have been made by figure-painters.

Pater's language has also led to misconceptions where
he writes of 'a merely poetical, or what may be called
literary interest', for he defines this interest in painting or sculpture as 'addressed to the pure intelligence'.
What he means here is the interest in the matter of a work
of art which can be distinguished and separated from the
interest in the form. But poetry is in precisely the same
condition with painting in this regard. It is never addressed to the pure intelligence. This passage is the
weak point of that beautiful essay.

Elsewhere in the same volume Pater often uses a fruitful phrase which very aptly suggests the primary relation
of the artist to his material; he writes of the 'virtue'
which is in things, in landscapes, in human character, in
the sense we give to the word in speaking of 'a herb, a
wine, a gem'; and it is this special 'virtue' which the
artist draws out from his material. For though in a sense
it is true that, as Mr Finberg(3) writes of Turner, 'natural facts' become in the making of a work of art 'the symbols of mere ideas and emotions', there must be some vital
relation between the facts, the concrete stuff, and the
ideas or emotions of the artist; and at times in Turner's
work, as often in that of lesser artists, this vital relation was lost. The artist expresses reality by identifying himself with the genius of the nature he contemplates,
at the same time that by ordering and recomposing these essential elements he makes them in their turn expressive of
his own mind.

Notes

1 See R, 135.
2 Executed (1522-3) by Titian.
3 Alexander Joseph Finberg (1866-1939), historian of English art, was invited by the Trustees of the National
  Gallery to complete the arrangement of the drawings of
  the Turner Bequest begun by Ruskin. Finberg wrote a
  number of books on the painter, among them 'Turner's
  Sketches and Drawings' (1910).

100. P.E. MORE, SIGNED REVIEW, 'NATION'

13 April 1911, xvii, 365-8

A slightly altered version is reproduced in the eighth
series of the 'Shelbourne Essays: The Drift of Romanticism' (New York, 1913), 83-115. See Introduction, pp. 5 and 39.

Paul Elmer More (1864-1937), the American critic, was
associated with Irving Babbitt (1865-1933) and T.S. Eliot
(1888-1965) in a philosophical and critical movement known
as the New Humanism, which flourished in the 1920s and
1930s and which espoused the ideals of tradition and classicism. From 1901 to 1914 he exerted a great influence as
journalist and editor of the 'Independent', the New York
'Evening Post' and the 'Nation'. He published eleven
volumes of 'Shelbourne Essays' (1904-21), in which he established the principles of the movement's doctrine.
     This review marks the decline of Pater's posthumous
reputation. More finds Pater a typical product of Oxford —
a writer with the wrong values and a critic with no sense
of discrimination.

Whatever else one may say of Pater, however one may like
or dislike him, he stands in the complex, elusive nineteenth century as a clear sign of something fixed and
known. But he performs this office not as a critic, as he
is commonly reckoned; indeed, of the critical mind, exactly speaking, he had little, being at once something more
and something less than this. It is, of course, legitimate
to take the expression of life as it comes to the critic in

literature, and from this to develop a philosophy and
vision of the critic's own; and this rather than any
weighing of relative values was the intention of Pater.
Such an aim is entirely justifiable, but it is not justifiable to misunderstand or falsify the basis on which the
critic's own fabric is to be reared. If he is true critic
his first concern must be the right interpretation of the
documents before him, and whatever else he may have to
offer must proceed from primary veracity of intention or
vision. Just here Pater faulted, or defaulted. He has
much to say that is interesting, even persuasive, about
the great leaders and movements of the past, but too often
his interpretation, when the spell of his manner is broken,
will be found essentially perverted.

This may seem a harsh judgment to pass on a writer who
has been one of the main influences in later nineteenth
century literature, but it can be easily substantiated. In
his three greatest works — 'Plato and Platonism', 'Marius
the Epicurean', and 'The Renaissance' — Pater has dealt
with three crises of history; and in each case he has
gravely, though in varying degrees, falsified the reality.

I

'Plato and Platonism' is a book that every student of
Greek and life should read; it is in itself a beautifully
wrought work of art in which each detail is fitted into
its place as part of a total designed effect; but that
effect, presented as an interpretation of Plato, is of a
kind, it can scarcely be said too emphatically, that
differs *toto caelo*(1) from what Plato himself meant to
convey in his dialogues, and is gained by a wilful dis-
tortion of the facts of history. In one of his chapters,
Pater gives a picture, based largely on Karl Otfried
Müller,(2) of the Doric life in Lacedaemon as the actuality which Plato had in mind when he conceived his ideal
city-state. It is a picture of cool colors and deliciously
subdued harmonies, an idyl beautiful in itself and not without lessons for the youth of to-day in its insistence on
the sheer loveliness and exquisite pleasures that may flow
from austere discipline and self-suppression. It has its
own wisdom, as in the development of Müller's text, that
'in a Doric state, education was, on the whole, a matter of
more importance than government'.(3) But it has one serious
defect: it is not true. This city, as the picture finally
arranges itself, is simply not the cold, hard Sparta that
stood on the banks of the Eurotas, but some idyllic Auburn
wafted into some Arcadia of the imagination. At the end of

the chapter, after giving a noble account of the training,
or *askêsis*,(4) by which the Lacedaemonian youth were
drilled for life, Pater represents an Athenian visitor as
asking: 'Why this strenuous task-work day after day; why
this loyalty to a system, so costly to you individually,
though it may be thought to have survived its original
purpose; this laborious, endless education, which does
not propose to give you anything very useful or enjoyable
in itself?' The question is apt, and Pater puts the
answer into the mouth of a Spartan youth: 'To the end that
I myself may be a perfect work or art, issuing thus into
the eyes of all Greece.' The discipline of Lycurgus, that
is to say, was to the end that the young men of Sparta
might be 'a spectacle, aesthetically, at least, very interesting' (the words are Pater's) to the rest of Greece!
Really, a more complete perversion of history has not often
been conceived. The institutions of Sparta, as the Lacedaemonian in Plato's 'Laws' admits without hesitation, were
ordered to the end 'that Sparta might conquer the other
states in war'. Not the indulgence of vanity, however
chastely controlled, but the law of self-preservation and
the terrible survival of the fittest made the Lacedaemonians the most comely of the people of Hellas; they were
warriors and the mothers of warriors, not aesthetes.

And this same misrepresentation extends through much
of Pater's analysis of Platonism. Pater saw, as all who
study Plato are forced to see, that the heart of Plato's
doctrine lay in his conception of ideas, in his use and
enforcement of dialectic or the process of passing from
particulars to generals. But Pater saw also something in
this process that militated against his particular notion
of aesthetics, and he was bound, if he accepted Platonism,
as it was his desire to accept all the great movements of
history, to interpret Platonic ideas in his own way. The
result is a curious 'apology for general ideas — abstruse,
or intangible, or dry and seedy and wooden, as we may
sometimes think them' — as a means of heightening the
momentary perception of particular, beautiful phenomena.
Doubtless to represent Plato as an enemy of the decent
and comely things of life, as an iconoclast of art and
poetry and music in themselves, would be to forget some
of the great passages in his 'Republic' and other dialogues,
in which the practical effect of beautiful things upon conduct is largely recognized and in which beauty in the abstract is placed by the side of the True and the Good in
the supreme trinity of ideas. I would even admit that much
of what Pater says in regard to Plato's conception of
beauty is sound and worthy of emphasis. He has done well
in drawing out the element of discipline in the Platonic

aesthetics — the value of the capacity for correction, of
patience, of crafty reserve, of intellectual astringency,
which Plato demanded of the poet and the musician and of
every true citizen of the ideal republic. Plato, as Pater
rightly observes, was of all men faithful to the old Greek
saying, *beauty is hard to attain*. But Pater's interpretation of Plato ends in a creed which Plato would have rejected with utter indignation. To recommend the pursuit
of ideas for the sake of lending piquancy to the pheno-
menal, to use the intellectual apparatus in order to en-
hance the significance of the particular object, to undergo
philosophical discipline for the sake of adding zest to
sensuous pleasure; in a word, to make truth the servant
of beauty, and goodness the servant of pleasure, is to
uphold a doctrine essentially and uncompromisingly the contrary of everything that Plato believed and held sacred.
To follow such a course, however purely and austerely
beauty may be conceived, is, as Plato says, to be ἥττων
τῶν καλῶν, the subject of beautiful things and not their
master. Plato taught that the perception of beauty in the
particular object was one of the means by which a man might
rise to contemplation of the idea of beauty in the intellectual world, and wherever he saw the danger of inverting
this order, as Pater and many other self-styled Platonists
have inverted it, he could speak of art with all the austerity of a Puritan. There is no sentence in the dialogues
that cuts more deeply into the heart of his philosophy than
the foreboding exclamation: 'When any one prefers beauty
to virtue, what is this but the real and utter dishonor
of the soul?'

II

From the study of 'Plato and Platonism' we turn naturally
to the greatest of Pater's works, 'Marius the Epicurean',
and here again we are confronted by a false interpretation
of one of the critical moments of history. The theme of
'Marius', I need scarcely say, is the life of a young Italian who, in the age of Marcus Aurelius, is searching for
some guiding motive amid the dissolution of all traditions.
He sees the world about him, the world at least that has
outgrown the ancestral belief in the gods, and has not sunk
into frivolity or sad skepticism, divided between the two
sects of the Epicureans and the Stoics; and the larger part
of the story is really a disquisition on the effect of
these opposed philosophies upon the human soul. In the
choice of Epicureanism instead of the harsher Stoic creed
as a preparation for Christian faith, Pater, I think, shows

a true knowledge of the human heart. Pascal, it will be
remembered, found himself fifteen centuries later face to
face with the revived tenets of Epicurus and Zeno, which
are indeed the expression of the two main tendencies, not
of one time but of all times, of those who attempt to stop
in a religious philosophy just short of religion; and
Pascal, too, saw that the step from Epicureanism to Christianity was easier than from Stoicism. So far Pater in
his account of the relation of the Pagan philosophies and
Christianity was psychologically right, but his portrayal
of Christianity itself one is compelled to condemn in the
same terms as his portrayal of Platonism. Read the story
of Marius at the home of the Christian Cecilia and at the
service of the mass, and you will feel that here is no
picture of a militant faith in training for the conquest
of the world, of a sect looking for struggle and moral re-
generation, but the report of a pleasant scene where the
eye is charmed and the ear soothed by the same subdued and
languid loveliness that seemed to Pater to rule in Sparta
and the ideal city of Plato. No doubt it would be wrong,
as Pater asserts, to set over 'against that divine urban-
ity and moderation the old error of Montanus' (Montanism,
it may be observed by the way, was at that date quite
young, but in the romantic convention everything is 'old')
— to set up as the complete Christian ideal the 'fanatical revolt' of Montanus, 'sour, falsely anti-mundane, ever
with an air of ascetic affectation, and a bigoted distaste
in particular for all the peculiar graces of womanhood'.
It is well to avoid extremes in either direction. Yet if
choice had to be made between the dainty voluptuousness of
religion as it appeared to Marius, and the moral vigor of
Tertullian, the great Montanist preacher who was contemporary with Marius, it would not be hard to say on which
side lay the real Christianity of the second century.
Against Pater's 'elegance of sanctity', as he calls it, a
Christian might exclaim with Tertullian that 'truth is not
on the surface but in the inmost heart'. Pater, borrowing
the phrase from Tertullian, describes the death of Marius
as that of a soul naturally Christian. Beside that picture
of a soul daintily dreaming itself into eternity set the
apostrophe of Tertullian himself to the *anima naturaliter
Christiana*:(5)

> But I summon thee — not such as when moulded in
> schools, trained in libraries, fed in attic academies
> and porches, thou blurtest forth wisdom — I address
> thee simple, and rude, and uncultured, and untaught,
> such as he possesses thee, who possesses thee and
> nothing else; the bare soul, just as it is from the
> road, the street, the weaver's shop.

The simple fact is that in Marius we have no real conversion from Epicureanism to religion, no Christianity at
all as it would have been recognized by St Paul or St
Augustine, but that peculiarly languid aestheticism which
Pater sucked from the romantic school of his century and
disguised in the phraseology of an ancient faith.   To
write thus was to betray Christianity with a kiss.

III

In the third of Pater's major works, 'The Renaissance',
there is again a reading of Paterism into the past, but
without the offensiveness that is felt in his treatment of
Platonism and Christianity.   Not a little of the romanticism from which Pater drew his philosophy may be traced to
the Italy of Botticelli and Leonardo da Vinci;   but the
tone, the energy, the êthos, are changed.   The nature of
the change cannot be better displayed than in the famous
description of La Gioconda in the essay on Leonardo da
Vinci, which is too familiar for quotation.   Now I shall
not criticise this famous passage for its treatment of
plain facts.   Those who care to see how far Pater has de-
párted from the inconveniences of history may consult the
monograph of Salomon Reinach(6) in No 2 of the 'Bulletin
des Musées de France' for 1909.   And, after all, Pater
was not dealing with facts, but with emotions;   as a 'lover
of strange souls', to use his own phrase, he was analyzing
the impression made upon him by this picture, and trying
to reach through it a definition of the chief elements of
Leonardo's genius.   Yet viewed even in that light, the
description rings false — not so false as his interpretations of Platonism and Christianity, but still subtly
perversive of the truth.   It may be true in a way that the
genius of Leonardo, as Goethe said, had 'thought itself
weary' — müde sich gedacht; but the deadly and deliberate
languor that trails through the lines of Pater — not, I
admit, without its own ambiguous and troubling beauty —
has no correspondence in the virile art of Leonardo.   And
whatever may have been the sins of Leonardo in the flesh,
and whatever may have been his intellectual doubts or in-
differences, he would not have understood that strange and
frequent identification among the modern romantics of the
soul and disease.   Into the face of Mona Lisa, says Pater,
'the soul with all its maladies has passed'!   as if health
were incompatible with the possession of a soul.
    The simple truth is that Pater was in no proper sense of
the word a critic at all.   History was only an extension
of his own ego, and he saw himself withersoever he turned

his eyes. To form any just estimate of Pater's work, we
must forget the critical form in which so much of his writing is couched, and regard the substance of his own philosophy apart from any apparent relation to the period or
person to which it is transferred. And here we are aided
by the singular consistency of his nature. In his works
all is of a piece, and all is the perfectly lucid out-
growth of an unvarying design and of a single attitude
toward the world.

                          IV

   If we search for the sources of this design, apart from
the original character of the artist himself, we shall
find them without difficulty. Among English writers he
himself would probably have ascribed the chief influence
upon him to Ruskin, but as a matter of fact I suspect that
the more dominating personal influence came from another
and more insinuating mind. I do not certainly know that
Pater ever met Rossetti in the flesh, but he recognized
that great and sad genius as one of his teachers.
   But however Pater may seem to have lighted his torch at
Rossetti's flame, we must not overlook the strong impersonal influence that emanated from the memories and the
very stones of Oxford. We all know Matthew Arnold's apostrophe to the 'home of lost causes, and forsaken beliefs,
and unpopular names, and impossible loyalties'; to the
dream city that 'lies, spreading her gardens to the moonlight, and whispering from her towers the last enchant-
ments of the Middle Ages'.(7) The call of Oxford is, as
her lover says, to beauty and to higher ideals; but there
is an aspect of her appeal which is not without its fascinating danger. From the beginning she has been the home of
secluded causes as well as lost causes; she has stood always as a protest against the coarse and ephemeral changes
of civilization, but she has maintained this centre of
calm too much by a withdrawal from life rather than by
strong control. Hers at her origin was the ideal of monasticism and of faith fleeing the world; her loyalty to the
King was strongest when loyalty meant a separation from
the great powers of political expansion; her religious
revival in the nineteenth century was not only the desire
of resuscitating an impossible past, but sought also to
sever the forms of worship entirely from the influence of
the state and of the people. Certainly much good has come
out of this pride of seclusion, and waves of spiritual
force have continually emanated from this reservoir of
memory; but it is true also that these influences have

often ended in sterility or have tended to widen rather
than close up the unfortunate gap between the utilitarian
and the sentimental phases of English life. In a word,
they have been too often a reinforcement to the romantic
ideal of the imagination as a worship of beauty isolated
from, and in the end despised by, the real interests of
life, and too seldom a reinforcement of the classical
ideal of the imagination as an active power in life itself.
The very contrast of the enchanted towers of Oxford with
the hideous chimneys of one of England's great manufactur-
ing towns seems to give to the university an atmosphere of
aesthetic unreality. Ideas do not circulate here as they
do in a university like that of Paris, situated at the
heart of the national life, and in too many of the books
that come from Oxford one feels the breath of a fine traditional culture that has somehow every excellent quality
— except vitality. And so it was not strange to see the
Oxford Movement depart further and further from practical
and intellectual realities and lose itself in an empty and
stubborn ritualism. Thought is the greatest marrer of
good looks, said Oscar Wilde, and that is why there are so
many good-looking young curates in England. The aestheticism of William Morris and Burne-Jones was a conscious revolt from the vapidity of the later stages of the Oxford
Movement in a pure and Pagan sensuousness. Rossetti gave
body and passion to the revolt, and Pater, following in
their steps, lent a scholastic authority to their artistic
achievements. Paterism might without great injustice be
defined as the quintessential spirit of Oxford, emptied
of the wholesome intrusions of the world — its pride of
isolation reduced to sterile self-absorption, its enchant-
ment of beauty alembicated into a faint Epicureanism, its
discipline of learning changed into voluptuous economy of
sensations, its golden calm stagnated into languid elegance.

V

In more than one passage Pater gives direct expression
to his philosophy, nowhere else so explicitly as in the
conclusion to his volume on the Renaissance. The motto of
that chapter is the famous saying of Heracleitus, 'All
things are in a state of flux and nothing abides'; and
the chapter itself is but a brief exhortation to make the
most of our human life amidst this endless and ceaseless
mutation of which we are ourselves an ever-changing element. That is the sum of Pater's philosophy as it is
everywhere implicitly expressed in critical essay and fiction: the admonition to train our body and mind to the

highest point of acuteness so as to catch, as it were,
each fleeting glimpse of beauty on the wing, and by the
intensity of our perception and participation to compen-
sate for the brevity of the world's gifts;   in a word, the
admonition to make of life itself an art. Now, we ought,
I think, to be grateful first of all to anyone who recalls
to us and utters in manifold ways this lesson of the immediate perception of lovely things, of grace within an-
swering to grace without.   Perhaps no other philosophy to-
day has so completely passed out of our range of vision
as this doctrine of the art of living which has been one
of the guiding principles of the great ages of the past.
We are too hurried for this, a little too unbalanced between egotism and sentimental humanitarianism, a little
too uncertain, despite much optimistic brag, of any real
and immediate values in life.   And there is much also to
commend in the method Pater proposes for attaining this
ideal.   If he teaches that the art of life is to train our
emotions, like a well-trimmed lamp, 'to burn always with a
hard, gemlike flame', he also endlessly reiterates the
lesson that this joy of eager observation and swift response can be made habitual in us only by a severe self-
discipline and moderation.   Only when the senses have been
purified and sharpened by a certain chastity of use, only
when the mind has been exercised by a certain rigidity of
application, do we become fit instruments to record the
delicate impacts of evanescent beauty.   In his essay on
Raphael, one of the soundest of his critical estimates,
Pater refers to the 'saying that the true artist is known
best by what he omits';   and this, he adds, is 'because
the whole question of good taste is involved precisely in
such jealous omission'.   No one, indeed, has seen more
clearly than Pater that virtue is not acquired by a re-
bound from excess, but is the exquisite flower of the
habit of moderation.

Yet withal, the account with Pater cannot stop here, nor,
if we consider the fruit of his teaching in such men as
Oscar Wilde, can we admit that his teaching was altogether
without offence.   His error was not that he inculcated the
art of life at all seasons, but that his sense of values
was finally wrong;   his philosophy from beginning to end
might be called by a rhetorician a kind of hysteron-proter-
on. And this is visible in his treatment of the three great
movements of history.   Thus in his interpretation of Plato,
we have seen how he falsified Plato's theory and use of
facts by raising beauty, or aesthetic pleasure, above truth
as the goal to be kept in sight.   Now this may seem a slight
sin, when, in extolling the one, nothing is intentionally
taken away from the honor of the other.   Pater would even

say that as truth and beauty are the same, it makes no
difference which of them you set before your gaze, and in
this he would have the authority of many eminent predecessors. Are we not all fond of quoting the lofty words of
Keats? —

> 'Beauty is truth, truth beauty' — that is all
> Ye know on earth, and all ye need to know.(8)

Perhaps, in some high philosophical realm that is the case;
but it happens that in practice in this mundane sphere,
truth and beauty are by no means always identical; and it
makes a world of difference where you come out, according
to whether you hold this or the other as your first desire
when the divergence occurs. I have been struck by a passage on this theme in one of the recently published Japan-
ese letters of Lafcadio Hearn(9) — certainly no foe to
romantic beauty. 'They all [the romanticists] sowed a
crop of dragon's teeth', he says. 'Preaching without
qualification, the gospel of beauty — that beauty is
truth — provoked the horrible modern answer of Zolaism:
"Then truth must be beauty!"' Pater's misinterpretation of
Plato was equally a misinterpretation of life.

In like manner, when Pater in his treatment of Christianity placed aesthetic satisfaction before religious
duty, he really missed the goal of happiness he was aiming
at. The old Scotch preacher Blair pronounced the sure answer to such an error many years before Paterism existed:
'To aim at a constant succession of high and vivid sensations of pleasure, is an idea of happiness altogether chi-
merical.... Instead of those fallacious hopes of perpetual
festivity, with which the world would allure us, religion
confers upon us a cheerful tranquillity.'(10) Nor was
Pater's fault in regard to the Renaissance essentially different in its consequences; it may even be that here, where
his temperament would seem to be most at home, his subtle
inversion of the facts, in making beauty and pleasure the
sole purpose of life instead of the reward or efflorescence
of right living, is the most instructive of all. Read
Pater's exquisitely refined pages on Leonardo da Vinci,
with their constant implication that beauty is a kind of
malady of the soul, and then recall the strong, lusty soul
of the Renaissance as it speaks, for instance, in the ring-
ing lines of Chapman:

> Give me a spirit that on this life's rough sea
> Loves t'have his sails fill'd with a lusty wind ...
> There is no danger to a man that knows
> What life and death is — (11)

recall the whole magnificent passage, and you will see why
Pater's philosophy leads on inevitably to weariness, and
satiety, and impotence. This exaltation of beauty above
truth, and aesthetic grace above duty, and refined perception above action, this insinuating hedonism which would
so bravely embrace the joy of the moment, forgets to stay
itself on any fixed and unselfish principle, and forgetting
this, it somehow misses the enduring joy of the world and
empties life of its true values. It is for such reasons
as this that we cannot finally accept Pater's philosophy
of the art of life, notwithstanding all that may be said
in its favor; that even his lesson of moderation and self-
restraint, much as that lesson is needed to-day and always,
seems at least to proceed from some deep-seated taint of
decaying powers rather than from conscious strength. So
intimately are good and evil mingled together in human
ideals.

Notes

1 As the whole sky.
2 See p. 277n.
3 Quoted in PP, 220.
4 See p. 361n.
5 See p. 321n.
6 Saloman Reinach (1858-1932), archaeologist, was the
   Director of the Musée de Saint-Germain (from 1902).
7 From the Preface to the First Edition of 'Essays in
   Criticism: First Series' (1865).
8 Ode on a Grecian Urn, 11. 49-50.
9 American journalist and author (1850-1904).
10 This is a recurring theme in the sermons of Hugh Blair
   (1707-1800).
11 'Conspiracy of Charles, Duke of Byron' (1608), III, iii,
   135-41.

Select Bibliography

Based on d'Hangest (ii, 313-49), 'The New CBEL' (iii, 1214-16) and Evans (Walter Pater, 323-59).

Part I: a brief list of bibliographies, letters, biographies and critical accounts essential for further investigation into Pater's nineteenth-century reputation. The place of publication is London unless otherwise stated.

Part II: a short check-list of articles, notices, essays, chapters in books, parodies and testimonials about Pater in the period 1873 to 1910 not included in this volume. The entries appear in chronological order.

PART I

Benson, A.C., 'Walter Pater' (1906).

Bertocci, A.P., French Criticism and the Pater Problem, 'Boston University Studies in English' (Winter 1955), i, 178-94.

Boas, F.S., Critics and Criticism in the 'Seventies, 'The Eighteen-Seventies' (Cambridge, 1929), ed. Harley Granville-Barker, 192-209.

Brake, Laurel, The Early Work of Walter Pater (Ph.D. thesis, University of London, 1971).

Buchan, John, 'Brasenose College' (1898).

Charlesworth, B., 'Dark Passages: The Decadent Consciousness in Victorian Literature' (Madison and Milwaukee, 1965).

Croft-Cooke, Rupert, Wilde and Walter Pater, 'Feasting with Panthers' (1967), 163-90.

d'Hangest, Germain, 'Walter Pater: l'Homme et l'Oeuvre', 2 vols (Paris, 1961).

Dilke, Lady, 'The Book of the Spiritual Life' (1905).

Evans, Lawrence (ed.), 'Letters of Walter Pater' (Oxford, 1970).

Evans, Lawrence, Walter Pater, 'Victorian Prose: A Guide to Research' (New York, 1973), ed. David J. De Laura, 323–59.

Farnell, L.R., 'An Oxonian Looks Back' (1934).

'Field, Michael', 'Works and Days: From the Journal of Michael Field' (1933), ed. T. and D.C. Sturge Moore.

Fletcher, Ian, 'Walter Pater' (1959).

Graham, Walter, 'English Literary Periodicals' (New York, 1930).

Grosskurth, Phyllis, 'John Addington Symonds: A Biography' (1964).

Gunn, Peter, 'Vernon Lee: Violet Paget, 1856–1935' (1964).

Hart-Davis, Rupert, 'The Letters of Oscar Wilde' (1962).

Hough, Graham, 'The Last Romantics' (1947).

Jackson, W.W., 'Ingram Bywater: The Memoir of an Oxford Scholar, 1840–1914' (Oxford, 1917).

Johnson, R.V., Pater and the Victorian Anti-Romantics, 'Essays in Criticism' (January 1954), iv, 42–57.

Knight, William, 'A Memoir of John Nichol' (Glasgow, 1896).

'Lee, Vernon', 'Juvenalia' (1887).

'Lee, Vernon', 'Vernon Lee's Letters: With a Preface by her executor' (Privately printed, 1937), ed. Irene Cooper Willis.

Levey, Michael, 'The Case of Walter Pater' (1978).

Mallock, W.H., 'The New Republic' (1877).

Mallock, W.H., 'Memoirs of Life and Literature' (New York, 1920).

Monsman, Gerald, 'Walter Pater' (Boston, Mass., 1977).

Paul, J. Balfour, and Macdonald, W.R., 'John Miller Gray: Memoir and Remains' (Edinburgh, 1895).

Seiler, R.M., Walter Pater and the Reviewers (Ph.D. thesis, University of Liverpool, 1974).

Sharp, E.A., 'William Sharp: A Memoir Compiled by his Wife' (1910).

Small, Ian, The Reputation of Walter Pater (Ph.D. thesis, Reading University, 1971).

Sprigge, Sylvia, 'Berenson: A Biography' (1960).

Stanford, Derek, Walter Pater, 'Critics of the 'Nineties' (1970), 65–72.

Stonehill, C.A. and H.W., Walter Pater, 'Bibliographies of Modern Authors. Second Series' (1925), 129–41.

'The New Cambridge Bibliography of English Literature' (Cambridge, 1969–77), ed. George Watson, iii, 1412–16.

Tillotson, Geoffrey, 'Criticism and the Nineteenth Century' (1951).

Ward, Mrs Humphry, 'A Writer's Recollections' (1918).

Watson, W.E., 'Life of Bishop John Wordsworth' (1915).

Wright, Samuel, 'A Bibliography of the Writings of Walter Pater' (New York, 1975).

Wright, T. 'The Life of Walter Pater', 2 vols (1907).
Yeats, W.B., 'Autobiographies' (1926).
Yeats, W.B. (ed.), 'Oxford Book of Modern Verse' (Oxford, 1936).

PART II

1 Notice of 'The Renaissance', 'British Quarterly Review' (April 1873), cxiv, 548-9.
2 R.H., Review of 'The Renaissance', 'Penn Monthly' (June 1873), iv, 424-9.
3 Mr Pater's Critical Essays, 'Spectator' (14 June 1873), 764-5.
4 Pater's Studies of the Renaissance, 'Saturday Review' (26 July 1873), xxxvi, 123-4.
5 Notice of 'The Renaissance', 'Scribner's Monthly' (August 1873), vi, 506.
6 Review of 'The Renaissance', 'Atlantic Monthly' (October 1873), xxxii, 496-8.
7 Notice of 'The Renaissance', 'Art-Journal' (1873), xii, 160.
8 Capes, The Rev. W.W., Sermon printed in the 'Oxford Undergraduate's Journal' (27 November 1873), 98-9.
9 [Courthope, W.J.] Wordsworth and Gray, 'Quarterly Review' (January 1876), cxli, 105-36.
10 Saintsbury, George, Modern English Prose, 'Fortnightly Review' (February 1876), xxv, 243-59.
11 Quilter, Harry, The New Renaissance: or the Gospel of Intensity, 'Macmillan's Magazine' (September 1880), xlii, 391-400.
12 Sharp, William, Review of 'Marius the Epicurean', 'Time' (March 1885), n.s. i, 341-54.
13 Review of 'Marius the Epicurean', 'Saturday Review' (14 March 1885), lix, 351-2.
14 Review of 'Marius the Epicurean', 'Spectator' (28 March 1885), 420-1.
15 Review of 'Marius the Epicurean', 'British Quarterly Review' (April 1885), lxxxi, 461-3.
16 [Gray, J.M.] Review of 'Marius the Epicurean', Edinburgh 'Courant' (4 April 1885), 3.
17 [Mackail, J.W.] Review of 'Marius the Epicurean', 'Oxford Magazine' (29 April and 6 May 1885), iii, 191-2 and 207-8.
18 Goodwin, Alfred, notice of 'Marius the Epicurean', 'Mind' (July 1885), x, 442-7.
19 Review of 'Marius the Epicurean', 'Atlantic Monthly' (August 1885), lvi, 273-7.
20 Powers, H.N., review of 'Marius the Epicurean', 'Dial'

(August 1885), vi, 90-1.

21 Notice of 'Marius the Epicurean', 'Westminster Review'
   (January 1886), n.s. lxix, 594-5.

22 Review of 'Marius the Epicurean', 'Catholic World' (May
   1886), xliii, 222-31.

23 [Cox, G.W.] Two Roman Novels, 'Edinburgh Review' (January 1887), clxv, 248-55.

24 Lyster, T.W., review of 'Imaginary Portraits', 'Academy'
   (18 June 1887), xxxi, 423-4.

25 Review of 'Imaginary Portraits', 'Saturday Review' (25
   June 1887), lxiii, 920-1.

26 Review of 'Imaginary Portraits', 'Westminster Review'
   (July 1887), n.s. lxxii, 515.

27 Review of 'Imaginary Portraits', 'Dial' (September
   1887), viii, 102.

28 Review of 'Imaginary Portraits', 'Critic' (24 September
   1887), n.s. viii, 149.

29 Review of the third edition of 'The Renaissance',
   'Critic' (14 July 1888), n.s. x, 15-16.

30 Bradford, Gamaliel, Jr., Walter Pater, Boston 'Andover
   Review' (August 1888), x, 141-55.

31 Review of 'Appreciations', 'Nation' (26 December 1889),
   xlix, 542.

32 Review of 'Appreciations', 'Saturday Review' (28 December 1889), lxviii, 745-6.

33 Pater's 'Appreciations', 'Critic' (8 February 1890),
   n.s. xiii, 61-2.

34 A.G., notice of 'Appreciations', 'Oxford Magazine' (26
   February 1890), viii, 233.

35 Mr Pater's Minor Essays, 'Atlantic Monthly' (March
   1890), lxv, 424-7.

36 The Point of View, 'Scribner's Magazine' (May 1890),
   vii, 525-6.

37 Richards, C.A.L., Pater's 'Appreciations', 'Dial' (June
   1890), xi, 37-8.

38 [Pain, Barry] parody of Pater entitled Of Mr Walter
   Pater. Marius at Sloane Street, in The Sincerest Form
   of Flattery, 'Cornhill Magazine' (October 1890), n.s.
   xv, 374-5.

39 Review of 'Plato and Platonism', 'Saturday Review' (25
   February 1893), lxxv, 211-12.

40 [Innes, A.D.] Review of 'Plato and Platonism', 'Athenaeum' (18 March 1893), 339-40.

41 Notice of 'Plato and Platonism', 'Westminster Review'
   (April 1893), n.s. lxxxiii, 447-8.

42 Notice of 'Plato and Platonism', 'Catholic World'
   (April 1893), lvii, 139.

43 Notice of 'Plato and Platonism', 'Mind' (April 1893),
   n.s. ii, 251.

44 Dodgson, Campbell, review of 'Plato and Platonism', 'Academy' (15 April 1893), xliii, 317-18.
45 Review of 'Plato and Platonism', 'Critic' (1 July 1893), n.s. xx, 1-2.
46 Logan, Mary, The New Art Criticism, 'Atlantic Monthly' (August 1893), lxxvi, 263-70.
47 Mabie, H.W., The Dialogues of Plato as Literature, 'Outlook' (9 September 1893), xlviii, 465-6.
48 Review of 'Plato and Platonism', 'Nation' (30 November 1893), lvii, 413-14.
49 Notice of 'Plato and Platonism', 'Popular Science Monthly' (May 1894), xlv, 132.
50 Walter Pater. By an Undergraduate, 'Pall Mall Gazette' (2 August 1894), 3.
51 Saunders, T.B., obituary notice in the 'Athenaeum' (4 August 1894), 161-2.
52 Mr Walter Pater, 'Saturday Review' (4 August 1894), lxxviii, 118-19.
53 Obituary notice, 'Illustrated London News' (4 August 1894), cv, 135.
54 Cotton, J.S., Obituary. Walter Pater, 'Academy' (11 August 1894), xlvi, 102.
55 Waugh, Arthur, Walter Pater, 'Critic' (11 August 1894), n.s. xii, 93-4.
56 Walter Pater, 'Dial' (16 August 1894), xvii, 84-5.
57 Dyer, Louis, Walter Pater, 'Nation' (23 August 1894), lix, 137-9.
58 A Note on Walter Pater. By One Who Knew Him, 'Bookman' (September 1894), vi, 173-5.
59 Johnson, Lionel, The Work of Mr Pater, 'Fortnightly Review' (September 1894), lxii, 352-67; reprinted in 'Post Liminium' (1911).
60 Waugh, Arthur, London Letter, 'Critic' (1 September 1894), xxv, 145-6.
61 Zangwill, I., Men, Women and Books, 'Critic' (15 September 1894), xxii, 165-7.
62 Titchener, E.B., Walter Horatio Pater, 'Book Reviews' (October 1894), ii, 201-5.
63 W.B.D., An Imaginary Portrait, 'Oxford Magazine' (28 November 1894), xiii, 128.
64 Gosse, Edmund, Walter Pater: A Portrait, 'Contemporary Review' (December 1894), lxvi, 795-810; reprinted in 'Critical Kit-Kats' (1896).
65 Sharp, William, Some Personal Reminiscences of Walter Pater, 'Atlantic Monthly' (December 1894), lxxiv, 801-14; reprinted in 'Papers Critical and Reminiscent' (1912).
66 [Sharp, William] Review of 'Greek Studies', 'Realm' (25 January 1895), i, 417-19.

67 Mr Pater's Last Book, 'Daily Chronicle' (4 February 1895), 3.
68 Mr Pater's 'Greek Studies', 'Saturday Review' (9 February 1895), lxxix, 191.
69 Baldwin, Montagu, review of 'Greek Studies', 'Educational Review' (March 1895), ix, 291-4.
70 Dodgson, Campbell, review of 'Greek Studies', 'Academy' (16 March 1895), xlvii, 229-30.
71 Verrall, A.W., Pater's 'Greek Studies', 'Classical Review' (May 1895), ix, 225-8.
72 Pater's Greek Studies, 'Nation' (13 June 1895), lx, 464-5.
73 [Barry, W.F.] Latter-Day Pagans, 'Quarterly Review' (July 1895), clxxxii, 31-58; reprinted in 'Heralds of Revolt' (1909).
74 Escott, T.H.S., Some Oxford Memories of the Prae-Aesthetic Age, 'National Review' (October 1895), xxiv, 232-44.
75 Hale, E.E., Jr, Walter Pater's Last Volume, 'Dial' (16 November 1895), xix, 279-81.
76 Beerbohm, Max, Be it Cosiness, 'Pageant' (1 December 1895); reprinted as Diminuendo in 'The Works of Max Beerbohm' (1896), 129-38.
77 [Saunders, T.B.] Review of 'Miscellaneous Studies', 'Athenaeum' (7 December 1895), 783.
78 Notice of 'Miscellaneous Studies', 'Westminster Review' (January 1896), cxlv, 229.
79 Jacobus, R.P., The Blessedness of Egoism: Maurice Barrès and Walter Pater, 'Fortnightly Review' (January and March 1896), lxv, 40-57 and 384-96.
80 Dodgson, Campbell, review of 'Miscellaneous Studies', 'Academy' (8 February 1896), xliv, 110-12.
81 Mr Pater's 'Miscellaneous Studies', 'Saturday Review' (1 August 1896), lxxxii, 107-9.
82 Symons, Arthur, Walter Pater: Some Characteristics, 'Savoy' (December 1896), iii, 33-41; reprinted in 'Studies in Verse and Prose' (1904).
83 Notice of 'Gaston de Latour', 'Westminster Review' (December 1896), cxlvi, 706.
84 Review of 'Gaston de Latour', 'Critic' (5 December 1896), n.s. xxvi, 359.
85 Mr Pater's Last Work, supplement to the 'Spectator' (30 January 1897), lxxviii, 144-5.
86 Sillard, P.A., Theology of Walter Pater, 'Christian Literature' (February 1897), xvi, 407-12.
87 Hale, E.E., Jr, A Last Volume from Walter Pater, 'Dial' (1 February 1897), xxii, 85-7.
88 Pater's Unfinished Romance, 'Nation' (4 March 1897), lxiv, 166-7.

89 Notice of 'Gaston de Latour', 'Atlantic Monthly' (May 1897), lxxix, 711-12.

90 Eno, H.L., Walter Pater: An Appreciation, Philadelphia 'Citizen' (January 1898), iii, 248-50.

91 Kaufman, M., Humanism and Christianity, 'Quarterly Review' (April 1901), cxciii, 458-81.

92 Mountain, W., Walter Pater, 'Poet-Lore' (April 1901), xiii, 275-81.

93 Symons, Arthur, Mr Pater's 'Essays from "The Guardian"', 'Athenaeum' (21 September 1901), 384.

94 Bourdillon, Mr Pater's 'Essays from "The Guardian"', 'Athenaeum' (28 September 1901), 416.

95 Notice of 'Essays from "The Guardian"', 'Contemporary Review' (October 1901), lxxx, 603.

96 Symons, Arthur, Mr Pater's 'Essays from "The Guardian"', 'Athenaeum' (5 October 1901), 453.

97 Bourdillon, F.W., Mr Pater's 'Essays from "The Guardian"', 'Athenaeum' (12 October 1901), 493.

98 F.E.H., Pater's Philosophy of Life, 'Macmillan's Magazine' (January 1902), lxxxv, 193-8.

99 Dowden, Edward, Walter Pater, 'New Liberal Review' (July 1902), iii, 777-94; reprinted in 'Essays Modern and Elizabethan' (1910).

100 Zangwill, I., Pater and Prose, 'Without Prejudice' (1902), 207-19.

101 Moore, George, Avowals. VI. Walter Pater, 'Pall Mall Magazine' (August 1904), xxxiii, 527-33; reprinted in 'Avowals' (1919).

102 Benson, A.C., Walter Pater, 'The Times' (29 January 1906), 3.

103 The Magic of Walter Pater's Style, 'Current Literature' (July 1906), xli, 51-2.

104 Saintsbury, George, Walter Pater, 'Bookman' (August 1906), xxx, 165-70.

105 Symons, Arthur, Walter Pater, 'Monthly Review' (September 1906), xxiv, 14-24.

106 Hammell, G.M., Walter Pater and his Philosophy of Life, 'Methodist Review' (September 1906), lxxxviii, 796-801.

107 Harris, Frank, Walter Pater the Pagan, 'John Bull' (8 September 1906), i, 329-30.

108 Manson, Edward, Recollections of Walter Pater, 'Oxford Magazine' (7 November 1906), xxv, 60-1.

109 Pater and his Circle, 'Current Literature' (June 1907), xlii, 644-5.

110 A Legendary Personality, 'Harper's Weekly' (12 June 1907), li, 41.

111 Bowen, E., Walter Pater: Prose Artist, 'Sewanee Review' (July 1907), xv, 271-84.

112 The Aesthetic Outlook: Walter Pater, 'Edinburgh Review'

(July 1907), ccvi, 23-49.

113 Orton, W.A., Walter Pater, 'Westminster Review' (November 1908), clxx, 536-41.

114 Buchan, John, Nine Brasenose Worthies, 'Brasenose College Quatercentenary Monographs', 2 vols (Oxford, 1909), Part XIV, 2(a), 23-30.

115 Ward, T. Humphry, Reminiscences. Brasenose, 1864-72, 'Brasenose College Quatercentenary Monographs', 2 vols (Oxford, 1909), Part XIV, 2(c), 71-8.

116 Notice of the Library Edition, 'Athenaeum' (18 June 1910), 732.

117 Tanner, H.B., Perfection in Prose Style: A Modern English Instance, 'Dial' (1 August 1910), xlix, 58.

118 Notice of the Library Edition, 'Athenaeum' (3 September 1910), 263.

119 Notice of the Library Edition, 'Athenaeum' (22 October 1910), 487.

120 The Oxford Spirit, 'Outlook' (19 November 1910), xcvi, 621-3.

Select Index

The index is divided into three parts: I Works by Pater;
II Topics; III General Index.

I. WORKS BY PATER

II. TOPICS

III. GENERAL INDEX

THE CRITICAL HERITAGE SERIES

GENERAL EDITOR: B. C. SOUTHAM

Volumes published and forthcoming